Aaron Thompson • Joseph B. Cuseo
John Robert Roush • Shane Shope

Thriving in HIGH SCHOOL *and Beyond*
Strategies for Academic Success
and Personal Development

Kendall Hunt
publishing company

Cover image © Shutterstock, Inc.

www.kendallhunt.com
Send all inquiries to:
4050 Westmark Drive
Dubuque, IA 52004-1840

Copyright © 2018 by Kendall Hunt Publishing Company

Text alone ISBN 978-1-5249-4990-7
Text with web ISBN 978-1-5249-5436-9

All rights reserved. No part of this publication may be reproduced,
stored in a retrieval system, or transmitted, in any form or by any means,
electronic, mechanical, photocopying, recording, or otherwise,
without the prior written permission of the copyright owner.

Published in the United States of America

BRIEF CONTENTS

CHAPTER 1 High School Knowledge   1

CHAPTER 2 Making Connections: Four Steps to Your Success   23

CHAPTER 3 Preparing for High School   47

CHAPTER 4 Time Management   73

CHAPTER 5 Deep Learning   99

CHAPTER 6 Higher-Level Thinking   135

CHAPTER 7 Test-Taking Skills and Strategies   165

CHAPTER 8 Financial Literacy   193

CHAPTER 9 Diversity and the High School Experience   223

CHAPTER 10 Career Exploration, Preparation, and Readiness   261

CONTENTS

CHAPTER 1 HIGH SCHOOL KNOWLEDGE 1

    Top Tips for Academic Success 6
    Transitioning from Middle School to High School 9
    Your First Year in High School 9
    High School Attendance 10
    Effective Classroom Behavior: The Fundamentals 11
    How to E-mail (or not) your Teacher 14
        An example of what not to do 14
        An example of an appropriate e-mail 14
    Career Paths 16
    High School and Beyond 16
    Chapter Summary and Highlights 17
    Chapter 1 Exercises 20

CHAPTER 2 MAKING CONNECTIONS: FOUR STEPS TO YOUR SUCCESS 23

    Four Steps to High School Success 24
    First Step to High School Success: Active Involvement (Engagement) 24
        Active Involvement in the Learning Process 25
        Active Listening and Note Taking in Class 25
        Active Class Participation 27
        Active Reading 27
    Second Step to High School Success:
    Capitalizing on School Resources (Resourcefulness) 29
        Disability Services 29
        Media Center Library 29
        Guidance Counseling 30
        Student Development Opportunities 30
        Seek Advice 31

Third Step to High School Success: Interpersonal Interaction and Collaboration (Social Integration) 31
- Interacting with High School Teachers 32
- Interacting with Your Guidance Counselor 33
- Interaction with Peers (Student–Student Interaction) 34
- Collaborative Learning 35

Fourth Step of High School Success: Reflection and Self-Awareness (Mindfulness) 38
- Self-Awareness 38
- Self-Monitoring 39
- Self-Assessment 39

Chapter Summary and Highlights 40

Chapter 2 Exercises 44

CHAPTER 3 PREPARING FOR HIGH SCHOOL 47

Start Planning Your Career Transition 48

Transition to High School—the Work and Experience 48
- Outside-of-School Choices 48
- Manage Your Time 48
- Organizational Tips—Being Ready Everyday Requires You to Manage the Work 49
- Tips to Transitioning to High School 49

The Relationship Between Goal Setting and Success 49

Characteristics of a Well-Designed Goal 50

Strategies for Maintaining Motivation and Progress Toward Your Goals 54

Characteristics of Successful People 57
- Internal Locus of Control 57
- Self-Efficacy 58
- Grit 59
- Growth Mindset 63

Chapter Summary and Highlights 65

Chapter 3 Exercises 69

CHAPTER 4 TIME MANAGEMENT 73

The Importance of Time Management 74
Strategies for Managing Time and Tasks 75
Creating a Time-Management Plan 80
Dealing with Procrastination 85
Myths That Promote Procrastination 86
- Psychological Causes of Procrastination 87

Strategies for Preventing and Overcoming Procrastination 88
Chapter Summary and Highlights 91
Chapter 4 Exercises 95

CHAPTER 5 DEEP LEARNING 99

What Is Deep Learning? 100
Effective Class-Listening and Note-Taking Strategies 101
Pre-Class Strategies: What to Do *Before* Class 102
Listening and Note-Taking Strategies: What to Do *During* Class 103
Post-Class Strategies: What to Do *After* Class 105
Strategic Reading 107
- Pre-Reading Strategies: What to Do *Before* Reading 108
- Strategies to Use *During* the Reading Process 109
- Post-Reading Strategies: What to Do *After* Reading 111

Strategic Studying: Learning Deeply and Remembering Longer 114
- Give Studying Your Undivided Attention 114

Make Meaningful Associations 116
- Integrate Information from Classes and Readings 118
- Distribute Study Time across Separate Study Sessions 118
- Use the "Part-to-Whole" Study Method 119
- Capitalize on the Power of Visual Learning 120
- Build Variety into the Study Process 122
- Learning Styles: Identifying Your Learning Preferences 122
- Learn with Emotion 125

Self-Monitor: Reflect on What You're Learning and Assess Whether You're Learning it Deeply 125

Chapter Summary and Highlights   127
Chapter 5 Exercises   131

CHAPTER 6 HIGHER-LEVEL THINKING   135

Defining and Describing the Major Forms of Higher-Level Thinking   136
- Analysis (Analytical Thinking)   137
- Synthesis (Integrative Thinking)   138
- Application (Applied Thinking)   138
- Multidimensional Thinking   139
- Balanced Thinking   140
- Critical Thinking (Evaluation)   142
- Creative Thinking   148

Using Higher-Level Thinking Skills to Improve Academic Performance   150
Strategies for Increasing Creativity   154
Chapter Summary and Highlights   155
Chapter 6 Exercises   160

CHAPTER 7 TEST-TAKING SKILLS AND STRATEGIES   165

Pre-Test Strategies: What to Do *in Advance* of Tests   166
- Recitation   167
- Creating Retrieval Cues   167

Strategies to Use *Immediately Before* a Test   169
Strategies to Use *During* Tests   171
Strategies for Answering Multiple-Choice Test Questions   173
Strategies for Answering Essay Questions   176
Strategies for Online Tests   179
Post-Test Strategies: What to Do *After* Receiving Your Test Results   180
Strategies for Reducing Test Anxiety   184
Chapter Summary and Highlights   186
Chapter 7 Exercises   189

CHAPTER 8   FINANCIAL LITERACY   193

Sources of Income for Financing a College Education   194
    Student Loans   195
    Student Loans and Credit Scores   196
    Scholarships   197
    Grants   197
    Planning on joining the Armed Services?   197

Developing a Money Management Plan   197
    Gain Financial Self-Awareness   197
    Track Your Cash Flow   198

Developing a Plan for Managing Money and Minimizing Debt   204
Chapter Summary and Highlights   215
Chapter 8   Exercises   218

CHAPTER 9   DIVERSITY AND THE HIGH SCHOOL EXPERIENCE   223

What Is Diversity?   224
What Is Racial Diversity?   225
What Is an Ethnic Group?   228
The Relationship between Diversity and Humanity   229
What Is Individuality?   232
Major Forms or Types of Diversity in Today's World   232
    Ethnic and Racial Diversity   232
    Socioeconomic Diversity   235
    Generational Diversity   236
    Sexual Diversity   237

The Benefits of Experiencing Diversity   238
    Diversity Increases Self-Awareness and Self-Knowledge   238
    Diversity Deepens Learning   238
    Diversity Promotes Critical Thinking   239
    Diversity Stimulates Creative Thinking   239
    Diversity Enhances Career Preparation and Career Success   239

Overcoming Barriers to Diversity   241
- Stereotyping   241
- Prejudice   242
- Discrimination   244

Strategies for Overcoming Stereotypes and Prejudices   247

Chapter Summary and Highlights   252

Chapter 9 Exercises   257

CHAPTER 10   CAREER EXPLORATION, PREPARATION, AND READINESS   261

The Importance of Career Planning   262

Strategies for Career Exploration and Preparation   263
- Step 1. Awareness of Self   263
- Multiple Intelligences   265
- Step 2. Awareness of Career Options   270
- Step 3. Awareness of Career Options that Provide the Best "Fit" for You   278
- Step 4. Awareness of the Major Steps Needed to Reach Your Career Goal   279
- Personal Resume   284

Chapter Summary and Highlights   289

Chapter 10 Exercises   293

INDEX   299

College & Career Ready: Are You?

For decades, American businesses have been critical of the career readiness skills that high school graduates have brought to the workplace. A shift from a manufacturing-based economy to a more service-oriented job market has created a demand for a labor force that possesses these critical skills. Moreover, what has been lacking are programs that can address this issue. Gewertz (2016) found that only 8% of U.S. high school graduates completed a Career College Readiness program. Also, only 25% of students have a clear idea about how to move into a career pathway and have a limited amount of information about choosing a career path (Cuseo, Thompson, & McLaughlin, 2016).

How Do We Address This Issue?

This book supplies you with resources to help you make a smooth transition from middle school to high school and equip you with skills for success in high school, college and career. The book offers a model for success that centers on three key components: Career READINESS, Self-AWARENESS and Cultural DIVERSITY (R.A.D.). The model is designed to promote your success, both academically and personally, and help you identify a career pathway that best matches your interests and talents.

R.A.D. Model

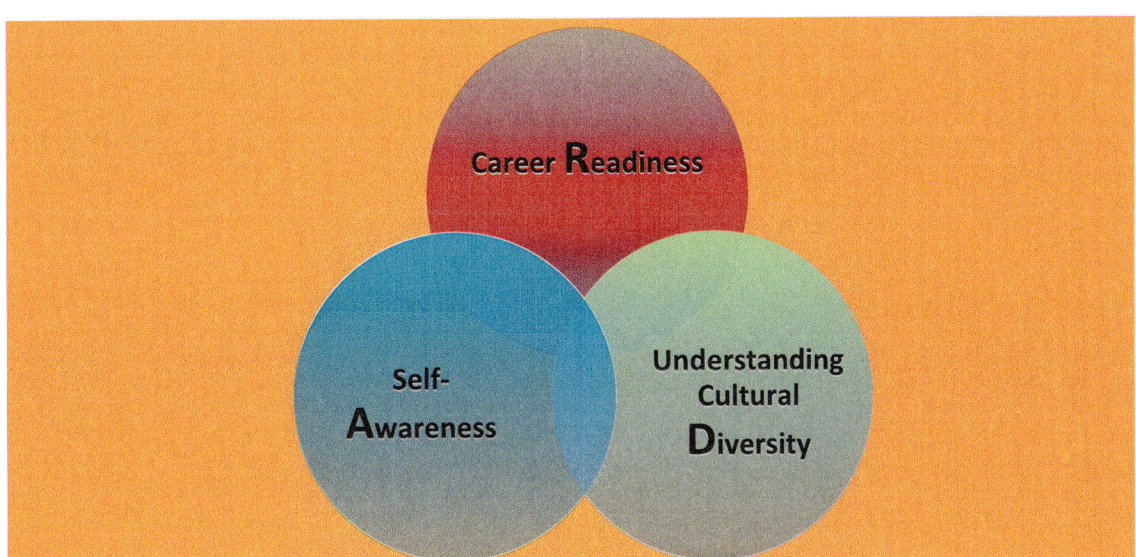

    This book will enable you to demonstrate career readiness and develop work-ethic competencies, including problem-solving, teamwork, time management, and money management. The book's content is aligned with the National Association of Colleges and Employer Competencies and the Council for Economic Education's National Standards for Financial Literacy. After completing the book's ten chapters, you will be provided with a College and Career Basic Skills Certificate to include in your professional portfolio and present to potential employers and colleges.

CHAPTER 1

HIGH SCHOOL KNOWLEDGE

Effective High School Behavior in Class and Online

CHAPTER PREVIEW

This chapter identifies top tips for academic success you can implement immediately, including what to do inside and outside the classroom. It also alerts you to in-class and out of class behavior that should be avoided in high school.

LEARNING GOALS

Equip yourself with key academic strategies for getting off to a good start in high school and increase your awareness of behaviors that reflect academic incivility and lack of academic integrity.

THOUGHT STARTER

 Think About It—Journal Entry 1.1

1. In what three major ways do you think high school will differ from middle/Junior high school? What are the biggest challenges you think you will experience?
   _____
   _____
   _____
   _____

2. What three personal characteristics, qualities and strategies do you think will be most important for high school success?
   _____
   _____
   _____
   _____

From *Thriving in the Community College & Beyond: Strategies for Academic Success and Personal Development*, Third Edition, by Joseph Cuseo, Aaron Thompson, and Julie McLaughlin. Copyright © 2016 by Kendall Hunt Publishing Company. Reprinted by permission.

Chapter 1: High School Knowledge

3. What do I want to do when I...? You are about to begin a look into your postsecondary plans; this process will be a "peek" into your future. These questions might show up again, so take a moment to think about and write:

   - Where have you been? (What experiences have you had that might help you in the future?)
   _____

   - Where are you now? (What are you currently doing to help yourself right now?)
   _____

   - Where are you heading? (What do you have planned, and what tools do you have to get there?)
   _____

BOX 1.1

Middle school	High school	College
You have more choices than you did in elementary school, but your classes are arranged for you.	Your classes are mostly arranged for you.	You arrange your own schedule in consultation with your advisor. Schedules tend to look lighter than they really are.
Your time is structured by others.	Your time is structured by others.	You manage your own time.
Your classes are divided into specialty areas that you will attend with different teachers.	You go from one class directly to another, spending six hours per day—30 hours per week—in class.	Youi have free time between classes; class times vary throughout the day and evening; and you spend 12–16 hours each week in class if you are a full-time student.
The school year is 36 weeks long with classes that typically last the entire school year.	The school year is 36 weeks long with classes that typically last the entire school year. Some high schools offer block schedules with semester-long courses, or trimesters rather than nine week courses.	The academic year may be divided into separate semesters or quarters.
Teachers monitor class attendance.	Teachers monitor class attendance.	Professors may not formally monitor class attendance: you're expected to have the self-discipline to show up and get down information that's presented in class.
Often teachers write notes on the board for you to copy down or provide you with a study guide. You may have an "agenda" or book that you are expected to keep updated to help keep your organized.	Often teachers write notes on the board for you to copy down or provide you with a study guide.	Professors may lecture non-stop, expecting you to identify and write down important information in your notes. Professors don't record all their key points on the board. Notes that professors write on the board are used to supplement or complement the lecture, not summarize the lecture.

BOX 1.1 (CONT)

Middle school	High school	College
Teachers provide you the missing work when you are absent, and will ask you to turn it in.	Teachers provide you the missing work when you are absent.	Professors expect you to get information you missed from classmates.
You may be asked to read short passages that are often reviewed then discussed in class or you might be asked to share your thoughts with the class.	You read short passages that are then often reviewed and then discussed in your class.	You're assigned substantial amounts of reading and writing that may not be directly addressed in class.
Teachers present material in class that helps explain the textbook.	Teachers present material in class that helps explain the textbook.	Professors may not follow the textbook, but you may be expected to relate the class sessions to textbook readings.
You may have studied outside of class zero to two hours (or had some support on projects outside of class). You may have a designated study hall in middle school.	You may have studied outside of class zero to two hours.	You need to study for at least two to three hours outside of class for each hour spent in class.
You seldom need to read anything more than once and sometimes listening in class is enough.	You seldom need to read anything more than once and sometimes listening in class is enough.	You will need to review your class notes and read material regularly.
On rare occasions, you may have older students in your class. For example, you may been in a middle school band class with sixth, seventh, and eighth graders.	You may have been in classes with students that are older than you.	Your classes likely will be diverse as far as ethnicity, age, gender, and beliefs.
Social and playtime are eliminated or reduced significantly.	Social and playtime are eliminated or reduced significantly.	As stated before, your will have total control of your free time.
Middle Schools typically have fewer students than elementary schools.	High schools have more students than a traditional middle school.	Depending on the college or university you could see several hundred or thousands of people daily walking to class.
Teachers continuously remind you of work due dates and requirements. Increase in homework and expectations.	Increase in homework and expectations.	Homework will take on a new meaning for you. A lot of work to prepare for class will be self-directed.
Behavior expectations increase.	Behavior expectations increase.	You're no longer considered a child, you're an adult now.
Experience a transition from being 'on top' at the end of elementary school, to rebuilding your identity as a middle school student.	Experience a transition from being "on top" in 8th grade to rebuilding your identity in the 9th grade.	The transition to college is not as difficult from a social aspect but the work and responsibility are; start off on the right foot.

Chapter 1: High School Knowledge

BOX 1.1 (CONT)

Middle school	High school	College
You are expected to take more responsibility for your school work.	You are expected to take more responsibility for your school work.	You're totally responsible for your work. Your parents can't help you here.
The academic expectations and demands will likely increase through your middle school years.	Increases in rigor; it's going to get difficult at times. Academic demands will increase as you progress in high school.	Don't come in expecting it to be easy. Get ready mentally to handle the demands of college work.
Teachers will communicate with your parents regarding your work, but you will be expected to be responsible for your work.	You are expected to do your work; you're responsible for your work!	<u>You are expected to do your work; you're responsible for your work!</u>
You may start taking more specific courses toward your career path. Career options and discussions may become more frequent. You might even take a course in middle school that may count as high school credit, or potentially college credit. Your final grades carry more importance than ever before. Familiarize yourself with GPAs (Grade Point Average).	You will more than likely begin taking courses that fit your career interest. You may even take courses that count toward college credit. Your final grades count toward your cumulative high school GPA (Grade Point Average). You may find certain courses are weighted more heavily than others.	As you progress through college your course choices will become focused on courses that lead to your graduation in a field of study you choose.

Adapted from : Southern Methodist University (2006)

 Think About It—Journal Entry 1.2

Look back at the differences between middle school and high school in Box 1.1.

Which differences were you least aware or were most surprised to see?

_____
_____
_____
_____
_____

Why?

_____
_____
_____
_____

Transitioning from middle school to high school will present several new challenges in your life. Your parents and teachers will expect you to become increasingly independent and take more responsibilities as you progress into your ninth grade year and beyond. Reflect on how you will manage these responsibilities with your high school work (Chapter 4 on time management will give you some strategies). You will notice that the classroom environment has changed from your middle school days. Now you will have classes with students that are older than you. You will rely on technology much more to assist with your education than you did years ago. If you need help with your technology skills, see if your school offers a basic technology course or has a technology help desk. You might also want to ask some of your more tech savvy classmates for some technology tips.

> "College teachers don't tell you what you're supposed to do. They just expect you to do it. High school teachers tell you about five times what you're supposed to do."
> —High School sophomore
> (Appleby, 2008)

BOX 1.2

What's in a syllabus?

What's in a syllabus? A course syllabus is a document created by instructors that will probably be given to you on the first day of class. The syllabus has been called a contract between the student and the instructor. Please pay careful attention to all parts of the syllabus and make a copy to keep with you always. You are responsible for adhering to this contract. However, your instructor can change the syllabus as he or she deems necessary. A syllabus usually contains the following components (not necessarily in the order listed below). Keep in mind that if you are in middle school or high school, you may not receive a syllabus for your course. You might receive a course map, course description, or course outline instead. Don't be afraid to ask for one of these documents. Some of the items listed below may not be included on your syllabus:

1. Course department, prefix, number, title, credit hours, semester and year, and course reference number.
2. Meeting times and location, instructor information (name, office location, office hours, contact information).
3. Catalog course description, including prerequisites and/or co-requisites (courses students need to have taken before the course or at the same time); prerequisite skill sets (e.g., programming languages, familiarity with software).
4. Text(s) with dates, supplemental text(s), other required readings, and references reading (books, reserve readings, course readers, software, and supplies with information about where they can be obtained). You are expected to have these on the first day or soon after the first day.
5. Student learning outcomes and/or course objectives (this is what the instructor is telling you that he or she will work the lectures around, and you will have learning opportunities around them throughout the course). The tests, quizzes, papers and so on are based on the objectives.
6. Skills and knowledge the student will gain. These are the additional items you will have learned after the course is completed. You may hear these referred to as competencies, or as MS/HS proficiencies, outcomes, or skills.

BOX 1.2 (CONT)

7. Course organization. This tells you step-by-step how this course will be taught.
8. Explanation of the topical organization of the course. This will give you an idea of the specific topics that will be covered in class.
9. Course requirements (what student will have to do in the course: assignments, exams, projects, performances, attendance, participation, etc.). Usually the nature and format of assignments and the expected length of written work, as well as due dates for assignments and dates for exams, will be explained.
10. Evaluation and grading policy: what grades are based on, especially your final grade. Always keep up on what grade you have in class and discuss how to improve it with the instructor on a regular basis.
11. Course policies and expectations: may include academic integrity, missing homework, missed exams, recording classroom activities, food in class, laptop use, cell phone use, etc.
12. Other expectations such as student behavior (e.g., respectful consideration of one another's perspectives, open-mindedness, creative risk-taking).
13. Course calendar/schedule (sometimes the instructor will put "tentative" before these words, letting you know it is subject to change). However, this is a class-to-class breakdown of topics and assignments (readings, homework, project due dates).

As a high school student, you are responsible for knowing the contents of the course syllabus. It is not the instructor's responsibility to go over it with you. Be sure to read and understand your syllabi for all your courses. If you have any questions, be sure to ask your instructor right away.

If you are a middle school or high school student, you may find yourself receiving a little more guidance or support, but the syllabus provides a look into what future expectations may look like, and responsible practices for your current setting. You may find your course outline or map may have more general benchmarks for the teacher to follow, but you are encouraged to take the initiative to begin looking ahead and seeing how all these pieces fit together. You are building skills for your career and/or high school experiences.

Top Tips for Academic Success

1. **Don't miss class.** Not surprisingly, the total amount of time you spend on learning is associated with how much you learn and how deeply you learn. This association leads to a straightforward recommendation: Attend all your classes in all your courses. It may be tempting to skip school but the short-term impact will only build momentum and hurt your grades and if becomes a habit then you jeopardize not graduating from high school. Over the past 75 years, numerous studies have shown a direct relationship between class attendance and course grades—as one goes up or down, so does the other (Credé, Roch, Kieszczynka, 2010; Launius, 1997; Shimoff & Catania, 2001; Tagliacollo, Volpato, & Pereira, 2010).

2. **Adopt a seating location in class that maximizes attention and minimizes distraction.** Many years of research show that students who sit in the front and center of class tend to earn higher test scores and course grades (Benedict & Hoag, 2004; Rennels & Chaudhair, 1988; Tagliacollo, Volpato, & Pereira, 2010). These results have been found even when students are assigned seats by their teacher, so it's not just a matter of more motivated and studious students sitting in the front of the room. Instead, the better academic performance achieved by students sitting front and center stems from learning advantages associated with this seating location.

> **NOTE**
> Look at going to class like going to work. If you miss work days, it lowers your pay; if you miss classes, it lowers your grades.

> "Eighty percent of success is showing up."
> —Woody Allen, Oscar & Golden Globe winning film director, writer, and author

> "I like to sit up front so I am not distracted by others and I don't have to look around people's heads to see the chalkboard."
> —college student

Front-and-center seating benefits your academic performance by improving your vision of material written on the board or screen and your ability to hear the teacher's voice. In addition, sitting in the front means you don't have to peer over or around the heads of other students. This results in more direct eye contact with the teacher, which increases your focus of attention, reduces your sense of anonymity, and increases your level of involvement in class.

Lastly, sitting in the front of class can also reduce your level of anxiety about speaking in class because you will not have numerous classmates sitting in front of you turning around to look at you when you speak.

The *bottom line:* When you enter a classroom, get in the habit of heading for a seat in the front and center of class. It allows you to develop a relationship with your teachers and depending on the size of your high school it can lead to a familiarity that later will benefit you through references and letters of recommendation.

3. **Sit by people who will enable (not disable) your ability to listen and learn.** Intentionally sit near classmates who will not distract you or interfere with the quality of your note taking. The human attention span has a limited capacity; we can give all or part of our attention to whatever task we're performing. Actively listening to and taking notes on lecture information is a demanding task that demands undivided attention.

> "I tend to sit at the very front of my classrooms. It helps me focus and take notes better. It also eliminates distractions."
> —college student

NOTE

When you enter class, you have a choice about where you're going to sit. Choose wisely by selecting a location that will maximize your attentiveness to the teacher and your effectiveness as a note-taker.

Think About It—Journal Entry 1.3

When you enter a classroom, where do you usually sit?

_____
_____

Why do you sit there? Is it a conscious choice or more like an automatic habit?

_____
_____
_____

Do you think that the seat you usually choose places you in the best possible position for listening and learning in the classroom? Why or why not?

_____
_____
_____
_____

4. **Adopt a seating posture that screams attention.** Sitting upright and leaning forward increases attention because these signs of physical alertness reach the brain and stimulate mental alertness. If your body is in an alert and ready position, your mind picks up these physical cues and follows your body's lead. Baseball players get into a ready position before a pitch is delivered to ready themselves to catch batted balls; similarly, learners who assume a ready position in the classroom put themselves in a better position to catch ideas batted around in class. Studies show that when humans are mentally alert and ready to learn, a greater amount of C-kinase (a brain chemical) is released at the connection point between brain cells, which increases the likelihood that neurological (learning) connections are formed between them (Howard, 2014).

   Another advantage to being attentive in class is that it sends a clear message to your teacher that you're a courteous and conscientious student. This can influence your teacher's perception and evaluation of your academic performance; if at the end of the course you're on the border between a higher and lower grade, you're more likely to get the benefit of the doubt.

5. **Be a self-aware learner.** One characteristic of successful learners is that they self-monitor (check themselves) while learning to remain aware of:
   - Whether they're using effective learning strategies (e.g., if they're giving their undivided attention to what they're learning)
   - Whether they're truly comprehending what they are learning (e.g., if they're understanding it at a deep level or memorizing it at a surface level)
   - How they're regulating or adjusting their learning strategies to meet the demands of different academic tasks and subjects (e.g., if they're reading technical material in a science textbook, they read at a slower rate and check their understanding more frequently than when reading a novel) (Pintrich & Schunk, 2002).

   You can begin to establish good self-monitoring habits by getting in the routine of periodically pausing to reflect on the strategies you're using to learn and how you "do" high school. For instance, you can ask yourself the following questions:
   - Am I listening attentively to what my teacher is saying in class?
   - Am I comprehending what I'm reading outside of class?
   - Am I effectively using school resources designed to support my success?
   - Am I interacting with school professionals who can contribute to my current success and future development?
   - Am I interacting and collaborating with peers who can support (not sabotage) my learning and development?
   - Am I effectively implementing high school success strategies (such as those identified in this book)?

Look at the high school website, what information is available?

    Academics?
    Athletics?
    Student Services?

> "We learn neither by thinking nor by doing; we learn by thinking about what we are doing."
> —George Stoddard, Professor Emeritus, University of Iowa

NOTE

Successful students and successful people are mindful—they watch what they're doing and remain aware of whether they're doing it effectively and to the best of their ability.

Pick a few examples that you think would help you transition to the first year of high school.

Transitioning from Middle School to High School

Your first day of high school will be exciting and might make you a little anxious. You will have a lot of questions such as; Where is my homeroom? Where is my first class of the day? When do I eat lunch? The list will continue throughout the day. As the week progresses, you will learn the written and unwritten rules of high school. Your teachers and principal are there to help you so don't be afraid to ask questions.

> **NOTE**
>
> Key activities to participate
>
> - High school web pages have a host of valuable information. Make yourself familiar with what they offer.
> - Look over the student handbook that you can find online.
> - Consult teacher web pages and make sure that you pay close attention to any classroom rules that are posted on the internet.
> - Attend an open house or any back-to-school events.
> - Some schools have evening activities so that you can get acquainted with the building, staff and your fellow peers.
> - Join a club or get involved with athletics.

Your First Year in High School

The beginning of any transition you have in life is crucial to your success in the long term. Starting off on the right foot during your first year in high school will impact future opportunities and influence the kind of choices you are provided in the future. Keep in mind, your freshman year in high school is more than just a move to a different building; it's a part of transitioning through stages of your life. No matter what your circumstances, you have an opportunity to start fresh and begin a path to lifelong success.

Academically, your time as a middle school student will be different from high school. Your grades for each course are linked to earning credits for grade level advancement and ultimately graduation. It is imperative to understand that your first year in high school is arguably the most important. For starters, your grade point average (GPA), which is an average of all the grades you will receive in high school is a crucial part of your success path. The cumulative GPA is the grade point average of all the grades you earned in a semester or term, and an overall GPA is an average of all your cumulative GPAs, which you earned in all your high school coursework. Why is this important? Simply put, your freshman year GPA is a roadmap to success or regrettable failure. Research has shown that the freshman year of high school on average has the lowest GPA, highest absenteeism, the highest level of failing grades and the most discipline referrals (McCallumore & Sparapani, 2010).

What does that mean to you? Transitions are difficult for reasons mentioned previously; your classes will have a more rigorous approach than what you experienced in middle school, in other words, the work will be more difficult. When you do poorly in classes, you become disengaged, and that leads to missing school. Stay engaged for your well-being. Don't miss school, despite what you might think, teachers do want to help you. Your behavior and attitude can go a long way in helping your performance in school. Ask for help, and no matter what challenges you face your teachers are always there to support you.

High School Attendance

You wouldn't think there's a need to mention attendance but something so obvious must be addressed. Students with chronic absenteeism are more likely to see drops in their grade point averages and see a significant increase in disciplinary problems. Keep in mind, as you enter your freshman year there are many pitfalls that can keep you from graduating. In fact, it is estimated that one in four high school freshmen will not graduate.

Think About It—Journal Entry 1.4

How would you rate your academic self-confidence at this point in your high school experience? (Circle one.)

very confident   somewhat confident
somewhat unconfident   very unconfident

Why?

_____
_____
_____
_____

AUTHOR'S EXPERIENCE

When I went to high school, I had to work to assist my family. Although I was a kid, I came from a very poor family and it was part of my obligation to assist them financially. It was more important to me to go to school and graduate so I could have a higher standard of living than my mother and father. Juggling my work life and school life quickly became a reality to which I had to adjust. Thus, I made sure I made the time to study and attend class my first priority. By placing my future above my immediate present, I was able to finish high school and go to college and achieve way beyond my parents' earnings.

—*Aaron Thompson*

Effective Classroom Behavior: The Fundamentals

In high school, there will be expectations regarding appropriate behavior inside and outside the classroom. These expectations will vary, depending on the type of course you're taking—traditional face-to-face, online, technology-enhanced, or hybrid. With a few exceptions (e.g., you can wear pajamas while participating in an online course at home), the following expectations apply to all high school courses.

Regardless of the type of course you take, you will be expected to know basic computer skills such as how to save, download, and send documents. If you have minimal computer skills refer to the Learn Free Basic Computer Skills website (http://www.gcflearnfree.org/basic-computer-skills) for helpful information.

1. **Avoid inappropriate and "uncivil" classroom behavior.** The following behaviors indicate to the teacher and to your classmates that you're an unmotivated student. In addition, they create a classroom climate that disturbs or disrupts the learning process. Be sure not to engage in any of them.
   - Coming to class late and/or leaving early
   - Walking in and out of the classroom during class
   - Talking with classmates while the teacher (or another classmate) is speaking
   - Disregarding deadlines set by your teacher
   - Using electronic devices for personal purposes
   - Acting disinterested in class (e.g., looking at the window or putting your head on your desk)
   - Doing homework during class time
   - Sleeping in class
   - Using electronic devices. (See **Box 1.3**)

BOX 1.3

Guidelines for Civil and Responsible Use of Personal Technology in the High School Classroom

Behavior that interferes with the right of others to learn or teach in the classroom is referred to as classroom incivility. Listed below are forms of classroom incivility that involve student use of personal technology. Be sure to avoid them.

Using Cell Phones

Keeping a cell phone on in class is a clear form of classroom incivility because it can interfere with the right of others to learn. In a study of high school students who heard a cell phone ringing during class and were later tested on information presented in class, they scored approximately 25% lower for information that was presented at the time a cell phone rang. This drop in performance was found even if the material was covered by the professor just prior to the cell phone ringing and if it was projected on a slide while the phone rang. The study also showed that students' attention to information presented in class is significantly reduced when classmates frantically search through handbags or pockets to find and silence a ringing (or vibrating) phone (Shelton et al., 2009). These findings clearly suggest that cell phone use in class disrupts the learning process and the civil thing to do is:

BOX 1.3 (CONT)

> "The right to do something does not mean that doing it is right."
> —William Safire, American author, journalist, and presidential speech writer

- Turn your cell phone off before entering class, or keep it out of the classroom altogether. (You can use *studiousapp.com* to automatically silence your phone at times of the day when you're in class.) In rare cases where you may need to leave class to respond to an emergency, ask your teacher for permission in advance.
- Don't check your cell phone during the class period by turning it off and on.
- Don't look at your cell phone at any time during a test because your teacher may suspect that you're looking up answers to test questions.

Text Messaging

Although this form of electronic communication is silent, it still can distract or disturb your classmates. It's also discourteous or disrespectful to teachers when you put your head down and turn your attention away from them while they're speaking in class. The bottom line: Be sensitive to your classmates and your teacher—don't text in class!

Surfing the Web

Although this can be done without creating distracting sounds, it still can still create visual distractions. Unless you're taking class notes on it, keep your laptop closed to avoid distracting your classmates and raising your teachers' suspicion that you're a disinterested or disrespectful student.

Cyberbullying

Bullying has long been a troubled aspect of schooling. Technology has added a cruel twist on this troubling trend referred to as cyberbullying. This form of psychological cruelty is not only mentally stressful, it's dangerous. For some, it's crippling and debilitating, pushing some children to feel so hopeless that they hurt themselves, or worse, end their lives. Don't be a part of it, in fact, intervene, be a friend and more than anything else show your humanity. Life is precious and so short, don't be a part of the crowd that has no respect for others or themselves. Ask yourself how you would feel in that same spot. Show empathy and support.

Final Note: In addition to technological incivilities, other discourteous classroom behaviors include personal grooming, holding side conversations, and doing homework for other classes. Even if your attendance is perfect, "little things" you do in class that reflect inattention or disinterest can send a strong message to your teachers that you're an unmotivated and discourteous student. Many schools have different policies on student usage of cell phones during school hours and others allow teachers to create their own classroom rules. As stated earlier, always adhere to school and classroom policies.

 Think About It—Journal Entry 1.6

Have you observed any recent examples of classroom incivility that you thought were particularly distracting or discourteous? What was the uncivil behavior and what consequences did it have on others?

_____
_____
_____
_____

Technology should be used sensitively and civilly not only inside the classroom, but outside the classroom as well. There are common rules of courtesy for Internet use (referred to as "netiquette") that should be used in social media. These rules are summarized in **Box 1.4**.

BOX 1.4

Top 20 Rules to Follow for Appropriate Netiquette

1. The Internet is not private. What goes out on the airwaves stays on the airwaves! Do not post pictures to the Internet that you would not want your mom or younger cousin to see.
2. Avoid saying anything that could be interpreted as derogatory (e.g., no cursing).
3. Do not say harsh or mean things to someone over e-mail or text (this could be considered cyber bullying) and do not post nasty, mean, or insulting items about someone.
4. Do not respond to nasty e-mails sent to you.
5. Do not break up with a significant other via text or e-mail.
6. When you receive an e-mail that says to forward it to everyone you know, please don't.
7. Do not use ALL CAPITALS. IT IMPLIES YOU ARE SHOUTING!!!
8. When you send messages online, make sure you proofread and correct mistakes before sending.
9. Do not forward other people's e-mails without their permission.
10. Do not forward virus warnings. They are generally hoaxes.
11. Ask before you send huge attachments.
12. Keep your communications short and to the point.
13. Do not leave the subject field blank in e-mails.
14. Avoid posting personal messages to a listserv.
15. Avoid using texting language for e-mails or social media sites (use correct spellings and correct language mechanics).
16. Remember to treat others online as you would like to be treated.
17. Use the Internet in ways that do not take away from your learning, but add to it.
18. Allow an appropriate amount of time for a person to respond to a message (24–48 business hours).
19. Be sure to have an appropriate salutation (i.e., *good morning, hello*) and closing (i.e., *goodbye, see you tomorrow,* etc.) in your e-mails.
20. Avoid slang (i.e., *wha's up, yo,* etc.) and acronyms (*btw, lol,* etc.)

Also, be sure your communication with your teacher, both in and out of the classroom is appropriate. E-mailing and text messaging are very different forms of communication. Texting is very informal. E-mail, especially to an teacher is considered a professional form of communication. Be sure to treat it that way. First, be sure to send the e-mail from your school e-mail address. Other e-mails often go to spam or junk folders. Do not leave the subject line blank and be sure the subject pertains to your e-mail. Address your teacher appropriately. State your question or concern (be aware of your tone). Avoid all slang and close your e-mail appropriately. Appropriate response time for an e-mail is 24 business hours. Give your teachers enough time to respond to your e-mail and do not inundate their inbox with multiple e-mails about the same issue. See box below for an example of an appropriate e-mail to an teacher and one that could use some work.

How to E-mail (or not) your Teacher

An example of what not to do:

To: highschoolteacher@xyzhighschoo.edu

From: pimpdaddy@bade-mail.com

Subject: WHATEVER!

Yo teach! Wha's up?
I know you did not give me an F on that test!!!! I studied all night for that and I know I should not have failed. Tell me how you are gonna fix this cuz I gotta pass your class.

Peace!

An example of an appropriate e-mail:

To:

From: concernedstudent@

Subject: My test grade

Good morning teacher (name),
I am concerned about my grade on the last test. I got an F and I don't know what I did wrong. I studied all night for that test! Can I meet with you to discuss some strategies about how I might do better on the next test? I really want to pass this class.

Please let me know when you are available to meet. I appreciate your time.

Sincerely,

Concerned Student

It is important to pay attention to your behavior on social media (Facebook, Instagram, Twitter, etc.) as well. Once you post something on the Internet it is always out "in the cloud." Even when you delete a post, highly skilled people can find it. Coaches, potential employers, colleges, etc. are taking a closer look at social media profiles to aid in their decision making process. Just as you think before you speak, you should think before you post. Refrain from posting anything illegal, rude, disrespectful, or in poor taste. Also be sure to refrain from cyberbullying. People tend to be much more brave when they can hide behind a computer. Don't post anything online that you would not say in person. All of these things could affect your future in far more ways than you realize.

2. **Avoid plagiarism.** Plagiarism is a violation of academic integrity that involves intentional or unintentional use of someone else's work without acknowledging it, which gives the reader the impression that it's your own work. Listed below are common forms of plagiarism.
    - Paying someone, or paying a service, for a paper and turning it in as your own work.

- Submitting an entire paper, or portion thereof, that was written by someone else.
- Copying sections of someone else's work and inserting it into your own work.
- Cutting paragraphs from separate sources and pasting them into the body of your own paper.
- Paraphrasing or rewording someone else's words or ideas without citing that person as a source. (Good strategies for paraphrasing without plagiarizing may be found at: http://www.upenn.edu/academicintegrity/ai_paraphrasing.html.)
- Placing someone else's exact words in the body of your paper and not placing quotation marks around them.
- Failing to cite the source of factual information in your paper that's not common knowledge.

Good examples of different forms of plagiarism may be found at: http://www.princeton.edu/pr/pub/integrity/pages/plagiarism/

Two other things to keep in mind:
- If you include information in your paper and just list its source in your reference (works cited) section—without citing the source in the *body* of your paper—this still qualifies as plagiarism.
- Be sure only to include sources in your reference section that you actually used and cited in the body of your paper. Although including sources in your reference section that aren't cited in your paper isn't technically a form of plagiarism, it may be viewed as being deceitful because you're "padding" your reference section, giving the reader the impression that you incorporated more sources into your paper than you actually did.

> "When a student violates an academic integrity policy no one wins, even if the person gets away with it. It isn't right to cheat and it is an insult to everyone who put the effort in and did the work, and it cheapens the school for everyone. I learned my lesson and have no intention of ever cheating again."
> —First-year student's reflection on an academic integrity violation.

> "I understood what I did was morally wrong and now I have to overcome it and move on living morally and ethically. It's really amazing that integrity is in everything we do in our lives."
> —First-year student's reflection on an academic integrity violation

Think About It—Journal Entry 1.7

Reflect back at the different forms of plagiarism just described. Were there any you were surprised to see, or didn't realize were plagiarism?

_____

_____

_____

_____

_____

_____

Career Paths

Increasingly, students are asked to look at career pathways at an earlier age. More often the responses from students, parents, and teachers will say "I didn't know what I wanted to do for a career until I was out of high school." For some, this may be true but consider how much the workforce has changed in the last 50 years. Manufacturing jobs are no longer a guarantee. You cannot depend on getting a job where your parents work. Why? Mostly, because the job market has changed significantly in last several decades, the U. S. economy has shifted from a manufacturing-based economy to one that is more suited to a service oriented economy, creating a demand for a labor force that possesses critical skills that companies desire. American businesses have been critical of the workplace readiness skills that high school graduates have brought to the workplace for quite some time. This need has placed more responsibility on schools to meet this critical piece of student development. The purpose of this book is to support you through this process in becoming ready to work or move on to college as soon as you graduate high school. Throughout your formal years of education, you have been taught the basics—reading, math, science and social studies to name a few. In the proceeding chapters, we discuss these critical skill sets and provide you with a roadmap for navigating high school successfully.

> **NOTE**
>
> What do you need to know and look for as you begin your career path journey?
> 8th grade
>
> - Inventory of interests
> - Mentorships (Rural areas—look for reaching out to local companies for opportunities)
> - Service learning in areas that interest you (grades 9-12)
> - Job shadowing experiences
> - Explore Career Technical Education options
> - Attend career fairs
> - Visit college campuses
> - Work during the summer
> - Mock interviews
> - Duel enrollment and post-secondary opportunities

High School and Beyond

For some, attending college has been an expectation with a select few viewing it as a birth right. For others, college seems an impossibility because of life circumstances and others have no interest in going to college. The key to success is not necessarily earning a college degree, but planning a path to a self-fulfilling career. You may choose to enter the workforce, join the military or enroll in a trade-related training program. Individual choices you make regarding your future depend entirely on your talents, interests, and passion. No matter what path you decide, the work you do is important. For example, some of you will choose to join the military in service of our country or choose to enter the workforce. Either choice is of vital importance to you as far as a career choice and to the overall well-being of our nation.

CHAPTER SUMMARY AND HIGHLIGHTS

This chapter highlighted the fact that successful students understand:

1. The differences between middle school and high school
2. Know the rules and understand the differences in expectations regarding their behavior and the increase in rigor they will face in high school.
3. What constitutes responsible classroom behavior
4. The dos and don'ts of technology

More specifically, this chapter suggested a number of "top tips" for getting off to a good start in high school. These tips are summarized below.

Don't miss class. Attendance studies repeatedly show that students who go to class earn higher grades. Look at going to school like going to work. If you miss work, you get lower pay; if you cut class, you get lower grades.

Intentionally choose a seat in class that maximizes attention and minimizes distraction. When you enter class, you have a choice about where you're going to sit. Choose wisely by selecting a location that will maximize your attentiveness to the teacher and your effectiveness as a note-taker. Many years of research show that students who sit in the front and center of class tend to earn higher exam scores and course grades.

Sit by people who will enable your ability to listen and learn. Intentionally sit near classmates who will not distract you or interfere with the quality of your note taking.

Be a self-aware learner. Successful students and successful people are *mindful*—they watch what they're doing and remain aware of whether they're doing it effectively and to the best of their ability. You can be a self-aware learner by asking yourself questions such as:

- Am I listening attentively to what my teacher is saying in class?
- Am I comprehending what I'm reading outside of class?
- Am I effectively using school resources designed to support my success?
- Am I interacting with school professionals who can contribute to my current success and future development?

- Am I interacting and collaborating with peers who can support (not sabotage) my learning and development?
- Am I effectively implementing high school success strategies (such as those identified in this book)?

Avoid inappropriate classroom behavior, such as the following:

- Coming to class late
- Talking with classmates while the teacher is speaking
- Disregarding deadlines set by your teacher
- Using electronic devices for personal purposes
- Acting disinterested in class (e.g., looking out the window or putting your head on your desk)
- Doing homework during class time
- Using electronic devices in class (e.g., texting or surfing the web)

Avoid plagiarism. Plagiarism is a violation of academic integrity that involves intentional or unintentional use of someone else's work without acknowledging it, which gives the reader the impression that it's your own work. Common forms of plagiarism include:

- Paying someone, or paying a service, for a paper and turning it in as your own work.
- Submitting an entire paper, or portion thereof, that was written by someone else.
- Copying sections of someone else's work and inserting it into your own work.
- Cutting paragraphs from separate sources and pasting them into the body of your own paper.
- Paraphrasing or rewording someone else's words or ideas without citing that person as a source. (Good strategies for paraphrasing without plagiarizing may be found at: http://www.upenn.edu/academicintegrity/ai_paraphrasing.html.)
- Placing someone else's exact words in the body of your paper and not placing quotation marks around them.
- Failing to cite the source of factual information in your paper that's not common knowledge.

Learning More through the World Wide Web: Internet-Based Resources

For additional information on strategies for high school success, see the following websites:

Resources to find a career path
USA jobs
https://www.usajobs.gov/

Bureau of Labor Statistics
https://www.bls.gov/careeroutlook/2015/article/career-planning-for-high-schoolers.htm

Dictionary of Occupational Titles
www.occupationalinfo.org

Occupational Outlook Handbook
www.bls.gov/oco

Occupational Information Network
www.online.onetcenter.org

References

Appleby, D. C. (2008, June). *Diagnosing and treating the deadly 13th grade syndrome*. Paper presented at the Association of Psychological Science Convention, Chicago, IL.

Benedict, M. E., & Hoag, J. (2004). Seating location in large lectures: Are seating preferences or location related to course performance? *Journal of Economics Education, 35*, 215–231.

Credé, M., Roch, S. G., & Kieszczynka, U. M. (2010). Class attendance in college: A meta-analytic review of the relationship of class attendance with grades and student characteristics. *Review of Educational Research, 80*(2), 272–295.

Howard, P. J. (2014). *The owner's manual for the brain: Everyday applications of mind-brain research* (4th ed.). New York: HarperCollins.

Kuh, G. D. (2005). Student engagement in the first year of college. In M. L. Upcraft, J. N. Gardner, B. O. Barefoot, & Associates, *Challenging and supporting the first-year student: A handbook for improving the first year of college* (pp. 86–107). San Francisco: Jossey-Bass.

Launius, M. H. (1997). College student attendance: Attitudes and academic performance. *College Student Journal, 31*(1), 86–93.

National Survey of Student Engagement. (2009). *NSSE Annual Results 2009. Assessment for improvement: Tracking student engagement over time*. Bloomington, IN: Author.

Pace, C. (1990). *The undergraduates: A report of their activities*. Los Angeles: University of California, Center for the Study of Evaluation.

Pace, C. (1995, May). *From good processes to good products: Relating good practices in undergraduate education to student achievement*. Paper presented at the meeting of the Association for Institutional Research, Boston.

Pascarella, E., & Terenzini, P. (1991). *How college affects students: Findings and insights from twenty years of research*. San Francisco: Jossey-Bass.

Pascarella, E., & Terenzini, P. (2005). *How college affects students: A third decade of research* (Vol. 2). San Francisco: Jossey-Bass.

Pintrich, P. R., & Schunk, D. H. (2002). *Motivation in education: Theory, research, and applications*. Upper Saddle River, NJ: Merrill-Prentice Hall.

Pryor, J. H., De Angelo, L., Palucki-Blake, B., Hurtado, S., & Tran, S. (2012) *The American freshman: National norms fall 2011*. Los Angeles: Higher Education Research Institute, UCLA.

Rennels, M. R., & Chaudhair, R. B. (1988). Eye-contact and grade distribution. *Perceptual and Motor Skills, 67* (October), 627–632.

Shelton, J. T., Elliot, E. M., Eaves, S. D., & Exner, A. L. (2009). The distracting effects of a ringing cell phone: An investigation of the laboratory and the classroom setting. *Journal of Environmental Psychology*, (March). Retrieved from http://news-info.wustl.edu/news/page/normal/14225.html.

Shimoff, E., & Catania, C. A. (2001). Effects of recording attendance on grades in Introductory Psychology. *Teaching of Psychology, 23*(3), 19–195.

Tagliacollo, V. A., Volpato, G. L., & Pereira, A., Jr. (2010). Association of student position in classroom and school performance. *Educational Research, 1*(6), 198–201.

Walsh, K. (2005). *Suggestions from more experienced classmates*. Retrieved from http://www.uni.edu/walsh/introtips.html.

CHAPTER 1 EXERCISES

1.1 QUOTE REFLECTIONS

Review the sidebar quotes contained in this chapter and select two that were especially meaningful or inspirational to you.

For each quote, provide a three- to five-sentence explanation why you chose it.

1.2 REALITY BITE

Crime and Punishment: Plagiarism and Its Consequences

In an article that appeared in an Ohio newspaper, titled "Plagiarism persists in classrooms," an English professor is quoted as saying: "Technology has made it easier to plagiarize because students can download papers and exchange information and papers through their computers. But technology has also made it easier to catch students who plagiarize." This professor works at a high school that subscribes to a website that matches the content of students' papers with content from books and online sources. Many professors now require students to submit their papers through this website. If students are caught plagiarizing, for a first offense, they typically receive an F for the assignment or the course. A second offense can result in dismissal or expulsion from high school, which has already happened to a few students.

Reflection and Discussion Questions

1. What do you suspect are their primary motives or reasons why students plagiarize from the web?
2. What would you say is a fair or just penalty for those found guilty of a first plagiarism violation? What do you think would be fair penalty for a second violation?
3. How might web-based plagiarism be minimized or prevented from happening in the first place?

1.3 SYLLABUS REVIEW

Review the syllabus (course outline) for all classes you're enrolled in this term, and complete the following information for each course.

Self-Assessment Questions

1. Is the overall workload what you expected? Are your surprised by the amount of work required in any particular course(s)?
2. At this point in the term, what do you see as your most challenging or demanding course or courses? Why?
3. Do you think you can handle the total workload required by the full set of courses you're enrolled in this term?
4. What adjustments or changes do you think you'll make to your previous learning and study habits to accommodate your academic workload this term?

1.4 IS IT OR IS IT NOT PLAGIARISM?

The following four incidents were brought to a judicial review board to determine if plagiarism had occurred and, if so, what the penalty should be. After reading each case, answer the questions listed below it.

Case 1. A student turned in an essay that included substantial material copied from a published source. The student admitted that he didn't cite the sources properly, but argued that it was because he misunderstood the directions, not because he was attempting to steal someone else's ideas.

Is this Plagiarism?

How severe is it? (Rate it on a scale from 1 = low to 5 = high)

What should the consequence or penalty be?

How could the accusation of plagiarism been avoided?

Case 2. A student turned in a paper that was identical to a paper submitted by another student for a different course.

Is this plagiarism?

How severe is it? (Rate it on a scale from 1 = low to 5 = high)

What should the consequence or penalty be?

How could the accusation of plagiarism been avoided?

Case 3. A student submitted a paper he wrote in a previous course as an extra credit paper for a current course.

Is this plagiarism?

How severe is it? (Rate it on a scale from 1 = low to 5 = high)

What should the consequence or penalty be?

How could the accusation of plagiarism been avoided?

Case 4. A student submitted a paper in an art history that contained some ideas from art critics she read about and whose ideas she agreed with. The student didn't cite the critics as sources, but claimed it wasn't plagiarism because their ideas were merely their own subjective judgments or opinions, not facts or findings; furthermore, they were opinions she agreed with.

Is this plagiarism?

How severe is it? (Rate it on a scale from 1 = low to 5 = high)

What should the consequence or penalty be?

How could the accusation of plagiarism been avoided?

1.5 CHAPTER 1 REFLECTION

List five strategies discussed in this chapter that you intend to use to achieve high school success, and explain HOW you plan to put them into practice.

CHAPTER 2

MAKING CONNECTIONS: FOUR STEPS TO YOUR SUCCESS

Using Powerful Principles of Student Success and Key School Resources

CHAPTER PREVIEW

This chapter focuses on the "big picture": powerful principles you can implement to promote your own success and key school resources you can use to help you succeed. It describes what these key principles and resources are, why they're effective, and how to capitalize on them.

LEARNING GOAL

Alert you to the most powerful strategies and resources you can use immediately to get off to a fast start in high school and continually to achieve excellence throughout your high school experience.

THOUGHT STARTER

Think About It—Journal Entry 2.1

1. What excites you about starting high school?

   _____
   _____
   _____
   _____
   _____

2. What concerns do you have about starting high school?

   _____
   _____
   _____
   _____
   _____
   _____

From *Thriving in the Community College & Beyond: Strategies for Academic Success and Personal Development*, Third Edition, by Joseph Cuseo, Aaron Thompson, and Julie McLaughlin. Copyright © 2016 by Kendall Hunt Publishing Company. Reprinted by permission.

Four Steps to High School Success

Research points to four powerful principles of high school success:

1. Active Involvement (Engagement)
2. Capitalizing on School Resources (Resourcefulness)
3. Interpersonal Interaction and Collaboration (Social Integration)
4. Reflection and Self-Awareness (Mindfulness)

(Sources: Astin, 1993; Kuh et al., 2005; Light, 2001; Pascarella & Terenzini, 1991, 2005; Tinto, 1993.)

These four principles are presented in the beginning of this book because they represent the foundational basis for all success strategies discussed throughout the book.

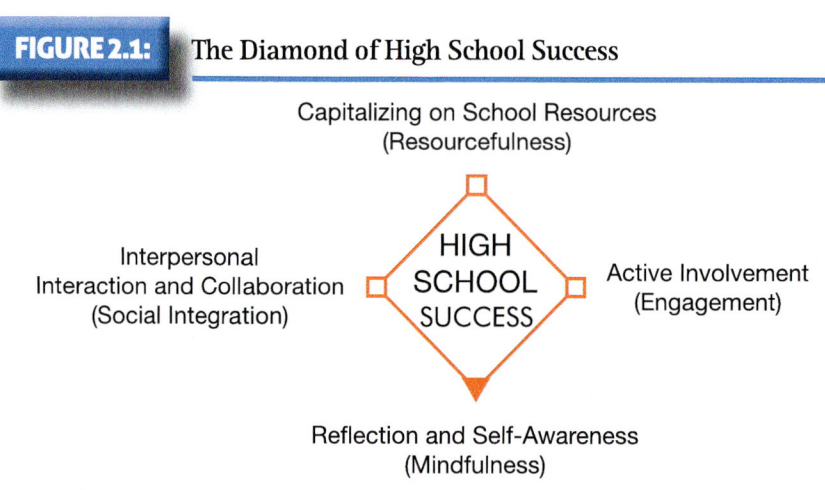

FIGURE 2.1: The Diamond of High School Success

© Kendall Hunt Publishing Company

> "Tell me and I'll listen. Show me and I'll understand. Involve me and I'll learn."
> —Teton Lakota Indian saying

First Step to High School Success: Active Involvement (Engagement)

Research indicates that active involvement may be the most powerful principle of human learning and academic success (Astin, 1993; Kuh et al., 2005). Although this research was done on college students, it can be extrapolated to high school. To succeed in high school, you can't be a passive spectator; you need to be an active player.

Active involvement includes the following key components:

- The amount of *time* you devote to the high school experience—inside and outside the classroom.
- The degree of *effort or energy* (mental and physical) you invest in the learning process.

Think of something you do with intensity, passion, and commitment. If you were to approach high school in the same way, you would be faithfully implementing the principle of active involvement. Here's how you can apply both key components of active involvement—time and energy—to the major learning challenges you'll face in high school.

Active Involvement in the Learning Process

Success will require that you work harder (put in more time than middle school) and work smarter (learn more strategically and effectively). Probably the most powerful principle of effective learning is active involvement (engagement); there's simply no such thing as "passive learning." You can ensure you're actively involved in the learning process by engaging in some form of *action* on what you're learning, such as the actions listed below.

- *Writing*. For example, when reading, take notes on what you're reading rather than passively highlighting sentences.
- *Speaking*. For example, rather than studying silently, explain what you're learning to a study group partner.
- *Organizing*. For example, create an outline, diagram, or concept map that pulls together the ideas you're learning.

Active Listening and Note Taking in Class

You will that find that high school teachers will spend 30–40 minutes reviewing the material by lecturing, group or individual work. Focus on taking careful notes and reviewing the material covered in class that day. The lecture method of instruction places great demands on your ability to listen actively and take notes that are both accurate and complete. Research consistently shows that most questions on high school tests are aligned with content standards material generated from the available curriculum and from classroom activities (Fives & Barnes, 2016).

The best way to apply the principle of active involvement during a class lecture is to engage in the physical action of writing notes. Writing down what your teacher is saying in class "forces" you to pay closer attention to what is being said and reinforces your retention of what was said. By taking notes, you not only hear the information (auditory memory), you also see it on paper (visual memory) and feel it in the muscles of your hand as you write it (motor memory).

NOTE

Your role in the high school classroom is not that of a passive spectator or an absorbent sponge who sits back and soaks up information through osmosis. Instead, it's like being an aggressive detective or investigative reporter on a search-and-record mission. Your job is to actively search for information by picking your teacher's brain, picking out the teacher's key points, and recording your "pickings" in your notebook.

> "All genuine learning is active, not passive. It is a process in which the student is the main agent, not the teacher."
> —Mortimer Adler, American professor of philosophy and educational theorist

Box 2.1 contains a summary of top strategies for classroom listening and note taking that you can put into action right now.

BOX 2.1

Top Tips for Active Listening and Note Taking in the High School Classroom

One task that you'll be expected to perform during the very first week of college is taking notes in class. Studies show that many college professors utilize their lecture content to create their exams. High school teachers generally follow the same pattern when constructing their assessments. You can improve the quality of your note taking and your course grades by using the following strategies.

1. **Attendance, get to school!** – Studies about attendance always have the obvious results. Attending school leads to graduation. If you consider your days at school like it's your job then its not as bad as you think. High school is a time for you to plan ahead. When you leave high school a number of choices will be provided to you. College, career or joining the military are choices to consider during your four years of high school. So make your time in high school count for something.
2. **Get to every class on time.** During the first few minutes of a class session, teachers often share valuable information—such as important reminders, reviews, and previews. So don't be tardy to class!
3. **Get organized.** Bring the right equipment to class. Get a separate notebook for each class, write your name on it, date each class session, and store all class handouts in it.
4. **Get in the right position.**
   - The ideal place to sit in class is at the front and center of the room—where you're in the best position to hear and see what's going on.
   - The ideal posture to adopt is sitting upright and leaning forward—because your body influences your mind; if your body is in an alert and ready position, your mind is likely to follow.
   - The ideal social position to occupy in class is near motivated classmates who will not distract you, but motivate you to listen actively and take notes aggressively.

NOTE

These attention-focusing strategies are particularly important in large classes where you're likely to feel more anonymous, less accountable, and less engaged.

5. **Get in the right frame of mind.** Come to class with the attitude that you're there to pick your teacher's brain, pick up answers to test questions, and pick up points to elevate your course grade.
6. **Get it down (in writing).** Actively look, listen, and record important points at all times in class. Pay special attention to whatever information teachers put in writing, whether it appears on the board, on a slide, or in a handout.
7. **Don't let go of your pen (or keyboard).** When in doubt, write it out (or type it out); it's better to have it and not need it than to need it and not have it.
8. **Finish strong.** During the last few minutes of class, teachers often share valuable information, such as timely reminders, reviews, and previews.

 Think About It—Journal Entry 2.2

When you enter a classroom, where do you usually sit?

Why do you sit there? Is it a conscious choice or more like an automatic habit?

___

Do you think that the seat you usually choose places you in the best possible position for listening and learning in the classroom?

___

Active Class Participation

You can implement the principle of active involvement in the classroom by not only taking notes in class, but also by being an engaged participant who comes to class well prepared (e.g., having done the assigned reading), asks relevant questions, and contributes thoughtful comments during class discussions. Class participation increases your ability to stay alert and attentive in class, and it sends a clear message to your teachers that you are a motivated student who wants to learn. Class participation is also likely to account for a portion of your grade in many courses, so your attentiveness and involvement in class can have a direct, positive effect on your grades. Consider these as skills you can develop during high school that translate well in the future, whether you attend college or move into a career.

Active Reading

Note-taking not only promotes active listening in class, it also promotes active reading out of class. Taking notes on what you're reading (or on information you've highlighted while reading) keeps you actively involved in the reading process because it requires more mental and physical energy than merely reading the material or passively highlighting sentences.

High school teachers will support you and help you develop these important study skills. Thus, it's important to start developing good reading habits now. You can do so by using the top tips suggested in **Box 2.2**.

BOX 2.2

Top Tips for Strengthening Textbook Reading Comprehension and Retention

1. **High school teachers often will lecture based on the readings assigned in class.** In fact, reading assignments ranks right behind lectures as a source of test questions. Many teachers deliver their lectures with the expectation that you've done the assigned reading and assume you can build on that knowledge to understand their lectures. If you haven't done the reading, you'll have more difficulty following what your teacher is saying in class. Thus, by not doing the assigned reading you pay a double penalty: you miss information from the reading that's not covered in class which will likely appear on exams, and you miss understanding ideas presented in class that build on the reading.

2. **Read with the right equipment.**
   - Bring a writing tool (pen, pencil, or keyboard) to record important information and a storage space (notebook or computer) in which you can save and later retrieve information found in your reading.
   - Use online resources as well, but consider asking your teacher what a trusted or respected source might be. Have a dictionary nearby to quickly find the meaning of unfamiliar words that may interfere with your ability to comprehend what you're reading. Looking up definitions of unfamiliar words helps you understand what you're reading and also builds your vocabulary. A strong vocabulary will improve your reading comprehension in all high school courses, as well as your performance on standardized tests, such as those required for admission to careers, college, graduate and professional schools.
   - Check the back of your textbook for a glossary (list) of key terms included in the book. Each subject and academic discipline has its own special language, and decoding it is often the key to understanding the concepts covered in the course. The glossary that appears at the end of your textbook is more than an ancillary add-on, it's a valuable tool that you can use to improve your comprehension of course concepts. Consider making a photocopy of the glossary at the back of your textbook so you can access it easily while you're reading—without having to repeatedly stop, hold your place, and go to the back of the text to find it.

3. **Get in the right position.** Sit upright and have light coming from behind you, over the side of your body opposite your writing hand. This will reduce the distracting and fatiguing effects of glare and shadows.

4. **Get a sneak preview.** Approach the chapter by first reading its boldface headings and any chapter outline, summary, or end-of-chapter questions that may be provided. This will supply you with a mental map of the chapter's important ideas before you start your trip through it. Getting an overview of the chapter will help you keep track of its chapter's major ideas (the "big picture") and reduce your risk of getting lost in all the smaller details you encounter along the way.

5. Finish each of your reading sessions with a short review. Rather than using the last few minutes of a reading session to cover a few more pages, end it with a review of what you've highlighted or noted as important information. Since most forgetting takes place immediately after you stop processing (taking in) information and start doing something else, it's best to use your last minutes of reading time to "lock in" the most important information you've just read.

NOTE

When reading, your goal is to discover or uncover the most important ideas, so the final step in the reading process should be to review (and lock in) the most important ideas you've discovered.

For a more detailed discussion of reading comprehension and retention, see Chapter 5 (pp. 113–114).

Think About It—Journal Entry 2.3

Which of the five reading strategies listed in **Box 2.2** have you used in the past? Which of these strategies do you intend to use in the future?

_____

_____

_____

_____

_____

Second Step to High School Success: Capitalizing on School Resources (Resourcefulness)

Successful people are *resourceful*; they seek out and take advantage of resources to help them reach their goals. Your school is chock full of resources that have been intentionally designed to support your quest for educational and personal success. Studies show that students who utilize school resources report higher levels of satisfaction with their educational experience and get more out of their education (Pascarella & Terenzini, 1991, 2005).

Utilizing school resources is a natural extension of the principle of active involvement. Successful students are *involved* students, both inside and outside the classroom.

NOTE

Capitalizing on school resources is not only valuable, it' also "free"! Your high school guidance counselor is a huge resource of information for career, college and advice for course choices.

Disability Services

If you have a physical or learning disability that's interfering with your performance in high school, or you think you may have such a disability, Disability Services is the campus resource to consult for assistance and support. Programs and services typically provided by this office include:

- Assessment for learning disabilities;
- Verification of eligibility for disability support services;
- Authorization of academic accommodations for students with disabilities; and
- Specialized counseling, advising, and tutoring.

NOTE

Using a tutor or other support services doesn't mean you're helpless, need remedial repart work, or require academic life support because you're on the verge of failing a class. Instead, it's a that you're a motivated and resourceful student who is striving for academic success.

Media Center Library

This is your school resource for finding information and completing research assignments (e.g., term papers and group projects). Librarians are professional educators who provide instruction outside the classroom; you can learn from them just as you can learn from faculty inside the classroom. They can help you develop research skills for accessing, retrieving, and evaluating information.

These are lifelong learning skills that promote your educational success at all stages of the high school as well as your college and professional life.

Guidance Counseling

Whether or not you have an assigned guidance counselor, the guidance counselor office is your school resource for help with course selection, educational planning, and choosing or changing a college and career paths. Be sure to find out who your guidance counselor is and where he or she is located. Studies show that students who develop clear educational and career goals are more likely to persist in school and complete their degree (Lotkowski, Robbins, & Noeth, 2004). Research also indicates that most beginning students need help clarifying their educational goals and identifying career options (Cuseo, 2005; Tinto, 2012). Being undecided or uncertain about your educational and career goals is nothing to be embarrassed about. However, you should start thinking about your future now. Start now, talk to your guidance counselor and connect early and often with a counselor to help you clarify your educational goals and choose a career pathway that best complements your interests, talents, and values.

Student Development Opportunities

Involvement in student life outside the classroom, including student clubs and organizations, recreational programs, leadership activities, and volunteer experiences is part of the educational process in high school. Research consistently shows that experiential learning outside the classroom contributes as much to your personal development and career success as class work (Kuh, 1995; Kuh et al., 1994; Pascarella & Terenzini, 2005). This is one reason why most schools no longer refer to out-of-class experiences as "*extra*curricular" activities; instead they are referred to as "*co*-curricular" experiences—which conveys the message they're equally important as classroom-based learning. Studies show that students who become actively involved in school life are more likely to:

- Enjoy their school experience;
- Graduate and
- Develop leadership skills that enhance career performance beyond high school (Astin, 1993).

Devoting some out-of-class time to co-curricular experiences should not interfere with your academic performance. Research indicates that students' academic performance and progress to degree completion aren't impaired if they spend 20 or fewer hours on co-curricular and part-time work experiences (Advisory Committee on Student Financial Assistance, 2008). In fact, they earn higher grades than students who don't get involved in any out-of-class activities (Pascarella, 2001; Pascarella & Terenzini, 2005).

NOTE

Co-curricular experiences are also resume-building experiences, and when you move forward to apply for jobs and college it demonstrates skill sets that are valued by employers.

Although co-curricular involvement is valuable, limit your involvement to no more than two or three co-curricular activities at a time. Restricting the number of your out-of-class activities will not only enable you to keep up with your studies, it will be more impressive to future schools or employers because a long list of involvement in numerous activities may send the message that you're padding your resume with activities you participated in superficially (or never participated in at all).

> "Just a [long] list of club memberships is meaningless; it's a fake front. Remember that quality, not quantity, is what counts."
> —Lauren Pope, former director of the National Bureau for College Placement

 Think About It—Journal Entry 2.4

If you were to join one school club or student organization, what would it be? How would participating in this club or organization contribute to your educational development?

_____
_____
_____
_____
_____

Seek Advice

Here's where you can get ideas and strategies for managing high school stress, gaining greater self-awareness, and reaching your full potential. Guidance counselors are professionals who do more than just help students maintain mental health; they also develop students' emotional intelligence, interpersonal skills, and personal growth.

NOTE

Counseling is not just for students experiencing emotional problems. It's for all students who want to enrich the quality of their life.

Third Step to High School Success: Interpersonal Interaction and Collaboration (Social Integration)

Students who become socially integrated or connected with other members of the school community are more likely to complete their degree (Pascarella & Terenzini, 2005; Tinto, 1993). (For effective ways to make interpersonal connections with key members of your high school community, see **Box 2.3**.)

Four particular forms of interpersonal interaction have been found to promote student learning and motivation.

1. Student–teacher interaction,
2. Student–advisor interaction,
3. Student–mentor interaction, and
4. Student–student (peer) interaction.

> **BOX 2.3**
>
> ### Social Integration: Making Connections with Members of Your High School Community
>
> Listed below are top tips for making key social connections in high school. Start developing these relationships right now so you can build a base of social support to help you succeed during the critical first year of high school.
>
> - Join a club, student organization, student government or volunteer service group whose members share the same personal or career interests as you. If you can't find a club or organization you were hoping to join, consider starting it on your own. For example, if you enjoy or excel at English, consider starting a Writing Club or Book Club.
> - Connect with classmates and team up with them to take notes, complete reading assignments, and study for exams. Look especially to team up with a peer who may be in more than one class with you. (For more detailed information on forming collaborative learning teams, see Chapter 5, **pp. 105–106.**)
> - Connect with a high school librarian to get early assistance or a head start on any research
> - Connect with a personal counselor or school minister to discuss high school adjustment or personal challenges you may be experiencing.

Strategies for capitalizing on each of these key forms of interaction are provided below.

Interacting with High School Teachers

High school success is strongly influenced by the frequency and quality of student–teacher interaction outside the classroom. Out-of-class contact with teachers is associated with the following positive outcomes:

- Improved academic performance;
- Increased critical thinking skills;
- Increased likelihood of graduating;
- Stronger desire to pursue further education (Astin, 1993; Pascarella & Terenzini, 1991, 2005).

These positive outcomes are so powerful, strong, and widespread that we encourage you to immediately begin making connections with your teachers outside of class time. Here are some of the easiest ways to do so.

1. **Seek contact with your teachers after school lets out.** Ask for time after school to discuss material covered during the day. If something covered in class captures your interest, approach your teacher to discuss it further. You could ask a quick question about something you weren't sure you understood, or have a short conversation about how the material covered in class really hit home for you or connected with something you learned in another course. Interacting briefly with teachers after class can help them get to know you as an individual and help you gain the confidence to approach them during at other times.

2. **Connect with your teacher during their planning time.** Teachers often have designated time dedicated to class planning.

Try to visit with them during this time if your other classes do not interfere. Even if your early contact with teachers is only for a few minutes, it can be a valuable icebreaker and help you in the future.

3. **Connect with your teachers through e-mail.** Electronic communication is another effective tool for experiencing the benefits of student—teacher interaction outside the classroom, particularly if you're involved in a lot of after-school activities. Keep in mind, there are some guidelines to follow when emailing your teachers (see Chapter 1, **Box 1.4**). E-mail may also be a good way to initially communicate with teachers and build self-confidence to eventually seek out face-to-face interaction with them. In one national survey, almost half of college students reported that e-mail enabled them to communicate their ideas with professors on subjects they would not have discussed in person (Pew Internet & American Life Project, 2002). However, if you miss class, don't use e-mail to ask such questions as:
    - Did I miss anything important in class today?
    - Could you send me your PowerPoint slides from the class I missed?

Also, when using e-mail to communicate with your teachers, be sure to:
- Include your full name in the message.
- Mention the class.
- Use complete sentences, correct grammar, and avoid informal "hip" expressions (e.g., "yo," "whatup").
- Spell check and proofread your message before sending it.
- Include your full contact information. (If you're communicating via Facebook, make sure your screen name is appropriate.)
- Give your instructor time to reply. (Don't expect an immediate response, particularly if you send your message in the evening or on a weekend.) (See Chapter 1, **pp. 11–12**, for more netiquette guidelines.)

Interacting with Your Guidance Counselor

If you need some help understanding the policies and procedures, or navigating the organizational maze of course options and course requirements, a guidance counselor is the person to see. Counselors also serve as key referral agents who can direct you to, and connect you with, support services that best meet your educational needs and career goals. Often they have access to upcoming events to college and career fairs that local agencies sponsor for your benefit. Don't be afraid to ask questions.

Your academic advisor or guidance counselor should be someone whom you feel comfortable speaking with, someone who knows your name, and someone who's familiar with your personal interests and abilities. Give them the opportunity to get to know you personally, and seek their input on courses, majors, and any academic difficulties you may be experiencing.

NOTE

Advisors and guidance counselors can be much more than course schedulers; they can be mentors. Your guidance counselor may be the one professional at school with whom you have regular contact and a continuous relationship throughout your high school experience.

Think About It—Journal Entry 2.5

Have you planned a meeting with the high school guidance counselor?

If yes, do you know who this person is and where he or she can be found?

If you don't have any contact with the guidance counselor, where will you go if you have questions about your class schedule or educational plans?

Interaction with Peers (Student–Student Interaction)

Your peers can be more than competitors or a source of negative peer pressure; they can also be collaborators, a source of positive social influence, and a resource for high school success. Peer support is important at any stage of the high school experience, but it's especially valuable during the first year of high school. It's at this stage when new students have a strong need for belongingness and social acceptance because they're in the midst of a major life transition. As a new student, it may be useful to view your first-year experience through the lens of psychologist Abraham Maslow's hierarchy of human needs (see **Figure 2.2**). According to Maslow, humans only reach their full potential and achieve peak performance after their more basic emotional and social needs have been met (e.g., needs for personal safety, social acceptance, and self-esteem). Making early connections with your peers helps you meet these basic human needs, provides you with a base of social support that eases your integration into the high school environment, and prepares you to move up to higher levels of the need hierarchy (e.g., achieving academic excellence and reaching your educational goals).

Getting involved with school organizations or activities is one way to connect with other students. Also, try to interact with experienced students who have spent more time in school than you. Sophomores, juniors, and seniors can be valuable social resources for a new student. In particular, seek out contact with students who have been selected and trained as peer mentors or peer leaders.

Research clearly demonstrates that students learn as much from peers as they do from instructors and textbooks (Astin, 1993; Pascarella, 2005). One study of more than 25,000 college students

FIGURE 2.2: Maslow's Theory of Self-Actualization

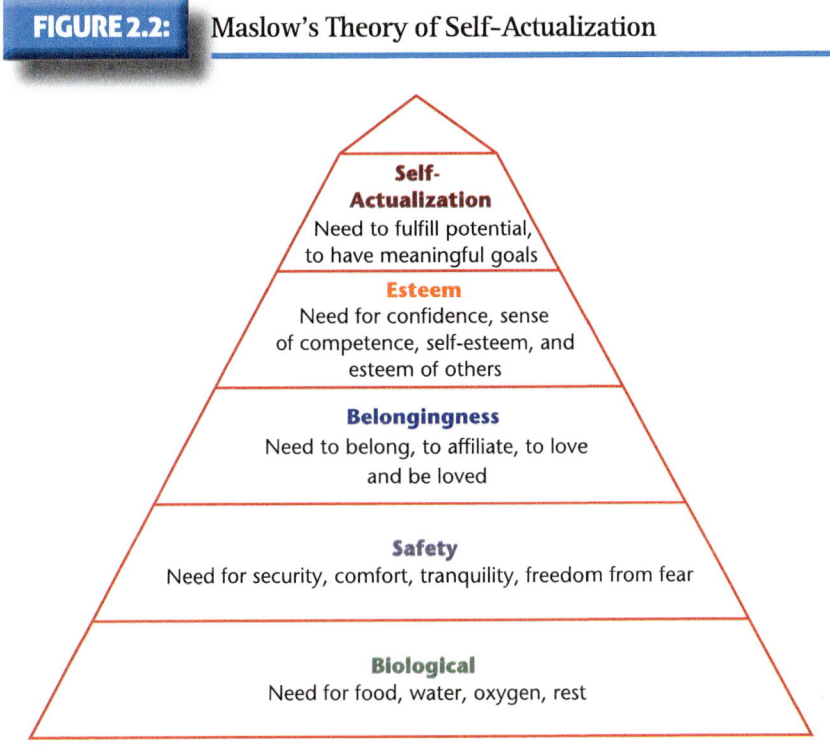

© Kendall Hunt Publishing Company

revealed that when peers interact with one another while learning, they achieve higher levels of academic performance and are more likely to persist to degree completion (Astin, 1993).

Be observant—keep an eye out for peers who are successful. Start building your social support network by surrounding yourself with success-seeking and success-achieving students. Learn from them, emulate their productive habits and strategies, and use them as a social resource to promote your own success.

Collaborative Learning

Simply defined, collaborative learning is the process of two or more people working *interdependently* to advance each other's success—as opposed to working independently or competitively. Learning is strengthened when it takes place in a social context that involves interpersonal interaction. As scholars put it, human knowledge is "socially constructed" or built up through dialogue and an exchange of ideas; conversations with others become internalized as ideas in your mind and influence your way of thinking (Bruffee, 1993). Thus, by having frequent, intelligent conversations with others, you broaden your knowledge base, deepen your learning, and elevate the quality of your thinking.

Research from kindergarten through college shows that students who learn collaboratively in teams experience significant gains in both academic performance and interpersonal skills (Cross, Barkley, & Major, 2005; Cuseo, 1996; Gilles & Adrian, 2003; Johnson, Johnson, &

> "Surround yourself with only people who are going to lift you higher."
> —Oprah Winfrey, actress and talk-show host

> "If you want to go quickly, go by yourself—if you want to go farther, go in a group."
> —African proverb

> "TEAM = Together Everyone Achieves More"
> —Author unknown

Chapter 2: Making Connections: Four Steps to Your Success

> **AUTHOR'S EXPERIENCE**
>
> During my time as a high school principal, I observed many students who surrounded themselves with students who were involved in many positive and healthy choices and peers. Those students began planning their career path early on. Many of their counterparts who struggled to fit in, or made unhealthy personal choices or relationships, found themselves trying to figure out how to get out of trouble or spending more energy on getting negative recognition than planning ahead for a career. Most of those students were not engaged in clubs, organizations or activities associated with the school. I would encourage you to talk with a school representative about what opportunities might exist, or could be developed to help fit your interest. Connect with school professionals who will help guide you in a positive direction, and associate yourself with people who will help you reach your career and life goals.
>
> I actually asked every senior to pick any employee in the district to mentor them. The employee had to agree to commit to helping that student succeed. In the fall, winter (mid-year), and spring each senior was asked three simple questions:
>
> Where have you been? Where are you at? Where are you going? The mentor was charged with helping the student build a plan and making sure the student had the resources to put the plan into action.
>
> *–J.R. Roush*

Smith, 1998). In one national study that involved in-depth interviews with more than 1,600 college students, it was discovered that almost all students who struggled academically had one particular study habit in common: they always studied alone (Light, 2001).

Whether it is succeeding in high school or your future career, you need to be able to work as a member of a team. This is a crucial skill for long-tem advancement in your career and life.

To maximize the power of collaboration, use the following pair of guidelines to choose teammates who will enhance the quality and productivity of your learning team:

1. Observe your classmates with an eye toward identifying potentially good teammates. Look for motivated students who will actively contribute to your team's success (rather than those whom you suspect may just be hitchhikers looking for a free ride).
2. Don't team up exclusively with peers who you are familiar with or who are similar to you in terms of personal characteristics, backgrounds, and experiences. This familiarity can actually interfere with your team's performance by turning your learning team into a social group or gabfest that gets off track and onto topics that have nothing to do with studying (e.g., what you did last weekend or what you're planning to do next weekend). Instead, include teammates who differ from you with respect to such characteristics as: gender, race or ethnicity, and cultural or geographical background. Such variety brings different life experiences, styles of thinking strategies, and learning styles to your team, which enriches your team's diversity and learning capacity.

Keep in mind that collaborative learning can be much more than just forming study groups the night before an exam. You can team up with classmates more regularly to work on a variety of academic tasks, such as those listed below.

> **NOTE**
>
> Capitalize on the advantages of collaborating with peers of varied backgrounds and lifestyles. Studies show that we learn more from people who are different from us than from people similar to us (Pascarella, 2001; Thompson & Cuseo, 2014). In addition, these are skills that are transferable to your career and college experience.

Note-Taking Teams. Since listening and note-taking are demanding tasks, it's likely that a classmate will pick up an important point you missed and vice versa. By teaming up after school or during a study hall, if you and your teammates find missing or confusing information, consult your teacher.

Reading Teams. After completing reading assignments, team up with classmates to compare your highlighting and margin notes. See what you both identified as the most important material to be studied for upcoming exams.

Writing Teams. Students can provide each other with feedback to revise and improve their own writing. Studies show that when peers assess each other's writing, the quality of their individual writing gets better and they develop a more positive attitude about the writing process (Topping, 1998). You can form peer writing teams to help at any or all of the following stages in the writing process:

1. Topic selection and refinement: to help one another come up with a list of possible topics and subtopics to write about;
2. Pre-writing: to clarify your writing purpose and audience;
3. First draft: to improve your general writing style and tone; and
4. Final draft: to proofread, detect, and correct clerical errors before submitting your written work.

Library Research Teams. Many first-year students are unfamiliar with the process of using a library to conduct academic research. Some experience "library anxiety" and avoid even stepping foot into the library, particularly if it's a large and intimidating place (Malvasi, Rudowsky, & Valencia, 2009). Forming library research teams is an effective way to develop a social support group that can make library research less intimidating by converting it from a solitary experience done alone to a collaborative venture done as a team. Working together with peers on any research task can reduce anxiety, create collective energy, and result in a final product that's superior to what could have been produced by a single person working independently.

> **NOTE**
>
> It's perfectly acceptable and ethical to team up with others to search for information and share resources. This isn't cheating or plagiarizing—as long as your final product is completed individually and what you turn into the teacher represents your own work.

Study Teams. When seniors at Harvard University were interviewed, nearly every one of them who had participated in study groups considered the experience to be crucial to their academic progress and success (Light, 1990, 1992, 2001). These same principles can be applied to high school and your school work.

Additional research on study groups indicates that they are effective only if each member has done the required course work in advance of team meetings—for example, if all teammates attended class consistently and completed required readings (Light, 2001). To fully capitalize and maximize the power of study teams, each team member should study individually *before* studying with the group and come to the group prepared with answers and ideas to share with teammates, as well as specific questions or points of confusion about which they hope to receive help from other members of the team. This ensures that all team members are individually accountable for

> "I would suggest students get to know [each] other and get together in groups to study or at least review class material. I find it is easier to ask your classmates with whom you are comfortable 'dumb' questions."
> —Advice to first-year students from a college sophomore (Walsh, 2005)

38 Chapter 2: Making Connections: Four Steps to Your Success

their own learning and equally responsible for contributing to their teammates' learning.

Test Review Teams. After receiving your results on course examinations (and assignments) you can collaborate with peers to review your performance as a team. When you compare your answers to the answers of other students, you're better able to identify what you did well and where you lost points. By seeing the answers of teammates who received maximum credit on certain questions, you get a clearer picture of what went wrong and what you can do next time to get it right next time.

> **NOTE**
>
> Don't forget that team learning goes beyond late-night study groups. Students could and should form learning teams in advance of exams to help each other with other academic tasks—such as note-taking, reading, writing, and library research.

Think About It—Journal Entry 2.6

Think about classmates in courses you're taking this term. Would you be willing to ask any of them if they'd like to form a learning team? Why?

_____
_____
_____
_____
_____

Fourth Step of High School Success: Reflection and Self-Awareness (Mindfulness)

The final step in the learning process, whether it be learning in the classroom or learning from experience, is to step back from the process, thoughtfully review it, and connect it to what you already know. Reflection is the flip side of active involvement; both processes are necessary for learning to be complete. Active involvement ensures attention—it enables information to enter your brain—and reflection ensures consolidation—it converts that information into knowledge and remains in your brain on a long-term basis (Bligh, 2000; Roediger, Dudai, & Fitzpatrick, 2007).

Self-Awareness

In addition to reflecting on what you're learning, it's also important to reflect on yourself. This process is known as *introspection*—it involves turning inward to gain deeper self-awareness and understanding of who you are, what you're doing, and where you're going. Two forms of self-awareness are particularly important for success in high school: (a) self-monitoring and (b) self-assessment.

Self-Monitoring

One characteristic of successful learners is that they self-monitor (check themselves) while learning to remain aware of:

- Whether they're using effective learning strategies (e.g., if they're giving their undivided attention to what they're learning);
- Whether they're truly comprehending what they are learning (e.g., if they're understanding it at a deep level or memorizing it at a surface level);
- How they're regulating or adjusting their learning strategies to meet the demands of different academic tasks and subjects (e.g., if they're reading technical material in a science textbook, they read at a slower rate and check their understanding more frequently than when reading a novel) (Pintrich & Schunk, 2002).

> "We learn neither by thinking nor by doing; we learn by thinking about what we are doing."
> —George Stoddard, Professor Emeritus, University of Iowa

You can begin to establish good self-monitoring habits by getting in the routine of periodically pausing to reflect on the strategies you're using to learn and how you "do" high school. For instance, you can ask yourself the following questions:

- Am I listening attentively to what my teacher is saying in class?
- Am I comprehending what I'm reading outside of class?
- Am I effectively using school resources designed to support my success?
- Am I interacting with school professionals who can contribute to my current success and future development?
- Am I interacting and collaborating with peers who can support (not sabotage) my learning and development?
- Am I effectively implementing high school success strategies (such as those identified in this book)?

NOTE

Successful students and successful people are mindful—they watch what they're doing and remain aware of whether they're doing it effectively and to the best of their ability.

Self-Assessment

Simply defined, self-assessment is the process of reflecting on and evaluating your personal characteristics. The following are key target areas for self-assessment because they enable you to accurately identify and achieve your educational and personal goals:

- **Personal interests.** What you like to do or enjoy doing.
- **Personal values.** What's important to you and what you care about doing.
- **Personal abilities or aptitudes.** What you do well or have the potential to do well.
- **Learning habits.** What approaches, methods, or techniques you use to learn.
- **Learning styles.** How you like or prefer to learn.
- **Personality traits.** Your temperament, emotional characteristics, and social tendencies (e.g., whether you lean toward being outgoing or reserved).

> "Successful students know a lot about themselves."
> —Claire Weinstein and Debra Meyer, professors of educational psychology at the University of Texas

Think About It—Journal Entry 2.7

How would you rate your academic self-confidence at this point in your high school experience? (Circle one.)

very confident   somewhat confident   somewhat unconfident
very unconfident

Why?
_____
_____
_____
_____

CHAPTER SUMMARY AND HIGHLIGHTS

The key ideas contained in this chapter are summarized in the following self-assessment checklist of success promoting principles and practices.

A Checklist of Success-Promoting Principles and Practices

1. **Active Involvement (Engagement)**
   Inside the classroom, I will:
   - ☑ *Get to class.* I'll treat it like a job and be there on all days I'm expected to.
   - ☑ *Get involved in class.* I'll come prepared, listen actively, take notes, and participate. Outside the classroom, I will:
   - ☑ *Read actively.* I'll take notes while I read to increase attention and retention.

2. **Capitalizing on School Resources**
   I will capitalize on academic and student support services available to me, such as the:
   - ☑ Academic Support Services
   - ☑ School Library
   - ☑ Guidance Counseling
   - ☑ Student Development Services

3. **Interpersonal Interaction & Collaboration (Social Integration)**
   I will interact and collaborate with the following members of my high school community:
   - ☑ Peers. I'll join student clubs and participate in school organizations.
   - ☑ Faculty members. I'll connect with my course teachers and other faculty members after class, in their offices, or via e-mail.
   - ☑ Guidance Counselors. I'll see a counselor for more than course registration, and I'll find an counselor whom I can relate to and develop an ongoing relationship.

4. **Reflection & Self-Awareness (Mindfulness)**
   I will engage in:
   - ☑ Reflection. I'll step back from what I'm learning, review it, and connect it to what I already.
   - ☑ Self-Monitoring. I'll maintain self-awareness of how I'm learning in high school and if I'm using effective strategies.
   - ☑ Self-Assessment. I'll reflect on and evaluate my personal interests, talents, learning styles, and learning habits.

In short, successful students are:
- **Involved.** They *get into* it by investing time and effort in the experience;
- **Interactive.** They *team up* for it by interacting and collaborating with others;
- **Resourceful.** They *get help* with it by capitalizing on their surrounding resources; and
- **Reflective.** They *step back* from it to think about their performance and themselves.

Think About It—Journal Entry 2.8

Identify one way in which you will put each of the following four principles of college success into practice during the next few weeks.

1. Active Involvement (Engagement)
   _____
   _____
   _____

2. Utilizing School Resources (Resourcefulness)
   _____
   _____
   _____

3. Interpersonal Interaction and Collaboration (Social Integration)

_____
_____
_____

4. Reflection and Self-awareness (Mindfulness)

_____
_____
_____

Learning More through the World Wide Web: Internet-Based Resources

For additional information on strategies for success, see the following websites:

http://www.cgcc.edu/success

http://www.dartmouth.edu/~acskills/success/

www.studygs.net

References

Advisory Committee on Student Financial Assistance (2008, September). *Apply to succeed: Ensuring community college students benefit from need-based financial aid*. Washington DC: Author. Retrieved from https://www2.ed.gov/about/bdscomm/list/acsfa/applytosucceed.pdf

Astin, A. W. (1993). *What matters in college?* San Francisco: Jossey-Bass.

Bailey, G. (2009). *University of North Carolina, Greensboro application for NADE certification, tutoring program*. NADE Certification Council Archives. Searcy, AR: Harding University.

Bligh, D. A. (2000). *What's the use of lectures?* San Francisco: Jossey Bass.

Bradshaw, D. (1995). Learning theory: Harnessing the strength of a neglected resource. In D. C. A. Bradshaw (Ed.), Bringing learning to life: *The learning revolution, the economy and the individual* (pp. 79–92). London: Falmer Press.

Brown, R. D. (1988). Self-quiz on testing and grading issues. Teaching at UNL (*University of Nebraska–Lincoln*), 10(2), 1–3.

Bruffee, K. A. (1993). *Collaborative learning: Higher education, interdependence, and the authority of knowledge.* Baltimore: Johns Hopkins University Press.

Cross, K. P., Barkley, E. F., & Major, C. H. (2005). *Collaborative learning techniques: A handbook for college faculty.* San Francisco: Jossey-Bass.

Cuseo, J. B. (1996). *Cooperative learning: A pedagogy for addressing contemporary challenges and critical issues in higher education.* Stillwater, OK: New Forums Press.

Cuseo, J. B. (2003). Comprehensive academic support for students during the first year of college. In G. L. Kramer et al. (Eds.), *Student academic services: An integrated approach* (pp. 271–310). San Francisco: Jossey-Bass.

Cuseo, J. B. (2005). "Decided," "undecided," and "in transition": Implications for academic advisement, career counseling, and student retention. In R. S. Feldman (Ed.), *Improving the first year of college: Research and practice* (pp. 27–50). Mahwah, NJ: Lawrence Erlbaum.

Cuseo, J. B., & Thompson, A., Campagna, M., & Fecas, V. S. (2013). *Thriving in college & beyond: Research-based strategies for academic success and personal development* (3rd ed.). Dubuque, IA: Kendall Hunt.

Erickson, B. L., Peters, C. B., & Strommer, D. W. (2006). *Teaching first-year college students.* San Francisco: Jossey-Bass.

Gilles, R. M., & Adrian, F. (2003). *Cooperative learning: The social and intellectual outcomes of learning in groups*. London: Farmer Press.

Gordon, V. N., & Steele, G. E. (2003). Undecided first-year students: A 25-year longitudinal study. *Journal of the First-Year Experience and Students in Transition, 15*(1), 19–38.

Johnson, D., Johnson, R., & Smith, K. (1998). Cooperative learning returns to college: What evidence is there that it works? *Change, 30*, 26–35.

Kiewra, K. A. (2000). Fish giver or fishing teacher? The lure of strategy instruction. *Teaching at UNL (University of Nebraska–Lincoln), 22*(3), 1–3.

Kuh, G. D. (1995). The other curriculum: Out-of-class experiences associated with student learning and personal development. *Journal of Higher Education, 66*(2), 123–153.

Kuh, et al. (2005). Student engagement in the first year of college. In M. L. Upcraft, J. N. Gardner, B. O. Barefoot, & Associates (Eds.), *Challenging and supporting the first-year student: A handbook for improving the first year of college* (pp. 86–107). San Francisco: Jossey-Bass.

Kuh, G. D., Douglas, K. B., Lund, J. P., & Ramin-Gyurnek, J. (1994). *Student learning outside the classroom: Transcending artificial boundaries*. ASHE-ERIC Higher Education Report No. 8. Washington, DC: George Washington University, School of Education and Human Development.

Light, R. L. (1990). *The Harvard assessment seminars*. Cambridge, MA: Harvard University Press.

Light, R. L. (1992). *The Harvard assessment seminars, second report*. Cambridge, MA: Harvard University Press.

Light, R. J. (2001). *Making the most of college: Students speak their minds*. Cambridge, MA: Harvard University Press.

Lotkowski, V. A., Robbins, S. B., & Noeth, R. J. (2004). *The role of academic and non-academic factors in improving student retention*. ACT Policy Report. Retrieved from https://www.act.org/research/policymakers/pdf/college_retention.pdf.

Malvasi, M., Rudowsky, C., & Valencia, J. M. (2009). *Library Rx: Measuring and treating library anxiety, a research study*. Chicago: Association of College and Research Libraries.

Pascarella, E. T. (2001, November/December). Cognitive growth in college: Surprising and reassuring findings from the National Study of Student Learning. *Change*, pp. 21–27.

Pascarella (2005). *How College Affects Students: Ten Directions for Future Research*.

Pascarella, E., & Terenzini, P. (1991). *How college affects students: Findings and insights from twenty years of research*. San Francisco: Jossey-Bass.

Pascarella, E., & Terenzini, P. (2005). *How college affects students: A third decade of research* (Vol. 2). San Francisco: Jossey-Bass.

Pew Internet & American Life Project. (2002). *The Internet goes to college: How students are living in the future with today's technology*. Retrieved from http://www.pewinternet.org/files/old-media/Files/Reports/2002/PIP_College_Report.pdf.pdf.

Pintrich, P. R., & Schunk, D. H. (2002). *Motivation in education: Theory, research, and applications*. Upper Saddle River, NJ: Merrill-Prentice Hall.

Roediger, H. L., Dudai, Y., & Fitzpatrick, S. M. (2007). *Science of memory: concepts*. New York, NY: Oxford University Press.

Smith, J. B., Walter, T. L., & Hoey, G. (1992). Support programs and student self-efficacy: Do first-year students know when they need help? *Journal of the Freshman Year Experience, 4*(2), 41–67.

Thompson, A., & Cuseo, J. (2014). *Diversity and the college experience*. Dubuque, IA: Kendall Hunt.

Tinto, V. (1993). *Leaving college: Rethinking the causes and cures of student attrition* (2nd ed.). Chicago: University of Chicago Press.

Tinto, V. (2012). *Completing college: Rethinking institutional action*. Chicago: The University of Chicago Press.

Topping, K. (1998). Peer assessment between students in colleges and universities. *Review of Educational Research, 68*(3), 249–276.

Walsh, K. (2005). *Suggestions from more experienced classmates*. Retrieved from http://www.uni.edu/walsh/introtips.html

Walter, T. L., & Smith, J. (1990, April). *Self-assessment and academic support: Do students know they need help?* Paper presented at the annual Freshman Year Experience Conference, Austin, Texas.

CHAPTER 2 EXERCISES

2.1 QUOTE REFLECTIONS

Review the sidebar quotes contained in this chapter and select two that were especially meaningful or inspirational to you.

For each quote, provide a three- to five-sentence explanation why you chose it.

2.2 REALITY BITE-CASE STUDY

Alone and Disconnected: Feeling like Calling It Quits

Josephine is a first-year student in her second week of high school. She doesn't feel like she's fitting in with other students on her school. She also feels a little guilty about the time she's taking time away from family and friends, and she fears that her ties with them will be weakened or broken if she continues spending so much time on schoolwork. Josephine is feeling so torn between school work her old friends that she's beginning to think about quitting school altogether.

Reflection and Discussion Questions

1. What would you say to Josephine that might persuade or motivate her to stay in school?
2. What could Josephine do to get more connected with her school and feel less disconnected from her family and hometown friends?
3. What could Josephine do for herself right now to minimize the conflict she's experiencing between her commitment to her education and her friends who quit school last year?
4. Can you relate to Josephine's situation? If yes, in what way? If no, why not?

2.3 CREATING A MASTER LIST OF RESOURCES ON YOUR SCHOOL

1. Construct a master list of all support services that are available to you on your school by consulting the following sources:
   - Printed information about your school
   - Information posted on your school's website
   - Information obtained by visiting with a professional in different offices or centers at your school

2. Your final product will be a list that includes the following:

School Support Service	Type of Support Provided	Contact Person	School Location
_____	_____	_____	_____
_____	_____	_____	_____
_____	_____	_____	_____
_____	_____	_____	_____

etc.

Notes
- You can team up with other classmates to work collaboratively on this assignment. Members of your team could identify different school resources to research and then share their findings with teammates.
- After completing this assignment, save your master list of support services for future use.

2.4 UTILIZING SCHOOL RESOURCES

Look back at the school resources you identified in the previous exercise, or those described on **pp. 29–31** of this chapter. Which of these resources do you plan to use this term?

Why did you identify these resources as your top priorities right now?

Ask your course teacher for recommendations about what resources you should consult during your first few weeks in high school. Compare their recommendations with your selections.

2.5 CHAPTER 2 REFLECTION

WHAT do you believe is the most important principle of high school success?

WHY do you believe this is the most important one?

Explain HOW you will use this principle to help you succeed in high school.

CHAPTER 3

PREPARING FOR HIGH SCHOOL

Transitioning from Middle School to High School

CHAPTER PREVIEW

The path to success begins with goals and finding the means (succession of steps) to reach those goals. People who set specific goals are more likely to experience success than people who simply tell themselves they're going to try hard and do their best. Understanding how to organize your goals will help you transition into high school. Each year will bring a new set of challenges but the time to start planning is now, not after you graduate high school. This chapter lays out the key steps involved in the process of setting effective goals, identifies key self-motivational strategies for staying on track and sustaining progress toward goals, and describes how personal qualities such as self-efficacy, grit, and growth mindset are essential for achieving goals.

LEARNING GOAL

Help you set meaningful goals and maintain motivation to achieve your goals.

THOUGHT STARTER

 Think About It—Journal Entry 3.1

Complete the following sentence:

For me, success in high school is . . .

_____
_____
_____
_____

From *Thriving in the Community College & Beyond: Strategies for Academic Success and Personal Development*, Third Edition, by Joseph Cuseo, Aaron Thompson, and Julie McLaughlin. Copyright © 2016 by Kendall Hunt Publishing Company. Reprinted by permission.

> "What keeps me going is goals."
> —Muhammad Ali, philanthropist, social activist, and Hall of Fame boxer

> "Stopping a long pattern of bad decision-making and setting positive, productive priorities and goals."
> —College sophomore's answer to the question: "What does being successful mean to you?"

> "Don't let others define success for you."
> —J.R. Roush (words offered to former high school students of Dr. J.R. Roush, Principal)

> "No matter what you do, do it well."
> —J.R. Roush (words offered to former high school students of Dr. J.R. Roush, Principal)

Start Planning Your Career Transition

Things to do and think about....

Before you enter high school....

Take an interest inventory and find out what you are interested in for a possible career. An interest inventory will ask you questions that pertain to your personal qualities and your favorite subjects in school. In some cases, the interest survey will provide you with a few career clusters that can aid you in determining your long-term career goals. You can locate many online versions by doing a simple search.

Once you have your interest inventory results, start exploring how your skills and interests apply to a career choice. There are so many sources available online to help you narrow your focus. Keep in mind, the idea is to create an action plan so you can plan your high school course work and guide you to additional opportunities. Part of transitioning to high school is lining up where you are headed after high school. Whether you decide to attend college, obtain training beyond high school, enter the military, or enter the workforce, the time to plan is now not when you graduate.

Transition to High School—the Work and Experience

Do your best in class. Remember more will be expected of you now.

1. DO NOT MISS School!
2. Know the school rules and be acquainted with the student code of conduct.
3. Familiarize yourself with the district and high school webpages.
4. If available, look at your future teacher webpages as well.
5. Sit in the front or as close as possible. Politely request to be moved if you have an assigned seat.
6. Stay current with your work.
7. Participate in class.
8. Work on your note-taking skills; compare your work to others so you can improve.
9. Develop your test-taking skills; your teachers will help you.

Outside-of-School Choices

1. Study, study and study some more.
2. Use the library if accessible. If you cannot get to a physical library, your school probably has some on-line resources.
3. Read the materials provided by your teachers.

Manage Your Time

1. Never procrastinate; don't wait—get busy with your school work. If you wait to the last minute, it shows up in the quality of your work and performance.
2. Find ways to record due dates for your coursework; if you have a planner or electronic device, record and make sure you review your calendar daily.

Chapter 3: Preparing for High School — 49

3. Reflect on your personal attributes. Are you a person that does better later at night or early in the evening? Regardless, work out a plan that meets your needs.

Organizational Tips—Being Ready Everyday Requires You to Manage the Work

1. Organize each class using a three-ring binder and folders.
2. Date your notes daily and make sure you place the notes in your binders and folders. Sometimes, rewriting your notes after class helps you remember and organize your work even more.
3. Before you go to bed, get everything ready to go for tomorrow.
4. Get some sleep. You may not think you need it but plenty of research links productivity levels amount of sleep (This means shutting down your electronic devices).
5. Take notes in every class daily. On days you are absent, ask to borrow a classmate's notes so you aren't missing any material.

Be prepared for an increase in the amount of homework you are assigned.

1. Get a routine established for what you do right after school or right before bedtime.
2. Understand the work assigned; consider a tutor for subjects that are challenging.
3. Organize a study group with friends from class.
4. It's okay to take a few minutes to give your mind a break; grab a snack and get back at it.
5. Manage your homework time. Extracurricular activities can take up a lot of your after-school time so be an efficient user of your after-school hours.

Tips on Transitioning to High School

1. Take an interest inventory and match your results to a career
2. For your career match: Is training required? College required? Or can you be employed immediately after high school?
3. Do some job shadowing in an area related to your career interests. (No, it's not too early.)
4. Attend college and career fairs.
5. Do online research for your areas of interest.
6. Ask teachers to clarify questions you may have about a specific career.
7. Begin to look at high school course offerings.
8. Visit a college campus or business that relates to some of your interest areas

The Relationship between Goal Setting and Success

Achieving success begins with setting goals. Success in high school depends on how you approach your transition from middle school. In this chapter, you will find information that will help you transition to high school and succeed in high school. Research shows that

> "The tragedy of life doesn't lie in not reaching your goal. The tragedy of life lies in having no goal to reach."
>
> —Benjamin Mays, minister, scholar, activist, president of Morehouse College

people who set goals and develop plans to reach them are more likely to reach them (Halvorson, 2010), and successful people set goals on a regular basis (Locke & Latham, 1990). In fact, the word *success* derives from the Latin root *successus*—meaning "to follow or come after"—as in the word *successive*. Thus, by definition, success involves a sequence of actions that leads to a desired outcome; the process starts with identifying an end (goal) and then finding a means (sequence of steps) to reach that goal.

Motivation begins with dreams and great intentions that get turned into realistic goals. Depending on the length of time it takes to reach them and the order in which they are to be achieved, goals may be classified into three general categories: long-range, mid-range, and short-range. Short-range goals need to be completed before a mid-range goal can be reached, and mid-range goals must be reached before a long-range goal can be achieved. For example, if your long-range goal is a successful career that requires a college degree, your mid-range goal is completing all the coursework required for a degree that will allow you entry into that career. To reach your mid-range goal of a college degree, you need to start by successfully completing the courses you're taking this term (your short-range goal).

This goal-setting process is called *means-end analysis*; it involves working backward from your long-range goal (the end) and identifying what mid-range and short-range subgoals (the means) must be reached in order to achieve your long-range goal (Brooks, 2009; Newell & Simon, 1959). Engaging in this process doesn't mean you're locking yourself into a premature plan that will restrict your flexibility or options. It's just a process that (a) gets you to think about where you want to go, (b) provides some sense of direction about how to get there, and (c) starts moving you in the right direction.

These strategies can be a game changer for you if school has been a struggle in the past. Keep in mind, it is never to late to change behaviors. During your time in school your teachers have always found ways to target your interests to motivate you to learn. As you progress through high school you will have the opportunity to make decisions that will impact your future. Goal setting is a big part of that process.

> "You've got to be careful if you don't know where you're going because you might not get there."
> —Yogi Berra, Hall of Fame baseball player

Characteristics of a Well-Designed Goal

Studies show that people who set specific, well-designed goals are more likely to succeed than are people who simply tell themselves they're going to try hard and do their very best (Halvorson, 2010; Latham & Locke, 2007). The acronym "SMART" is a well-known mnemonic device (memory strategy) for recalling all the key components of a well-designed goal (Doran, 1981; Meyer, 2003). **Box 3.1** describes the different components of a SMART goal. Talk to your teacher about SMART goals. Educators devise goals for each unit and daily lesson to make sure they are meeting state and national standards.

BOX 3.1

The *SMART* Method of Goal Setting

A *SMART* goal is one that's:

*S*pecific—it states precisely what the goal is, targets exactly what needs to be done to achieve it, and provides a clear picture of what successfully reaching the goal looks like.

Example: By spending 10 hours per week on my coursework outside of class and by using the effective learning strategies (such as those recommended in this book), I'll achieve at least a 3.0 grade point average this term. (Note that this is a much more specific goal than saying, "I'm really going to work hard this term.")

*M*eaningful (and *M*easurable)—the goal really matters to you (not someone else) and the progress you're making toward the goal can be clearly measured (tracked).

Example: Achieving at least a 3.0 grade point average this term is important to me because it will enable me to get into the field I'd like to major in. I'll measure my progress toward this goal by calculating the grade I'm earning in each of my courses this semester at regular intervals throughout the term.

Note: At *www.futureme.org* you can set up a program to send future e-mails to yourself that remind you to check and reflect on whether you're making steady progress toward the goals you set.

*A*ctionable (i.e., *A*ction-Oriented)—the actions or behaviors that will be taken to reach your goal are clearly specified.

Example: I will achieve at least a 3.0 grade point average this term by (a) attending all classes, (b) taking detailed notes in all my classes, (c) completing all reading assignments before their due dates, and (d) avoiding cramming by studying in advance for all my major exams.

*R*ealistic—there is a good chance of reaching the goal, given the time, effort, and skills needed to get there.

Example: Achieving a 3.0 grade point average this term is a realistic goal because my courses are manageable. I will be working no more than 15 hours per week at my part-time job, and I'll be able to get help from school support services for any academic skills or strategies that need to be strengthened.

*T*ime-framed—the goal has a deadline plus a timeline or timetable that includes short-range (daily), mid-range (weekly), and long-range (monthly) steps).

Example: To achieve at least a 3.0 grade point average this term, first I'll acquire all the information I need to learn by taking complete notes in my classes and complete all reading assignments (short-range step). Second, I'll learn the information I've acquired from my notes and readings, break it into parts and study the parts in separate sessions in advance of major exams (mid-range step). Third, on the day before exams, I'll review all the information I previously studied in parts so I avoid cramming and get a good night's sleep (long-range step).

Note: The SMART process can be used to set goals in any area of your life or dimension of personal development, such as:

- self-management (e.g., time management and money management goals),
- physical development (e.g., health and fitness goals),
- social development (e.g., relationship goals),
- emotional development (e.g., stress management or anger management goals),
- intellectual development (e.g., learning and critical thinking goals),
- career development (e.g., career exploration and preparation goals),

> "Dreams can be fulfilled only when they've been defined."
>
> —Ernest Boyer, former United States Commissioner of Education

Think About It—Journal Entry 3.2

If you were to set a SMART goal for some aspect of your life right now, what would it be and why would you set it?

_____

_____

_____

_____

_____

In addition to the effective goal-setting properties associated with the SMART method, research reveals that the following goal-setting features characterize people who set and reach important goals.

> "Nothing ever comes that is worth having, except as a result of hard work."
> —Booker T. Washington, born-in-slavery Black educator, author, and advisor to Republican presidents

1. Effective goal-setters set *improvement (get-better) goals* that emphasize progress and growth, rather than perfection (be-good) goals. Studies show that when people pursue get-better goals, they pursue them with greater interest and intensity, and they are more likely to enjoy the process (Halvorson, 2010). This is likely because get-better goals give us a sense of accomplishment about how far we've come—even when we still have a long way to go.

2. Effective goal-setters focus on outcomes they have *influence or control over*, not on outcomes that are beyond their control. For example, a controllable goal for an aspiring actress would be to improve her acting skills and opportunities, rather than to become a famous movie star—which will depend on factors that are beyond her control.

> "Accomplishing something hard to do. Not something that has just been handed to me."
> —First-year student's response to the question: "What does being successful mean to you?"

3. Effective goal-setters set goals that are *challenging and effortful*. Goals worth achieving require that we stretch ourselves and break a sweat; they require endurance, persistence, and resiliency. Studies of successful people in all occupations indicate that when they set goals that are attainable but also *challenging*, they pursue those goals more strategically, with more intensity, and with greater commitment (Latham & Locke, 2007; Locke & Latham, 2002). There's another advantage of setting challenging goals: Achieving them supplies us with a stronger sense of accomplishment, satisfaction, and self-esteem.

> "I never liked using the word obstacle, it always sounded like I would not be able to overcome it. I always look at obstacles as a challenge which I always loved taking on."
> Shane Shope, co-author of this book

4. Effective goal-setters anticipate *obstacles* they may encounter along the path to their goal and have a plan in place for dealing with them. Successful people often imagine what things will be like if they don't reach their goals, which drives them to anticipate problems and setbacks before they arise (Gilbert, 2006; Harris, Griffin, & Murray, 2008). They're optimistic about succeeding, but they're not blind optimists; they realize the road will be tough and they have a realistic plan in place for dealing with the rough

spots (Oettingen, 2000; Oettingen & Stephens, 2009). Thus a well-designed goal should not only include specific information about how the goal will be achieved, but also specific plans to handle anticipated impediments along the way—for example, identifying what resources and social support networks may be used to keep you on track and moving forward.

Capitalize on resources that can help you stay on track and moving toward your goal. Research indicates that success in school involves a combination of what students do for themselves (personal responsibility) and how they to capitalize on resources available to them (Pascarella & Terenzini, 1991, 2005). Successful people are resourceful; they seek out and take advantage of resources to help them reach their goals. Use your school (and community) resources to help you achieve your long-range goals (e.g., guidance counseling and career counseling).

Don't forget that your peers can serve as a resource to help you reach your goals. Much has been said about the dangers of "peer pressure," but much less attention has been paid to the benefits of "peer power." The power of social support groups for helping people achieve personal goals is well documented by research in different fields (Brissette, Cohen, & Seeman, 2000; Ewell, 1997). There's also a long historical trail of research pointing to the power of peers for promoting the development and success of students (Astin, 1993; Feldman & Newcomb, 1994; Pascarella & Terenzini, 2005). Be sure to ask yourself: Who can help me stick to my plan and complete the steps needed to reach my goal? You can harness the power of social support by surrounding yourself with peers who are committed to successfully achieve their educational goals and by avoiding "toxic" people who are likely to poison your plans or dampen your dreams.

Find motivated peers with whom you can make mutually supportive "pacts" to help one another reach your respective goals. These mutual support pacts may be viewed as "social contracts" signed by "co-witnesses" who help them stay on track and moving toward their long-range goals. Studies show that making a commitment to a goal in the presence of others increases our commitment to that goal because our successful pursuit of it is viewed not only through our own eyes, but through the eyes of others as well (Hollenbeck, Williams, & Klein, 1989; Locke, 2000).

> "Develop an inner circle of close associations in which the mutual attraction is not sharing problems or needs. The mutual attraction should be values and goals."
> —Denis Waitley, former mental trainer for U.S. Olympic athletes and author of Seeds of Greatness

Think About It—Journal Entry 3.3

What *obstacles* or *impediments* do you anticipate may interfere with your goal of succeeding in high school and graduating?

_____

_____

_____

What *school resources* do you think would be most helpful for dealing with your anticipated obstacles?

_____

_____

_____

_____

What *social support networks* (family members, friends, or mentors) do you think could help you overcome your anticipated obstacles?

_____

_____

_____

_____

Strategies for Maintaining Motivation and Progress Toward Your Goals

The word *motivation* derives from the Latin *movere*, meaning "to move." Success comes to those who overcome inertia—they start moving toward their goal; then they maintain momentum until their goal is reached. Goal-setting only creates the potential for success; it takes motivation to turn this potential into reality by converting intention into action. We can have the best designed goals and know the way to succeed, but if we don't have the *will* to succeed, there's no way we will succeed. Studies show that goal-setting is just the first step in the process; it must be accompanied by a strong commitment to achieve the goal that has been set (Locke, 2000; Locke & Latham, 1990).

Reaching challenging goals requires that you maintain motivation and sustain effort over an extended period of time. Listed below are strategies for doing so.

Put your goals in writing and make them visible. Written goals can serve almost like a written contract that holds you accountable for following through on your commitments.

By placing written goals where you can't help but see them on a daily basis (e.g., your laptop, refrigerator, and bathroom mirror), you're less likely to "lose sight" of them and more likely to continue pursuing them. What's kept in sight is kept in mind.

Keep your eye on the prize. Visualize reaching your long-range goals; picture it by creating vivid mental images of your future success. For example, if your goal is to earn your high school diploma. Visualize a crowd of cheering family, friends, and faculty at your

> "You can lead a horse to water, but you can't make him drink."
> —*Author unknown*

NOTE

The next best thing to doing something you intend to do is to write down your intention to do it.

graduation. (You could even add musical accompaniment to your visualization by playing a motivational song in your head—e.g., "We are the Champions" by Queen.) Imagine cherishing this proud memory for the rest of your life and being in a career your high school graduation enabled you to enter. Picture a typical workday going something like this: You wake up on a Monday morning and are excited about the upcoming workweek. When you're at work, time seems to fly by; before you know it, the day is over. When you go home after work and reflect on your day, you feel great about what you did and how well you did it. Finding your passion in life allows you to define your purpose. No matter what you decide to do in life be the best and you will never work a day in your life.

In addition to visualizing the positive consequences of achieving your goal, you can also motivate yourself by visualizing the negative consequences of not achieving it—as illustrated by the following experience.

AUTHOR'S EXPERIENCE

My father, who spent 50 years working in the coal mines of eastern Kentucky, always had a simple, motivating statement for me to gain more education than he had. He would always say, "Son, I did not have the chance to go to school, so I have to write my name with an X and work in the coal mines. You have the opportunity to get an education and you do not have to break your back in those mines." What my father was telling me was that education would give me options in life that he did not have and that I should take advantage of those options by going to college. My dad's lack of education supplied me with drive and dedication to pursue education. My experience suggests that when you are developing your goals and motivating yourself to achieve them, it may be as important to know what you don't want as it is to know what you do want.

—*Aaron Thompson*

Visualize completing the steps leading to your goal. For visualization to be really effective, you need to visualize not just the success itself (the end goal), but also the steps you'll take along the way. "Just picturing yourself crossing the finish line doesn't actually help you get there—but visualizing how you run the race (the strategies you will use, the choices you will make, the obstacles you will face) not only will give you greater confidence, but also leave you better prepared for the task ahead" (Halvorson, 2010, p. 208).

Thus, reaching a long-term goal requires focusing on the prize—your dream and *why* it's important to you; this "big picture" view provides the inspiration. At the same time, however, you have to focus on the little things—*what* it will take to get there—the nitty-gritty of due dates, to-do lists, and day-to-day tasks. This is the perspiration that transforms inspiration into action, enabling you to plug away and stay on track until your goal is achieved.

It could be said that successfully achieving a long-term goal requires two lenses, each of which provides you with a different focus point: (a) a wide-angle lens that gives you a big picture view of a future

> "Whether you think you can or you can't, you're right."
> —Henry Ford, founder of Ford Motor Co. and one of the richest people of his generation.

> "You've got to think about 'big things' while you're doing small things, so that all the small things go in the right direction."
> —Alvin Toffler, American futurologist and author who predicted the future effects of technology on our society

that's far ahead of you (your ultimate goal), and (b) a narrow-angle lens that allows you to focus intently on the here and now—on the steps that lie immediately ahead of you. Alternating between these two perspectives allows you to view your small, short-term chores and challenges (e.g., completing an assignment that's due next week) in light of the larger, long-range picture (e.g., college graduation and a successful future).

AUTHOR'S EXPERIENCE

I once helped coach a youth soccer team (five to six year olds) and noticed that many of the less successful players tended to make one of either two mistakes when they tried to advance the ball toward the goal. Some spent too much time looking down, focusing on the ball at their feet, trying to be sure that they didn't lose control of it. By not occasionally lifting their head and looking ahead, they often missed open territory, open teammates, or an open goal. Other unsuccessful players made the opposite mistake: They spent too much time with their heads up, trying to see where they were headed. By not periodically glancing down at the ball in front of them, they often lost control of it, moved ahead without it, or sometimes stumbled over it and fell flat on their face. In contrast, the more successful players had developed the habit of shifting their focus between looking down to maintain control of the ball immediately in front of them and lifting their eyes to see where they were headed.

The more I thought about how these successful soccer players alternated their perspective between looking at the ball right in front of them and looking at the goal farther ahead, it struck me that this was a metaphor for success in life. Successful people alternate between long-range and short-range perspectives; they don't lose sight of how executing the tasks immediately in front of them connect with the ultimate goal further ahead of them.

—*Joe Cuseo*

NOTE

Keep pursuit of your future dreams and completion of your current tasks in dual focus. Integrating these two perspectives provides you with the inspiration to set goals and the determination to reach them.

"Writing my resume was a real ego booster—I've actually done stuff!"

—College student
(quoted in Brooks, 2009)

Keep a record of your progress. Research indicates that the mere act of monitoring and recording progress toward your goals increases your motivation to continue pursuing them (Locke & Latham, 2005; Matsui, Okada, & Inoshita, 1983). Keeping a regular record of your personal progress increases motivation by providing you with frequent *feedback* about whether you're on track and positive *reinforcement* for staying on track (Bandura & Cervone, 1983; Schunk, 1995).

Mark down your accomplishments in red on a calendar, or keep a journal of the short- and mid-range goals you've reached. These markings serve as benchmarks, supplying you with concrete evidence and a visible reminder of your progress. You can also mark your progress on a chart or graph, or list your achievements in a resume or portfolio. Place these displays of progress where you can see them on a daily basis and use them as a source of motivation to keep striving toward your ultimate goal (Halvorson, 2010).

This practice of ongoing (daily) assessment of our personal progress toward goal completion is a simple, yet powerful form of self-reflection that's associated with success. Research on successful people reveals that they reflect regularly on their daily progress to ensure they're on track and progressing steadily toward their goals (Covey, 1990).

Reward yourself for reaching milestones on the path toward your goal. Reaching a long-range goal is clearly rewarding because it marks the end of the trip and arrival at your desired destination. However, reaching short- and mid-range goals are not as self-rewarding because they're merely the means to the end. Thus, you need to make intentional attempts to reward yourself for climbing these smaller, yet essential stepping stones on the path to the mountain peak.

The behaviors needed to persist and persevere through all the intermediate steps needed to reach a long-range goal is more likely to take place if these behaviors are followed by reward (positive reinforcement). The process of setting small goals, moving steadily toward them, and rewarding yourself for reaching them is a simple, yet powerful self-motivational strategy. It helps you maintain momentum over an extended period of time, which is exactly what's required to reach a long-range goal. When you achieve short- and mid-range goals, check them off as milestones and reward yourself for reaching them (e.g., celebrate successful completion of midterms or finals by treating yourself to something you really enjoy).

> "Whoever wants to reach a distant goal must take many small steps."
> —Helmut Schmidt, former chancellor of West Germany

 Think About It—Journal Entry 3.4

For you, what would be effective rewards for making progress toward your goals and serve as motivators to keep you going?

_____

_____

_____

_____

Characteristics of Successful People

Achieving success involves effective use of goal-setting and motivational strategies, but it takes something more. Ultimately, success emerges from the inside out; it flows from personal qualities and attributes found within a person. Studies of successful people who achieve their goals reveal they possess the following personal characteristics. Keep these characteristics in mind as you set and pursue your goals.

Internal Locus of Control

Successful people have what psychologists call an "internal locus of control"; they believe that the locus (location or source) of control for events in their life is *internal*—"inside" them and within their control—rather than *external*—outside them and beyond their control. They believe that success is influenced more by attitude, effort, commitment, and preparation than by inherited ability, inborn intelligence, luck, chance, or fate (Carlson, et al., 2009; Jernigan, 2004; Rotter, 1966).

> "If you do not find it within yourself, where will you go to get it?"
> —Zen saying (Zen is a branch of Buddhism that emphasizes seeing deeply into the nature of things and ongoing self-awareness)

Research shows that individuals with a strong internal locus of control display the following positive qualities:

1. Greater independence and self-direction (Van Overwalle, Mervielde, & De Schuyer, 1995),
2. More accurate self-assessment of strengths and weaknesses (Hashaw, Hammond, & Rogers, 1990), and
3. Higher levels of learning and achievement (Wilhite, 1990).

Self-Efficacy

An internal locus of control contributes to the development of another positive trait that psychologists refer to as *self-efficacy*—the belief that you have power to produce a positive effect on the *outcomes* of your life (Bandura, 1994). People with low self-efficacy tend to feel helpless, powerless, and passive; they think (and allow) things to happen to them rather than taking charge and making things happen for them. High school students with a strong sense of self-efficacy believe they're in control of their educational success and can shape their future, regardless of their past experience or current circumstances.

People with a strong sense of self-efficacy initiate action and exert effort. They believe success is something that's earned and the harder they work at it, the more likely they'll get it. If they encounter setbacks or bad breaks along the way, they don't give up or give in; they persevere and push on (Bandura, 1986, 1997).

> "I'm a great believer in luck, and I find the harder I work the more I have of it."
> —Thomas Jefferson, third president of the United States

Students with a strong sense of *academic self-efficacy* have been found to:

1. Put considerable effort into their studies;
2. Use active learning strategies;
3. Capitalize on school resources; and
4. Persist in the face of obstacles (Multon, Brown, & Lent, 1991; Zimmeman, 1995, 2000).

Students with a strong sense of self-efficacy also possess a strong sense of personal responsibility. As the breakdown of the word "responsible" implies, they are "response" "able"—they believe they're able to respond to personal challenges, including academic challenges.

 Think About It—Journal Entry 3.5

In what area or areas of your life do you feel that you've been able to exert the most control and achieve the most positive results?

_____

_____

_____

_____

In what area(s) do you wish you had more control and were achieving better results?

_____

_____

_____

_____

What strategies have you used in the area of your life where you've been able to exert the most personal control and achieve the most positive outcomes?

_____

_____

_____

_____

Could you apply any of these same strategies to those areas in which you need to gain more control? How?

_____

_____

_____

_____

Grit

When you expend significant effort, energy, and sacrifice over a sustained period of time to achieve a goal, you're demonstrating grit (Stoltz, 2014). People with grit have been found to possess the following qualities (Duckworth, et al., 2007).

Persistence. They hang in there and persevere effort until they reach their goals. When the going gets tough, they don't give up—they step it up. They have the fortitude to persist in the face of frustration and adversity.

Tenacity. They pursue their goals with relentless determination. If they encounter something along the way that's hard to do, they work harder to do it.

Resilience. They bounce back from setbacks and keep striving to reach their goals. They adopt the mindset that they'll bounce back from setbacks and turn them into comebacks. How you react

> "Grit is perseverance and passion for long-term goals. Sticking with your future day in, day out, not just for the week, not just for the month, but for years and working really hard to make that future a reality."
> —Angela Duckworth,
> psychologist, University
> of Pennsylvania

> "How smart you are will influence the extent to which you experience something as difficult (for example, how hard a math problem is), but it says nothing about how you will deal with difficulty when it happens. It says nothing about whether you will be persistent and determined or feel overwhelmed and helpless."
> —Heidi Grant Halvorson, social psychologist, and author of *Succeed: How We Can Reach Your Goals*

> "The harder you fall, the higher you bounce."
> —Chinese proverb

mentally and emotionally to a setback affects what action you take in response to it. For instance, you can react to a poor test grade by knocking yourself down with self-putdowns ("I'm a loser") or by building yourself back up with positive self-talk ("I'm going to learn from my mistakes on this test and rebound with a stronger performance on the next one").

As you can see in **Figure 3.1**, information passes through the emotional center of the human brain (lower, shaded area) before reaching the center responsible for rational thinking and future planning (upper area). As a result, when we encounter setbacks, our initial (and subconscious) tendency is to react emotionally and defensively. To counteract this tendency, we need to slow down, calm down, and make a conscious attempt to respond rationally to setbacks—thinking about how we can overcome them, learn from them, and make use of them to continue progressing toward our goal.

It's noteworthy that the word *problem* derives from the Greek root *proballein*, meaning "to throw forward." This suggests that a problem is an opportunity to move ahead. You can take this approach to problems by rewording or rephrasing the problem you're experiencing in terms of a positive goal statement. (For example, "I'm flunking math" can be reframed as: "My goal is to get a grade of C or better on the next test to pull my overall course grade into passing territory.")

Similarly, the root of the word *failure* is *fallere*—meaning to "trip or fall." Thus, failing at something doesn't mean we've been defeated, it just means we've stumbled and taken a temporary spill. Success can still be achieved after a fall if we don't give up, but get up and get back to taking the next step needed to reach our goal. By viewing poor academic performances and other setbacks (particularly those occurring early in your high school experience) not as failures but as learning opportunities, you put yourself in a position to bounce back and

> "What happens is not as important as how you react to what happens."
> —Thaddeus Golas, *Lazy Man's Guide to Enlightenment*

FIGURE 3.1: The Brain's Emotional Filter

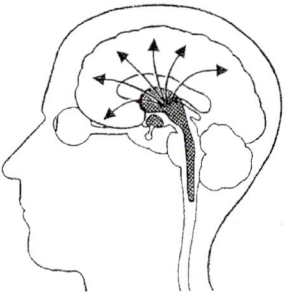

Information entering the human brain is first processed emotionally (lower shaded area) before reaching higher areas of rational thinking and future planning.

© Kendall Hunt Publishing Company

transform your setbacks into comebacks. Here are some notable people who did so:

- Louis Pasteur, famous bacteriologist, failed his admission test to the University of Paris;
- Albert Einstein, Nobel Prize–winning physicist, failed math in elementary school;
- Thomas Edison, prolific inventor, once expelled from school as "uneducable";
- Johnny Unitas, Hall of Fame football player, cut twice from professional football teams early in his career;
- Michael Jordan, Hall of fame basketball player, cut from his high school team as a sophomore.

> "When written in Chinese, the word 'crisis' is composed of two characters. One represents danger, and the other represents opportunity."
> —John F. Kennedy, 35th president of the United States

NOTE

Don't let early setbacks bring you down emotionally or motivationally. Reflect on them, learn from them, and make sure they don't happen again.

 Think About It—Journal Entry 3.6

What would you say is the biggest setback or obstacle you've overcome in your life thus far?

_____

_____

_____

_____

How did you overcome it? (What enabled you to get past it, or what did you do to prevent it from stopping you?)

_____

_____

_____

_____

Self-Discipline. People with grit have the *self-control*—they keep their actions aligned with their goal, staying on course and moving in the right direction—despite distractions and temptations (Halvorson, 2010). They resist the impulse to pursue instant gratification and do what they feel like doing instead of what needs to be done to reach their goal. They're able to sacrifice immediate, short-sighted needs and desires to do what has to be done to get where they want to be in the long run.

The ability to delay short-term (and short-sighted) gratification is distinctive human characteristic that sets us apart from other animals. As can be seen in **Figure 3.2**, the upper front part of the human brain, which is responsible for long-range planning and impulse control, is much larger in humans than chimpanzees—one of the most intelligent of all nonhuman animals.

> "Self-discipline is the ability to make yourself do the thing you have to do, when it ought be done, whether you like it or not."
> —Thomas Henry Huxley, 19th-century English biologist

Chapter 3: Preparing for High School

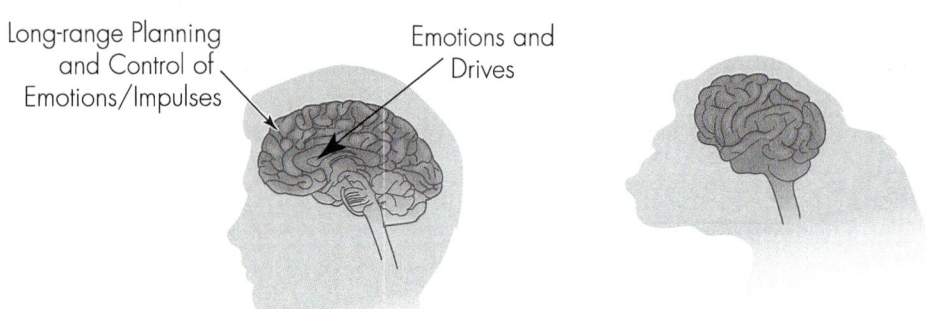

FIGURE 3.2: Where Thoughts, Emotions, and Drives are Experienced in the Brain

The part of the brain responsible for long-range planning and controlling emotions and impulses is much larger in humans than in other animals, including the highly intelligent chimpanzee.

© Kendall Hunt Publishing Company

Setting long-range goals is important but having the self-discipline to reach them is another matter. Each day, whether we're aware of it or not, we're tempted to make choices and decisions that interfere with our ability to reach our goals. We need to remain mindful about whether these choices are moving us in the direction of our goals or taking us off course.

AUTHOR'S EXPERIENCE

When I entered college in the mid-1970s, I was a first-generation student from an extremely impoverished background. Not only did I have to work to support my education, I also needed to assist my family financially. I stocked grocery store shelves at night during the week and waited tables at a local country club on the weekends. Managing my time, school, work, and life required a lot of self-discipline. However, I always understood that my goal was to graduate from college and all of my other commitments supported that goal. One of my greatest achievements in life was to keep my mind and body focused on the ultimate prize of getting a college education. That achievement has paid off for me many times over the course of my life.

—*Aaron Thompson*

NOTE

Doing what you *have* to do now allows you to do what you *want* to do later. Sacrifices made for a short time can bring benefits that last a lifetime.

 Think About It—Journal Entry 3.7

Think about something in your life that you sacrificed for and persisted at for the longest period of time before getting there. What is it? Do you see ways in which you could apply the same approach to achieving your goals in high school? Explain.

_____

_____

_____

Growth Mindset

A *mindset* is a powerful belief. People with a *growth mindset* believe that intelligence and other positive qualities can be grown or developed. People with a *fixed mindset* believe just the opposite: they think that intelligence and personal characteristics are deep-seated traits that are set and unlikely to change (Dweck, 2006).

Listed below are opposing pairs of traits—one representing a fixed mindset (FM) and the other representing a growth mindset (GM). As you read through them, honestly assess whether you lean more toward a fixed or growth mindset by circling either FM or GM for each pair of traits.

I try to get better at what I do. (GM)
I try to show others (including myself) how good I am. (FM)

I try to validate myself by proving how smart or talented I am. (FM)
I validate myself by stretching myself to become smarter and more talented. (GM)

I believe that if I cannot learn to do something easily, I'm not smart. (FM)
I believe that I can learn to do something well even if it doesn't come easily at first. (GM)

I evaluate my performance by comparing it to the performance of others. (FM)
I evaluate my performance by comparing it to my past performances. (GM)

I believe I have a certain amount of intelligence and not much can be done to change it. (FM)
I believe that the amount of intelligence I start with isn't the amount I'll end up with. (GM)

I think that intelligence and personal qualities are inherited and hard to change. (FM)
I think that intelligence and personal qualities are learned and changeable. (GM)

I think success is a matter of having ability. (FM)
I think success is a matter of getting ability. (GM)

I focus on demonstrating my skills to others. (FM)
I focus on developing my skills. (GM)

I focus on proving myself (as being good or smart). (FM)
I focus on improving myself (by getting better). (GM)

I feel smart when I complete tasks quickly and without mistakes. (FM)
I feel smart when I work on something for awhile before figuring it out. (GM)

I avoid seeking constructive criticism from others because it will expose my weaknesses. (FM)
I seek out constructive criticism from others to improve myself. (GM)

I feel threatened by the success of others. (FM)
I feel I can be inspired by and learn from the success of others. (GM)

> "If you believe you can develop yourself, then you're open to accurate information about your current abilities, even if it's unflattering."
> —Carol Dweck, Growth Mindset: The New Psychology of Success

I tend to peak early and don't continually progress to higher levels of achievement. (FM)
I tend to keep progressing toward increasingly higher levels of achievement. (GM)

I think success should be effortless. (FM)
I think success should be effortful. (GM)

I view challenges as threatening because they may prove I'm not smart. (FM)
I view challenges as opportunities to develop new skills. (GM)

I believe effort creates talent. (GM)
I believe effort is for those who can't make it on talent. (FM)

I focus on self-improvement—about becoming the best I can be. (GM)
I focus on self-validation—about proving I'm already good. (FM)

I look at grades as labels that judge or measure my intelligence. (FM)
I look at grades as a source of feedback for improving my performance. (GM)

> "No matter what your ability is, effort is what ignites that ability and turns it into accomplishment."
> —Carol Dweck, Stanford psychologist and author of Mindset

> "SUCCESS is peace of mind which is a direct result of self-satisfaction in knowing you made the effort to become the best that you are capable of becoming."
> —John Wooden, college basketball coach and author of the Pyramid of Success

Think About It—Journal Entry 3.8

Look back at the above pairs of statements and compare the total number of fixed mindset (FM) and growth mindset (GM) statements you circled.

Do your totals suggest that, in general, you lean more toward a growth or fixed mindset?

_____
_____
_____
_____

Do you see any patterns in your responses that suggest you're more likely to hold a growth mindset for certain characteristics or situations and a fixed mindset for others?

_____
_____
_____
_____

Numerous studies show that a growth mindset is strongly associated with goal achievement and personal success (Dweck, 2006). In one study, the mindset of pre-med students taking a difficult chemistry course was measured at the start of the semester and their performance was tracked throughout the term. Students with a growth mindset consistently earned higher grades in the course. Even when students with a growth mindset did poorly on a particular test, they improved on the next one. In contrast, the performance of students with a fixed mindset showed no pattern of improvement from one exam to the next (Dweck, 2006).

In another study, students with a growth mindset (who believed their goal in high school courses was to improve their grade as the course progressed) were compared to students with a fixed mindset (who believed their goal was to prove how smart they were). Students with a growth mindset achieved higher overall course grades and did so because they improved with each exam. They didn't have higher grades on the first exam, but began earning higher grades on later exams. The opposite pattern was true for fixed mindset students—their performance actually remained the same or declined over time—particularly if their first exam score was low (Halvorson, 2010).

It's been found that students can have different mindsets for different subjects and situations. Some students may have a fixed mindset for learning math, but a growth mindset for learning other subjects. However, the most important thing to remember about mindsets is that, although they're powerful, they're just beliefs held in our mind. Thus, mindsets can be changed from fixed to growth for any subject or situation. By so doing, we increase the likelihood of achieving our goals and reaching our full potential (Dweck, 2006).

> "When we change the way we look at things, the things we look at change."
> —Max Planck, Nobel Prize-winning physicist

CHAPTER SUMMARY AND HIGHLIGHTS

A key to success is challenging ourselves to set ambitious, yet realistic goals. Studies consistently show that goal-setting is a more effective self-motivational strategy than simply telling ourselves to "try hard" or "do our best." Achieving success begins with setting goals and successful people set goals on a regular basis.

The acronym "SMART" is a popular mnemonic device (memory strategy) for recalling all the key components of a well-designed goal. A **SMART** goal is one that is:

Specific—it states precisely what the goal is and what you will do to achieve it.
Meaningful (and **M**easurable)—it's a goal that really matters to you and your progress toward reaching it can be steadily measured or tracked.
Actionable (or **A**ction-Oriented)—it identifies concrete actions and specific behaviors you'll engage in to reach the goal.
Realistic—the goal is attainable and you're aware of the amount of time, effort, and skill it will take to attain it, as well as obstacles you'll need to overcome along the way.
Time-framed—the goal has a deadline and a timeline that includes a sequence of short-range, mid-range, and long-range steps.

In addition to the effective goal-setting properties associated with the SMART method, research reveals that the following goal-setting features characterize people who set and reach important goals.

1. Effective goal-setters set *improvement (get-better) goals* that emphasize progress and growth, rather than perfection (be-good) goals.
2. Effective goal-setters focus on what outcomes can *influence or control*, not on outcomes that are beyond their control.
3. Effective goal-setters set goals that are *challenging and effortful*.
4. Effective goal-setters anticipate *obstacles* they may encounter along the path to their goal and have a plan in place for dealing with them.

Setting goals ignites motivation, but maintaining motivation after it's been ignited requires use of effective self-motivational strategies. You can maintain your motivation by using such strategies as:

- Visualizing reaching your long-range goals;
- Putting your goals in writing;
- Creating a visual map of your goals;
- Keeping a record of your progress toward your goals;
- Rewarding yourself for milestones you reach along the path to your goals;
- Converting setbacks into comebacks by learning from mistakes and maintaining positive expectations.

Studies of successful people who achieve their goals reveal they possess the following personal characteristics.

Internal Locus of Control. They believe that the locus (location or source) of control for events in their life is *internal*—"inside" them and within their control—rather than *external*—outside them and beyond their control.

Self-Efficacy. They believe they have power to produce a positive effect on the *outcomes* of their lives. They believe success is something that's earned and the harder they work at it, the more likely they'll get it.

Grit. They expend significant effort, energy, and sacrifice over an extended period of time to achieve their goals. People with grit have been found to possess the following qualities:

- *Persistence*—when the going gets tough, they don't give up, they step it up; they have the fortitude to persist in the face of frustration and adversity.
- *Tenacity*—they pursue their goals with relentless determination; if they encounter something along the way that's hard to do, they work harder to do it.
- Resilience—they bounce back from setbacks and turn them into comebacks.
- *Self-Discipline*—they have *self-control*—they resist the impulse to pursue instant gratification and do what they feel like doing instead of what should be done to reach their goal; they're able to sacrifice immediate, short-sighted needs and desires to do what has to be done to get where they want to be in the long run.

Growth Mindset. They believe that intelligence and other positive qualities can be grown or developed. In contrast, people with a "fixed mindset" believe that intelligence and personal characteristics are deep-seated traits that are set and unlikely to change.

NOTE

Achieving success isn't a short sprint; it's a long-distance run that takes patience and perseverance. Goal-setting is the key that gets us off the starting blocks and motivation is the fuel that keeps us going until we cross the finish line.

Learning More through the World Wide Web: Internet-Based Resources

For additional information on goal-setting and motivation, see the following websites.

Goal Setting:
https://www.mindtools.com/page6.html

Self-Motivational Strategies:
www.selfmotivationstrategies.com

Self-Efficacy:
www.psychologytoday.com/blog/flourish/201002/if-you-think-you-can-t-think-again-the-sway-self-efficacy

Grit & Resilience:
https://undergrad.stanford.edu/resilience

Growth Mindset:
www.ted.com/talks/carol_dweck_the_power_of_believing_that_you_can_improve?language=en

References

Astin, A. W. (1993). *What matters in college?* San Francisco: Jossey-Bass.
Bandura, A. (1986). *Social foundations of thought and action: A social cognitive theory*. Englewood Cliffs, NJ: Prentice Hall.
Bandura, A. (1994). Self-efficacy. In V. S. Ramachaudran (Ed.), *Encyclopedia of human behavior* (Vol. 4, pp. 71–81). New York: Academic Press.
Bandura, A. (1997). *Self-efficacy: The exercise of control*. New York: Freeman.
Bandura, A., & Cervone, D. (1983). Self-evaluative and self-efficacy mechanisms governing the motivational effects of goal systems. *Journal of Personality and Social Psychology, 45*(5), 1017–1028.
Brissette, I., Cohen, S., & Seeman, T. E. (2000). Measuring social integration and social networks. In S. Cohen, L. G. Underwood, & B. H. Gottlieb (Eds.), *Social support measurement and intervention* (pp. 53–85). New York: Oxford University Press.
Brooks, K. (2009). *You majored in what? Mapping your path from chaos to career*. NY: Penguin.
Carlson, N. R., Miller, H., Heth, C. D., Donahoe, J. W., & Martin, G. N. (2009). *Psychology: The science of behaviour* (7th ed.). Toronto, ON: Pearson Education Canada.
Covey, S. R. (1990). Seven habits of highly effective people (2nd ed.). New York: Fireside.
Doran, G. T. (1981). "There's a S.M.A.R.T. Way to Write Management's Goals and Objectives", Management Review, Vol. 70, Issue 11, pp. 35–36.
Duckworth, A. L., Peterson, C., Matthews, M. D., & Kelly, D. R. (2007). Grit: Perseverance and passion for long-term goals. *Journal of Personality and Social Psychology, 92*(6), 1087–1101.
Dweck, C. S. (2006). *Mindset: The new psychology of success*. New York: Random House.
Ewell, P. T. (1997). Organizing for learning. *AAHE Bulletin, 50*(4), 3–6.
Feldman, K. A., & Newcomb, T. M. (1994). *The impact of college on students*. New Brunswick, NJ: Transaction Publishers. (Original work published 1969).
Gilbert, P. T. (2006). *Stumbling on happiness*. New York: Alfred A. Knopf.
Halvorson, H. G. (2010). *Succeed: How we can reach our goals*. New York: Plume.

Harris, P., Griffin, D., & Murray, S. (2008). Testing the limits of optimistic bias: Event and person moderators in a multilevel framework. *Journal of Personality and Social Psychology, 95,* 1225–1237.

Hashaw, R. M., Hammond, C. J., & Rogers, P. H. (1990). Academic locus of control and the collegiate experience. *Research & Teaching in Developmental Education,* 7(1), 45–54.

Hollenbeck, J. R., Williams, C. R., & Klein, H. J. (1989). An empirical examination of the antecedents of commitment to difficult goals. *Journal of Applied Psychology,* 74(1), 18–23.

Jernigan, C. G. (2004). What do students expect to learn? The role of learner expectancies, beliefs, and attributions for success and failure in student motivation. *Current Issues in Education* [On-line], 7(4). Retrieved January 16, 2012, from cie.asu.edu/ojs/index.php/cieatasu/article/download/824/250

Latham, G., & Locke, E. (2007). New developments in and directions for goal-setting research. *European Psychologists, 12,* 290–300.

Locke, E. A. (2000). Motivation, cognition, and action: An analysis of studies of task goals and knowledge. *Applied Psychology: An International Review, 49,* 408–429.

Locke, E. A., & Latham, G. P. (1990). *A theory of goal setting and task performance.* Englewood Cliffs, NJ: Prentice Hall.

Locke, E. A., & Latham, G. P. (2002). Building a practically useful theory of goal setting and task motivation. *American Psychologist, 57,* 705–717.

Locke, E. A., & Latham, G. P. (2005). Goal setting theory: Theory building by induction. In K.G. Smith & M.A. Mitt (Eds.), *Great minds in management: The process of theory development.* New York: Oxford.

Matsui, T., Okada, A., & Inoshita, O. (1983). Mechanism of feedback affecting task performance. *Organizational Behavior and Human Performance, 31,* 114–122.

Meyer, P. J. (2003). "What would you do if you knew you couldn't fail? Creating S.M.A.R.T. Goals". *In Attitude Is Everything: If You Want to Succeed Above and Beyond.* Meyer Resource Group, Incorporated.

Multon, K. D., Brown, S. D., & Lent, R. W. (1991). Relation of self-efficacy beliefs to academic outcomes: A meta-analytic investigation. *Journal of Counseling Psychology,* 38(1), 30–38.

Newell, A., & Simon, H. A. (1959). *The simulation of human thought.* Santa Monica, CA: Rand Corporation.

Oettingen, G. (2000). Expectancy effects on behavior depend on self-regulatory thought. *Social Cognition, 14,* 101–129.

Oettingen, G., & Stephens, E. (2009). Mental contrasting future and reality: A motivationally intelligent self-regulatory strategy. In G. Moskowitz & H. Grant (eds.), *The psychology of goals.* New York: Guilford.

Pascarella, E., & Terenzini, P. (1991). *How college affects students: Findings and insights from twenty years of research.* San Francisco: Jossey-Bass.

Pascarella, E., & Terenzini, P. (2005). *How college affects students: A third decade of research* (Vol. 2). San Francisco: Jossey-Bass.

Rotter, J. (1966). Generalized expectancies for internal versus external controls of reinforcement. *Psychological Monographs: General and Applied,* 80(609), 1–28.

Schunk, D. H. (1995). Self-efficacy and education and instruction. In J. E. Maddux (Ed.), *Self- efficacy, adaptation, and adjustment: Theory, research, and application* (pp. 281–303). New York: Plenum Press.

Snyder, C. R. (1995). Conceptualizing, measuring, and nurturing hope. *Journal of Counseling and Development,* 73 (January/February), 355–360.

Stoltz, P. G. (2014). *Grit: The new science of what it takes to persevere, flourish, succeed.* San Luis Obispo: Climb Strong Press.

Van Overwalle, F. I., Mervielde, I., & De Schuyer, J. (1995). Structural modeling of the relationships between attributional dimensions, emotions, and performance of college freshmen. *Cognition and Emotion,* 9(1), 59–85.

Wilhite, S. (1990). Self-efficacy, locus of control, self-assessment of memory ability, and student activities as predictors of college course achievement. *Journal of Educational Psychology,* 82(4), 696–700.

Zimmerman, B. J. (1995). Self-efficacy and educational development. In A. Bandura (Ed.), *Self-efficacy in changing societies.* New York: Cambridge University Press.

Zimmerman, B. J. (2000). Self-efficacy: An essential motive to learn. *Contemporary Educational Psychology* 25, 82–91.

CHAPTER 3 EXERCISES

3.1 QUOTE REFLECTIONS

Review the sidebar quotes contained in this chapter and select two that were especially meaningful or inspirational to you.

For each quote, write a three- to five-sentence explanation why you chose it.

3.2 REALITY BITE

Goals and Motivation

Lorraine has decided to go to her local community college to become an RN. She knows that nurses make good money and it is easy to get a job in the profession right now. All she really cares about is having a good job and making money. She did not realize the classes would be difficult and she had a hard time getting through them. Also, she was not really interested in the courses. She started her clinicals and HATED what she was being asked to do. She was not prepared for all the bodily fluids she would see in one day. Lorraine decides nursing is not for her and is angry that no one told her she would hate it this much! She has to find a different major now that will still make a lot of money, but she is angry that she wasted more than a year of her life as well as the money she spent on her education.

1. Why do you think Lorraine is really unhappy with the events that have unfolded during the past year?
2. What could Lorraine have done differently to avoid this situation?
3. What goals would you suggest Lorraine set for herself?

Lorraine is clearly motivated by money. Do you think that will make her happy? Why or why not?

3.3 CLARIFYING YOUR GOALS

- Take a moment to answer the following questions as honestly as possible:
- What are my highest priorities?
- What competing needs and priorities do I need to keep in check?
- How will I maintain balance across different aspects of my life?
- What am I willing and able to give up in order to achieve my educational and personal goals?
- How can I maintain motivation on a day-to-day basis?
- Who can I collaborate with to reach my goals and what will that collaboration involve?

3.4 SETTING A SMART GOAL TO REDUCE THE GAP BETWEEN YOUR IDEAL FUTURE AND YOUR CURRENT REALITY

Think of an aspect of your life where there's a significant gap between what you'd like it to be (the ideal) and where you are (the reality).

Use the following form to identify a goal you could pursue to reduce this gap.

Goal: _____

What specific *actions* will be taken?

When will these actions be taken?

What *obstacles or roadblocks* do you anticipate?

What *resources* could you use to overcome your anticipated obstacles or roadblocks?

How will you *measure your progress*?

How will you know when you *reached or achieved* your goal?

3.5 CONVERTING SETBACKS INTO COMEBACKS: TRANSFORMING PESSIMISM INTO OPTIMISM THROUGH POSITIVE SELF-TALK

In Hamlet, Shakespeare wrote: "There is nothing good or bad, but thinking makes it so." His point was that experiences have the potential to be positive or negative, depending on how people interpret them and react to them.

Listed below is a series of statements representing negative, motivation-destroying interpretations and reactions to a situation or experience:

a) "I'm just not good at this."
b) "There's nothing I can do about it."
c) "Nothing is going to change."
d) "This always happens to me."
e) "Everybody is going to think I'm a loser."

For each of the preceding statements, replace the negative statement with a statement that represents a more positive, self-motivating interpretation or reaction.

3.6 SELF-ASSESSMENT OF HOPE

Studies of people who have changed their lives in productive ways indicate they exhibit "high hope" by engaging in certain behaviors that enable them to find the will and the way to reach their personal goals (Snyder, 1995). A sample of hopeful behaviors is listed below. Assess yourself on these behaviors, using the following scale:

1 = Never
2 = Rarely
3 = Frequently
4 = Almost Always

Behavior Exhibited by People Possessing High Levels of Hope

___ When I think of goals, I think of challenges, rather than setbacks and failures.

___ I seek out stories about how other people have succeeded to inspire me and give me new ideas on how to be successful.

___ I find role models I can emulate and who can advise, guide, or mentor me.

___ I tell my friends about my goals and seek their support to help me reach my goals.

___ I use positive self-talk to help me succeed.

___ I think that mistakes I make along the way to my goals are usually the result of using a wrong strategy or making a poor decision, rather than lack of talent or ability on my part.

___ When I struggle, I remember past successes and things I did that worked.

___ I reward myself when reaching smaller, short-term goals I accomplish along the way to larger, long-term goals.

Adapted from: Snyder, C. R. (1995). Conceptualizing, measuring, and nurturing hope. *Journal of Counseling and Development*, 73 (January/February), 355–360.

Self-Assessment Reflections

For any item you rated "1" or "2," explain:

(a) *Why* you "rarely" or "never" engage in the practice;

(b) *If* you intend to engage in the practice more frequently in the future;

(c) *How likely* is it that you'll engage in the practice more frequently in the future;

(d) *When do* you plan to begin engaging in the practice.

3.7 CHAPTER 3 REFLECTION

What is the one thing that motivates you the most in high school?

HOW and WHY does this motivate you?

What is the one obstacle that gets in the way of your success?

How can you motivate yourself to overcome this obstacle?

TIME MANAGEMENT

Prioritizing Tasks, Preventing Procrastination, and Promoting Productivity

CHAPTER PREVIEW

Time is a valuable personal resource—if you gain greater control of it, you can greater control of your life. Time managed:
- Enables you to get work done in a timely manner,
- Enables you to attain personal priorities, and
- Maintain balance in your life.

This chapter offers a comprehensive set of strategies for managing time, combating procrastination, and ensuring that your time-spending habits are aligned with your educational goals and priorities.

LEARNING GOAL

Equip you with a powerful set of strategies for setting priorities, planning time, and completing tasks in a timely and productive manner.

THOUGHT STARTER

Think About It—Journal Entry 4.1

Complete the following sentence with the first thought that comes to your mind:
For me, time is . . .

_____
_____
_____
_____

From *Thriving in the Community College & Beyond: Strategies for Academic Success and Personal Development*, Third Edition, by Joseph Cuseo, Aaron Thompson, and Julie McLaughlin. Copyright © 2016 by Kendall Hunt Publishing Company. Reprinted by permission.

The Importance of Time Management

For many freshmen the beginning of high school means the beginning of more responsibility and self-management. Managing time is an important skill to possess because you're likely juggling multiple responsibilities, including school, family, and work. To have any realistic chance of achieving our goals, we need an intentional and strategic plan for spending our time in a way that aligns with our goals and enables us to make steady progress toward them. Thus, setting goals, reaching goals, and managing time are interrelated skills.

Most high school students struggle to at least some extent with time management, particularly first-year students who are transitioning from the a regimented middle school schedule to a broader experience in high school. In high school, time management skills grow in importance. High school students have more freedom and choices. In addition, during this time students will begin to drive a car for the first time. These factors can make time management a challenge for students when prioritizing family responsibilities, school work, and social activities. This added freedom to roam and the challenges many high school students face with peer pressure place more demands on student schedules. The key is prioritize your time. Your high school is regimented and is dictated to you daily but after-school time is a challenge because of other commitments. A worst-case scenario is if you don't have other activities after school. Extracurricular activities and even a part-time job have real-life skill benefits in addition to your high school curriculum. These experience teach you about proper time management and also interpersonal skills, such as communication and collaboration. These skills are portable and over time you will learn to use these skills throughout your career. Don't sell these simple ideas short. Soft skills are an important part of your personal and career development. No matter what vocation or career you choose in life, your ability to adapt and work effectively with others will shape your long-term economic outlook.

Simply stated, high school students who have difficulty managing their time have difficulty managing high school. One study compared college sophomores who had an outstanding first year (both academically and personally) with sophomores who struggled in their first year. Interviews with both groups revealed there was one key difference between them: sophomores who experienced a successful first year repeatedly brought up the topic of time during the interviews. The successful students said they had to think carefully about how they spent their time and that they needed to budget their time. In contrast, sophomores who experienced difficulty in their first year of college hardly talked about the topic of time during their interviews, even when they were specifically asked about it (Light, 2001). The same can be said for high school students.

Studies also indicate that people of all ages report time management to be a critical element of their life. Working adults report

> "The major difference [between high school and college] is time. You have so much free time on your hands that you don't know what to do for most of the time."
> —First-year college student (Erickson & Strommer, Teaching College Freshmen)

> "I cannot stress enough that you need to intelligently budget your time."
> —Advice to new college students from a student finishing his first year in college

that setting priorities and balancing multiple responsibilities (e.g., work and family) can be a stressful juggling act (Harriott & Ferrari, 1996). For them, time management and stress management are interrelated.

These findings suggest that time management is more than just a high school success skill; it's also as a life management and life success skill. When we gain greater control of our time, we gain greater control of our life. Studies show that people who manage their time well report being happier (Myers, 1993, 2000).

Each Sunday, before the start of the school week think through what you have going on at school (assignments and tests) and what you have planned with your family and friends. Plan your week, preferably writing out what you need to accomplish. Remember, the long-term goal is to graduate and everything that contributes to that end goal should appear on the list near the top. Obviously, your family is a priority as well so look for a balance to meet both aspects of your life.

AUTHOR'S EXPERIENCE

I started the process of earning my doctorate a little later in life than other students. I was a married father with a preschool daughter (Sara). Since my wife left for work early in the morning, it was always my duty to get up and get Sara's day going in the right direction. In addition, I had to do the same for myself. Three days of my week were spent on campus in class or in the library. (We didn't have quick access to research on home computers then as you do now.) The other two days of the workweek and the weekend were spent on household chores, family time, and studying.

I knew that if I was to have any chance of finishing my Ph.D. in a reasonable amount of time, I had to adopt an effective schedule for managing my time. Each day of the week, I held to a strict routine. I got up in the morning, ate breakfast while reading the paper, got Sara ready for school, and got her to school. Once I returned home, I put a load of laundry in the washer, studied, wrote, and spent time concentrating on what I needed to do to be successful from 8:30 a.m. to 12:00 p.m. every day. At lunch, I had a pastrami and cheese sandwich and a soft drink while rewarding myself by watching *Perry Mason* reruns until 1:00 p.m. I then continued to study until it was time to pick up Sara from school. Each night I spent time with my wife and daughter and then prepared for the next day. I lived a life that had a preset schedule. By following that schedule, I was able to successfully complete my doctorate in a reasonable amount of time while giving my family the time they needed. (By the way, I still watch *Perry Mason* reruns.)

—*Aaron Thompson*

Strategies for Managing Time and Tasks

Effectively managing our time and our tasks involves three key processes:

1. **Analysis.** breaking down time to see how much of it we have and what we're spending it on;
2. **Itemizing.** identifying and listing the tasks that we need to complete and when we need to complete them; and

3. **Prioritizing.** ranking our tasks in terms of their importance and attacking them in order of their importance.

The following strategies can be used to implement these three processes and should help you open up more time in your schedule, enabling you to discover new ways to use your time more productively.

Think About It—Journal Entry 4.2

1. What is your greatest time waster?

   _____
   _____
   _____
   _____

2. Is there anything you can do right now to stop or eliminate it?

   _____
   _____
   _____
   _____

Become more aware of how your time is spent by breaking it into smaller units. How often have you heard someone say, "Where did all the time go?" or "I just can't seem to find the time!" One way to find out where all our time goes and find more time to get things done is by doing a *time analysis*—a detailed examination of how much total time we have and where we're spending it—including patches of wasted time when we get little done and nothing accomplished. This time analysis only has to be done for a week or two to give us a pretty good idea of where our time is going and to find better ways to use our time productively.

Identify *what* specific tasks you need to accomplish and when you need to accomplish them. When we want to remember items we need to buy at the grocery store or people we want to invite to a party, we make a list. This same list-making strategy can be used for tasks we need to complete so we don't forget about them, or forget to do them on time. One characteristic of successful people is that they are list makers; they make lists for things they want to accomplish each day (Covey, 2004).

⊖ **Think About It—Journal Entry 4.3**

Do you make a to-do list of things you need to get done each day? (Circle one.)

        never   seldom   often   almost   always

If you circled "never" or "seldom," why don't you?

_____

_____

_____

_____

> **NOTE**
>
> When we write out things we need to do, we're less likely to block them out and forget to do them.

Take advantage of time planning and task management tools, such as the following:

- *Small, portable planner.* You can use this device to list all your major assignments and exams for the term, along with their due dates. By pulling together all work tasks required in each of your courses and getting them in one place, it will be much easier to keep track of what you have to do and when you have to do it throughout the entire term.
- *Large, stable calendar.* In the calendar's date boxes, record your major assignments for the term. The calendar should be posted in a place you can see every day (e.g., bedroom or refrigerator). If you repeatedly see the things you have to do, you're less likely to overlook them, forget about them, or subconsciously push them out of your mind because you'd really prefer not to do them.
- *Smartphone.* These devices can be used for more than checking social networking sites and sending or receiving text messages. They can be used as a calendar tool to record due dates and set up alert functions to remind you of deadlines. Many smartphones also allow you to set up task or to-do lists and set priorities for each item entered. A variety of apps are now available for planning tasks and tracking time spent on tasks (e.g., see: http://www.rememberthemilk.com; other apps available include cozi, an organization app, and pomodoro, an app intended to boost productivity). Take advantage of cutting edge tools, but at the same time, keep in mind that planners don't plan time, people do. Effectively planning time and tasks flows from a clear vision of your goals and priorities.

AUTHOR'S EXPERIENCE

My mom ensured I got up for school on time. Once I got to school the bell would ring to let me know to move on to the next class. When I returned home, I had to do my homework and chores. My daily and weekly schedules were dictated by someone else.

When I entered college, I quickly realized that I needed to develop my own system for being organized, focused, and productive without the assistance of my mother or school authorities. Since I came from a modest background, I had to work my way through college. Juggling schedules became an art and science for me. I knew the things that I could not miss, such as work and school, and the things I could miss—TV and girls. (OK, TV, but not girls.)

After college, I spent 10 years in business—a world where I was measured by being on time and delivering a productive "bottom line." It was during this time that I discovered a scheduling book. When I became a professor, I had other mechanisms to make sure I did what I needed to do when I needed to do it. This was largely based on when my classes were offered. Other time was dedicated to working out and spending time with my family. Now, as an administrator, I have an assistant who keeps my schedule for me. She tells me where I am going, how long I should be there, and what I need to accomplish while I am there. Unless you take your parents with you or have the luxury of a personal assistant, it's important to schedule your time. Use a planner!

—*Aaron Thompson*

 Think About It—Journal Entry 4.4

Do you have a calendar that you carry with you or use the calendar tool on your cell phone?

___

If yes, why? If no, why not?

___
___
___
___

> "Things that matter most must never be at the mercy of things that matter least."
> —Johann Wolfgang von Goethe, German poet, dramatist, and author of the epic *Faust*

Prioritize: rank tasks in order of their importance. After you itemize your work tasks by identifying and listing them, the next step is to *prioritize* them—determine the order or sequence in which they get done. Prioritizing basically involves ranking tasks in terms of their importance, with the highest priority tasks placed at the top of the list to ensure they're tackled first.

How do you decide on what tasks are to be ranked highest and tackled first? Here are two key criteria (standards of judgment) for determining your highest priority tasks:

- **Urgency.** Tasks that are closest to their deadline or due date should receive highest priority. Finishing an assignment that's due tomorrow should receive higher priority than starting an assignment that's due next month.

- **Gravity.** Tasks that carry the greatest weight (count the most) should receive highest priority. If an assignment worth 100 points and an assignment worth 10 points are due at the same time, the 100-point task should receive higher priority. We want to be sure to invest our work time on tasks that matter most. Similar to investing money, we should invest our time on tasks that yield the greatest pay-off.

An effective strategy for prioritizing tasks is to divide them into "A," "B," and "C" lists (Lakein, 1973; Morgenstern, 2004). The "A" list is reserved for *essential* (nonnegotiable) tasks—those that that *must* be done now. The "B" list is for *important* tasks—those that *should* be done soon. The "C" list is for *optional* tasks—those that *could* or *might* be done if there's time remaining after the more important tasks on lists A and B have been completed. Organizing tasks and time in this fashion helps you decide how to divide your labor in a way that ensures you "put first things first." You shouldn't waste time doing unimportant things to deceive yourself into thinking that you're "getting stuff done"—when, in reality, all you're doing is "keeping busy" and distracting yourself (and subtracting time) from doing the things that should be done.

> **NOTE**
> Put first things first: Plan your work by identifying your most important and most urgent tasks, and work your plan by attacking these tasks first.

> "When I have lots of homework to do, I suddenly go through this urge to clean up and organize the house. I'm thinking, 'I'm not wasting my time. I'm cleaning up the house and that's something I have to do.' But all I'm really doing is avoiding school work."
> —College sophomore

AUTHOR'S EXPERIENCE

Growing up I had learned a lot on my own. My mom worked continuously to provide for me and my younger brother—that left us a lot of time to learn how to do things on our own. I was not the greatest student; I struggled in reading but excelled in math. Over time, I learned everything about time management the hard way. Mostly because I never had a mentor or any guidance to navigate the "system". Eventually, I learned how to manage my time effectively. I didn't realize the people who loved me the most were providing an example of prioritizing and managing time effectively. My mom worked in a bakery, which required her to get up early and work late, often missing a lot of her sons' after school activities. My grandparents, even though they were both retired, still woke up early each day and worked. Why? For my mom it was love; she wanted to make sure we (my brother and I) were clothed and fed. For my grandparents, who lived through the depression and World War II, it was because they didn't know any other way to live. Hard work was not a choice as they grew up, it was a part of their daily lives. In both cases, they learned to manage their time and prioritize to provide for their families and survive. Who are your role models? And why?

—Shane Shope

> **NOTE**
> Developing awareness of how our time is spent is more than a brainless, clerical activity. When it's done well, it becomes an exercise in self-awareness and values clarification—how we spend our time is a true test of who we are and what we really value.

> "Time = Life. Therefore waste your time and waste your life, or master your time and master your life."
> —Alan Lakein, international expert on time management and author of the bestselling book How to Get Control of Your Time and Your Life (1973)

> "If you fail to plan, you are planning to fail."
> —Benjamin Franklin, renowned author, inventor, civic activist, and a founding father of the United States

Creating a Time-Management Plan

You may have heard of the old proverb, "A stitch in time saves nine." Planning your time represents the "stitch" (unit of time) that saves you nine additional stitches (units of time). Similar to successful chess players, successful time managers plan ahead and anticipate their next moves.

Don't buy into the myth that taking time to plan takes time away from getting started and getting things done. Time management experts estimate that the amount of time planning your total work actually reduces your total work time by a factor of three: for every one unit of time you spend planning, you save three units of time working (Goldsmith, 2010; Lakein, 1973). For example, 5 minutes of planning time will typically save you 15 minutes of total work time, and 10 minutes of planning time will save you 30 minutes of work time.

Planning your time saves you time because it ensures you start off in the right direction. If you have a plan of attack, you're less vulnerable to "false starts"—starting your work and then discovering you're not on the right track or not doing things in the right sequence, which forces you to retreat and start all over again.

Once you have accepted the idea that taking time to plan your time will save you time in the long run, you're ready to create a plan for effectively managing time. Listed below are specific strategies for doing so.

Be mindful of time by wearing a watch or carrying a phone that can accurately and instantly tell you the date and time. This may seem like an obvious "no-brainer", but time can't be managed if we don't know what time it is, and we can't plan a schedule if we don't know what day it is. Consider setting the time on your watch or phone slightly ahead of the actual time to help ensure that you arrive to class, work, or meetings on time. You can also equip your phone with apps to remind you of times when tasks are to be completed (e.g., *remindme.com* or *studiousapp.com*).

Carry a *small calendar, planner,* or *appointment book* at all times. This will allow you to record appointments that you may make on the run as well as enable you to jot down creative ideas or memories of things you need to do—which can sometimes pop into your mind at the most unexpected times.

Take *portable work* with you during the day that you can work at any place at any time. This will enable you to take advantage of "dead time" such as time spent sitting and waiting for appointments or transportation. Portable work allows you to resurrect dead time and transform it into productive work time. Not only is this a good time management strategy, it's a good stress management strategy because you replace the frustration and boredom associated with having no control over "wait time" with a sense of accomplishment.

> "Only boring people get bored."
> —Graffiti appearing in a bathroom stall at the University of Iowa, circa 1977

Make good use of your *free time between classes* by working on assignments and studying in advance for upcoming exams. See **Box 4.1** for a summary of how you can use your out-of-class time to improve your academic performance and course grades.

> **NOTE**
>
> High school teachers won't always be on you about your work so plan, plan and plan ahead. Write down what you need to do and create good study habits. The resources you have today make it very difficult for you to blame others for your own shortcomings. Your work is your responsibilty.

BOX 4.1

Making Productive Use of "Free Time" Outside the Classroom

As a high school student, your schedule is laid out for you. Depending on your situation, your classes will start early each day and end in the mid-afternoon. How will you manage the time you have at school and after school?

Think back to elementary and middle school, the academic work was manageable and your teachers always made sure you understood the material. In high school, you have to take ownership of your schoolwork.

As you progress in life, whether it's college or a career, you will be expected and to complete the task assigned. Will you do this work on your own and without supervision?

> "In high school we were given a homework assignment every day. Now we have a large task assigned to be done at a certain time. No one tells [us] when to start or what to do each day.""
> —*First-year college student*

Listed in this box are strategies for working independently and in advance of high school exams and assignments. By building time for each of these activities into your regular schedule, you'll make more productive use of out-of-class time, decrease your level of stress, and strengthen your academic performance.

Doing Out-of-Class Work in Advance of Exams

- **Complete reading assignments** relating to class topics *before* the topic is discussed in class. This will make classes easier to understand and enable you to participate intelligently in class (e.g., by asking meaningful questions and making informed comments during class discussions).
- **Review class notes** from your last class before the next class to build a mental bridge from one class to the next. Many students don't look at their class notes until they study them right before an exam. Don't be one of those students; instead, review your notes before the next class. Rewrite any class notes that may have been sloppily written the first time. If you find notes related to the same point all over the place, reorganize them into the same section. Lastly, if you find any information gaps or confusing points in your notes, seek out the course teacher or a trusted classmate to clear them up before the next class takes place.

  By reviewing your class notes on a regular basis, you will improve your ability to understand each upcoming class and reduce the total time you'll need to spend studying your notes the night before an exam.
- **Review your reading notes and highlights** to improve retention of important material. If you find certain points in your reading to be confusing, discuss them with your course teacher during office hours or with a fellow classmate outside of class.

BOX 4.1 (CONT)

- **Integrate class material with reading material.** Connect related information from your class notes and reading notes and get them in the same place (e.g., on the same index card).
- **Use a "part-to-whole" study method** whereby you study material from your class notes and assigned reading in small pieces (parts) during short, separate study sessions in advance of the exam; then make your last study session before the exam a longer review session during which you re-study all the small parts (the whole) at the same time. Don't buy into the myth that studying in advance is a waste of time because you'll forget everything you studied by test time. Material studied in advance of an exam remains in your brain and is still there when you later review it. Even if it doesn't immediately come back to mind when you first start reviewing it, you'll relearn it much faster than you did the first time.

Doing Out-of-Class Work in Advance of Term Papers and Research Reports

Work on large, long-range assignments due at the end of the term by breaking them into smaller, short-term tasks completed at separate times during the term. For instance, a large term paper may be broken up into the following smaller tasks and completed in separate installments.

1. Search for and decide on a topic.
2. Locate sources of information on the topic.
3. Organize information obtained from your sources into categories.
4. Develop an outline of your paper's major points and the order or sequence in which you plan to present them.
5. Construct a first draft of your paper (and, if necessary, a second or third draft).
6. Write a final draft of your paper.
7. Proofread your final draft for spelling and grammatical errors before turning it in.

Think About It—Journal Entry 4.5

Think about how you utilize your free time, do you use your study period or time after school wisely? How do you use your free time?

_____
_____
_____
_____

What would you say is your greatest between-class time waster?

_____
_____
_____
_____

Do you see a need to stop or eliminate it?

_____
_____

If yes, what could you do to convert your wasted time into productive time?

_____

_____

_____

_____

A good time management plan transforms intention into action. Once you've planned the work, the next step is to work the plan. A time management plan turns into an action plan when you: (a) preview what you intend to do, (b) review whether you actually did what you intended to do, and (c) close the gap between your intentions and actions. The action plan begins with your *daily to-do list*, bringing that list with you as the day begins, and checking off items on the list as they're completed during the day. At the end of the day, the list is reviewed to determine what got done and what still needs to be done. The uncompleted tasks then become high priorities on the following day's to-do list.

If, at the end of each day, you find many unchecked items still remaining on your daily to-do list, this probably means you're spreading yourself too thin by trying to do too many things in a single day. You may need to be more realistic about how much you can accomplish per day by shortening your daily to-do lists. Not being able to complete many of your intended daily tasks may also mean that you need to modify your time management plan by adding more work time or subtracting some non-work activities that are drawing time and attention away from your work (e.g., responding to phone calls and text messages during your planned work times). If you're consistently falling short of achieving your daily goals, honestly ask yourself if you're spending too much time on less important things (e.g., TV, video games, Facebook).

Think About It—Journal Entry 4.6

At the end of a typical day, how often do you find that you accomplished most of the tasks you intended to accomplish? (Circle one.)

      never   seldom   often   almost   always

If you circled "never" or "seldom," what strategies could you use to move the bar toward "often" or "almost always"?

_____

_____

_____

> **Supreme Effort Rule**
>
> "No matter what the goal, consider the time you think is needed to accomplish the task at hand and then multiply it by two and that's the amount of effort it will take to make it happen."
>
> —*Shane Shope, co-author of this book*

> "Murphy's Laws:
> 1. Nothing is as simple as it looks.
> 2. Everything takes longer than it should.
> 3. If anything can go wrong, it will."
> —Author unknown (Murphy's Laws were named after Captain Edward Murphy, a naval engineer)

A good time management plan includes reserving time for the unexpected. Always hope for the best, but prepare for the worst. Your plan should include a buffer zone or safety net that contains extra time in case you encounter unforeseen developments or unexpected emergencies. Just as you should plan to have extra funds in your account to pay for unexpected expenses (e.g., auto repair), you should plan to have extra time in your schedule for unexpected events (e.g., personal illness or family emergency).

A good time management plan contains time for work and play. Your plan shouldn't consist solely of a daunting list of work tasks you have to do; it should also include fun things you like to do. Plan time to relax, refuel, and recharge. Your overall time management plan shouldn't turn you into an obsessive-compulsive workaholic. Instead, it should represent a balanced blend of work and play, including activities that promote your mental and physical wellness—such as relaxation, recreation, and reflection. Consider following the daily "8-8-8 rule"—8 hours for sleep, 8 hours for school, and 8 hours for other activities.

If you schedule things you like to do, you're more likely do to the things you have to do. You're much more likely to faithfully execute your plan if play time is scheduled along with work time, allowing play activities to serve as a reward for completing your work tasks.

NOTE

An effective time management plan helps you stress less, learn more, and earn higher grades while reserving time for other things that are important to you, enabling you to attain and maintain balance in your life.

Think About It—Journal Entry 4.7

What activities do you engage in for fun or recreation?
_____
_____
_____
_____

What do you do to relax or relieve stress?
_____
_____
_____
_____

Do you build these activities into your daily or weekly schedule?
_____
_____
_____
_____

A good time management plan has some flexibility. A time management plan shouldn't enslave you to a rigid work schedule. The plan should be flexible enough to allow you to occasionally bend it without breaking it. Just as work commitments and family responsibilities can crop up unexpectedly, so, too, can opportunities for fun and enjoyable activities. Your plan should allow you the freedom to modify your schedule to take advantage of these enjoyable opportunities and experiences. However, you should plan to make up the work time you lost. In other words, you can borrow or trade work time for play time, but don't "steal" it; plan to pay back the work time you borrowed by substituting it for play time that was planned for another time. If you decide not to do work you planned, the next best thing to do is re-plan when you'll do it.

> **NOTE**
> When you create a personal time management plan, remember it's *your* plan—you own it and you run it. It shouldn't run you.

Dealing with Procrastination

A major enemy of effective time management is procrastination. Procrastinators don't abide by the proverb: "Why put off till tomorrow what can be done today?" Instead, their philosophy is just the opposite: "Why do today what can be put off till tomorrow?" Adopting this philosophy promotes a perpetual pattern of postponing what needs to be done until the last possible moment, forcing the procrastinator to rush frantically to finish work on time and turn in work that's inferior or incomplete (or not turn anything in at all).

> "Many people take no care of their money 'til they come nearly to the end of it, and others do just the same with their time."
> —Johann Wolfgang von Goethe, German poet, dramatist, and author of the epic Faust

©Kendall Hunt Publishing Company.

Next time I'll start sooner!

A procrastinator's idea of planning ahead and working in advance often boils down to this scenario.

AUTHOR'S EXPERIENCE

Procrastination story

In high school, I would often wait until the last minute, usually the night before a big project was due, and often times I would just get by with the least amount of preparation and work. I soon realized that when I broke the work up over a couple of weeks, the final product was always of better quality and my grade was substantially higher. When I moved on to college and work I was expected to meet the expectations of my professors and supervisors. Always prepare and plan accordingly to meet the expectations provided by your teachers.

—*Shane Shope*

> "Haste makes waste."
> —Benjamin Franklin

Myths That Promote Procrastination

To have any hope of putting a stop to procrastination, procrastinators need to let go of two popular myths or misconceptions about time and performance.

Myth 1. "I work better under pressure" (e.g., on the day or night before something is due). Procrastinators often confuse desperation with motivation. Their belief that they work better under pressure is usually a rationalization to justify the fact that they *only* work under pressure—when they have to work because they've run out of time and are under the gun of a looming deadline.

It's true that when people are under pressure, they will start working and work with frantic energy, but that doesn't mean they're working more *effectively* and producing work of better *quality*. Because procrastinators are playing "beat the clock," they focus less on doing the job well and more on beating the buzzer. This typically results in a work product that's incomplete or inferior to what could have been produced if they had begun the work process sooner.

Myth 2. "Studying in advance is a waste of time because you will forget it all by test time." This myth is used by procrastinators to justify putting off all studying until the night before an exam. Studying that's distributed (spread out) over time is more effective than massed (crammed) studying all at one time. Furthermore, last minute studying before exams often involves pulling "late-nighters" or "all-nighters" that result in sleep loss. This fly-by-night strategy deprives the brain of dream sleep (a.k.a. REM sleep), which it needs to retain information and manage stress (Hobson, 1988; Voelker, 2004). Research indicates that procrastinators suffer from higher rates of stress-related physical disorders, such as insomnia, stomach problems, colds, and flu (McCance & Pychyl, 2003). Working under time pressure also increases performance pressure by leaving the procrastinators with (a) no margin of error to correct mistakes, (b) no time to seek help on their work, and (c) no chance to handle random catastrophes or setbacks that may arise at the last minute.

Psychological Causes of Procrastination

Sometimes, procrastination has deeper psychological roots. People may procrastinate for reasons that relate more to emotional issues than poor time management habits. Studies show that some people procrastinate as a psychological strategy to protect their self-esteem. Referred to as *self-handicapping* (Rhodewalt & Vohs, 2005), this strategy is used by some procrastinators, often unconsciously, to give themselves a "handicap," or disadvantage. By starting their work at the last possible moment, if their performance turns out to be less than spectacular, they can always conclude (rationalize) that it was because they were performing under a handicap—lack of time rather than lack of ability (Chu & Cho, 2005).

For example, if they receive a low grade on a test or paper, they can "save face" (self-esteem) by concluding that it was because they waited until the last minute and didn't put much time or effort into it. In other words, they had enough ability or intelligence to earn a high grade, they just didn't put in enough time. Better yet, if they happen to get a good grade—despite their last-minute, last-ditch effort—it proves just how smart they are. It shows they were able to earn a high grade, even without putting in much time at all. Thus, self-handicapping creates a fail-safe or win–win scenario that always protects the procrastinators' self-image.

> "Procrastinators would rather be seen as lacking in effort than lacking in ability."
> —Joseph Ferrari, professor of psychology and procrastination researcher

 Think About It—Journal Entry 4.8

Do you tend to put off work for so long that getting it done turns into an emergency or panic situation?

If your answer is yes, why do you think you put yourself in this position?

If your answer is no, what motivates or enables you to avoid this scenario?

In addition to self-handicapping, other psychological factors have been found to contribute to procrastination, including the following:

- **Fear of failure.** The procrastinator feels better about not turning in work than turning it in and getting negative feedback (Burka & Yuen, 2008; Solomon & Rothblum, 1984);
- **Perfectionism.** The procrastinator has unrealistically high personal standards or expectations, which leads to the belief that it's better to postpone work or not do it than to risk doing it less than perfectly (Kachgal, Hansel, & Nuter, 2001);
- **Fear of success.** The procrastinator fears that doing well will show others that he has the ability to achieve success, leading others to expect him to maintain those high standards in the future (Beck, Koons, & Milgram, 2000; Ellis & Knaus, 2002);
- **Indecisiveness.** The procrastinator has difficulty making decisions, including decisions about what to do first, when to do it, or whether to do it (Anderson, 2003; Steel, 2007), so they delay doing it or don't do it at all; and
- **Thrill seeking.** The procrastinator is hooked on the adrenaline rush triggered by rushing around to get things done just before a deadline (Szalavitz, 2003).

If these psychological issues are at the root of procrastination, they must be uprooted and dealt with before the problem can be solved. This may take some time and assistance from a counselor (either on or off school) who is professionally trained to deal with emotional issues, including those that underlie procrastination.

> *"Striving for excellence motivates you; striving for perfection is demoralizing."*
> —Harriet Braiker, psychologist and best-selling author

Think About It—Journal Entry 4.9

How often do you procrastinate? (Circle one.)

    rarely   occasionally   frequently   consistently

When you do procrastinate, what's the usual cause?

_____

_____

_____

_____

_____

Strategies for Preventing and Overcoming Procrastination

Consistently use effective time management strategies. When effective time management practices (such as those cited in this chapter) are implemented consistently, they turn into regular habits. Research indicates that procrastinators are less likely to procrastinate

> *"We are what we repeatedly do. Excellence, then, is not an act, but a habit."*
> —Aristotle, influential Ancient Greek philosopher

when they convert their intentions or vows ("I swear I'm going to start tomorrow") into concrete action plans (Gollwitzer, 1999; Gollwitzer & Sheeran, 2006). When they repeatedly practice effective time management strategies with respect to tasks they tend to procrastinate on, their bad procrastination habits gradually fade and are replaced by good time management habits (Ainslie, 1992; Baumeister, Heatherton, & Tice, 1994).

Make the start of work as inviting or appealing as possible. Starting work—getting off the starting blocks—is often the major stumbling block for procrastinators. It's common for procrastinators to experience what's known as "start-up stress"—when they're about to start a task, they start having negative feelings about it, expecting it to be difficult, stressful, or boring (Burka & Yuen, 2008).

If you have trouble starting your work, sequence your work tasks in a way that allows you to start on tasks you find more interesting or are more likely to do well. Beginning with these tasks can give you a "jump start," enabling you to overcome inertia and create momentum. You can ride this initial momentum to motivate you to attack less appealing or more daunting work tasks that come later in your work sequence, which often turn out not to be as unpleasant or time-consuming as you thought they would be. Like many events in life, anticipation of the event turns out to be worse than the event itself. In one study of high school students who didn't start a project until just before its due date, it was found that they experienced anxiety and guilt while they were procrastinating, but once they began working, these negative emotions subsided and were replaced by more positive feelings of progress and accomplishment (McCance & Pychyl, 2003).

You can also reduce start-up stress by beginning your work in an environment you find pleasant and relaxing (e.g., working in your favorite coffee shop while sipping your favorite beverage). In other words, if you have trouble starting work, start it in a place you enjoy while doing something you enjoy.

Organization matters. Research indicates that disorganization is a factor that contributes to procrastination (Steel, 2007). How well you organize your workplace and manage your work materials can reduce your tendency to procrastinate. Having the right materials in the right place at the right time can make it easier to get started. Once you decide to start working, you don't want to delay acting on that decision by looking for the tools you need to work with. If you're a procrastinator, this slight delay may provide the time (and excuse) to change your mind and not start working.

One simple, yet effective way to organize academic materials is to develop your own filing system. Start by filing (storing) materials from different courses in different colored folders or notebooks. This not only enables you to keep all materials related to the same course in the same place, it also gives you immediate access to them when you need them. A filing system helps get you organized, gets rid of the stress associated with having things all over the place, and reduces your risk of procrasting by reducing the time and effort it takes to get started.

> "The secret to getting ahead is getting started."
> —Mark Twain (Samuel Clemens), American humorist and author of the Adventures of Huckleberry Finn (1885), a.k.a. "the Great American Novel"

> "Did you ever dread doing something, then it turned out to take only about 20 minutes to do?"
> —Conversation between two college students overheard in a coffee shop

NOTE

The less time and effort it takes to start working, the more likely the work will be started.

Location matters. *Where* you choose to work can influence *whether* your work gets done. Research indicates that distractions promote procrastination (Steel, 2007). Thus, working in an environment that minimizes distraction and maximizes concentration will reduce the risk of procrastination.

Arrange your work environment in a way that minimizes social distractions (e.g., people nearby who are not working), and media distractions (e.g., cell phones, e-mails, text messages, music, and TV). Remove everything from your work site that's not relevant or directly related to the work you're doing.

Your concentration will also improve if you work in an environment that allows you easy access to (a) work-support materials— (e.g., class notes, textbooks, and a dictionary), and (b) social support networks (e.g., working with a group of motivated students who help you stay focused, on task, and on track toward completing your work).

> "To reduce distractions, work at a computer on campus rather than using one in your room or home."
> —Advice to new college students from a student finishing her first year in college

Think About It—Journal Entry 4.10

List your two most common sources of distraction while working. Next to each distraction, identify a strategy you might use to reduce or eliminate it.

Source of Distraction   *Strategy for Reducing this Distraction*

1. _____

2. _____

> "I'm very good at starting things but often have trouble keeping a sustained effort."
> —First-year college student

If you have difficulty maintaining or sustaining commitment to your work until it's finished, schedule easier and more interesting work tasks *in the middle or toward the end* of your planned work time. Some procrastinators have difficulty starting work, others have trouble continuing and completing the work they've started (Lay & Silverman, 1996). As previously mentioned, if you have trouble starting work, it might be best for you to start with tasks you find most interesting or easiest. In contrast, if you tend to experience procrastination by not completing your work once you've started, it might be better to schedule tasks of greater interest and ease at later points during your work session. Doing so can restore or revive your interest and energy. Tackling enjoyable and easier tasks last can also provide you with an incentive or reward for completing your less enjoyable and more difficult tasks first.

If you're close to completing a task, don't stop until you complete it. Just do it! Completing a task that's almost done allows you to build on the momentum you've already generated. In contrast, postponing work on a task that's near completion means that you have to overcome inertia and regenerate momentum all over again. As the old saying goes, "There's no time like the present."

Furthermore, finishing a task gives you a sense of *closure*—the feeling of personal accomplishment and self-satisfaction that comes from knowing you've "closed the deal." Checking off a completed task can motivate you to keep going and complete the unfinished tasks ahead of you.

Divide large work tasks into smaller, bite-sized pieces. Work becomes less overwhelming and stressful when it's handled in small chunks or segments. You can conquer procrastination for large tasks by using a "divide and conquer" strategy: divide the large task into smaller, more manageable subtasks, then tackle and complete these subtasks one at a time.

Don't underestimate the power of short work sessions. They're often more effective than longer sessions because it's easier to maintain concentration and momentum for shorter periods of time. By dividing work into short sessions, you can take quick jabs at a tall task, poke holes in it, and shrink its overall size with each successive jab. This reduces the pressure of having to deliver one, big knockout punch right before the final bell (deadline date).

> "Just do it."
> —Commercial slogan of Nike, athletic equipment company named after the Greek goddess of victory

> "To eat an elephant, first cut it into small pieces."
> —Author unknown

AUTHOR'S EXPERIENCE

The two biggest projects I've had to complete in my life were writing my doctoral thesis and writing this book. The strategy that enabled me to complete both of these large tasks was to set short-term deadlines for myself (e.g., complete five to ten pages each week). I psyched myself into thinking that these little, self-imposed due dates were really drop-dead deadlines that I had to meet. This strategy allowed me to divide one monstrous chore into a series of smaller, more manageable mini-tasks. It was like taking a huge, indigestible meal and breaking it into small, bite-sized pieces that could be easily ingested and gradually digested over time.

—*Joe Cuseo*

> "I long to accomplish some great and noble task, but it is my chief duty to accomplish small tasks as if they were great and noble."
> —Helen Keller, seeing- and hearing-impaired author and activist for the rights of women and the handicapped

CHAPTER SUMMARY AND HIGHLIGHTS

Effective goal-setting gets you going, but effective time management gets things done. To manage time effectively, we need to

- *Analyze* it. Break down time and become aware of how we spend it;
- *Itemize* it. Identify the tasks we need to accomplish and their due dates; and
- *Prioritize* it. Tackle our tasks in order of their importance.

Developing a comprehensive time management plan for academic work involves long-, mid-, and short-range steps that involve:

- Planning the total term (long-range step);
- Planning your week (mid-range step); and
- Planning your day (short-range step).

A good time management plan includes the following features:

- It transforms intention to action.
- It includes time to take care of unexpected developments.
- It contains time for work and play.
- It gives you the flexibility to accommodate unforeseen opportunities.

The enemy of effective time management is procrastination. Overcoming it involves letting go of two major myths:

- Better work is produced "under pressure"—on the day or night before it's due.
- Studying in advance is a waste of time—because you'll forget it all by test time.

Effective strategies for beating the procrastination habit include the following:

- Organize your work materials to make it easy and convenient for you to start working.
- Organize your work place or space so that you work in a location that minimizes distractions and temptations not to work.
- Intentionally arrange your work schedule so that you are working on more enjoyable or stimulating tasks at times when you're less vulnerable to procrastination.
- If you're close to finishing a task, finish it, because it's often harder to restart a task than to complete one that's already been started.
- Divide large tasks into smaller, more manageable units and tackle them in separate work sessions.

Mastering the skill of managing time is critical for success in high school and beyond. Time is one of our most powerful personal resources; the better we manage it, the more likely we are to achieve our goals and gain control of our life.

> "Doesn't thou love life? Then do not squander time, for that is the stuff life is made of."
> —Benjamin Franklin, 18th-century inventor, newspaper writer, and cosigner of the Declaration of Independence

Learning More through the World Wide Web: Internet-Based Resources

For additional information on managing time, and preventing procrastination, see the following websites:

Time-Management Strategies for All Students:
www.studygs.net/timman.htm
www.pennstatelearning.psu.edu/resources/study-tips/time-mgt

Time-Management Strategies for Adult Students:
www.essortment.com/lifestyle/timemanagement_sjmu.htm

Beating Procrastination:
www.mindtools.com/pages/article/newHTE_96.htm
http://success.oregonstate.edu/learning-corner/time-management/managing-procrastination

References

Ainslie, G. (1992. Specious reward: A behavioral theory of impulsiveness and impulse control. *Psychological Bulletin, 82,* 463–496.

American Association of Community Colleges 2009 Fact Sheet. (2009). Retrieved from http://www.aacc.nche.edu/About/Documents/factsheet2009.pdf.

Anderson, C. J. (2003). The psychology of doing nothing: Forms of decision avoidance result from reason and emotion. *Psychological Bulletin, 129,* 139–167.

Baumeister, R. F., Heatherton, T. F., & Tice, D. M. (1994). *Losing control: How and why people fail at self-regulation.* San Diego, CA: Academic Press.

Beck, B. L., Koons, S. R. & Milgram, D. L. (2000). Correlates and consequences of behavioural procrastination: The effects of academic procrastination, self-consciousness, self-esteem and self-handicapping [Special issue], *Journal of Social Behaviour & Personality, 15*(5) (2000), pp. 3–13

Burka, J. B., & Yuen, L. M. (2008). *Procrastination: Why you do it, what to do about it now.* Cambridge, MA: De Capo Press.

Chu, A. H. C., & Cho, J. N. (2005). Rethinking procrastination: Positive effects of "active" procrastination behavior on attitudes and performance. *The Journal of Social Psychology, 145*(3), 245–264.

Covey, S. R. (2004). *Seven habits of highly effective people* (3rd ed.). New York: Fireside.

Ellis, A., & Knaus, W. J. (2002). *Overcoming procrastination* (Rev. ed.). New York: New American Library.

Goldsmith, E. B. (2010). *Resource management for individuals and families.* (4th ed.). Upper Saddle River, NJ: Prentice Hall.

Gollwitzer, P. M. (1999). Implementation intentions: Strong effects of simple plans. *American Psychologist, 54*(7), 493–503.

Gollwitzer, P. M., & Sheeran, P. (2006). Implementation intentions and goal achievement: A meta-analysis of effects and processes. *Advances in Experimental Social Psychology, 38,* 69–119.

Harriot, J. & Ferrari, J. R. (1996). Prevalence of procrastination among samples of adults. *Psychological Reports, 78* (1996), pp. 611–616.

HERI (Higher Education Research Institute) (2014). *Your first college year survey 2014.* Los Angeles, CA: Cooperative Institutional Research Program, University of California-Los Angeles.

Hobson, J. A. (1988). *The dreaming brain.* New York: Basic Books.

Kachgal, M. M., Hansen, L. S., & Nutter, K. T. (2001). Academic procrastination prevention/intervention: Strategies and recommendations. *Journal of Developmental Education, 25*(1), 2–12.

Lakein, A. (1973). *How to get control of your time and your life.* New York: New American Library.

Lay, C. H., & Silverman, S. (1996). Trait procrastination, time management, and dilatory behavior. *Personality & Individual Differences, 21,* 61–67.

Light, R. J. (2001). *Making the most of college: Students speak their minds.* Cambridge, MA: Harvard University Press.

McCance, N., & Pychyl, T. A. (2003, August). *From task avoidance to action: An experience sampling study of undergraduate students' thoughts, feelings and coping strategies in relation to academic procrastination.* Paper presented at the Third Annual Conference for Counseling Procrastinators in the Academic Context, University of Ohio, Columbus.

Morgenstern, J. (2004). *Time management from the inside out: The foolproof system for taking control of your schedule—and your life* (2nd ed.). New York: Henry Holt & Co.

Myers, D. G. (1993). *The pursuit of happiness: Who is happy—and why?* New York: Morrow.

Myers, D. G. (2000). *The American paradox: Spiritual hunger in an age of plenty.* New Haven, CT: Yale University Press.

Onwuegbuzie, A. J. (2000). Academic procrastinators and perfectionistic tendencies among graduate students. *Journal of Social Behavior and Personality, 15,* 103–109

Rhodewalt, F., & Vohs, K. D. (2005). Defensive strategies, motivation, and the self. In A. Elliot & C. Dweck (Eds.), *Handbook of competence and motivation* (pp. 548–565). New York: Guilford Press.

Solomon, L. J., & Rothblum, E. D. (1984). Academic procrastination: Frequency and cognitive-behavioral correlates. *Journal of Counseling Psychology, 31*(4), 503–509.

Steel, P. (2007). The nature of procrastination: A meta-analytic and theoretical review of quintessential self-regulatory failure. *Psychological Bulletin, 133*(1), 65–94.

Szalavitz, M. (2003, July/August). Tapping potential: Stand and deliver. *Psychology Today*, 50–54.

Voelker, R. (2004). Stress, sleep loss, and substance abuse create potent recipe for college depression. *Journal of the American Medical Association, 291*, 2177–2179.

CHAPTER 4 EXERCISES

4.1 QUOTE REFLECTIONS

Review the sidebar quotes contained in this chapter and select two that were especially meaningful or inspirational to you.

For each quote, provide a three- to five-sentence explanation why you chose it.

4.2 REALITY BITE

You have a paper due tomorrow for your 10:00 a.m. class. You stay up late writing the paper, and then your friends call and ask you to go out. The paper is finished, and you decide you can print it off when you get to school tomorrow. You have a great time with your friends and oversleep, waking at 9:45 a.m. You go straight to the computer lab and experience difficulties printing off your paper. You find a lab technician to help you, but it takes him 40 minutes to retrieve the paper. You run into class (45 minutes late) and give the paper to your teacher, who informs you that she will take the paper for late credit because the class policy states that any papers handed in after the beginning of class are considered late.

1. Who is primarily responsible for this paper being late? Why?
2. How could the situation have been avoided or handled differently?

4.3 TERM AT A GLANCE

Review with your teachers the critical assignments and projects for the term. (course outline) for each course you're enrolled in this term, and complete the following information for each:

Term _____ Year _____

Course ↓	Teacher ↓	Exams ↓	Projects & Papers ↓	Other Assignments ↓	Late & Makeup Assignment Policy ↓

1. Is the overall workload what you expected? Are you surprised by the amount of work required in any particular course or courses?

2. At this point in the term, what do you see as your most challenging or demanding course or courses? Why?

3. Do you think you can handle the total workload required for the full set of courses you're enrolled in this term?

4. What adjustments or changes could you make to your personal schedule that would make it easier to accommodate your academic workload this term?

4.4 DEVELOPING A TASK MANAGEMENT PLAN FOR YOUR FIRST TERM IN HIGH SCHOOL

1. Review each class you are enrolled in this term and highlight all major exams, tests, quizzes, assignments, and papers and the dates on which they are due.

2. Obtain a *large calendar* for the academic term (available at your school bookstore or learning center) and record all the highlighted information for your exams and assignments for all your courses in the calendar boxes that represent their due dates. To fit this information within the calendar boxes, use creative abbreviations to represent different tasks, such as RA for reading assignment, E for exam, and TP for term paper. When you're done, you'll have a detailed chart or map of deadline dates and a master schedule for the entire term. There are several online calendars that can assist in managing your schedule (e.g., http://www.cozi.com/family-calendar.htm and http://pomodorotechnique.com/).

3. Activate the calendar and task lists functions on your PDA or smartphone. Enter your schedule, important dates, deadlines, and set alert reminders. By carrying your PDA or cell phone with your regularly, you will always have this information at your fingertips.

Reflections

1. Is your overall workload what you expected? Are your surprised by the amount of work time you will need to devote to your courses?

2. At this point in the term, what course is demanding the greatest amount of out-of-class work time? Have you been able to put in this time?

3. What adjustments or changes (if any) could you make to your personal schedule this term to create more time to handle your academic workload?

4.5 TIME ANALYSIS INVENTORY

1. Go to the following website: *pennstatelearning.psu.edu/resources/study-tips/time-mgt* Click on the link for the "time-management exercise."

2. Complete the time management exercise at this site. The exercise asks you to estimate the hours per day or week that you engage in various activities (e.g., sleeping, employment, and commuting). When you enter the amount of time devoted to each activity, this website will automatically compute the total number of remaining hours you have available in the week for academic work.

3. After completing your entries, answer the following questions (or provide your best estimate).

    a) How many hours per week do you have available for academic work?

    b) Do you have enough time available for homework outside of class? If you don't, what activities could be eliminated or reduced to create more time for academic work outside of class?

4.6 DEVELOPING A TIME MANAGEMENT PLAN FOR YOUR FIRST YEAR IN HIGH SCHOOL

> "Always have a weekly study schedule to go by. Otherwise, time slips away and you will not be able to account for it."
> —Advice to new college students from a first-year student (Rhoads, 2005)

Keep in mind the task management plan you developed in Exercise 4.3, use the following *Week-at-a-Glance Grid* to map out your typical or average week for this term. Start by recording what you usually do on these days, including the times you're in class, when you work, and when you relax or recreate. You can use abbreviations (e.g., CT for class time, HW for homework, J for job, and R&R for rest and relaxation). List the abbreviations you created at the bottom of the page so that your teacher can follow them.

Week-at-a-Glance Grid

	Sunday	Monday	Tuesday	Wednesday	Thursday	Friday	Saturday
7:00 a.m.							
8:00 a.m.							
9:00 a.m.							
10:00 a.m.							
11:00 a.m.							
12:00 p.m.							
1:00 p.m.							
2:00 p.m.							
3:00 p.m.							
4:00 p.m.							
5:00 p.m.							
6:00 p.m.							
7:00 p.m.							
8:00 p.m.							
9:00 p.m.							
10:00 p.m.							
11:00 p.m.							
8:00 a.m.							

Reflections:

1. How likely are you to put this time management plan into practice? Circle one: Definitely Probably Unlikely
2. What would *promote or encourage* you to put this plan into practice?
3. What would *prevent or discourage* you from putting this plan into practice?
4. How do you think other students would answer the above three questions?

4.7 RANKING PRIORITIES

Look at the tasks below and decide if they are A, B, or C priorities:

_____ Going for a run

_____ Writing a paper that is due tomorrow

_____ Checking out what your friends are doing on Facebook

_____ Getting your haircut

_____ Making an appointment with your academic advisor to register for classes

_____ Playing your favorite video game

_____ Making it to your doctor's appointment

_____ Helping your sister plan her wedding

_____ Studying for your final exams

_____ Calling your cousin to catch up on family gossip

_____ Making reservations for your vacation

_____ Going to see the hot new movie that has come out

_____ Getting your oil changed in your car

_____ Getting your car washed

4.8 REALITY BITE

Procrastination: The Vicious Cycle

Delayla has a major paper due at the end of the term. It's now past midterm and she still hasn't started to work on it. She keeps telling herself, "I should have started sooner," but she continues to postpone her work and is becoming increasingly anxious and guilty. To relieve her growing anxiety and guilt, Delayla starts doing other tasks instead, such as cleaning her room and returning e-mails. This makes her feel a little better because these tasks keep her busy, take her mind off the term paper, and give her the feeling that at least she's getting something accomplished. Time continues to pass; the deadline for the paper grows dangerously close. Delayla now finds herself in the position of having lots of work to do and little time in which to do it.

Adapted from *Procrastination: Why You Do It, and What to do about It* (Burka & Yuen, 2008)

Reflection and Discussion Questions

1. What do you expect Delayla will do at this point? Why?
2. What grade do you think she'll end up receiving on her paper?
3. Other than simply starting sooner, what else could Delayla (and other procrastinators like her) do to break the cycle of procrastination?
4. Can you relate to this student's predicament, or do you know other students who often find themselves in this predicament?

CHAPTER 4 REFLECTION

Looking back on suggestions from this chapter, what are three things you can do start managing your time better?

1.

2.

3.

Explain how you are going to make these things happen.

CHAPTER 5

DEEP LEARNING

Strategic Note-Taking, Reading, and Studying

CHAPTER PREVIEW

This chapter will help you apply research on human learning and the human brain to become a more effective and efficient learner. It takes you through three key stages of the learning process—from the first stage of acquiring information through classes and readings, through the second stage of studying and retaining the information you acquire, through the final stage of retrieving (recalling) the information you studied. The ultimate goal of this chapter is to supply you with a set of powerful strategies that can be used to promote learning that's *deep* (not surface-level memorization), *durable* (long-lasting), and *retrievable* (accessible to you when you need it).

LEARNING GOAL

Develop a collection of effective strategies for studying smarter, learning deeply, and retaining longer what you have learned.

THOUGHT STARTER

Think About It—Journal Entry 5.1

What would you say is the key difference between learning and memorizing?

_____
_____
_____
_____
_____

From *Thriving in the Community College & Beyond: Strategies for Academic Success and Personal Development*, Third Edition, by Joseph Cuseo, Aaron Thompson, and Julie McLaughlin. Copyright © 2016 by Kendall Hunt Publishing Company. Reprinted by permission.

Learning is the fundamental mission of all institutions of learning. One of the major goals of education is to help students become independent, self-directed learners. Learning doesn't stop after graduation; it's a lifelong process that is essential for success in the 21st century. The ongoing information technology revolution, coupled with global interdependence, is creating a greater need for effective learning skills that can be used throughout life and in different cultural and occupational contexts. Today's employers value job applicants who have "learned how to learn" and will continue to be "lifelong learners" (SECFHE, 2006).

FIGURE 5.1: Network of Brain Cells

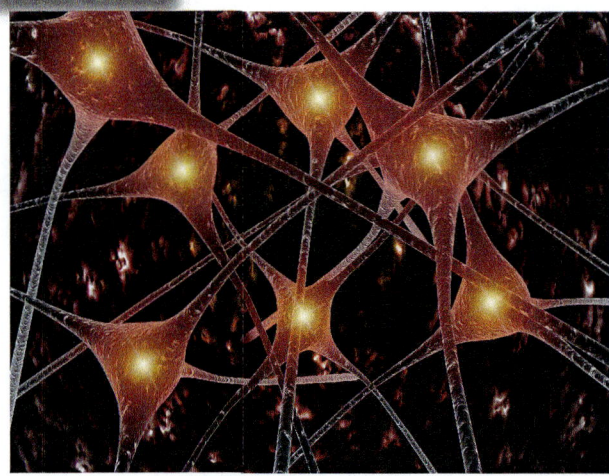

Deep learning involves making connections between what you're trying to learn and what you already know. When you learn something deeply, it's stored in the brain as a link in an interconnected network of brain cells.

©Jurgen Ziewe/Shutterstock.com

What Is Deep Learning?

When students learn deeply, they dive below the surface of shallow memorization; they go further by building mental bridges between what they're trying to learn and what they already know (Piaget, 1978; Vygotsky, 1978). Knowledge isn't acquired by simply pouring information into the brain as if it were an empty jar. It's a matter of attaching or connecting new ideas to ideas that are already stored in the brain. When this happens, facts are transformed into *concepts*—networks of connected or interrelated ideas. In fact, when something is learned deeply, the human brain actually makes a physical (neurological) connection between separate nerve cells (LeDoux, 2002) (see **Figure 5.1**).

Studies suggest that most students don't engage in deep learning (Arum & Roksa, 2011; Kuh, 2005; Nathan, 2005). They may show up for class most of the time, cram for their exams, and get their assignments done right before they're due. These learning strategies may enable students to survive high school, but not thrive in high school and achieve academic excellence.

Effective Class-Listening and Note-Taking Strategies

The importance of developing effective listening skills in the classroom was highlighted in a classic study of more than 400 students who were given a listening test at the start of their college experience. At the end of their first year in college, 49% of those students who scored low on the listening test were on academic probation—compared to only 4.4% of students who scored high on the listening test. On the other hand, 68.5% of students who scored high on the listening test were eligible for the honors program at the end of their first year—compared to only 4.17% of those students who had low listening test scores (Conaway, 1982). This is applicable to the high school classroom as well.

Think About It—Journal Entry 5.2

Do you think writing notes in class helps or hinders your ability to pay attention to and learn from your teachers' classes?

Why?

___

___

___

___

___

Studies show that information delivered during classes is the number one source of test questions (and answers) on exams (Brown, 1988; Kuhn, 1988). When class information isn't recorded in students' notes and appears on a test, it has only a 5% chance of being recalled (Kiewra et al., 2000). Students who write notes during classes achieve higher course grades than students who just listen to classes (Kiewra, 1985, 2005), and students with a more complete set of class notes are more likely to demonstrate higher levels of overall academic achievement (Johnstone & Su, 1994; Kiewra & DuBois, 1998). Same goes for you in high school, note taking is an important part of your study plan. Create outlines for the chapters in your textbook and add to those outlines by taking notes in class as the teacher covers the chapter material.

Contrary to a popular belief that writing while listening interferes with the ability to listen, students report that taking notes actually increases their attention and concentration in class (Hartley, 1998; Hartley & Marshall, 1974). Studies also show that when students write down information that's presented to them, they're more likely to remember the most important aspects of that information when tested later (Bligh, 2000). One study discovered that students with grade point averages (GPAs) of 2.53 or higher record more information in their notes and retain a larger percentage of the most important information than do students with GPAs of less than 2.53 (Einstein, Morris, & Smith, 1985). These findings aren't surprising when you consider that hearing information, writing it and then seeing it after it's been written produces three different memory traces (tracks) in the brain, thus tripling your chances of remembering it.

Furthermore, when notes are taken, you're left with a written record of class information that can be studied later to improve your test performance. In contrast, if you take few or no notes, you're left with little or no information to study for upcoming exams. As previously noted, the majority of questions on teachers' exams come from information contained in their classes. So, come to class with the attitude that your teachers are dispensing answers to test questions as they speak and your job is to pick out and record these answers so you can pick up points on the next exam.

Pre-Class Strategies: What to Do *Before* Class

1. **Always be aware what is upcoming in your classes.** At some point before the start of the week review what will be reviewed in each class. Review what was covered the previous week and think about how the upcoming week's material will add to that knowledge. This strategy capitalizes on the brain's natural tendency to seek larger patterns and see the "big picture." The human brain is naturally inclined to connect parts into a whole (Caine & Caine, 2011). It looks for meaningful patterns and connections rather than isolated bits and pieces of information (Jensen, 2008).
2. **Review your notes from the previous class session and from any reading assignments relating to the day's class topic.** Research indicates that when students review information related to an upcoming class topic, they take more accurate and complete class notes (Jairam & Kiewra, 2009; Kiewra, 2005). Thus, a good way to improve your ability to learn from classes is to review your notes from the previous class session and read textbook information related to the class topic—*before* hearing the class. Reviewing previously learned information activates your prior knowledge,

enabling you to connect class material to what you already know—a powerful way to promote deep learning (Bruner, 1990; Piaget, 1978; Vygotky, 1978).

Listening and Note-Taking Strategies: What to Do *During* Class

1. **Give classes your undivided attention.** As previously noted, research shows that in all subject areas, the majority of test questions appearing on exams come from the teacher's classes and students who take better class notes get better course grades (Brown, 1988; Cuseo et al., 2013; Kiewra, 2000). Studies also show that the more time students spend surfing the web or using Facebook during classes, the lower their test scores. These results hold true for all students, regardless of how they scored on high school admissions tests (Ravizza, Hambrick, & Fenn, 2014).

    Remember that like all humans, not all teachers are created equal. You'll have some that are more dynamic and easier to pay attention to than others. It's the less dynamic ones that will tempt you to lose attention and stop taking notes. Don't let the less engaging or less entertaining teachers lower your course grades. Instead view them as a challenge; step up your focus of attention, continue taking notes to keep yourself engaged, and leave the course with the satisfaction of earning a good grade.

2. **Take your own notes in class.** Don't rely on someone else to take notes for you. Taking notes in your own words focuses your attention and ensures the notes you take make sense to you. Research indicates that students who record and review their own notes on information presented to them earn higher scores on memory tests for that information than do students who review notes taken by others (Jairam & Kiewra, 2009; Kiewra, 2005). Taking your own notes in your own words makes them *meaningful to you*. While it's a good idea to collaborate with classmates to compare notes for completeness and accuracy, or to pick up points you may have missed, you shouldn't rely on someone else to do your note-taking for you.

3. **Take notes in longhand rather than typing them on a laptop.** Studies show that when students use a keyboard to type notes, they're more likely to mindlessly punch in the exact words used by the teacher, rather than transforming the teacher's words into words that are meaningful to them. When tested on understanding and memory for key concepts presented in class, students who took notes in longhand outperformed those who typed notes on a keyboard (Mueller & Oppenheimer, 2014). This may be due to the fact that the movements made during handwriting leave a motor (muscle) memory trace in the brain, which deepens learning and strengthens memory (Herbert, 2014).

4. **Be alert to cues for the most important information contained in classes.** Since the human attention span is limited, it's

impossible to attend to and make note of everything. Thus, we need to use our attention *selectively* to detect and select information that matters most. Here are some strategies for identifying and recording the most important information delivered by professors during classes:

- Pay particular attention to information your teachers put *in print*—on the board, on a slide, or in a handout. If your teacher has taken the time and energy to write it out or type it out, this is usually a good clue that the information is important and you'll likely see it again—on an exam.
- Pay special attention to information presented during the *first and last few minutes of class*. Teachers are most likely to provide valuable reminders, reviews, and previews at the start and end of a class session.
- Look for *verbal and nonverbal cues* that signal the teacher is delivering important information. Don't just tune in when your teachers are writing something down and tune out at other times. It's been found that students record almost 90% of material written on the board, but less than 50% of important ideas that professors state but don't write on the board (Johnstone & Su, 1994; Locke, 1977; Titsworth & Kiewra, 2004). So, don't fall into the reflex-like routine of just taking notes when you see your teacher writing notes. Instead, listen actively to ideas you *hear* your teacher saying and take notes on these ideas as well. **Box 5.1** contains strategies for detecting clues to important information that professors are delivering orally in class.

BOX 5.1

Detecting When Teachers Are Delivering Important Information during Classes

Look for *verbal* cues, such as:

- Phrases signaling important information (e.g., "The point here is . . ." or "What's most significant about this is . . .").
- Information that's repeated or rephrased in a different way (e.g., "In other words, . . .", or "To put it another way . . .").
- Stated information that's followed by a question to check understanding (e.g., "Is that clear?" "Do you follow that?" "Does that make sense?" or "Are you with me?").

Watch for *vocal* (*tone of voice*) cues, such as:

- Information delivered in a louder tone or at a higher pitch than usual—which may indicate excitement or emphasis.
- Information delivered at a slower rate or with more pauses than usual—which may be your teacher's way of giving you more time to write down these important ideas.

Keep an eye out for *nonverbal* cues, such as:

- Information delivered by your teacher with more than the usual:
  a. Facial expressiveness (e.g., raised or furrowed eyebrows);
  b. Body movement (e.g., gesticulation and animation);
  c. Eye contact (e.g., looking directly and intently at the faces of students to see if they're following or understanding what's being said).
- Your teacher moving closer to the students (e.g., moving away from the podium or blackboard).
- Your teacher orienting his or her body directly toward the class (i.e., both shoulders directly or squarely facing the class).

5. **Keep taking notes even if you don't immediately understand what your teacher is saying.** If you are uncertain or confused about the material being presented, don't stop taking notes. Having notes on that material will at least leave you with a record to review later—when you have more time to think about it and make sense of it. If you still don't understand it after taking time to review it, seek clarification from your teacher, a classmate, or your textbook.
6. **Take organized notes.** If your teacher continues to make points relating to the same idea, take notes on that idea within the same paragraph. When the teacher shifts to a new idea, skip a few lines and shift to a new paragraph. Be alert to phrases that your teacher may use to signal a shift to a new or different idea (e.g., "Let's turn to . . ." or "In addition to . . ."). Use these phrases as cues for taking notes in paragraph form.

    By recording different ideas in different paragraphs, the organizational quality of your notes improves as will your comprehension and retention of them. Be sure to leave extra space between paragraphs (ideas) to give yourself room to add information that you may have initially missed, or to later translate the teacher's words into your own words.

    Another popular strategy for taking organized notes is the *Cornell Note-Taking System*.

    There are several methods to take notes. It is important you find the note-taking method that works best for you. Examples include formal outlining, informal outlining, mapping, charting, and many others. Please refer to: http://www.redlands.edu/docs/Academics/1Five_Methods_of_Notetaking_2015.pdf for more information.

Post-Class Strategies: What to Do *After* Class

1. **As soon as class ends, quickly check your notes for missing information or incomplete thoughts.** Information delivered during a class is likely to be fresh in your mind immediately after class. A quick check of your notes at this time will allow you to take advantage of your short-term memory. By reviewing and reflecting on your notes, you can help move that information into long-term memory before forgetting takes place. This quick review can be done alone or, better yet, with a motivated classmate. If you both have gaps in your notes, check them out with your teacher before he or she leaves the classroom. Even though it may be weeks before you'll be tested on the material, the quicker you pick up missed points and clear up sources of confusion, the better; it will help you understand upcoming material—especially upcoming material that builds on previously covered material. Catching confusion early in the game also enables you to avoid the mad last-minute rush of students seeking help from the teacher just before test time. You want to reserve the critical time just before exams to study notes you know are complete and accurate, rather than rushing around trying to find missing information and seeking last-minute help on concepts presented weeks earlier.

Think About It—Journal Entry 5.3

Do you tend to stick around a few minutes after class sessions end to review your notes and clear up missing information or confusing points? Why?

_____
_____
_____
_____

What could you do immediately after class to be a more successful student?

_____
_____
_____
_____

2. **Before the next class session meets, reflect on and review your notes to make sense of them.** Your professors will often class on information that you may have little prior knowledge about, so it's unrealistic to expect that you will understand everything that's being said the first time you hear it. Instead, set aside time to reflect on and review your notes as soon as possible after class has ended. During this review process, take notes on your notes by:

   - translating technical information into your own words to make it more meaningful to you; and
   - reorganizing your notes to get ideas related to the same point in the same place.

Studies show that students who organize their class notes into meaningful categories demonstrate superior recall of that information on memory tests—compared to students who simply review the notes they took in class (Howe, 1970; Kiewra, 2005).

> **NOTE**
>
> Effective note taking is a two-stage process: Stage 1 involves actively taking notes in class and stage 2 takes places after class—when you take time to reflect on your notes and process them more deeply.

> **AUTHOR'S EXPERIENCE**
>
> I spent my first year in college spending a lot of time trying to manipulate my schedule to create large blocks of free time. I took all of my classes in a row without a break to preserve some time at the end of the day for relaxation and hanging out with friends. Seldom did I even look at my notes until it was time to be tested on them. Thus, on the day before the test I was in a panic trying to cram the class notes into my head for the upcoming exam. Needless to say, I didn't perform well on many of my first tests. Eventually, a professor told me that if I spent some time each day rewriting my notes I would retain the material longer, increase my grades, and decrease my stress at test time. I employed this system and it worked wonderfully.
>
> —*Aaron Thompson*

Think About It—Journal Entry 5.4

Rate yourself in terms of how frequently you use these note-taking strategies according to the following scale:

    4 = always, 3 = sometimes, 2 = rarely, 1 = never

1. I take notes aggressively in class.   4   3   2   1
2. I sit near the front of the class.   4   3   2   1
3. I sit upright and lean forward while in class.   4   3   2   1
4. I take notes on what my teachers say, not just what they write on the board.   4   3   2   1
5. I pay special attention to information presented at the start and end of class.   4   3   2   1
6. I take notes in paragraph form.   4   3   2   1
7. I review my notes immediately after class to check that they are complete and accurate.   4   3   2   1

What works for you? What might you try to improve your note-taking skills?

_____

_____

_____

_____

Strategic Reading

Expect to do more reading in high school than in middle school and be ready to be held accountable for the reading you're assigned. Information from assigned readings ranks right behind information from classes as a source of test questions on exams (Brown, 1988; Cuseo et al., 2013). You're likely to find exam questions relating to reading assignments that your professors didn't talk about specifically in class (or even mention in class). High school teachers often expect you to relate or connect their classes with material they've assigned you to read. Furthermore, teachers often deliver classes with the assumption that students have done the assigned reading, so if you haven't done it, you're more likely to have difficulty following what your teacher is saying in class. Thus, you should do the assigned reading but also do it according to the schedule the teacher has established. By completing assigned reading in a timely manner, you will (a) be better positioned to understand material covered in class, (b) acquire information that's likely to appear on exams but not covered in class, and (c) improve the quality of your participation in class.

The following research-based strategies can be used to improve your comprehension and retention of material you read.

Pre-Reading Strategies: What to Do *Before* Reading

1. **Before jumping into your assigned reading, first see how it fits into the overall organizational structure of the book and course.** You can do this efficiently by taking a quick look at the book's table of contents to see where the chapter you're about to read is placed in the overall sequence of chapters. Look especially at its relationship to the chapters that immediately precede and follow it. This strategy will give you a sense of how the particular part you're focusing on connects with the bigger picture. Research shows that if students have advanced knowledge about how material they're about to learn is organized—if they see how its parts relate to the whole before they start learning the specific parts—they're better able to comprehend and retain the material (Ausubel, Novak, & Hanesian 1978; Chen & Hirumi, 2009). Thus, the first step toward improving reading comprehension and retention of a book chapter is to see how it relates to the book as a whole.

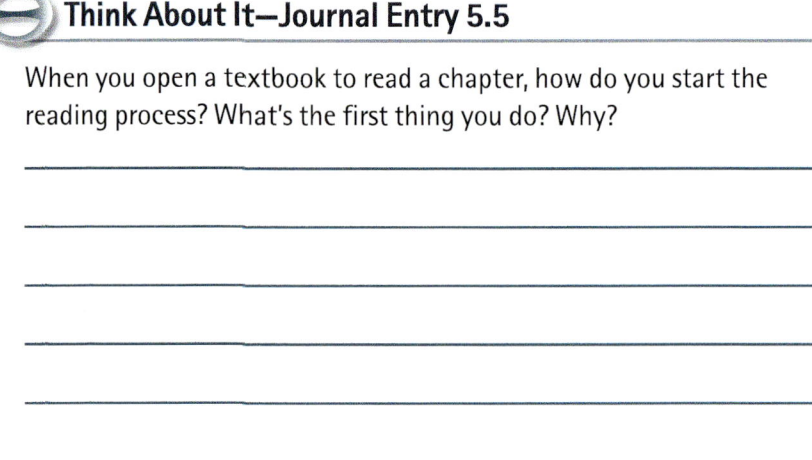

Think About It—Journal Entry 5.5

When you open a textbook to read a chapter, how do you start the reading process? What's the first thing you do? Why?

_____

_____

_____

_____

_____

2. **Preview the chapter by first reading its boldface headings and any chapter outline, objectives, summary, or end-of-chapter questions that may be included.** Before tackling the chapter's specific content, get in the habit of previewing what's in the chapter to get a general sense of its overall organization. If you dive into the specific details first, you may lose sight of how the smaller details relate to the larger picture. Since the brain's natural tendency is to perceive and comprehend whole patterns rather than isolated bits of information, start by seeing how the parts of the chapter relate to the whole. Just as looking at the whole picture of a completed jigsaw puzzle beforehand helps you connect its parts, so too does getting a picture of the whole chapter before reading its parts.

3. **Take a moment to think about what you may already know that relates to the main topic of the chapter.** This strategy will activate the areas of your brain where your prior knowledge about that topic is stored, thereby preparing it to make meaningful connections with the material you're about to read.

Strategies to Use *During* the Reading Process

1. **Read selectively to locate the most important information.** Effective reading begins with a plan for identifying what should be noted and remembered. Here are three key strategies you can use while reading to help you determine what information you should focus on and retain.
   - **Use boldface or dark-print headings and subheadings as cues for identifying important information.** These headings organize the chapter's major points; you can use them as "traffic" signs to direct you to the most important information in the chapter. Better yet, turn the headings into questions and read to find answers to them. This question-and-answer routine ensures that you read actively and with a purpose. (You can set up this strategy while previewing the chapter by placing a question mark after each heading contained in the chapter.) Creating and answering questions while reading also keeps you motivated because the questions stimulate curiosity and a desire to find answers to them (Walter, Knudsvig, & Smith, 2003). Another advantage of posing and answering questions about what you're reading is that it's an effective way to prepare for exams—you're practicing exactly what you'll be expected to do on exams—answering questions.
   - **Pay close attention to information that's *italicized*, underlined, CAPITALIZED, or bulleted.** These features call attention to key terms that must be understood and built on before you can proceed to understand higher-level concepts covered later in the reading. Don't simply highlight these words because their special appearance suggests they're important. Read these terms carefully and be sure you understand them before you continue reading.
   - **Pay special attention to the first and last sentences in each paragraph.** These sentences provide an important introduction and conclusion to the key point contained in the paragraph. It's a good idea to reread the first and last sentences of each paragraph before you move on to the next paragraph, particularly when reading material that's cumulative (builds on previously covered material), such as science and math.
2. **Take written notes on important information you find in your reading.** A good way to stop and think deeply about key ideas in your reading is to take notes on those ideas in your own words. Research shows that the common student practice of just highlighting the text (the author's words) is not a particularly

NOTE

Your goal when reading is not just to cover the assigned pages, but to uncover the most important ideas contained on those pages.

"I would advise you to read with a pen in your hand, and enter in a little book of short hints of what you find that is curious, or that might be useful; for this will be the best method of imprinting such particulars in your memory, where they will be ready."
—*Benjamin Franklin, 18th-century inventor, newspaper writer, and cosigner of the Declaration of Independence*

effective strategy (Dunlosky et al., 2013). Highlighting is a passive learning process, whereas note-taking actively engages you in the reading process and enables you to transform the text into your own words. Don't slip into the habit of using your textbook simply as a coloring book in which the artistic process of highlighting information in spectacular, kaleidoscopic colors distracts you from the more important process of learning actively, and thinking deeply about what you're reading. Highlighting is okay as long it's not the only thing you do while reading; take time to make notes on the material you've highlighted—in your own words—to ensure that you reflect on it and make it personally meaningful. Taking notes on information delivered during classes will improve your performance on exams; taking notes on your reading assignments will do the same.

When you transform what someone else has written into your own words, you're implementing a powerful principle of deep learning: relating what you're trying to learn to what you already know (Demmert & Towner, 2003). A good time for pausing and writing a brief summary of what you've read in your own words is when you encounter a boldface heading because it indicates you're about to encounter a new topic; this is the ideal time to deepen your knowledge of what you just finished reading and use that knowledge to help you understand what's coming next.

> "I had the worst study habits and the lowest grades. Then I found out what I was doing wrong. I had been highlighting with a black magic marker."
> —Jeff Altman, American comedian

 Think About It—Journal Entry 5.6

When reading a textbook, do you usually have the following tools on hand?

Pen or pencil:	yes	no
Notebook:	yes	no
Class notes:	yes	no
Dictionary:	yes	no
Glossary:	yes	no

If you don't usually have one or more of the above tools on hand while reading, which one(s) do you plan to have on hand in the future?

_____
_____
_____
_____
_____

3. **Make use of visual aids that accompany the written text.** Don't fall into the trap of thinking that visual aids can or should be skipped because they're merely supplemental or ornamental. Visual aids, such as charts, graphs, diagrams, and concept maps are powerful learning and memory tools for a couple of reasons: (a) they enable you to "see" the information in addition to reading (hearing) it, and (b) they pull together separate ideas into a unified snapshot.

    Visual aids also improve learning and memory of written material by delivering information to the brain through a different sensory modality. In addition, periodically pausing to view visual aids adds variety and a change of pace to the reading process. Breaking up sustained periods of reading with a change of pace and different sensory input helps maintain your interest and attention (Malmberg & Murname, 2002; Murname & Shiffrin, 1991).

4. **Regulate or adjust your reading speed to the type of subject matter you're reading.** As you know, academic subjects vary in terms of their level of technicality and complexity. Reading material in a math or science textbook requires reading at a slower rate with more frequent pauses to check for understanding than reading a novel or a short story.

Post-Reading Strategies: What to Do *After* Reading

1. **End your reading sessions with a short review of the key information you've highlighted and taken notes on.** Rather than ending your reading session by trying to cover a few more pages, reserve the last five minutes to review the key ideas you already covered. Most forgetting of information takes place immediately after we stop focusing on the information and turn our attention to another task (Averell & Heathcote, 2011; Baddeley, 1999). By taking a few minutes at the end of a reading session to review the most important information you've just read, you help your brain "lock" that information into long-term memory before getting involved with another task.

    The graph in **Figure 5.2** represents the results of a classic experiment that tested how well information is recalled at various times after it was originally learned. As you can see on the far left of the graph, most forgetting occurs soon after information has been taken in (e.g., after 20 minutes, more than 60% of it was forgotten). The results of this classic study have been confirmed multiple times (Schacter, 2001) and they underscore the importance of reviewing key information acquired through reading *immediately* after you've read it. By doing so, your memory for that information improves dramatically because you're intercepting the human "forgetting curve" at its steepest point of memory loss—just after information has been taken in.

2. **After completing a reading assignment, if you're still confused about an important idea or concept contained in the reading, go to another source.** The problem may not be you—it may be the way the author has presented or explained it. You may

Chapter 5: Deep Learning

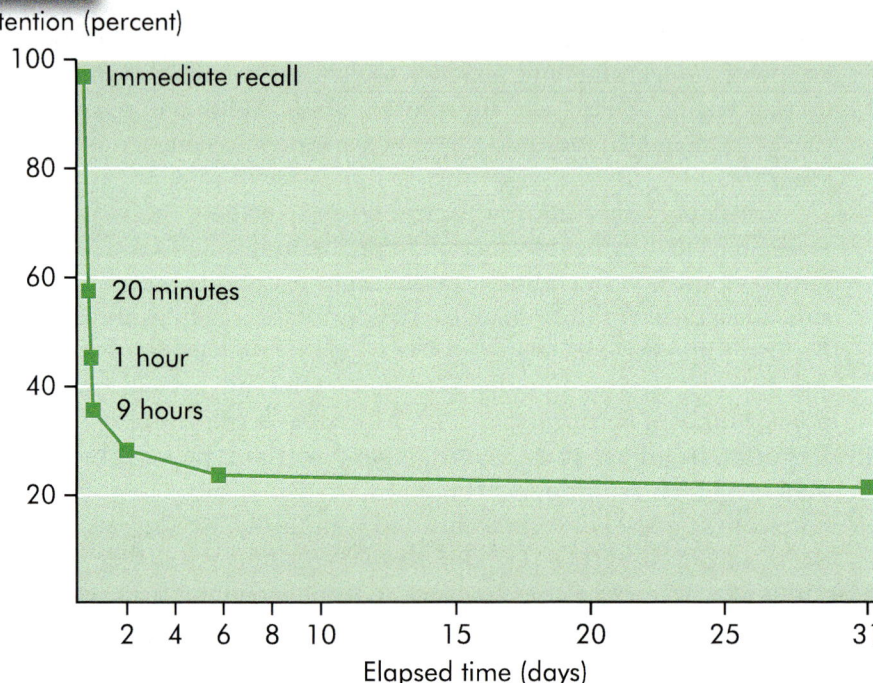

FIGURE 5.2: The Forgetting Curve

Source: Hermann Ebbinghaus, *Memory: A Contribution to Experimental Psychology*, 1885/1913

be able to clear up your confusion by simply consulting another source or resource, such as those listed below.

- **Look at how another book explains it.** Not all textbooks are created equal; some do a better job of explaining certain concepts than others. Check to see whether your library or school bookstore has other texts dealing with the same subject as your course. A different book may be able to explain a hard-to-understand concept much better than your assigned textbook.
- **Seek help from your teacher.** If you completed the reading assignment and made every effort to understand a particular concept but still can't grasp it, most teachers should be willing to assist you.
- **Seek help from learning assistance professionals or peer tutors in your Learning Center (Academic Support Center).** This is your key school resource for help with reading assignments, particularly if your teacher is unavailable or unwilling to provide assistance.

AUTHOR'S EXPERIENCE

Believe or not, being busy during school is not a bad thing. I found that when I had to plan my daily schedule to accommodate my schoolwork, practice, and job, I performed better in the classroom. It forced me to manage my time efficiently to meet the commitments I had made to school, my team and work. I learned to prioritize and meet the expectations I set for myself.

—*Shane Shope*

BOX 5.2

SQ3R: A Method for Improving Reading Comprehension and Retention

A popular system for organizing and remembering key reading strategies, such as those discussed in this chapter, is the *SQ3R* system. SQ3R is an acronym for five steps that can be taken to increase textbook reading comprehension and retention, particularly when reading highly technical or complex material. The following sequences of steps comprise this method:

1. Survey
2. Question
3. Read
4. Recite
5. Review

S = Survey: Get a preview and overview of what you're about to read.

1. Use the chapter's title to activate your thoughts about the subject and get your mind ready to receive information related to it.
2. Read the introduction, chapter objectives, and chapter summary to become familiar with the author's purpose, goals, and key points.
3. Note the boldface headings and subheadings to get a sense of the chapter's organization before you begin reading. This supplies you with a mental structure or framework for making sense of the information you're about to read.
4. Take note of any graphics—such as charts, maps, and diagrams; they provide valuable visual support and reinforcement for the material you're reading.
5. Pay special attention to reading aids (e.g., italics and boldface font); use them to identify, understand, and remember key concepts.

Q = Question: Stay active and curious.

As you read, use boldface headings to formulate questions and read to find answers to those questions. When your mind is actively searching for answers, it becomes more engaged in the learning process. As you read, add any questions of your own that come to mind.

R = Read: Find answers to questions you've created.

Read one section at a time—with your questions in mind—and search for answers to these questions.

R = Recite: Rehearse your answers.

After you complete reading each section, recall the questions you asked and see if you can answer them from memory. If not, look at the questions again and practice your answers until you can recall them without looking. Don't move onto the next section until you're able to answer all questions in the section you've just completed.

R = Review: Look back and get a second view of the whole picture.

Once you've finished the chapter, review all the questions you've created for different parts or sections. See whether you can still answer them without looking. If not, go back and refresh your memory. Also, read the Chapter Summary. If any of the information in the summary seems unfamiliar, go back and find it and make sure you can relate it to what is in the summary.

 Think About It—Journal Entry 5.7

Rate yourself in terms of how frequently you use the following reading strategies, using the following scale:

4 = always, 3 = sometimes, 2 = rarely, 1 = never

1. I read chapter outlines and summaries before I start reading the chapter content.   4 3 2 1

2. I preview a chapter's boldface headings and subheadings before I begin to read the chapter.   4 3 2 1

3. I adjust my reading speed to the type of subject I am reading. 4 3 2 1

4. I look up the meaning of unfamiliar words and unknown terms that I come across before I continue reading. 4 3 2 1

5. I take written notes on information I read. 4 3 2 1

6. I use the visual aids included in my textbooks. 4 3 2 1

7. I finish my reading sessions with a review of important information that I noted or highlighted. 4 3 2 1

What works for you? What might you do to improve your reading strategies?

_____
_____
_____
_____
_____
_____

Strategic Studying: Learning Deeply and Remembering Longer

Studying isn't a short sprint that takes place just before test time. Instead, it's more like a long-distance run that takes place over time. Studying the night before an exam should be the last step in a sequence of test-preparation steps that take place well before test time, which include: (a) taking accurate and complete notes in class, (b) doing the assigned reading, and (c) seeking help from professors or peers along the way for any concepts that are unclear or confusing. After these steps have been taken, you are then well-positioned to study the material you've acquired and learn it deeply.

Described below is a series of study strategies you can use to promote deep and durable (long-lasting) learning.

Give Studying Your Undivided Attention

The human attention span has limited capacity—we have only so much of it available to us at any point in time and we can give all or part of it to whatever task(s) we're working on. As the phrase "paying

> "You can do several things at once, but only if they are easy and undemanding. You are probably safe carrying on a conversation with a passenger while driving on an empty highway [but] you could not compute the product of 17 x 24 while making a left turn into dense traffic, and you certainly should not try."
> —Daniel Kahneman, professor emeritus of Psychology, and author of Thinking Fast and Slow

Multitasking while studying interferes with learning by dividing up attention and driving down comprehension and retention.

attention" suggests, it's like paying money, we only have so much of it to spend. Thus, if attention while studying is spent on other activities at the same time (e.g., listening to music, watching TV, or text messaging friends), there's a deduction in the amount of attention paid to studying. In other words, studying doesn't receive our undivided attention.

Studies show that when people multitask they don't pay equal attention to all tasks at the same time; instead, they divide their attention by shifting it back and forth between tasks (Howard, 2014). Their performance on the task that demands the most concentration or deepest thinking is the one that suffers the most (Crawford & Strapp, 1994). When performing complex mental tasks that cannot be done automatically or mindlessly, the brain needs quiet, internal reflection time for permanent connections to form between brain cells—which is what must happen if deep, long-lasting learning is to take place (Jensen, 2008). If the brain must simultaneously engage in other tasks or process other sources of external stimulation, this connection-making process is interfered with and learning is impaired.

So, give study time your undivided attention by unplugging all your electronic accessories. You can even use apps to help you do so (e.g., to silence your phone). Another strategy would be to set aside a short block of time to check electronic messages after you've completed a longer block of study time (e.g., as a study break); this allows you to use social media as a reward *after* putting in a stretch of focused study time. Just don't do both at the *same* time.

AUTHOR'S EXPERIENCE

When I was in college there were so many distractions for me. I had a job that I could work as many hours as I wanted to work. I had organizations where I was offered leadership positions. In addition, there were so many attractive girls. Then there were all these demanding classes that required me to study. To be honest, I enjoyed some of these distractions more than others. Well, that's another story for another day and another book. What I did know was that my education was the most important thing to me so I had to prioritize it. Thus, I had to study, learn, and do well in order to graduate. To do this I had to **REDUCE MY DISTRACTIONS!!** So, I developed Thompson's plan of action. They were: 1. Find motivated friends who could be study partners. What I realized was that my primary learning style is auditory (this worked well when I needed to study for a test). 2. If I was studying alone, find a place that was quiet where I could not listen to music or turn on the TV (the library was my favorite place to do this). BTW, in today's terms, that means no internet, text, phone, etc. 3. Never study when I am hungry and tired. 4. Give myself enough time to complete the assigned study task where I did not feel I had to rush through the material.

—*Aaron Thompson*

> "When you have to do work, and you're getting it. It's linking what I already know to what I didn't know."
> —*Student's description of a "good class"*

Make Meaningful Associations

Deep learning doesn't take place by simply absorbing information like a sponge—in exactly the same, prepackaged form as you received it from a textbook or class. Instead, deep learning involves actively translating the information you receive into a form that makes sense to you (Biggs & Tang, 2007; Mayer, 2002).

NOTE

Deep learning is not about teachers transmitting information to students; it's about students *transforming* that information into *knowledge* that's meaningful to them.

The brain's natural learning tendency is to translate unfamiliar information into a familiar form that makes sense and has personal meaning. This is illustrated in the experience.

AUTHOR'S EXPERIENCE

When my son was about three years old, we were riding in the car together and listening to a song by the Beatles titled, *Sergeant Pepper's Lonely Hearts Club Band*. You may be familiar with this tune, but in case you're not, there's a part in it where the following lyrics are sung repeatedly: "Sergeant Pepper's Lonely, Sergeant Pepper's Lonely, Sergeant Pepper's Lonely . . . ."

When this part of the song was being played, I noticed that my three-year-old son was singing along. I thought it was pretty amazing for a boy his age to be able to understand and repeat those lyrics. However, when that part of the song came on again, I listened to him more closely and noticed he wasn't singing "Sergeant Pepper's Lonely, Sergeant Pepper's Lonely . . ." Instead, he was singing: "Sausage Pepperoni, Sausage Pepperoni . . ." (which were his two favorite pizza toppings).

My son's brain was doing what all human brains tend to naturally do. It took unfamiliar information—song lyrics that didn't make any sense to him—and transformed it into a form that was meaningful to him.

—*Joe Cuseo*

You can experience the brain's natural inclination for meaning-making by reading the following passage, which once appeared anonymously on the Internet.

Aoccdrnig to rscheearch at Cmabridge Uinverstisy, it deos't mattaer in what order the ltteers in a word are, the only iprmoetnt thing is that the frist and lsat ltteer be at the rghit pclae. The rset can be a total mses and you can still raed it wouthit a porbelm. This is bcusae the human mind deos not raed ervey lteter by istlef, but the word as a wlohe. Amzanig huh?

Notice how easily you made meaning out of unfamiliar, misspelled words by naturally transforming them into familiar, meaningful words—which were already stored in your brain. Whenever you're learning something new, capitalize on the brain's natural tendency to find meaning by trying to connect what you're trying to understand to what you already know.

Learning the specialized terminology associated with different academic subjects may seem like learning a foreign language for a student with little or no experience with these terms. However, before you start brutally beating these terms into your brain through sheer repetition, try to find meaning in them. One way to do so is by looking up the term's word root in the dictionary or by identifying its prefix or suffix, which may give away the term's meaning. For instance, suppose you're taking a biology course and studying the autonomic nervous system—the part of the nervous system that operates without conscious awareness or voluntary control (e.g., your heart and lungs). The meaning of this biological term is found in its prefix "auto," meaning self-controlling or "automatic" (e.g., automatic transmission). Once you find meaning in a term, you can learn it faster and retain it longer than by memorizing it through sheer repetition.

If looking up an academic term's root, prefix, or suffix doesn't reveal its meaning, see if you can make it meaningful to you in some other way. Suppose you looked up the root of the term "artery" and nothing about the origins of this term helped you understand its meaning or purpose. You could create your own meaning for this term by taking its first letter (a), and have it stand for "away"—to help you remember that arteries carry blood away from the heart. By so doing, you take a meaningless term and make it personally meaningful and memorable.

 Think About It—Journal Entry 5.8

Think of a technical academic term or concept you're learning in a course this term, and create a meaningful association you could use to remember it.

Another way you can make learning meaningful is by *comparing and contrasting* what you're learning with what you already know. When you're studying, get in the habit of asking yourself the following questions:

1. How is this idea similar or comparable to something that I've already learned? (Compare)
2. How is this idea different from what I've already learned? (Contrast)

Research indicates that this simple strategy is one of the most powerful ways to promote learning of academic information (Marzano, Pickering, & Pollock, 2001). When you ask yourself the question, "How is this similar to and different from concepts I already know?" you make the learning process more meaningful and relevant because you're relating what you're trying to learn to what you already know or have already experienced.

Integrate Information from Classes and Readings

Connect ideas from your class notes and reading assignments that relate to the same concept. Get them in the same place by recording them on the same index card under the same category heading. Index cards can be used like a portable file cabinet, whereby each card functions like the hub of a wheel, around which individual pieces of related information can be attached like spokes. In contrast, when ideas pertaining to the same point or concept are spread all over the place, they're more likely to take that form in your mind—leaving them mentally disconnected and leaving you more confused or overwhelmed (and stressed out).

Distribute Study Time across Separate Study Sessions

Learning deeply depends not only on how you learn (your method), but when you learn (your timing). Equally important as how much time you spend studying is how you distribute or spread out your study time. Research consistently shows that for students of all abilities and ages, distributing study time across several shorter sessions results in deeper learning and longer retention than channeling all study time into one long session (Brown, Roediger, & McDaniel, 2014; Carey, 2014; Dunlosky et al., 2013). Distributed practice improves your learning and memory in two major ways:

- It minimizes loss of attention due to fatigue or boredom.
- It reduces mental interference by giving the brain some downtime to cool down and lock in information it has received before being interrupted by the need to deal with additional information (Malmberg & Murnane, 2002; Murname & Shiffrin, 1991). Memory works like a muscle: after it's been exercised, if given some "cool down" time before it's exerted again, it builds greater strength—that is, stronger memory for what it previously learned (Carey, 2014). On the other hand, if the brain's downtime is interfered with by the arrival of additional information, it gets

> **NOTE**
> When learning, go for meaning first, memorization last. If you can connect what you're trying to learn to what you already know, the deeper you'll learn it and the longer you'll remember it.

> **NOTE**
> Deep learners ask questions like: How can this specific piece of information be categorized or classified into a larger concept? How does this particular idea relate to or "fit into" something bigger?

overloaded and its capacity for handling information becomes impaired. That's what cramming does—it overloads the brain with lots of information in a limited period of time. In contrast, distributed study does just the opposite—it uses shorter sessions with downtime between sessions—giving the brain time to slow down and retain the information it's previously processed (studied) and more time to move that information from short-term to long-term memory (Willis, 2006).

Distributed study is also less stressful and more motivating than cramming. You're more likely to start studying when you know you won't be doing it for a long stretch of time (or lose any sleep doing it). It's also easier to sustain attention for tasks that are done for a shorter period of time.

Although cramming just before exams is better than not studying at all, it's far less effective than studying that's spread out across time. Instead of frantically cramming total study time into one long session ("massed practice"), use *distributed practice*—"distribute" or space out your study time over several shorter sessions.

> "Hurriedly jam-packing a brain is akin to speed-packing a cheap suitcase—it holds its new load for a while, then most everything falls out."
> —Benedict Carey, author, How We Learn: Throw Out the Rule Book and Unlock Your Brain's Potential

Think About It—Journal Entry 5.9

Are you more likely to study in advance of exams or cram just before exams? Explain.

_____
_____
_____
_____

How do you think most students would answer this question?

_____
_____
_____
_____

Use the "Part-to-Whole" Study Method

A natural extension of distributed practice is the part-to-whole method. This method involves breaking up the material you need to learn into smaller parts and studying those parts in separate sessions in advance of the exam; then you use your last study session just before the exam to review (restudy) the parts you previously studied in separate sessions. Thus, your last session isn't a cram session or even a study session, it's a review session.

Research shows that students of all ability levels learn material in college courses more effectively when it's studied in small units and when progression to the next unit takes place only after the previous unit has been mastered or understood (Pascarella & Terenzini, 1991, 2005).

Don't buy into the myth that studying in advance is a waste of time because you'll forget it all by test time. (Procrastinators often use this argument to rationalize their habit of putting off studying until the very last moment, which forces them to cram frantically the night before exams.) Even if you aren't able to recall what you previously studied when you look at it again closer to test time, research shows that once you start reviewing it, you can relearn it in a fraction of the time it took the first time. Since it takes much less time to relearn the material because the brain still has a memory trace for information studied in the earlier sessions (Kintsch, 1994), it proves you didn't completely forget it and that studying it in advance wasn't a waste of time. Another key advantage of breaking material you're learning into smaller parts and studying those parts in advance of major exams is that it allows you to check your understanding of the part you studied before moving on to learning the next part. This is a particularly important advantage in courses where learning the next unit of material builds on your understanding the previous unit (e.g., math and science).

Capitalize on the Power of Visual Learning

The human brain consists of two hemispheres (half spheres)—left and right (see **Figure 5.3**). Each of these hemispheres specializes in a different type of learning. The left hemisphere specializes in verbal learning; it deals primarily with words. In contrast, the right hemisphere specializes in visual–spatial learning; it deals primarily with perceiving images, patterns, and objects that occupy physical place or space. If you involve both hemispheres of the brain while studying, two different memory traces are recorded—one in each major hemisphere (half) of the brain. This process of laying down dual memory traces (verbal and visual) is referred to as *dual coding* (Paivio, 1990). Since two memory traces are better than one, dual coding results in deeper learning and longer retention.

FIGURE 5.3:

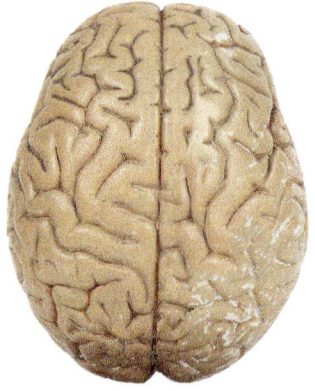

The human brain is comprised of two half spheres (hemispheres): the left hemisphere specializes in verbal learning, and the right hemisphere specializes in visual learning.

©JupiterImages Corporation.

To capitalize on the advantage of dual coding, be sure to use all the visual aids available to you, including those found in your textbook and those provided by your teacher in class. You can also create your own visual aids by representing what you're learning in the form of pictures, symbols, or concept maps—such as flowcharts, timelines, spider webs, wheels with hubs and spokes, or branching tree diagrams. (See **Figure 5.4** for an example of a concept map.) Visit https://coggle.it/ for help in creating your own concept/mind maps. When you transform material you're learning into a visual pattern, you're putting it into a form that's compatible with the brain's tendency to store information in neurological networks (Willis, 2006). Drawing also keeps you actively engaged in the process of learning, and by representing verbal information in visual form, you double the number of memory traces recorded in your brain. As the old saying goes, "A picture is worth a thousand words."

> **NOTE**
>
> Don't forget that drawings and visual illustrations can be more than just forms of artistic expression; they can also be powerful learning tools— you can draw to learn!

Think About It—Journal Entry 5.10

Think of a course you're taking this term in which related pieces of information could be joined together to form a concept map. Make a rough sketch of this map that includes the information you need to remember.

_____

_____

_____

_____

_____

_____

FIGURE 5.4: Concept Map for the Human Nervous System

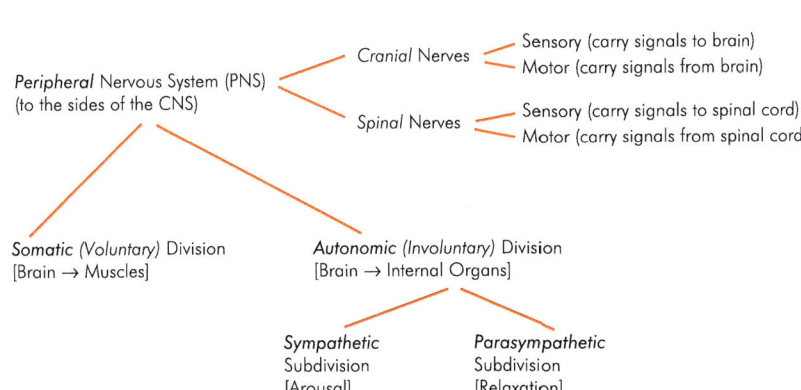

©Kendall Hunt Publishing Company

Build Variety into the Study Process

Infusing variety and change of pace into your study routine can increase your motivation to study and your concentration while studying. Here are some practical strategies for doing so.

Mix it up: periodically shift the type of academic tasks you perform during a study session. Changing the nature of the academic work you do while studying increases your alertness and concentration by reducing *habituation*—attention loss that occurs after repeatedly engaging in the same type of mental task (Thompson, 2009). You can combat attention loss due to habituation by varying the type of tasks you perform during a study session. For instance, you can shift periodically among tasks that involve reading, writing by hand, typing on a keyboard, reviewing, reciting, and solving problems. Similar to how athletes benefit from mixing different types of drills into their workouts (e.g., separate drills for building strength, speed, and endurance), studies of human learning show that "interleaving" (mixing) different academic subjects or academic skills while studying results in deeper learning and stronger memory (Brown, Roediger, & McDaniel, 2014; Carey, 2014).

Study in different places. In addition to spreading out your studying at different times, it's also a good idea to spread it out in different places. Studying in different locations provides different environmental contexts for learning; this reduces the amount of mental interference that normally builds up when all information is studied in the same place. The great public speakers in ancient Greece and Rome used this method of changing places to remember long speeches by walking through different rooms while rehearsing their speech, learning each major part of their speech in a different room (Higbee, 2001).

Although it's useful to have set times for studying so that you get into a regular work routine, this doesn't mean you learn best by always studying in the same place. Periodically changing the academic tasks you perform while studying, as well as the environment in which you perform them, has been found to improve attention to (and retention of) what you're studying (Carey, 2014; Druckman & Bjork, 1994).

Break up long study sessions with short study breaks that involve physical activity (e.g., a short jog or brisk walk). Study breaks that include physical activity refresh the mind by giving it a rest from studying. Physical activity also stimulates the mind by increasing blood flow to your brain—helping you retain what you've studied and regain concentration for what you'll study next.

Learning Styles: Identifying Your Learning Preferences

Your learning style is another important personal characteristic you should be aware of when choosing your major. Learning styles refer to individual differences in learning preferences—that is, ways in which individuals prefer to perceive information (receive or take it in) and process information (deal with it after taking it in). Individuals may differ in terms of whether they prefer to take it in information by reading about it, listening to it, seeing an image or diagram of it, or physically touching and manipulating it. Individuals may also vary in terms of whether they like to receive information in a structured and orderly format or in an unstructured form that allows them the freedom to explore, play with, and restructure it in their own way. Once information has been received, individuals may also differ in terms of how they prefer to process or deal with it mentally. Some might like to think about it on their own; others may prefer to discuss it with someone else, make an outline of it, or draw a picture of it.

Probably the most frequently used learning styles test is the Myers-Briggs Type Indicator (MBTI; Myers, 1976; Myers & McCaulley, 1985), which is based on the personality theory of psychologist Carl Jung. The test consists of four pairs of opposing traits and assesses how people vary on a scale (low to high) for each of these four sets of traits.

Learning styles are no more or no less common ways that people learn. We all have a mix of multiple learning styles, thus we have different and multiple ways of learning. Many students may find that they have a dominant learning style but using other styles that are less dominant. In many cases, you might use different styles for different learning circumstances. No style is set in concrete. They can change and there is no perfect mix for greater learning. You have the ability to increase your lesser used methods to make them more dominant while strengthening your dominant one.

Although there are many (multiple) learning styles, the three that are considered most common are:

- Visual-Spatial Learning (learning by seeing),
- Auditory-Sequential Learning (learning by hearing),
- Kinesthetic Learning (learning by doing).

In addition to taking formal tests to assess which or how many of these are your learning style(s), you can gain awareness of your learning styles through some simple introspection or self-examination. Take a moment to complete the following sentences that are designed to stimulate personal reflection on your learning style:

I learn best if . . .
I learn most from . . .
I enjoy learning when . . .

Knowing your preferred learning style can make studying easier for you. Once you discover your dominant learning style, research some ways you can incorporate your learning style into your study routine (i.e., if your learning style is visual, read over notes or use flashcards; if you are an auditory learner, read your notes out loud to yourself; if you are a kinesthetic learner, rewrite your notes).

Learn with and through a variety of senses. When memory is formed in the brain, different sensory aspects of it are stored in

> "I have to *hear* it, *see* it, *write* it, and *talk* about it."
> —First-year college student responding to the question: "How do you learn best?"

different areas. For example, if your brain receives auditory input (e.g., hearing your own words or the words of others), visual input (viewing images, maps, or charts), and motor input (movement made when writing, drawing, or manipulating), that information reaches your brain through multiple sensory modalities and is better retained because it: (a) creates more interconnections in areas of the brain where that information is stored, and (b) provides multiple cues for retrieving (recalling) the information (Shams & Seitz, 2011; Willis, 2006; Zull, 2002). Different forms of sensory input are stored as multiple neurological tracks in different parts of the brain, which deepens learning and strengthens memory.

Don't forget that movement is also a sensory channel. When you move, your brain receives kinesthetic stimulation—the sensations generated by your muscles. Memory traces for movement are commonly stored in an area of your brain (the cerebellum) that plays a major role for all types of learning (Middleton & Strick, 1994; Jensen, 2005). Thus, incorporating movement into the process of learning improves your ability to retain what you're studying by adding a motor (muscle) memory trace of it to your brain. You can use movement to help you learn and retain academic information by using your body to act out what you're studying or symbolize it with your hands (Kagan & Kagan, 1998). Suppose you're trying to remember five points about something (e.g., five consequences of the Civil War). When you're studying these points, count them on your fingers as you try to recall each of them.

> "When I have to remember something, it's better for me to do something with my hands so I could physically see it happening."
> —First-year college student

AUTHOR'S EXPERIENCE

I was talking about memory in class one day and mentioned that when I can't recall how to spell a word, its correct spelling comes back to me after I start writing it. One of my students raised her hand and said the same thing happens to her when she forgets a phone number—it comes back to her when she starts punching it in. Both of these experiences point to the power of movement for promoting learning and memory.

—*Joe Cuseo*

AUTHOR'S EXPERIENCE

As a high school teacher, I always tried to figure out ways to help students recall information on test days. A simple technique I learned going through high school was to create words out of the key concepts from the unit lessons. I learned later that this was called a mnemonic device. You may know a few from elementary school, such as "ROY G. BIV," HOME, the colors of the rainbow and the Great Lakes. Granted, this is a simple memory strategy but it can be used to help you organize and remember key concepts. It helped me remember the key concepts I needed to discuss in my written responses.

—*Shane Shope*

Also, remember that talking involves muscle movement of your lips and tongue. Thus, speaking aloud when you're studying, either to a friend or to yourself, can improve memory by supplying kinesthetic stimulation to your brain (in addition to the auditory stimulation your brain receives from hearing what you're saying).

Learn with Emotion

Neural connections run between the emotional and memory centers of the brain (Zull, 1998). Thus, the emotions we're experiencing while learning can affect how deeply we learn. Research indicates that emotional intensity, excitement, and enthusiasm strengthen memory of academic information just as they do for memory of life events and personal experiences. When we're emotionally excited about what we're learning, adrenaline is released and is carried through the bloodstream to the brain. Once adrenaline reaches the brain, it increases blood flow and glucose production, which stimulates learning and strengthens memory (LeDoux, 1998; Rosenfield, 1988). Thus, if you become passionate and enthused about what you're learning, you're more likely to learn it deeply and remember it longer (Howard, 2014; Minninger, 1984).

One way to do this is by keeping in mind the importance or significance of what you're learning. For instance, if you're learning about photosynthesis, remind yourself that you're not just learning a chemical reaction, you're learning about the driving force that underlies all plant life on the planet. If you don't know why the concept you're studying is significant, find out—do a computer search, talk it over with your teacher, or ask an advanced student majoring in the field.

> **NOTE**
>
> Make learning a "total body experience." Put your whole self into it—your mind, your body, and your heart.

Self-Monitor: Reflect on What you're Learning and Assess Whether You're Learning it Deeply

Deep learners are *reflective* learners—they are self-aware and mindful of how well they're learning what they're studying. They reflect, check, and self-assess whether they're really getting it. They monitor their comprehension by asking questions such as: "Am I actually understanding this?" and "Do I really know it?"

How do you know if you really know it? Probably the best answer to this question is: "I find meaning in it—I can relate to it personally or put it in terms that make sense to me" (Ramsden, 2003). Listed below are some strategies for checking whether you're truly (deeply) understanding what you're learning. These strategies can be used as indicators or checkpoints for determining whether you're just memorizing or learning at a deep level. They will help you answer the question: "How do I know if I really know it?"

Can you think of an *analogy* between the concept you're learning and something you already know or understand? (e.g., This concept is like _____ or is similar to _____.)

- **Can you paraphrase (restate or translate) what you're learning in your own words?** If you can take what you're learning and complete the following sentence: "In other words, . . .", it's very likely you've moved beyond surface memorization (and mental regurgitation) to a deeper level of comprehension, because you've transformed what you're learning into a form that makes sense to you. You know you know it if you're not stating it the same way your teacher or textbook stated it, but restating it in words that are your own.

> "When you know a thing, to recognize that you know it; and when you do not, to know that you do not know; that is knowledge."
> —Confucius, influential Chinese thinker and educator

> "Most things used to be external to me—out of a lecture or textbook. It makes learning a lot more interesting and memorable when you can bring your experiences into it. It makes you want to learn."
> —Returning adult student

> "You do not really understand something unless you can explain it to your grandmother."
> —Albert Einstein, considered the Father of Modern Physics

> "I learn best through teaching. When I learn something and teach it to someone else, I find that it really sticks with me a lot better."
> —College sophomore

- **Can you explain what you're learning to someone who is unfamiliar with it?** One of the best ways to gain awareness of how well we know or don't know something is to explain it to someone who's never heard it before (just ask any teacher). Studies show that students gain a deeper level of understanding for what they're learning when they're asked to explain it to someone else (Chi et al., 1994). If you can explain it to someone who's unfamiliar with it, that's a good sign you've moved to deeper comprehension because you're able to translate it into language that's understandable to anyone.

- **Can you think of an *example* of what you've learned?** If you can come up with an instance or illustration of what you're learning—that's your own—not one given by your teacher or textbook, this is a good sign that you truly understand it. It shows you've taken an abstract academic concept and connected it to a concrete experience (Bligh, 2000).

- **Can you apply what you're learning to solve a new problem that you haven't seen before?** The ability to apply what you've learned in a different situation is a good indicator of deep learning (Erickson & Strommer, 2005). Learning specialists refer to this mental process as *decontextualization*—taking what you learned in one context (situation) and transferring it to another context (Bransford, Brown, & Cocking, 2000). For instance, you know you've learned a mathematical concept deeply when you can use that concept to solve math problems different from those solved by your teacher or textbook. This is why math teachers rarely include on exams the exact problems they solved in class or were solved in your textbook. They're not trying to "trick" you at test time; they're trying to see whether you've learned the concept deeply.

 Think About It—Journal Entry 5.11

Rate yourself in terms of how frequently you use the following learning strategies:

4 = always, 3 = sometimes, 2 = rarely, 1 = never

1. I block out all distracting sources of outside stimulation when I study.   4 3 2 1

2. I try to find meaning in technical terms by looking at their prefix or suffix, or by looking up their etymology (word origin).   4 3 2 1

3. I compare and contrast what I'm currently studying with what I've already learned.   4 3 2 1

4. I organize the information I'm studying into categories or classes.   4 3 2 1

5. I pull together information from my class notes and readings that relate to the same concept or general category.   4 3 2 1

6. I distribute (spread out) my study time over several short sessions in advance of exams and use my last study session before the test to review the information I previously studied.   4   3   2   1

7. I participate in study groups with my classmates.   4   3   2   1

Which works best for you? Why?

_____

_____

_____

_____

_____

_____

CHAPTER SUMMARY AND HIGHLIGHTS

This chapter identified key principles of human learning and supplied specific strategies for learning effectively in high school and throughout life. Deep learning goes beyond surface-level memorization. It's connecting new ideas to ideas that have already been learned. Deep learners build mental bridges between what they're trying to learn and what they already know.

Information delivered during classes is the information that's most likely to appear as items on high school exams. Students who don't take good class notes have a slim chance of recalling the information at test time. Thus, effective note taking is critical to successful academic performance in high school.

Information from reading assignments is the second most common source of test questions on high school exams. Professors often don't discuss information in class that's contained in assigned reading. Thus, doing the assigned reading, and doing it in a way that maximizes comprehension and retention, is essential for academic success in high school.

Learning from classes requires active involvement (e.g., actively taking notes while listening to classes) as does learning from reading (e.g., actively taking notes while reading). Active involvement during the learning process engages your attention and enables information to enter the brain. Reflection on what you have learned keeps it in the brain by locking it into memory. Self-awareness also promotes deep learning. By reflecting on whether you truly understand what you're studying, you become a more self-aware learner and a more successful student.

Cramming total study time into one long session ("massed practice") immediately before exams doesn't promote deep learning or long-term retention. Research consistently shows that *distributed practice*, whereby study time is "distributed" or spread out over several shorter sessions, is more effective—particularly if the last study session just before an exam is used to review (restudy) the parts that were previously studied in separate sessions. Learning is also deepened by engaging as many senses as possible during the learning process.

Lastly, deep learning is enhanced when done *collaboratively*. Research from kindergarten through high school shows that students who learn in teams experience significant gains in both academic performance and interpersonal skills.

Learning More through the World Wide Web: Internet-Based Resources

For additional information on learning deeply and strategically, see the following websites:

Strategic Learning & Study Strategies:
https://www.khanacademy.org/coach-res/reference-for-coaches/case-studies-hied/a/help-students-build-study-plans
http://www.dartmouth.edu/~acskills/success/
http://www.isu.edu/success/strategies/handouts.shtml

Brain-Based Learning:
http://www.brainrules.net/the-rules

Learning Math and Overcoming Math Anxiety:
www.mathacademy.com/pr/minitext/anxiety
www.onlinemathlearning.com/math-mnemonics.html

References

Anderson, C. J. (2003). The psychology of doing nothing: Forms of decision avoidance result from reason and emotion. *Psychological Bulletin, 129,* 139–167.

Arum, R., & Roska, J. (2011). *Academically adrift: Limited learning on college campuses.* Chicago: The University of Chicago Press.

Ausubel, D., Novak, J., & Hanesian, H. (1978). *Educational psychology: A cognitive view* (2nd ed.). New York: Holt, Rinehart & Winston.

Averell, L., & Heathcote, A. (2011). The form of the forgetting curve and the fate of memories. *Journal of Mathematical Psychology, 55*(1), 25–35

Baddeley, A. D. (1999). *Essentials of human memory.* Hove: Psychology.

Biggs, J., & Tang, C. (2007) *Teaching for quality learning at university* (3rd ed.) Buckingham: SRHE and Open University Press.

Bligh, D.A. (2000). *What's the use of lectures?* San Francisco: Jossey Bass.

Bransford, J. D., Brown, A. L., & Cocking, R. R. (2000). *How people learn: Brain, mind, experience and school.* Washington, DC: National Academies Press.

Brown, R. D. (1988). Self-quiz on testing and grading issues. *Teaching at UNL (University of Nebraska–Lincoln), 10*(2), 1–3.

Brown, P. C., Roediger III, H. L., & McDaniel, M. A. (2014). *Make it stick: The science of successful learning.* Cambridge, MA: The Belknap Press of Harvard University Press.

Bruffee, K. A. (1993). *Collaborative learning: Higher education, interdependence, and the authority of knowledge.* Baltimore: Johns Hopkins University Press.

Bruner, J. (1990) *Acts of Meaning* Cambridge, MA: Harvard University Press.

Caine, R., & Caine, G. (2011). *Natural learning for a connected world: Education, technology and the human brain.* New York, NY. Teachers College Press

Carey, B. (2014). *How we learn*. London: Random House.

Chen, B., & Hirumi, A. (2009). Effects of advance organizers on learning for differentiated learners in a fully Web-based course. *International Journal of Instructional Technology & Distance Learning*. Retrieved from http://itdl.org/Journal/Jun_09/article01.htm

Chi, M., de Leeuw, N., Chiu, M. H., & LaVancher, C. (1994). Eliciting self-explanations improves understanding. *Cognitive Science, 18*, 439–477.

Conaway, M. S. (1982). Listening: Learning tool and retention agent. In A. S. Algier & K. W. Algier, (Eds.), *Improving reading and study skills*, (pp. 51–63). San Francisco: Jossey-Bass.

Crawford, H. J., & Strapp, C. H. (1994). Effects of vocal and instrumental music on visuospatial and verbal performance as moderated by studying preference and personality. *Personality and Individual Differences, 16*(2), 237–245.

Cuseo, J. B., Thompson, A., Campagna, M., & Fecas, V. S. (2013). *Thriving in college & beyond: Research-based strategies for academic success and personal development* (3rd ed.). Dubuque, IA: Kendall Hunt.

Demmert, W. G., Jr., & Towner, J. C. (2003). *A review of the research literature on the influences of culturally based education on the academic performance of Native American students.* Retrieved from the Northwest Regional Educational Laboratory, Portland, Oregon, website: http://educationnorthwest.org/sites/default/files/cbe.pdf.

Druckman, D., & Bjork, R. A. (Eds.). (1994). *Learning, remembering, believing: Enhancing human performance*. Washington, DC: National Academies Press.

Dunlosky, J., Rawson, K. A., Marsh, E. J., Nathan, M. J., & Willingham, D. T. (2013). Improving students' learning with effective learning techniques: Promising directions from cognitive and educational psychology. *Psychological Science in the Public Interest, 14*(1), 4–58.

Einstein, G. O., Morris, J., & Smith, S. (1985). Note-taking, individual differences, and memory for lecture information. *Journal of Educational Psychology, 77*(5), 522–532.

Erickson, B. L., & Strommer, D. W. (2005). Inside the fist-year classroom: Challenges and constraints. In J. L. Upcraft, J. N. Gardner, & B. O. Barefoot, (Eds.), *Challenging and supporting the first-year student* (pp. 241–256). San Francisco: Jossey-Bass.

Hartley, J. (1998). *Learning and studying: a research perspective*. London: Routledge.

Hartley, J., & Marshall, S. (1974). On notes and note taking. *Universities Quarterly, 28*, 225–235.

Hartman, H. J. (2001). *Metacognition in learning and instruction: Theory, research and practice*. Dordrecht: Kluwer Academic Publishers.

Herbert, W. (2014). Ink on paper: Some notes on note taking. Association for Psychological Science (APS). Retrieved from http://www.psychologicalscience.org/index.php/news/were-only-human/ink-on-paper-some-notes-on-note-taking.html

Higbee, K. L. (2001). *Your memory: How it works and how to improve it*. New York: Marlowe.

Howard, P. J. (2014). *The owner's manual for the brain: Everyday applications of mind-brain research* (4th ed.). New York: HarperCollins.

Howe, M. J. (1970). Note-taking strategy, review, and long-term retention of verbal information. *Journal of Educational Psychology, 63*, 285.

Jairam, D., & Kiewra, K. A. (2009). An investigation of the SOAR study method. *Journal of Advanced Academics* (August), 602–629.

Jensen, E. (2005). *Teaching with the brain in mind* (2nd ed.). Alexandria, VA: ASCD.

Jensen, E. (2008). *Brain-based learning*. Thousand Oaks, CA: Corwin Press.

Johnstone, A. H., & Su, W. Y. (1994). Lectures: a learning experience? *Education in Chemistry, 31*(1), 65–76, 79.

Kagan, S., & Kagan, M. (1998). *Multiple intelligences: The complete MI book*. San Clemente, CA: Kagan Cooperative Learning.

Kiewra, K. A. (1985). Students' note-taking behaviors and the efficacy of providing the instructor's notes for review. *Contemporary Educational Psychology, 10*, 378–386.

Kiewra, K. A. (2000). Fish giver or fishing teacher? The lure of strategy instruction. *Teaching at UNL (University of Nebraska–Lincoln), 22*(3), 1–3.

Kiewra, K. A. (2005). *Learn how to study and SOAR to success*. Upper Saddle River, NJ: Pearson Prentice Hall.

Kiewra, K. A., & DuBois, N. F. (1998). *Learning to learn: Making the transition from student to lifelong learner*. Needham Heights, MA: Allyn and Bacon.

Kiewra, K. A., Hart, K., Scoular, J., Stephen, M., Sterup, G., & Tyler, B. (2000). Fish giver or fishing teacher? The lure of strategy instruction. *Teaching at UNL (University of Nebraska–Lincoln)*, 22(3).

Kintsch, W. (1994). Text comprehension, memory, and learning. *American Psychologist*, 49, 294–303.

Kuh, G. D, (2005). Student engagement in the first year of college. In M. L. Upcraft, J. N. Gardner, B. O. Barefoot, & Associates, (Eds.), *Challenging and supporting the first-year student: A handbook for improving the first year of college* (pp. 86–107). San Francisco: Jossey-Bass.

Kuhn, L. (1988). What should we tell students about answer changing? *Research Serving Teaching*, 1(8).

LeDoux, J. (1998). *The emotional brain: The mysterious underpinnings of emotional life*. New York: Simon & Schuster.

LeDoux, J. (2002). *Synaptic self: How our brains become who we are*. New York: Penguin Books.

Locke, E. (1977). An empirical study of lecture note-taking among college students. *Journal of Educational Research*, 77, 93–99.

Malmberg, K. J., & Murnane, K. (2002). List composition and the word-frequency effect for recognition memory. *Journal of Experimental Psychology: Learning, Memory, and Cognition*, 28, 616–630.

Marzano, R. J., Pickering, D. J., & Pollock, J. (2001). *Classroom instruction that works: Research-based strategies for increasing student achievement*. Alexandria, VA: Association for Supervision and Curriculum Development.

Mayer, R. E. (2002). Rote versus meaningful learning. *Theory into Practice*, 41(4), 226–232.

Middleton, F., & Strick, P. (1994). Anatomical evidence for cerebellar and basal ganglia involvement in higher brain function. *Science*, 226(51584), 458–461.

Minninger, J. (1984). *Total recall: How to boost your memory power*. Emmaus, PA: Rodale.

Mueller, P. A. & Oppenheimer, D. M (2014). The pen is mightier than the keyboard: Advantages of longhand over laptop note taking. *Psychological Science*, 25(6), 1159–1168.

Murname, K., & Shiffrin, R. M. (1991). Interference and the representation of events in memory. *Journal of Experimental Psychology: Learning, Memory, & Cognition*, 17, 855–874.

Nathan, R. (2005). *My freshman year: What a professor learned by becoming a student*. Ithaca, NY: Cornell University Press.

Paivio, A. (1990). *Mental representations: A dual coding approach*. New York: Oxford University Press.

Pascarella, E., & Terenzini, P. (1991). *How college affects students: Findings and insights from twenty years of research*. San Francisco: Jossey-Bass.

Pascarella, E., & Terenzini, P. (2005). *How college affects students: A third decade of research* (Vol. 2). San Francisco: Jossey-Bass.

Piaget, J. (1978). *Success and understanding*. Cambridge, MA: Harvard University Press.

Ramsden, P. (2003). *Learning to teach in higher education* (2nd ed.). London: RoutledgeFalmer.

Ravizza, S. M., Hambrick, D. Z.. & Fenn, K. M. (2014). Non-academic internet use in the classroom is negatively related to classroom learning regardless of intellectual ability. *Computers & Education*, 78, 109–114.

Rosenfield, I. (1988). *The invention of memory: A new view of the brain*. New York: Basic Books.

Schacter, D. L. (2001). *The seven sins of memory: how the mind forgets and remembers*. Boston: Houghton Mifflin.

SECFHE (2006). *A national dialogue: The Secretary of Education's Commission on the future of higher education*. (U.S. Department of Education Boards and Commissions: A Draft Panel Report). Retrieved from http://www.ed.gov/about/bdscomm/list/hiedfuture/reports/0809-draft.pdf

Shams, W., & Seitz, K. (2011). Influences of multisensory experience on subsequent unisensory processing. *Frontiers in Perception Science*, 2(264), 1–9.

Thompson, R. F. (2009). Habituation: A history. *Neurobiology of Learning and Memory*, 92(2), 127–134.

Titsworth, S., & Kiewra, K. A. (2004). Organizational lecture cues and student notetaking. *Contemporary Educational Psychology*, 29, 447–461.

Vygotsky, L. S. (1978). Internalization of higher cognitive functions. In M. Cole, V. John-Steiner, S. Scribner, & E. Souberman (Eds. & Trans.), *Mind in society: The development of higher psychological processes* (pp. 52–57). Cambridge, MA: Harvard University Press.

Walter, T. W., Knudsvig, G. M., & Smith, D. E. P. (2003). *Critical thinking: Building the basics* (2nd ed.). Belmont, CA: Wadsworth.

Willis, J. (2006). *Research-based strategies to ignite student learning: Insights from a neurologist and classroom teacher*. Alexandria, VA: ASCD.

Zull, J. E. (1998). The brain, the body, learning, and teaching. *The National Teaching & Learning Forum*, 7(3), 1–5.

Zull, J. E. (2002). *The art of changing the brain: Enriching the practice of teaching by exploring the biology of learning*. Sterling, VA: Stylus.

CHAPTER 5 EXERCISES

5.1 QUOTE REFLECTIONS

Review the sidebar quotes contained in this chapter and select two that were especially meaningful or inspirational to you.

For each quote, provide a three- to five-sentence explanation why you chose it.

5.2 REALITY BITE

Too Fast, Too Frustrating: A Note-Taking Nightmare

Susan Scribe is a first-year student majoring in journalism. She's currently enrolled in an introductory course that is required for her major (Introduction to Mass Media). The teacher in this course classes at a rapid rate and uses vocabulary that goes right over her head. Since she cannot get all her teacher's words down on paper and cannot understand half the words she does manage to write down, she becomes frustrated and stops taking notes. She wants to do well in this course because it's the first course in her major, but she's afraid she'll fail it because her class notes are so pitiful.

Reflection and Discussion Questions

1. Can you relate to this case personally, or do know any students who are in the same boat as Susan?
2. What would you recommend that Susan do at this point? Why?

5.3 SELF-ASSESSMENT OF LEARNING HABITS

Look back at the ratings you gave yourself for effective note-taking **(Journal Entry 5.4, p. 107)**, reading **(Journal Entry 5.7, pp. 113–114)**, and studying **(Journal Entry 5.11, pp. 126–127)**. Add up your total score for these three sets of learning strategies (the maximum score for each set is 28):

Note Taking = _____

Reading = _____

Studying = _____

Total Learning Strategy Score = _____

Self-Assessment Questions

1. In which learning strategy area did you score lowest?
2. Do you think the area in which you scored lowest has anything to do with your lowest course grade at this point in the term?
3. Of the seven strategies listed under the area you scored lowest, which could you immediately put into practice to improve your performance in the course you're having most difficulty with this term?
4. What's the likelihood that you will put the preceding strategies into practice this term?

5.4 CONSULTING WITH A LEARNING SPECIALIST

Make an appointment to visit your Learning Center or Academic Support Center on school to discuss the results of your note-taking, reading, and studying self-assessment in Exercise 5.1 (or any other learning self-assessment you may have taken). Ask for recommendations about how you can improve your learning habits in your lowest score area. Following your visit, answer the following questions.

Learning Resource Center Reflection

1. Who did you meet with in the Learning Center?
2. What steps were recommended to you for improving your academic performance?
3. How likely is it that you will take the steps mentioned in the previous question?
    (a) definitely,
    (b) probably,
    (c) possibly, or
    (d) unlikely. Why?
4. Do you plan to see a learning specialist again? (If yes, why? If no, why not?)

CHAPTER 5 REFLECTION

5.6 LIST AND DESCRIBE AT LEAST FIVE PRINCIPLES DISCUSSED IN THIS CHAPTER THAT CAN HELP YOU TAKE BETTER NOTES IN CLASS AND IMPROVE YOUR READING COMPREHENSION.

1.

2.

3.

4.

5.

Now explain how you can put these principles into practice.

CHAPTER 6

HIGHER-LEVEL THINKING

Moving Beyond Basic Knowledge to Critical and Creative Thinking

CHAPTER PREVIEW

This chapter will help you understand what critical thinking is and develop your ability to think critically. You will be equipped with thinking strategies that move you beyond memorization to higher levels of thinking, and you will learn how to demonstrate higher-level thinking on exams and assignments.

LEARNING GOAL

Supply you with higher-level thinking skills for succeeding in high school and beyond.

THOUGHT STARTER

 Think About It—Journal Entry 6.1

To me, thinking critically means . . . .

_____
_____
_____
_____
_____
_____

From *Thriving in the Community College & Beyond: Strategies for Academic Success and Personal Development*, Third Edition, by Joseph Cuseo, Aaron Thompson, and Julie McLaughlin. Copyright © 2016 by Kendall Hunt Publishing Company. Reprinted by permission.

Chapte 6: Higher-Level Thinking

The number one educational goal of teachers is to help students think at a higher or more advanced level. In national surveys of college instructors teaching freshman-level through senior-level courses in various academic fields, more than 95% of faculty report that the most important goal of a college education is to develop students' ability to think critically (Gardiner, 2005; Milton, 1982). Similarly, college instructors teaching introductory courses for freshmen and sophomores report that the primary educational purpose of their courses is to develop students' critical thinking skills (Higher Education Research Institute, 2009; Stark et al., 1990). Simply stated, teachers are more concerned with teaching you *how* to think than teaching you *what* to think (i.e., what facts to remember). Studies show that memory for factual information acquired in school fades quickly with the passage of time. However, higher-level thinking is a *skill* (like learning to ride a bike) that's retained on a long-term basis and used for an entire lifetime (Pascarella & Terenzini, 1991, 2005). This is not to say that acquiring knowledge and basic comprehension are unimportant; they provide the stepping stones needed to climb to higher levels of thinking—as illustrated in **Figure 6.1**.

> "What is the hardest task in the world? To think."
> —Ralph Waldo Emerson, celebrated 19th-century American essayist and lecturer

FIGURE 6.1: The Relationship between Knowledge, Comprehension, and Higher-Level Thinking

- Higher-Level Thinking
- Comprehension
- Basic Knowledge

©Kendall Hunt Publishing Company.

NOTE

High school teachers expect students to do more than just retain or reproduce information; they want you to demonstrate higher levels of thinking with respect to what you learned (e.g., analyze it, evaluate it, apply it, or integrate it with other concepts you've learned).

NOTE

The focus of higher-level thinking is not just to answer questions but also to question answers.

Defining and Describing the Major Forms of Higher-Level Thinking

When your high school teachers ask you to "think critically," they're usually asking you to use one or more of the eight forms of thinking listed in **Box 6.1**. As you read the descriptions of each form of thinking, note whether you've heard of it before.

BOX 6.1

Seven Major Forms of Higher-Level Thinking

1. **Analysis (Analytical Thinking).** Breaking down information to identify its essential parts and underlying elements.
2. **Synthesis (Integrative Thinking).** Building up ideas by connecting them to form a larger whole or more comprehensive system.
3. **Application (Applied Thinking).** Putting thinking into practice to solve problems and resolve issues.
4. **Multidimensional Thinking.** Viewing issues from a variety of vantage points to gain a more complete or comprehensive perspective.
5. **Balanced Thinking.** Carefully considering arguments for and against a particular position or viewpoint.
6. **Critical Thinking (Evaluation).** Judging the quality of arguments, conclusions, and thought processes—including all forms of thinking on this list.
7. **Creative Thinking.** Generating ideas that are unique, original, or distinctively different.

Think About It—Journal Entry 6.2

Look back at the seven forms of thinking described in Box 6.1. Which of these forms of thinking have you used on high school exams or assignments?

_____
_____
_____
_____
_____

Analysis (Analytical Thinking)

The mental process of analysis is similar to the physical process of peeling an onion. When you analyze something, you take it apart and pick out its key parts, main points, or underlying elements. For example, if you were to analyze a chapter in this book, you would do more than cover its content; you would try to uncover or discover its main ideas by detecting its essential points and distinguishing them from background information or incidental details.

In an art course, you would use analytical thinking to identify the underlying elements or separate components of a painting or sculpture (e.g., its structure, texture, tone, and form). In the natural and social sciences, you would use analysis to identify underlying reasons or causes for natural (physical) phenomena and social events—known as "causal analysis." For instance, a causal analysis of the September 11, 2001, attack on the United States would involve identifying the key factors that led to the attack or the underlying reasons why the attack took place.

> "In physics, you have to be analytical and break it [the problem] down into its parts."
> —Physics student
> (quoted in Donald, 2002)

Think About It—Journal Entry 6.3

A TV commercial for a particular brand of liquor (which shall remain nameless) once showed a young man getting out of his car in front of a house where a party is going on. The driver gets out of his car, takes out a knife, slashes his tires, and goes inside to join the party. Using the higher-level thinking skill of analysis, what would you say are the underlying or embedded messages in this commercial?

_____

_____

_____

_____

_____

_____

_____

Synthesis (Integrative Thinking)

When you engage in *synthesis*, you're using a thought process that's basically the opposite of analysis. Instead of breaking down or taking apart ideas, you piece them together to form an integrated whole—like piecing together parts of a puzzle. Connecting ideas learned in different courses is a form of synthesis, such as integrating ethical concepts learned in a philosophy course with marketing concepts learned in a business course to develop a comprehensive set of ethical guidelines for marketing and advertising products.

Although synthesis and analysis are seemingly opposite thought processes, they complement one another. Analysis enables you to disassemble information into its key parts; synthesis allows you to reassemble those parts into a new whole. For instance, when writing this book, we analyzed published material in many fields (e.g., psychology, history, philosophy, and biology) to detect pieces of information in these different fields that were most relevant to promoting the success of high school students. We then synthesized or reassembled these parts to create a new whole—the textbook you're now reading.

Application (Applied Thinking)

When you learn something deeply, you transform information into knowledge; when you translate knowledge into practice, you engage

> **NOTE**
>
> Synthesis is not just a summary of ideas produced by someone else, it's a thought process that integrates isolated pieces of information to generate a comprehensive product of your own.

> "As gold which he cannot spend will make no man rich, so knowledge which he cannot apply will make no man wise."
> —Dr. Samuel Johnson, famous English literary figure and original author of the Dictionary of the English Language (1747)

in a higher-level thinking process known as *application*. It's a powerful form of higher-level thinking that allows you to transfer your knowledge to real-life situations and put it to use for practical purposes. For instance, you're engaging in application if you use knowledge you've acquired about human relations to become more assertive, or when you take knowledge acquired in an accounting course to help manage your personal finances.

Always be on the lookout for ways to take action on the knowledge you've acquired by applying it to your personal life experiences and current events or issues. When you use your knowledge for the practical purpose of doing something good, such as bettering yourself or others, you not only demonstrate application, you also demonstrate *wisdom* (Staudinger, 2008).

Multidimensional Thinking

When you view yourself and the world around you from different perspectives or vantage points to gain a comprehensive perspective, you're engaging in *multidimensional thinking*. For instance, multidimensional thinkers are able to think from the following four key perspectives and see how each of them influences, and is influenced by, the issue they're examining:

1. Perspective of **Person (Self):** How does this issue affect individuals on a personal basis?
2. Perspective of **Place:** What impact does this issue have on people living in different parts of the country or world?
3. Perspective of **Time:** How will future generations of people be affected by this issue?
4. Perspective of **Culture:** How is this issue likely to be interpreted or experienced by groups of people who share different social customs and traditions? (the perspective of culture)

> "To me, thinking at a higher level is when you approach a question or topic thoughtfully, when you fully explore every aspect of that topic from all angles."
> —First-year college student

Important issues don't exist in isolation but as parts of a complex, interconnected system that involves interplay of multiple factors and perspectives. For example, global warming (climate change) is an issue that involves the gradual thickening and trapping of more heat in the earth's atmosphere as a result of a buildup in gases generated by the burning fossil fuels for industrial purposes (Intergovernmental Council on Climate Change, 2013). The consensus among today's scientists is that this buildup of human-made pollution is causing temperatures to rise (and sometimes fall) around the world, resulting in more extreme weather conditions and more frequent natural disasters—such as droughts, wildfires, hurricanes, and dust storms (Joint Science Academic Statement, 2005; National Resource Defense Council, 2005, 2012). As depicted in **Box 6.2**, understanding and addressing this issue requires understanding interrelationships among the multiple perspectives of person, place, time, and culture.

BOX 6.2

Understanding Climate Change from Four Key Perspectives

Person

Climate change involves humans at a personal level because individual efforts to conserve energy in our homes and our willingness to purchase energy-efficient products can play a major role in resolving this issue.

Place

Climate change is an international phenomenon that extends beyond the boundaries of any one country; it affects all countries in the world and its solution requires the joint effort of different nations around the world to reduce their level of carbon emissions.

Time

If the current trend toward higher global warming isn't addressed soon, it could seriously threaten the lives of future generations inhabiting the planet.

Culture

Industries in technologically and industrially advanced cultures are primarily responsible for contributing to the problem of climate change, yet its potentially adverse effects will be greater for less technologically advanced cultures because they lack the resources to respond to it (Joint Science Academies' Statement, 2005). Industrially advanced cultures will need to use their advanced resources and technology to devise alternative methods for generating energy in ways that reduce the risk of global warming for all cultures.

Think About It—Journal Entry 6.4

Think of a current national or international problem (other than climate change) whose solution requires multiple perspective taking or systems thinking.

Balanced Thinking

When we seek out and carefully consider arguments *for* and *against* a particular position, we're engaging in balanced thinking. The process of finding supporting evidence or reasons for a position is referred to as *adduction*—when you adduce, you identify reasons *for* a position; the process of finding evidence or reasons that contradicts a position is called *refutation*—when you refute, you provide a rebuttal *against* a particular position.

Balanced thinking involves both adduction and refutation. Each position's stronger arguments are acknowledged, and its weaker ones are refuted (Fairbairn & Winch, 1996). The goal of a balanced thinker is not to stack up evidence for one position or the other but to be an impartial judge looking at supporting and opposing evidence for both sides of an issue, and striving to draw a conclusion that's neither biased nor one-sided. When you consider the strengths and weaknesses of opposing arguments at the same time, it reduces the likelihood that you'll fall prey to an overly simplistic form of thinking typical of many first-year students—known as *dualistic* thinking—seeking the "truth" in the form of clear-cut, black-or-white answers or solutions to complex issues—where one position or theory is "right" and the others "wrong" (Perry, 1970, 1999).

Don't be surprised and frustrated if you find scholars disagreeing about what particular positions or theories are more accurate or account for most of the "truth" in their field. This is a healthy thought process known as *dialectic* or *dialogic* thinking (deriving from the root "dialogue" or "conversation"). It's a productive form of intellectual dialogue (Paul & Elder, 2014) that acknowledges different sides of a complex issue and results in a more balanced, integrated understanding of it. In a study of leaders who excel in the field of business, it was discovered that one of their distinguishing qualities was their capacity for "integrative thinking"—the ability to hold opposing or conflicting ideas in their head and use that tension to create a new and superior idea—much like how humans use their opposable thumbs to excel at manual tasks (Martin, 2007).

Keep in mind that your first step in the process of solving problems and seeking truth shouldn't be to immediately jump in and take an either-or (for-or-against) position. Instead, take a balanced thinking approach by looking at arguments for and against each position, acknowledge the strengths and weaknesses of both sides of the argument, and seek to integrate the best points of both arguments.

Lastly, balanced thinking involves more than just totaling the number of arguments for and against a position; it also involves *weighing* the strength of each argument. Arguments can vary in terms of their degree of importance or level of support. When weighing arguments, ask yourself, "What is the quality and quantity of evidence supporting it?" Consider whether the evidence is:

1. **Definitive**—so strong or compelling that a definite conclusion should be reached;
2. **Suggestive**—strong enough to suggest that a tentative or possible conclusion may be reached; or
3. **Inconclusive**—too weak to reach any conclusion.

When making class presentations and writing papers or reports, be mindful of how much weight should be assigned to different arguments and explain how their weight has been factored into your conclusion.

In some cases, after reviewing both supporting and contradictory evidence for opposing positions, balanced thinking may lead you to suspend judgment and withhold drawing a conclusion that favors one position over another. A balanced thinker may occasionally reach the following conclusion: "The evidence doesn't strongly favor one

---

"The test of a first-rate intelligence is the ability to hold two opposed ideas in mind at the same time and still retain the ability to function."
—F. Scott Fitzgerald, regarded as one of the greatest American writers of the 20th century

"[Successful] business leaders have the capacity to hold two diametrically opposing ideas in their heads. And then, without panicking or settling for one alternative or the other, they're able to produce a synthesis that is superior to either opposing idea."
—Roger Martin, dean of the Rotman School of Management, University of Toronto

"For years I really didn't know what I believed. I always seemed to stand in the no man's land between opposing arguments, yearning to be won over by one side or the other but finding instead degrees of merit in both. But in time I came to accept, even embrace, what I called "my confusion" and to recognize it as a friend and ally, with no apologies needed."
—"In Praise of the 'Wobblies,'" by Ted Gup, journalist, who has written for Time Magazine, National Geographic, and The New York Times

position over the other" or "More information is needed before I can make a final judgment or reach a firm conclusion." These aren't wishy-washy answers; they're legitimate conclusions to reach after all the evidence has been carefully considered. In fact, it's better to hold an undecided but informed viewpoint based on balanced thinking than to hold definite opinions that are uninformed, biased, or based on emotion—such as those often expressed by people on radio talk shows.

If you find that the more you learn, the more complicated things seem to become, this is good news. It means you're moving from simplistic to complex thinking that's more multidimensional and balanced.

> "The more you know, the less sure you are."
> —Voltaire, French historian, philosopher, and advocate for civil liberty

Think About It—Journal Entry 6.5

Consider the following positions:

1. Course requirements should be eliminated; high school students should be allowed to choose the classes they want to take for their degree.

2. Course grades should be eliminated; high school students should take classes on a pass–fail basis.

Using balanced thinking, identify one or more arguments for and against each of these positions?

_____
_____
_____
_____
_____
_____
_____

NOTE

Balanced thinking enables you to become a more complex and comprehensive thinker capable of viewing issues from opposing sides and multiple perspectives.

Critical Thinking (Evaluation)

When we *evaluate* or *judge* the quality of an argument or work product, we're engaging in a form of higher-level thinking known as *critical thinking*. It's a skill highly valued by instructors teaching students at all stages in the college experience and all subjects in the college curriculum (Higher Education Research Institute, 2009; Stark et al., 1990). By working on developing your critical thinking skills as a first-year student, you will significantly improve you academic performance throughout your college experience.

> "Critical thinking is an evaluative thought process that requires deep thinking."
> —First-year college student

Critical thinking is used for many purposes beyond critiquing films, art, or music. It's a skill that enables you to "read between the lines" and cut through the fog or smog of ideas and arguments—including your own. Whether the evaluation is positive or negative (or some combination thereof), critical thinking involves backing up your evaluation with specific, well-informed reasons or evidence that support the critique. Failure to do so makes the criticism unfounded—that is, lacking any foundation or basis of support.

You can start developing the mental habit of critical thinking by using the following criteria as standards for evaluating ideas or arguments:

1. **Validity (Truthfulness).** Is it true or accurate?
2. **Morality (Ethics).** Is it fair or just?
3. **Beauty (Aesthetics).** Does it have artistic merit or value?
4. **Practicality (Usefulness).** Can it be put to use for practical or beneficial purposes?
5. **Priority (Order of Importance or Effectiveness).** Is it better than other ideas and alternative courses of action?

Critical Thinking and Inferential Reasoning

When we make arguments or arrive at conclusions, we use a mental process called *inferential reasoning*. We start with a premise (a statement or observation) and use it to infer (step to) a conclusion. Two major ways in which we use inferential reasoning to make arguments and reach conclusions are: (a) through logical reasoning, and/or (b) citing empirical (observable) evidence.

1. *Logical Reasoning.* Reaching a conclusion by showing that it logically follows from or is logically consistent with an established premise. In other words, if statement "A" is true, it can be concluded that statement "B" is also true.

    For example:
    Statement A. The constitution guarantees all U.S. citizens the right to vote. (Premise)
    Statement B. Women and people of color are citizens of the United States; therefore, they should have the right to vote. (Conclusion)

2. *Empirical (observable) evidence.* Reaching a conclusion by showing that it is supported with statistical data or scientific research findings. In other words, based on evidence "A," it can be concluded that "B" is true.

    For example:
    Statement A. There is statistical evidence that a much higher percentage of people who smoke experience cancer and heart disease. (Premise)
    Statement B. Based on this statistical evidence, smoking is a major health risk. (Conclusion)

Although using logic and empirical evidence are different routes to conclusions, they can be combined to support the same conclusion. For instance, in this book, we use both logical arguments and empirical evidence (research and statistics) to support our conclusions and recommendations. Similarly, advocates for lowering the legal drinking age to 18 have used the following forms of logical reasoning and empirical evidence to support their position:

(a) Logical reasoning: 18-year-olds in the United States are considered to be legal adults with respect to such rights and responsibilities as voting, serving on juries, joining the military, and being held responsible for committing crimes; therefore, 18-year-olds should have the right to drink.

(b) Empirical evidence: In other countries where drinking is allowed at age 18, statistics show that they have fewer binge-drinking and drunk-driving problems than the United States.

Think About It—Journal Entry 6.6

Can you think of arguments *against* lowering the drinking age to 18 that are based on logical reasoning and empirical evidence?

_____

_____

_____

_____

_____

Drawing inferences based on logic and empirical evidence are the primary thought processes that humans use to reach conclusions about themselves and the world around them. Inferential reasoning is also the form of thinking you will use to make arguments and reach conclusions in your college courses. You'll often be required to take positions and support your conclusions with sound reasoning and solid evidence. Adopt the mindset that you're a courtroom lawyer and be ready to prove your case with logical arguments and empirical evidence (exhibit A, exhibit B, etc.).

Logical Fallacies: Inferential Reasoning Errors

Unfortunately, errors can be made in the inferential reasoning process, which are commonly referred to as *logical fallacies*. Listed below is a summary of the major types of logical fallacies. Be mindful of them in your thinking and when evaluating the thinking of others. As you read the following reasoning errors, briefly note in the margin whether you've ever witnessed it or committed it.

- **Non sequitur.** Drawing a conclusion that doesn't follow from or connect with the premise—the initial statement or observation. (*Non sequitur* derives from Latin, which literally means, "it does

> "A very bad (and all too common) way to misread a newspaper: To see whatever supports your point of view as fact, and anything that contradicts your point of view as bias."
>
> —Daniel Okrent, first public editor of The New York Times

not follow.") Example: There was a bloody glove found at the murder scene and it doesn't fit the defendant, therefore the defendant must be innocent.
- **Selective Perception.** Seeing only examples and instances that support one's position while overlooking or ignoring those that contradict it. Example: Believers of astrology who only notice and point out people whose personalities happen to fit their astrological sign, but overlook those who don't.
- **Dogmatism.** Stubbornly clinging to a personal point of view unsupported by evidence while remaining closed-minded (nonreceptive) to other viewpoints better supported by evidence. Example: Arguing that adopting a national health system is a form of socialism that cannot work in a capitalistic economy, while ignoring the fact that there are many other nations in the world that have both a national health care system and a capitalistic economy.
- **Double Standard.** Having two sets of judgment standards—a higher standard for judging others and a lower standard for judging oneself. Example: Critically evaluating and challenging the opinions of others, but not our own.
- **Wishful Thinking.** Thinking something is true not because of logic or evidence, but because the person *wants* it to be true. Example: A teenage girl who believes she will not become pregnant, even though she and her boyfriend are having sex without any form of contraception.
- **Hasty Generalization.** Reaching a conclusion prematurely on the basis of a limited number of instances or experiences. Example: Concluding that people belonging to a racial or ethnic group are all "that way" on the basis of personal experiences with only one or two individuals.
- **Jumping to a Conclusion.** Making a leap of logic to a conclusion that's based on a single reason or factor while ignoring other possible reasons or contributing factors. Example: A shy person immediately concludes that a person who doesn't make eye contact with her doesn't like her, without considering the possibility that the lack of eye contact may be due to the fact that the other person was distracted or shy himself.
- **False Cause and Effect (a.k.a. Correlational Error).** Concluding that if two things co-occur at about the same time or in close sequence, one must *cause* the other. Example: The old belief that sexual activity causes acne because when children become teenagers, they are more sexually active and also are more likely to develop acne.
- **False Analogy.** Concluding that because two things are alike in one respect, they must be alike in another respect. This is the classic error of "comparing apples and oranges"—they're both alike in that they are fruits but they're not alike in other ways. Example: People who argue that government is a form of business, therefore it should be run like a business or run by a businessman. While it's true that government and business are societal institutions that have some similarities (e.g., budgets and payrolls), government is not a profit-making enterprise and it has purposes that are not fiscal in nature.

> "Facts do not cease to exist because they are ignored."
> —Aldous Huxley, English writer and author of *Brave New World*.

> "Belief can be produced in practically unlimited quantity and intensity, without observation or reasoning, and even in defiance of both by the simple desire to believe."
> —George Bernard Shaw, Irish playwright and Nobel Prize winner for literature

- **Glittering Generality.** Making a positive, general statement that isn't supported by specific details or evidence. Example: A letter of recommendation that describes the recommended person as a "wonderful person" with a "great personality," but provides little or no evidence to back up the claim.
- **Straw Man Argument.** Distorting an opponent's argument position and then attacking it. Example: Attacking an opposing political candidate for restricting civil liberties when, in fact, the opponent only supported a ban on concealed weapons.
- **Ad Hominem Argument.** Attacking the person, not the person's argument. (Literally translated, *ad hominem* means "to the man.") Example: discounting a young person's argument by saying: "you're too young and inexperienced to know what you're talking about," or discounting an older person's argument by stating: "you're too old-school to understand this issue."
- **Red Herring.** Bringing up an irrelevant issue that disguises or distracts attention from the real issue being discussed or debated. (The term "red herring" derives from an old practice of dragging a herring—a strong-smelling fish—across a trail to distract the scent of pursuing dogs.) Example: People who responded to criticism of former President Richard Nixon's involvement in the Watergate scandal by arguing, "He was a good president who accomplished many great things while he was in office." (Nixon's effectiveness as a president is an irrelevant issue or a red herring; the real issue being discussed is Nixon's behavior in the Watergate scandal.)
- **Smoke Screen.** Intentionally disguising or camouflaging the truth by providing confusing or misleading explanations. Example: A politician who opposes gun control legislation by arguing that it's a violation of the constitutional right to bear arms, when in reality, the reason for his position is that he's receiving financial support from gun manufacturing companies.
- **Slippery Slope.** Using fear tactics to argue that not accepting a position will result in a "domino effect"—bad things will happen one after another—like a series of falling dominoes. Example: Arguing that "if America allows communism to happen anywhere, it will eventually happen everywhere."
- **Rhetorical Deception.** Using deceptive language to conclude that something is true without actually providing reasons or evidence. Example: Using glib words such as: "*Clearly* this is . . ." "It's *obvious* that . . ." or "Any *reasonable* person can see . . .", without explaining why it's so "clear," "obvious," or "reasonable."
- **Circular Reasoning (a.k.a. "Begging the Question").** Drawing a conclusion by merely rewording or restating one's position without providing any supporting reasons or evidence, thus leaving the original question unanswered. This logical fallacy basically offers a conclusion that's simply a circular restatement of the premise—it's true because it's true. Example: Concluding that "stem cell research isn't ethical because it's morally wrong."
- **Appealing to Authority or Prestige.** Believing that if an authority figure or celebrity says it's true, it must be true. Example: Buying product X simply because a famous actor or athlete endorses

it. Or, concluding that a course of action should be taken simply because the president says so.
- **Appealing to Tradition or Familiarity.** Concluding that if something has been considered to be true for a long time, or has always been done in a certain way, it must be true or must be the best way to do it. Example: "Throughout history, marriage has been a relationship between a man and a woman; therefore, gay marriage should be illegal."
- **Appealing to Popularity or the Majority (a.k.a. Jumping on the Bandwagon).** Believing that if an idea is popular or held by the majority of people, it must be true. Example: "So many people believe in psychics, it must be true; they can't all be wrong."
- **Appealing to Emotion.** Believing in something based on the emotional intensity of our reaction to an argument, rather than the quality of reasoning or evidence used to support the argument. Example: "If I feel strongly about something, it must be true" or believing that I should "always trust my feelings" and "just follow my heart."

> "Political talk shows have become shouting matches designed to push emotional hot buttons and drive us further apart. We desperately need to exchange ideas with one another rationally and courteously."
> —David Boren, president, University of Oklahoma and longest-serving chairman of the U.S. Senate Intelligence Committee

Think About It—Journal Entry 6.7

Glance back at the reasoning errors just discussed. Identify the two most common errors you've witnessed or experienced.

_____
_____
_____

What were the situations in which these errors took place?

_____
_____
_____
_____
_____

Why do you think they took place?

_____
_____
_____
_____
_____
_____

AUTHOR'S EXPERIENCE

When I teach classes or give workshops, I often challenge students or participants to debate me on either politics or religion. I ask them to choose a political party affiliation, a religion or a branch of religion for their debate topic, or their stance on a social issue for which there are political or religious viewpoints. The ground rules are as follows: They choose the topic for debate; they can only use facts to support their argument, rebuttal, or both, and they must respond in a rational manner—without letting emotions drive their answers.

When I conduct this exercise, I usually discover that the topics people feel most strongly about are often those they haven't critically evaluated. For instance, people say they are Democrat, Republican, independent, and so on, and argue from this position; however, few of them have taken the time to critically examine whether their stated affiliation is actually consistent with their personal viewpoints. They almost always answer "no" to the following questions: "Have you read the core document (e.g., party platform) that outlines the party stance?" and "Have you engaged in self-examination of your party affiliation through reasoned discussions with others who say they have the same or a different political affiliation?"

> "Too often we enjoy the comfort of opinion without the discomfort of thought."
> —John F. Kennedy, 35th U.S. president

—*Aaron Thompson*

> "The principle mark of genius is not perfection but originality, the opening of new frontiers."
> —Arthur Koestler, Hungarian novelist and philosopher

> "The blues are the roots. Everything else are the fruits."
> —Willie Dixon, blues songwriter; commenting on how all forms of contemporary American music contain elements of blues music, which originated among African American slaves

> "Imagination should give wings to our thoughts, but imagination must be checked and documented by the factual results of the experiment."
> —Louis Pasteur, French microbiologist, chemist, and founder of pasteurization (a method for preventing milk and wine from going sour)

Creative Thinking

Creative thinking leads you to ask the question: "Why not?" (e.g., "Why not do it a different way?"). When you generate something new or different—an original idea, strategy, or work product—you're thinking creatively.

The process of creative thinking may be viewed as an extension or higher form of synthesis. Like synthesis, separate ideas are integrated, but they're combined in a way that results in something distinctively different (Anderson & Krathwohl, 2001). For instance, the musical genre of hard rock was created by combining elements of blues and rock and roll, and folk rock was born when Bob Dylan combined musical elements of acoustic blues and amplified rock (Shelton et al., 2003). Robert Kearns (subject of the film, "Flash of Genius") combined preexisting mechanical parts to create the intermittent windshield wiper (Seabrook, 2008).

Keep in mind that creative thinking is not restricted to the arts, it can occur in all subject areas—even in fields that seek precision and definite answers. In math, creative thinking involves using new approaches or strategies for arriving at a correct solution to a problem. In science, creativity takes place when a scientist first uses imaginative thinking to create a hypothesis or logical hunch ("What might happen if . . . ?") and then conducts an experiment to test out whether the hypothesis turns out to be true.

It could be said that thinking critically involves looking "inside the box" to evaluate the quality of its content. Thinking creatively involves looking "outside the box" to imagine other packages containing different content. Creative and critical thinking are two of the most important forms of higher-level thinking and they can work together in a cyclical and complementary fashion. Creative thinking is used to ask new questions and generate new ideas; critical thinking is used to evaluate or critique the ideas we generate (Paul & Elder, 2004). For an idea to be truly creative, it must not just be different or unusual, it must also be effective or significant (Runco, 2004; Sternberg, 2001). If our critique of what we've created reveals that it lacks quality or is ineffective, we shift back to creative thinking to generate something new and improved.

Or, the starting points for the cyclical process of creative and critical thinking may be reversed, whereby we begin by using critical thinking to evaluate an old idea or approach. If our evaluation indicates that it's not very good, we turn on the creative thinking process to come up with a quality of the new idea or different approach; then we turn back to critical thinking to evaluate the quality of the new idea we created.

Brainstorming is a problem-solving process that illustrates how creative and critical thinking work hand-in-hand. The steps or stages involved in the process of brainstorming are summarized in **Box 6.3**.

> "Creativity isn't 'crazytivity.'"
> —Edward De Bono, internationally known authority on creative thinking

BOX 6.3

The Process of Brainstorming

1. Generate as many ideas as you can, jotting them down rapidly without stopping to evaluate their validity or practicality. Studies show that worrying about whether an idea is correct often blocks creativity (Basadur, Runco, & Vega, 2000). So, at this stage of the process, just let your imagination run wild; don't be concerned about whether the idea you generate is impractical, unrealistic, or outrageous.
2. Review the ideas you generated and use them as a springboard to trigger additional ideas, or combine them into larger ideas.
3. After you run out of ideas, critically evaluate the list of ideas you've generated and eliminate those that you think are least effective.
4. From the remaining list of ideas, choose the best idea or best combination of ideas.

Note that the first two steps in the brainstorming process involve *divergent thinking*—a form of creative thinking that allows you to go off in different directions and generate diverse ideas. In contrast, the last two steps in the process involve *convergent thinking*—a form of critical thinking in which you converge (focus in) and narrow down the ideas, evaluating each of them for their effectiveness.

As this multistage process suggests, creativity doesn't just happen suddenly or effortlessly (the so-called "stroke of genius"); instead, it takes sustained mental effort (De Bono, 2007; Paul & Elder, 2004). Although creative thinking may occasionally involve spontaneous or intuitive leaps, it typically involves careful reflection and evaluation of whether any of those leaps actually land you on a good idea.

Chapte 6: Higher-Level Thinking

AUTHOR'S EXPERIENCE

I was once working with a friend to come up with ideas for a grant proposal. We started out by sitting at his kitchen table, exchanging ideas while sipping coffee; then we both got up and began to pace back and forth, walking all around the room while bouncing different ideas off each other. Whenever a new idea was thrown out, one of us would jot it down (whoever was pacing closer to the kitchen table at the moment).

After we ran out of ideas, we shifted gears, slowed down, and sat down at the table together to critique the ideas we generated during our "binge-thinking" episode. After some debate, we finally settled on an idea that we judged to be the best of all the ideas we produced, and we used this idea for the grant proposal—which, ultimately, was awarded to us.

> "Creativity is allowing oneself to make mistakes; art is knowing which ones to keep."
> —Scott Adams, creator of the Dilbert comic strip and author of The Dilbert Principle

Although I wasn't fully aware of it at the time, the stimulating thought process my friend and I were engaging in was called brainstorming: first we engaged in creative thinking—our fast-paced, idea-production stage—followed by critical thinking—our slower-paced, idea-evaluation stage.

—*Joe Cuseo*

NOTE

Creative thinking is about generating new answers and solutions. Critical thinking is about evaluating the quality of answers and solutions we generate.

Think About It—Journal Entry 6.8

Do you consider yourself to be a creative thinker? Why?

_____
_____
_____
_____

What could you do to improve your ability to think creatively?

_____
_____
_____
_____
_____

Using Higher-Level Thinking Skills to Improve Academic Performance

Thus far, this chapter has focused primarily on helping you get a clear idea of what higher-level thinking is and what its major forms are. The remainder of the chapter focuses on helping you develop habits of higher-level thinking that can be applied to improve your performance in high school and beyond.

Connect ideas you acquire in class with related ideas found in your assigned reading. When you discover information in your reading that relates to something you've learned about in class (or vice versa), make a note of it in the margin of your textbook or your class notebook. By integrating knowledge you've obtained from these two major sources, you're engaging in the higher-level thinking skill of synthesis, which you can then demonstrate on exams and assignments to improve your course grades.

When listening to lectures and completing reading assignments, pay attention not only to the content being covered but also the thought process used to cover the content. Periodically ask yourself what form of higher-level thinking your instructors are using during class presentations and authors are using when you're reading their writing. The more conscious you are of the type of higher-level thinking skills you're being exposed to, the more likely you are to develop those thinking skills yourself and demonstrate them on exams and assignments.

Periodically pause to reflect on your own thinking process. When working on different academic tasks, ask yourself what type of thinking you're doing (e.g., analysis, synthesis, or evaluation). Thinking about and becoming aware of how you're thinking while you're thinking is a mental process called *metacognition* (Flavell, 1979; Hartman, 2001). It's a mental habit that's associated with higher-level thinking and improved problem-solving skills (Halpern, 2013; Resnick, 1986).

Develop habits of higher-level thinking by asking yourself higher-level thinking questions. One simple yet powerful way to help you reflect on your thinking is through self-questioning. Since thinking often involves talking to ourselves silently (or aloud), if we ask ourselves high-quality, thought-provoking questions, you can train your mind to think at a higher level. A good question can launch you on a quest or voyage to answer it by using higher-level thinking skills. Getting in the habit of asking yourself higher-level thinking questions while learning will increase the likelihood you'll display higher levels of thinking during class discussions, as well as on course exams and assignments.

> "If you do not ask the right questions, you do not get the right answers."
> —Edward Hodnett, British poet

Box 6.4 contains key questions you can use to trigger different forms of higher-level thinking. The questions are constructed as incomplete sentences so you can fill in the blank with any topic or concept you're studying in any course you may be taking. Research indicates that when students get in the habit of using question stems such as these, they develop and demonstrate higher levels of thinking in college courses (King, 1990, 1995, 2002). As you read the questions under each of the seven forms of higher-level thinking in the following box, think about how they may be applied to material you're learning in courses this term.

BOX 6.4

Self-Questioning Strategies to Trigger Different Forms of Higher-Level Thinking

1. **ANALYSIS (ANALYTICAL THINKING)**—breaking down information into its essential elements or parts.

   Trigger Questions:
   - What are the main ideas contained in _____?
   - What are the important aspects of _____?
   - What are the key issues raised by _____?
   - What are the major purposes of _____?
   - What hidden assumptions are embedded in _____?
   - What are the reasons behind _____?

2. **SYNTHESIS (INTEGRATIVE THINKING)**—integrating separate pieces of information to form a more complete and coherent product or pattern.

   Trigger Questions:
   - How can this idea be joined or connected with _____ to create a more complete or comprehensive answer?
   - How could these different _____ be grouped together into a more general class or category?
   - How could these separate _____ be reorganized or rearranged to produce a comprehensive understanding of the big picture?

3. **APPLICATION (APPLIED THINKING)**—using knowledge for practical purposes to solve problems and resolve issues.

   Trigger Questions:
   - How can this idea be used to _____?
   - How can this theory be put into practice to _____?
   - What could be done to improve or strengthen _____?
   - What could be done to prevent or reduce _____?

4. **BALANCED THINKING**—carefully considering reasons for and against a particular position or viewpoint.

   Trigger Questions:
   - Have I considered both sides of _____?
   - What are the strengths (advantages) and weaknesses (disadvantages) of _____?
   - What evidence supports and contradicts _____?
   - What are arguments for and counterarguments against _____?

5. **MULTIDIMENSIONAL THINKING**—thinking that involves viewing yourself and the world around you from different angles or vantage points.

   Trigger Questions:
   - Have I taken into consideration all factors that could influence _____ or be influenced by _____?
   - How would _____ affect different dimensions of myself (emotional, physical, etc.)?
   - What broader impact would _____ have on the social and physical world around me?
   - How might people living in different times (e.g., past and future) experience _____?
   - How would people from different cultural backgrounds interpret or react to _____?

6. **CRITICAL THINKING (EVALUATION)**—making critical judgments or assessments.

   Trigger Questions for Evaluating *Empirical Evidence:*
   - What examples support the argument that _____?
   - What research evidence is there for _____?
   - What statistical data document or back up this _____?

   Trigger Questions for Evaluating *Logical Consistency:*
   - If _____ is true, does it follow that _____ is also true?
   - If I believe in _____, should I practice _____?
   - To draw this conclusion means I'm assuming that _____?

BOX 6.4 (CONT)

Trigger Questions for Evaluating *Morality* (Ethics):
- Is _____ fair?
- Is _____ just?
- Is this action consistent with the professed or stated values of _____?

Trigger Questions for Evaluating *Beauty* (Aesthetics):
- Does _____ meet established criteria for judging artistic beauty?
- What is the aesthetic merit or value of _____?
- Does _____ contribute to or detract from the beauty of the environment?

Trigger Questions for Evaluating *Practicality* (Usefulness):
- Will _____ work?
- What practical value does this _____ have?
- What potential benefits and drawbacks would result if this _____ were put into practice?

Trigger Questions for Evaluating *Priority* (Order of Importance or Effectiveness):
- Which one of these _____ is the most important?
- Is this _____ the best option or choice available?
- How do these _____ rank from first to last (best to worst) in terms of their effectiveness?

7. **CREATIVE THINKING**—generating ideas that are unique, original, or distinctively different. Trigger Questions:
   - What could be invented to _____?
   - Imagine what would happen if _____?
   - What might be a different way to _____?
   - How would this change if _____?
   - What would be an innovative approach to _____?

Note: Save these higher-level thinking questions and use them when completing different academic tasks required in your courses (e.g., preparing for exams, writing papers or reports, and participating in class discussions or study group sessions). Get in the habit of periodically stepping back to reflect on your thinking and ask yourself what form of thinking you're engaging in (analysis, synthesis, application, etc.). You could even keep a "thinking log" or "thinking journal" to increase self-awareness of the thinking strategies you're using and developing. This strategy will not only help you acquire higher-level thinking skills, it will also help you communicate these skills in job interviews and letters of application for career positions.

Think About It—Journal Entry 6.9

Review the higher-level thinking skills listed in questions in **Box 6.4**. Identify one trigger question listed under each of the seven forms of thinking and fill in the blank with an idea or issue being covered in a course you're taking this term.

_____

_____

_____

_____

Strategies for Increasing Creativity

In addition to self-questioning strategies, the following attitudes and practices can be used to stimulate creative thinking.

- **Be flexible.** Think about ideas and objects in alternative and unconventional ways. The power of flexible and unconventional thinking was well illustrated in the movie "*Apollo 13*," based on the true story of an astronaut who saved his life by creatively using duct tape as an air filter. The inventor of the printing press (Johannes Gutenberg) made his groundbreaking discovery while watching a machine being used to crush grapes at a wine harvest. He thought that the same type of machine could be used for a different purpose—to press letters onto paper (Dorfman, Shames, & Kihlstrom, 1996).

- **Be experimental.** Play with ideas; try them out to see whether they'll work or work better than the status quo. Studies show that creative people tend to be mental risk-takers who are willing to experiment with different ideas and techniques (Sternberg, 2001). Consciously resist the temptation to settle for the security of familiarity. When people cling rigidly to what's conventional or traditional, they're clinging to the comfort or security of what's most familiar and predictable; this often blocks originality, ingenuity, and openness to change. Tom Kelley, cofounder of the famous IDEO design firm in Palo Alto, California, has found that innovative thinking emerges from an exploratory mindset that's "open to new insights every day" (Kelley & Littman, 2005).

- **Get mobile.** Stand up and move around while you're thinking. Research shows that taking a walk—either inside or outside—stimulates the production of creative ideas (Oppezzo & Schwartz, 2014). Even by standing up, our brain gets approximately 10% more oxygen than it does when sitting down (Sousa, 2011). Since oxygen provides fuel for the brain, our ability to think creatively is energized when we're up on our feet and moving around.

- **Get it down.** Creative ideas can often pop into our mind at the most unexpected times. Scholars refer to the sudden birth of creative ideas as *incubation*—just like incubated eggs can hatch at any time, so too can original ideas suddenly hatch and pop into our consciousness. However, just as great ideas can suddenly come to mind, they can also slip out of mind as soon as we start thinking about something else. You can prevent this slippage from happening by having the right equipment on hand to record your creative ideas before they slip away. Carry a pen and a small notepad, a packet of sticky notes, or a portable electronic recording device at all times to immediately record original ideas the instant you have them.

- **Get diverse.** Seek ideas from diverse social and informational sources. Bouncing your ideas off of different people and getting their feedback about your ideas is a good way to generate mental energy, synergy (multiplication of ideas), and serendipity

> "All thinking begins with wonder."
> —Socrates, classic Greek (Athenian) philosopher and founding father of Western philosophy

> "I make progress by having people around who are smarter than I am—and listening to them. And I assume that everyone is smarter about something than I am."
> —Henry Kaiser, successful industrialist, known as the father of American shipbuilding

(accidental discoveries). Studies show that creative people venture well beyond the boundaries of their particular area of training or specialization (Baer, 1993; Kaufman & Baer, 2002). They have wide-ranging interests and knowledge, which they draw upon and combine to generate new ideas (Riquelme, 2002). So, be on the lookout to combine the knowledge and skills you acquire from different subjects and different people, and use them to create bridges to new ideas.

- **Take breaks.** If you're having trouble discovering a solution to a problem, stop working on it for a while and come back to it later. Creative solutions often come to mind after you stop thinking about the problem you're trying to solve. What often happens when you work intensely on a problem or challenging task for a sustained period of time, your attention can get rigidly riveted on just one approach to its solution (German & Barrett, 2005; Maier, 1970). By taking your mind off of it and returning to it later, your focus of attention is likely to shift to a different feature or aspect of the problem. This new focus may enable you to view the problem from a different angle or vantage point, which can lead to a breakthrough idea that was blocked by your previous perspective (Anderson, 2010). Furthermore, taking a break allows the problem to incubate in your mind at a lower level of consciousness and stress, which can sometimes give birth to a sudden solution.

> "Eureka! (literally translated: "I have found it!")"
> —Attributed to Archimedes, ancient Greek mathematician and inventor when he suddenly discovered (while sitting in a bathtub) how to measure the purity of gold

- **Reorganize the problem.** When you're stuck on a problem, try rearranging its parts or pieces. Reorganization can transform the problem into a different pattern that may enable you to suddenly see a solution you previously overlooked—similar to how changing the order of letters in a word jumble can help you find the hidden word. You can use the same strategy to change the wording of any problem you're working on, or by recording ideas on index cards (or sticky notes) and laying them out in different sequences and patterns.

> "Creativity consists largely of re-arranging what we know in order to find out what we do not know."
> —George Keller, prolific American architect and originator of the Union Station design for elevated train stations

If you're having trouble solving a problem that involves a sequence of steps (e.g., a math problem), try reversing the sequence and start by working from the end or middle. The new sequence makes you to take a different approach to the problem; this forces you to come at it from a different direction, which can lead you to an alternative path to its solution.

CHAPTER SUMMARY AND HIGHLIGHTS

Higher-level thinking (also known as higher-order thinking) refers to a more advanced level of thought than that used to acquire factual knowledge. It involves reflecting on knowledge acquired and taking it to a higher level—by performing additional mental action on it—such as evaluating its validity, integrating it with other ideas, or applying it to solve problems.

In this chapter, seven major forms of higher-level thinking skills were identified along with strategies for developing each of them:

1. *Analysis (Analytical Thinking)*—breaking down information to identify its key parts and underlying elements;
2. *Synthesis (Integrative Thinking)*—building up ideas by connecting them to form a larger whole or more comprehensive system;
3. *Application (Applied Thinking)*—putting knowledge into practice to solve problems and resolve issues;
4. *Multidimensional Thinking*—taking multiple perspectives (i.e., viewing issues from different vantage points);
5. *Balanced Thinking*—carefully considering arguments for and against a particular argument or position;
6. *Critical Thinking*—evaluating (judging the quality of) arguments, conclusions, and ideas;
7. *Creative Thinking*—generating ideas that are unique, original, or distinctively different.

Besides achieving academic excellence in college, there are other key benefits of developing higher-level thinking skills.

1. **Higher-level thinking is essential for success in today's "information age"—a time when new information is being generated at faster rates than at any other time in human history.** The majority of new workers in the information age no longer work with their hands, they will work with their heads (Miller, 2003). Employers now value college graduates who have inquiring minds and possess higher-level thinking skills (Harvey, et al., 1997; Peter D. Hart Research Associates, 2006).
2. **Higher-level thinking skills are vital for citizens in a democratic nation.** Authoritarian political systems, such as dictatorships and fascist regimes, suppress critical thought and demand submissive obedience to authority. In contrast, citizens of a democracy are able to control their political destiny by making wise choices about the political leaders they elect. Thus, effective use of higher-level thinking skills, such as critical thinking, is an essential civic responsibility for people living in a democratic nation.
3. **Higher-level thinking is an important safeguard against prejudice, discrimination, and hostility.** Racial, ethnic, and national prejudices are often rooted in narrow, self-centered or group-centered thinking (Paul & Elder, 2014). Oversimplified, dualistic thinking can lead individuals to categorizing others into either "in" groups (us) or "out" groups (them). Such dualistic thinking can lead, in turn, to ethnocentrism—the tendency to view one's own racial or ethnic group as the superior "in" group and see other groups as inferior "out" groups. Development of higher-level thinking skills, such as taking multiple perspectives and using balanced thinking, counteracts the type of dualistic, ethnocentric thinking that leads to prejudice, discrimination, and hate crimes.

4. **Higher-level thinking helps preserve mental and physical health.** Simply put: Those who use their mind don't lose their mind. As they age, mentally active people are less likely to suffer memory loss or experience dementia (Wilson, Mendes, & Barnes, 2002). Thinking is not only a mental activity, it's also a physical activity that exercises the brain, much like physical activity exercises muscles in other parts of the body. Thinking requires higher levels of energy, which stimulates biological activity among brain cells, invigorates them, and reduces the likelihood they will deteriorate with age.

Contrary to common belief, problem solving and other forms of higher-level thinking will not "fry" your brain but will stimulate and exercise it, reducing the likelihood that you'll experience Alzheimer's disease and other causes of memory loss in later life.

Learning More through the World Wide Web: Internet-Based Resources

For additional information on thinking skills, see the following websites:

Higher-Level Thinking Skills:
http://edorigami.wikispaces.com/Bloom%27s+Digital+Taxonomy

Critical Thinking:
www.criticalthinking.org

Creative Thinking:
www.amcreativityassoc.org

Thinking Errors:
www.psychologytoday.com/blog/what-mentally-strong-people-dont-do/201501/10-thinking-errors-will-crush-your-mental-strength
www.factcheck.org (site for evaluating the factual accuracy of statements made by politicians in TV ads, debates, speeches, interviews, and news releases)

References

Anderson, J. R. (2010). *Cognitive psychology and its implications*. New York: Worth Publishers.
Anderson, L. W., & Krathwohl, D. R. (Eds.). (2001). *A taxonomy for learning, teaching, and assessing: A revision of Bloom's taxonomy of educational objectives*. New York: Addison Wesley Longman.
Baer, J. M. (1993). *Creativity and divergent thinking*. Hillsdale, NJ: Erlbaum.
Basadur, M., Runco, M. A., & Vega, L. A. (2000). Under-standing how creative thinking skills, attitudes and behaviors work together: A causal process model. *Journal of Creative Behavior*, Vol. 34, (2), pp 77–100.
Conley, D. T. (2005). *College knowledge: What it really takes for students to succeed and what we can do to get them ready*. San Francisco: Jossey-Bass.
De Bono, E. (2007). *How to have creative ideas*. London, UK: Vermillion.
Donald, J. G. (2002). *Learning to think: Disciplinary perspectives*. San Francisco: Jossey-Bass.
Dorfman, J., Shames, J., & Kihlstrom, J. F. (1996). Intuition, incubation, and insight. In G. Underwood (Ed.), *Implicit cognition* (pp. 257–296). New York: Oxford University Press.
Ericsson, K. A. (2006). The influence of experience and deliberate practice on the development of superior expert performance. In K. A. Ericsson, N. Charness, P. Feltovich, & R. R. Hoffman, (Eds.). *Cambridge handbook of expertise and expert performance* (pp. 685–706). Cambridge, UK: Cambridge University Press.
Ericsson, K. A., & Charness, N. (1994). Expert performance: Its structure and acquisition. *American Psychologist*, 49(8), 725–747.
Fairbairn, G. J., & Winch, C. (1996). *Reading, writing and reasoning: A guide for students* (2nd ed.). Buckingham: OU Press.
Flavell, J. H. (1979). Metacognition and cognitive monitoring: A new area of cognitive- developmental inquiry. *American Psychologist*, 34(10), 906–911.
Gardiner, L. F. (2005). Transforming the environment for learning: A crisis of quality. *To Improve the Academy*, 23, 3–23.
German, T. P., & Barrett, H. C. (2005). Functional fixedness in a technologically sparse culture. *Psychological Science*, 16, 1–5.
Halpern, D. F. (2013). *Thought & knowledge: An introduction to critical thinking* (5th ed.). New York: Psychology Press.
Hartman, H. J. (Ed.) (2001). *Metacognition in learning and instruction: Theory, research and practice*. Dordrecht: Kluwer Academic Publishers.
Harvey, L., Moon, S., Geall, V., & Bower, R. (1997). *Graduates work: Organizational change and students' attributes*, Birmingham, Centre for Research into Quality, University of Central England.
Higher Education Research Institute (HERI) (2009). *The American college teacher: National norms for 2007–2008*. Los Angeles: HERI, University of California, Los Angeles.
Intergovernmental Council on Climate Change (2013). *Climate change 2013: The physical science basis*. Working Group I Contribution to the Fifth Assessment Report of the Intergovernmental Council on Climate Change. Switzerland: Intergovernmental Panel on Climate Change. Retrieved from http://www.ipcc.ch/report/ar5/wg1/.
Joint Science Academies Statement (2005). *Global response to climate change*. Retrieved from http://nationalacademies.org/onpi/06072005.pdf.
Kaufman, J. C., & Baer, J. (2002). Could Steven Spielberg manage the Yankees? Creative thinking in different domains. *Korean Journal of Thinking & Problem Solving*, 12(2), 5–14.
Kelley, T., & Littman, J. (2005). *The ten faces of innovation: IDEO's strategies for beating the devil's advocate & driving creativity throughout your organization*. New York: Currency/Doubleday.
King, A. (1990). Enhancing peer interaction and learning in the classroom through reciprocal questioning. *American Educational Research Journal*, 27(4), 664–687.
King, A. (1995). Guided peer questioning: A cooperative learning approach to critical thinking. *Cooperative Learning and College Teaching*, 5(2), 15–19.

King, A. (2002). Structuring peer interaction to promote high-level cognitive processing. *Theory into Practice, 41*(1), 33–39.

Maier, N. R. F. (1970). *Problem solving and creativity in individuals and groups.* Belmont, CA: Brooks/Cole.

Martin, R. L. (2007). *The opposable mind: How successful leaders win through integrative thinking.* Boston: Harvard Business School Press.

Miller, M. A. (2003, September/October). The meaning of the baccalaureate. *About Campus,* pp. 2–8.

Milton, O. (1982). *Will that be on the final?* Springfield, IL: Charles C. Thomas. National Resources Defense Council (2005). *Global warming: A summary of recent findings on the changing global climate.* Retrieved from http://www.nrdc.org/globalwarming/science/2005.asp.

National Resources Defense Council. (2012). *Global warming: An introduction to climate change.* Retrieved from www.nrdc.org/globalwarming.

Oppezzo, M., & Schwartz, D. L. (2014). Give your ideas some legs: The positive effect of walking on creative thinking. *Journal of Experimental Psychology: Learning, Memory, and Cognition, 40*(4), 1142–1152.

Pascarella, E., & Terenzini, P. (1991). *How college affects students: Findings and insights from twenty years of research.* San Francisco: Jossey-Bass.

Pascarella, E., & Terenzini, P. (2005). *How college affects students: A third decade of research* (Vol. 2). San Francisco: Jossey-Bass.

Paul, R., & Elder, L. (2004). *The nature and functions of critical and creative thinking.* Dillon Beach, CA: Foundation for Critical Thinking.

Paul, R., & Elder, L. (2014). *Critical thinking: Tools for taking charge of your professional and personal life.* Upper Saddle River, NJ: Pearson Education.

Perry, W. G. (1970, 1999). *Forms of intellectual and ethical development during the college years: A scheme.* New York: Holt, Rinehart & Winston.

Peter D. Hart Research Associates, 2006. *How should colleges prepare students to succeed in today's global economy?* The Association of American Colleges and Universities by Peter D. Hart Research Associates, Inc.

Resnick, L. B. (1986). *Education and learning to think.* Washington, DC: National Academy Press.

Riquelme, H. (2002). Can people creative in imagery interpret ambiguous figures faster than people less creative in imagery? *Journal of Creative Behavior, 36*(2), 105–116.

Runco, M. A. (2004). Creativity. *Annual Review of Psychology, 55,* 657–687.

Seabrook, J. (2008). *Flash of genius and other true stories of invention,* New York: St. Martin's Press.

Shelton, et al., 2003 Evaluation of parameters affecting quantitative detection of Escherichia coli O157 in enriched water samples using immunomagnetic electrochemiluminescence. *J. Microbiology Methods, Dec; 55*(3): 717–25.

Sousa, D. A. (2011). *How the brain learns.* Thousand Oaks, CA: Sage.

Stark, J. S., Lowther, R. J., Bentley, M. P., Ryan, G. G., Martens, M. L., Genthon, P. A., et al. (1990). *Planning introductory college courses: Influences on faculty.* Ann Arbor: National Center for Research to Improve Postsecondary Teaching and Learning, University of Michigan. (ERIC Document Reproduction Services No. 330 277 370.)

Staudinger, U. M. (2008). A psychology of wisdom: History and recent developments. *Research in Human Development, 5,* 107–120.

Sternberg, R. J. (2001). What is the common thread of creativity? *American Psychologist, 56*(4), 360–362.

Wilson, R., Mendes, C., Barnes, L., and others (2002). Participation in cognitively stimulating activities and risk of incident Alzheimer's disease. *Journal of the American Medical Association, 287*(6), 742–748.

CHAPTER 6 EXERCISES

6.1 QUOTE REFLECTIONS

Review the sidebar quotes contained in this chapter and select two that were especially meaningful or inspirational to you. For each quote, provide a three- to five-sentence explanation why you chose it.

6.2 REALITY BITE

Trick or Treat: Confusing Test or Challenging Test?

Students in a math course just got their first exam back and the teacher is going over the test in class. Some students are angry because they feel the teacher deliberately included "trick questions" to confuse them. The teacher responds by saying that the test questions were not intended to trick them, but to "challenge them to think."

Reflection and Discussion Questions

1. What do you think may have led some students to believe that the teacher was trying to trick or confuse them?
2. What type of test questions do you suspect the teacher created to "challenge students to think"?
3. On future tests, what might students do to reduce the likelihood that they will feel tricked again?

6.3 SELF-ASSESSMENT OF HIGHER-LEVEL THINKING QUALITIES

Thinking at a higher level is not just an intellectual process, it's also a personal attribute. Listed below are attributes of higher-level thinkers, accompanied by specific behaviors associated with each attribute. As you read the behaviors under each of the general attributes, place a checkmark (✓) next to any behavior that's true of you now and an asterisk (*) next to any behavior you think you need to work on.

1. *Tolerant and Accepting*

    ___ Don't tune out ideas that conflict with your own

    ___ Keep your emotions under control when someone criticizes your personal viewpoint

    ___ Feel comfortable discussing controversial issues

    ___ Try to find common ground with others holding opposing viewpoints

2. *Inquisitive and Open Minded*

    ___ Eager to continue learning new things from different people and different experiences

    ___ Willing to seek out others who hold viewpoints different than your own

    ___ Find differences of opinion and opposing viewpoints to be interesting and stimulating

    ___ Attempt to understand why people have opposing viewpoints

3. *Reflective and Tentative*

    ___ Take time to consider all perspectives or sides of an issue before drawing conclusions, making choices, or reaching decisions

    ___ Give fair consideration to ideas that others may instantly disapprove of or find distasteful

    ___ Acknowledge the complexity, ambiguity and uncertainty of certain issues, and am willing to say: "I need to give this more thought" or "I need more evidence before I can draw a conclusion"

    ___ Periodically reexamine your own viewpoints to determine whether they should be maintained or changed

4. *Honest and Courageous*

    ___ Willing to examine your views to see if they're biased or prejudiced

    ___ Willing to challenge others' ideas that are based on personal bias or prejudice

    ___ Willing to express viewpoints that may not conform to those of the majority

    ___ Willing to change previously held opinions and personal beliefs when they're contradicted by sound arguments or new evidence

Look back at the list and count the number of checkmarks and asterisks you placed in each of the four general areas:

	Checkmarks	Asterisks
Tolerant and Accepting:	_____	_____
Inquisitive and Open Minded:	_____	_____
Reflective and Tentative:	_____	_____
Honest and Courageous:	_____	_____

Reflection Questions:

- Under which of the four attributes did you place (a) the most *checkmarks*, (b) the most *asterisks*? What do you think accounts for the difference?

- What could you do in college to strengthen your weakest area (the attribute below which you had the most asterisks)?

6.4 CHAPTER REFLECTION

How can you use critical thinking to be a more successful student? List three action steps you can do to make this happen.

How can you use critical thinking to improve your personal life?

How can you use creative thinking to be a more successful student? List three action steps you can do to make this happen.

How can you use creative thinking to improve your personal life? Explain.

CHAPTER 7
TEST-TAKING SKILLS AND STRATEGIES

What to do before, during, and after tests

CHAPTER PREVIEW

This chapter supplies you with a systematic set of strategies for improving your performance on different types of tests that can be used before, during, and after exams, helping you to become more "test wise" and less "test anxious."

LEARNING GOALS

Acquire effective strategies to improve your performance on multiple-choice, true–false, and essay tests.

THOUGHT STARTER

 Think About It—Journal Entry 7.1

On which of the following types of tests do you tend to perform better?
a) Multiple-choice tests
b) Essay tests

Why?
_____
_____
_____
_____

From *Thriving in the Community College & Beyond: Strategies for Academic Success and Personal Development*, Third Edition, by Joseph Cuseo, Aaron Thompson, and Julie McLaughlin. Copyright © 2016 by Kendall Hunt Publishing Company. Reprinted by permission.

Learning in high school courses typically takes place in a three-stage process: (1) acquiring information from classes and readings; (2) studying that information and storing it in your brain as knowledge; and (3) demonstrating that knowledge on exams. The following sections of this chapter contain strategies relating primarily to the third stage of this learning process and they are divided into three categories:

- Strategies to use *in advance* of a test,
- Strategies to use *during* a test, and
- Strategies to use *after* test results are returned.

Pre-Test Strategies: What to Do *in Advance* of Tests

Your ability to remember material on a test that you studied prior to the test depends not only on how long and how well you studied, but also on the type of test questions used to test your memory. You may be able to remember what you've studied if you're tested in one format (e.g., multiple-choice) but not if tested in a different format (e.g., essay). Thus, the type of questions that will appear on an upcoming test should influence the type of study strategies you use to prepare for the test. Test questions can be classified into the following two major categories, depending on the type of memory required to answer them.

1. *Recognition test questions* ask you to select or choose the correct answer from choices that are provided for you. Falling into this category are multiple-choice, true–false, and matching questions. These test questions don't require you to supply or produce the correct answer on your own; instead, you're asked to recognize or pick out the correct answer—similar to picking out the "correct" criminal from a lineup of potential suspects.
2. *Recall test questions* require you to retrieve information you've studied and reproduce it on your own. As the word "recall" implies, you have to re-call ("call back") information and supply it yourself—as opposed to picking it out from information supplied for you. Recall test questions include essay and short-answer questions that require you to provide your own answer—in writing.

Since recognition test questions (e.g., multiple-choice or true–false) ask you to recognize or pick out the correct answer from answers provided for you, reading your class notes and textbook highlights and identifying key information may be an effective study strategy—because it matches the type of mental activity you'll be performing on the exam—reading test questions and identifying correct answers provided to you.

On the other hand, recall test questions, such as essay questions, require you to retrieve information and generate your own answers. They don't involve answer recognition; they require answer *production*—you produce the answer in writing. If you study for essay tests by just looking over your class notes and reviewing your reading highlights, you're using a study strategy that doesn't align with or match what you'll be expected to do on the test itself, which is to supply the correct information yourself. To prepare for essay test questions, you need to practice *retrieval*—recalling the information on your own—without looking at it.

Two essay-test preparation strategies that ensure you engage in memory retrieval are: (a) recitation and (b) creation of retrieval cues. Each of these strategies is described below.

Recitation

Stating aloud the information we want to remember—without looking at that information—is a memory-improvement strategy known as *recitation*. Memory is strengthened substantially when we reproduce on our own what we're trying to remember, instead of simply looking it over or rereading it (Roediger & Karpicke, 2006). Research consistently indicates that this type of self-testing may be the most powerful of all test-preparation strategies (Carey, 2014). Recitation strengthens memory and better prepares you for essay tests because it:

- Requires *more mental effort* to dig out (retrieve) the answer on its own, which strengthens memory for the answer and allows the brain to practice exactly what it's expected to do on essay tests.
- Gives you clear *feedback* about whether or not you know the material. If you can't retrieve and recite it without looking at it, you know for sure that you won't be able to recall it at test time and need to study it further. You can provide yourself with this feedback by putting the question on one side of an index card and the answer on the flip side. If you find yourself flipping over the index card to look at the answer in order to remember it, this shows you can't retrieve the information on your own and you need to study it further. (To create electronic flash cards, see: www.studystack.com or studyblue.com)
- Encourages you to *use your own words*. If you can paraphrase it—rephrase what you're studying in your own words—it's a good indication you really understand it; and if you really understand it, you're more likely to recall it at test time.

Recitation can be done silently, by speaking aloud, or by writing out what you're trying to recall. Speaking aloud or writing out what you're reciting are particularly effective essay-test preparation strategies because they involve physical activity, which ensures that you're actively involved and engaged in the learning process.

Creating Retrieval Cues

Suppose you're trying to remember the name of a person you know; you know you know it, but just can't recall it. If a friend gives you a clue (e.g., the first letter of the person's name or a name that rhymes with it), it's likely to suddenly trigger your memory of that person's name. What your friend did was provide a retrieval cue. A *retrieval cue* is a type of memory reminder (like a string tied around your finger) that brings back to mind what you've temporarily forgotten.

Research shows that students who can't remember previously studied information are better able to recall that information if they're given a retrieval cue. In a classic study, students studied a long list of items, some of which were animals (e.g., giraffe, coyote, and turkey). After they finished studying, students were given a blank sheet of paper and asked to write down the names of those animals. None of the students were able to recall all of the animals that appeared on the list they previously studied. However, when the word "animals" was written on top of the answer sheet to provide students with a retrieval cue, they were able to recall many of the animals they had forgotten (Tulving, 1983). Research findings such as these suggest that category names can serve as powerful retrieval cues. By taking pieces of information you need to recall on an essay test and organizing it into categories, you can then use the category names as retrieval cues at test time. Retrieval cues work because memories are stored in the brain as part of an interconnected network. So, if you're able to recall one piece or segment of the network (the retrieval cue), it can trigger recall of other pieces of information linked to it in the same network (Willingham, 2009).

Think About It—Journal Entry 7.2

Think about items of information you need to remember in a course you're taking this term. Group these items into a category that can be used as a retrieval cue to help you remember them.

1. What's the course?

   _____
   _____
   _____
   _____

2. What's the category you've created as a retrieval cue?

   _____
   _____
   _____
   _____

3. What items of information would this retrieval cue help you recall?

   _____
   _____
   _____
   _____

Another strategy for creating retrieval cues is to come up with your own catchword or catchphrase to "catch" or batch together all related ideas you're trying to remember. Acronyms can serve as catchwords, with each letter acting as a retrieval cue for a batch of related ideas. For instance, suppose you're studying for an essay test in abnormal psychology that will include questions testing your knowledge of different forms of mental illness. You could create the acronym SCOT as a retrieval cue to help you remember to include the following key elements of mental illness in your essay answers: Symptoms (S), Causes (C), Outcomes (O), and Therapies (T).

Strategies to Use *Immediately Before* a Test

1. **Before the exam, take a brisk walk or light jog.** Physical activity increases mental alertness by increasing oxygen flow to the brain; it also decreases tension by increasing the brain's production of emotionally "mellowing" brain chemicals (e.g., serotonin and endorphins).
2. **Come fully armed with all the test-taking tools you need.** In addition to the basic supplies (e.g., no. 2 pencil, pen, blue book, Scantron, calculator, etc.), bring backup equipment in case you experience equipment failure (e.g., an extra pen in case your first one runs out of ink or extra pencils in case your original one breaks).
3. **Get to the classroom as early as possible.** Arriving early allows you to take a few minutes to get into a relaxed pretest state of mind by thinking positive thoughts, taking slow, deep breaths and stretching your muscles.
4. **Sit in the same seat you normally occupy in class.** Research indicates that memory is improved when information is recalled in the same place where it was originally received or reviewed (Sprenger, 1999). Thus, taking a test in the same place where you heard the information delivered will likely improve your test performance.

> "Avoid flipping through notes (cramming) immediately before a test. Instead, do some breathing exercises and think about something other than the test."
> —Advice to first-year students from a college sophomore

Studies also show that when students take a test on material in the same environment where they studied the material, they tend to remember more of it at test time than do students who study the material in one place and take a test on that material in a different place (Smith & Vela, 2001). While it's unlikely you will be able to do all your studying in the same room where your test will be taken, it may be possible to do a short, final review session in your classroom or in an empty classroom with similar features. This should strengthen your memory because the physical features of the room become associated with the material you're trying to remember. Seeing these features again at test time can help trigger your memory of that material.

A classic, fascinating study supporting this recommendation was once conducted on a group of deep sea divers. Some divers learned a list of words on a beach, while the others learned the list underwater. They were later tested for their memory of the words. Half the divers who learned the words on the beach remained there to take the test; the other half were tested underwater. Half the divers who studied the words underwater took the test in the same place; the other half took the test on the beach. The results showed that the divers who took the test in the same place where they learned the list recalled 40% more of the items than the divers who did their learning and testing in different places (Godden & Baddeley, 1975). This study provides strong evidence that memory is strengthened when studying and testing takes place in the same location.

Other intriguing studies have shown that if students are exposed to a certain aroma while they're studying (e.g., the smell of chocolate) and they're later exposed to that same smell during a memory test for what they studied, they display better memory for the information they studied (Schab & Crowder, 2014). One possible, practical application of this finding to improve your memory during a test is to put on a particular cologne or perfume while studying, and put in on again on the day of the test. This may improve your memory for the information you studied by matching the scent of your study environment with the scent of your test environment. Although this strategy may seem silly, keep in mind that the area of the human brain where humans perceive smell has connections with the brain's memory centers (Jensen, 2005). These neurological connections probably explain why people often report that certain smells can trigger long-ago memories (e.g., the smell of a summer breeze triggering memories of summer games played during childhood).

Since smell is related to memory, you may be able to use smell as a retrieval cue to stimulate recall for information you've studied. In so doing, you may improve your performance on essay tests.

BOX 7.1

Nutritional Strategies for Strengthening Academic Performance

Is there a "brain food" that can enhance our test performance? Can we "eat to learn" or "eat to remember"? Some animal studies suggest that memory can be improved by consumption of foods containing lecithin—a substance that helps the brain produce acetylcholine—a chemical that plays an important role in the formation of memories (Ueda et al., 2011; Ulus & Wurtman, 1977). Fish contains high amounts of lecithin, which may explain why fish is sometimes referred to as "brain food."

Despite the results of some animal studies, not enough human research evidence is available to conclude that consuming certain foods will dramatically increase our ability to retain information or knowledge. However, the following nutritional strategies can improve mental performance on days when our knowledge is tested.

1. Eat breakfast on the day of the exam. Studies show that when students eat a nutritious breakfast on the day they are tested, they achieve higher test scores (Phillips, 2005; Schroll, 2006). Breakfast on the day of an exam should include grains, such as whole wheat toast, whole grain cereal, oatmeal, or bran, because those foods contain complex carbohydrates that deliver a steady stream of energy to the body throughout the day. These complex carbohydrates also help your brain produce a steady stream of serotonin—a brain chemical that reduces tension and anxiety.

BOX 7.1 (CONT)

> "No man can be wise on an empty stomach."
> —George Eliot, 19th-century English novelist

2. **Make the meal you eat before a test a light meal.** The meal you consume nearest test time should not be a large one because it will elevate your blood sugar to a high level, causing large amounts of insulin must be released into the bloodstream to reduce the blood sugar level. This draws blood sugar away from the brain, causing mental fatigue.

3. **If you need an energy boost prior to a test, eat a piece of fruit rather than a candy bar.** Candy bars are processed sweets that infuse synthetic sugar into the bloodstream, which provides a short and sudden burst of energy. That's the good news; the bad news is that this short-term rush of blood sugar and sudden jolt of energy can also increase bodily tension followed by a sharp drop in energy and feelings of sluggishness (Haas, 1994; Thayer, 1997). The key is to find a food that elevates energy without elevating tension and sustains this energy level over an extended period of time. The best nutritional option for producing such a steady, sustained state of higher energy is *natural* sugar contained organically in a piece of fruit, not processed sugar artificially slipped into a candy bar.

4. **Avoid consuming caffeine before a test.** Although caffeine increases alertness, it's a stimulant that elevates bodily tension and nervousness. These are feelings you don't want to experience during a test, particularly if you're prone to test anxiety. Also, caffeine is a diuretic, which means it will increase your urge to urinate. You certainly want to avoid this urge during an exam—when you're confined to a classroom and can't afford to take time to tend to urological needs (or be distracted by them).

Consuming large doses of caffeine or other stimulants before exams is likely to increase your alertness, but it's also likely to increase your level of stress and test anxiety.

Strategies to Use *During* Tests

1. **Before you receive a copy of the test, write down any hard-to-remember terms, formulas, and equations and any memory-retrieval cues you may have created as soon as you start the exam.** This will help ensure you don't forget this important information when you start focusing your attention on the test itself.

2. **First answer questions you know well and carry the most points.** Before automatically attacking the first question that appears on test, take a moment to check out the overall layout of the test and note the questions that are worth the most points and the questions you're best prepared to answer. Tackle these questions first. Put a checkmark next to questions whose answers you're unsure of and come back to them later—after you've answered the questions you're sure of—to ensure you get these points added to your total test score before you run out of test time.
3. **If you experience "memory block" for information you know, use the following strategies to unlock it.**
   - Mentally put yourself back in the environment in which you studied. Recreate the situation by mentally picturing the place where you first heard or saw the information and where you studied it—including sights, sounds, smells, and time of day. This memory-improvement strategy is referred to as *guided retrieval*, and research supports its effectiveness for recalling information of any kind, including information recalled by eyewitnesses to a crime (Glenberg, 1997; Glenberg et al., 1983).
   - Think of any idea or piece of information that relates to the information you can't remember. Studies show that when students forget information they studied, they're more likely to suddenly remember that information if they first recall a piece related to it in some way (Reed, 2013). This strategy works because related pieces of information are typically stored in the same area of the brain—as part of an interconnected neural network.
   - Take your mind off the question by turning to another question. This frees your subconscious to focus on the forgotten information, which can suddenly trigger your conscious memory of it. Moving on to other test questions also allows you to find information included in later test questions that may enable you to recall information related to the earlier question that you previously forgot.
   - Before turning in your test, carefully review and double-check your answers. This is the critical last step in the test-taking process. Sometimes the performance pressure and anxiety associated with test taking can cause students to overlook details, misread instructions, unintentionally skip questions, or make absentminded mistakes. So take time to look over your answers and check for any mindless mistakes you may have made. Avoid the temptation to immediately cut out of class after answering the last test question because you're pooped out or stressed out. When you think about the amount of time and effort you put into preparing for the exam, it's foolish not to take a little more time to detect and correct any silly mistakes you made that could cost you points and lower your test score.

Think About It—Journal Entry 7.3

I'm most likely to experience memory block during exams in the following subjects:

_____

_____

_____

_____

_____

During tests, when I experience memory block, I usually . . .

_____

_____

_____

_____

_____

Strategies for Answering Multiple-Choice Test Questions

You're likely to encounter multiple-choice questions on high school tests (particularly in large classes), on certification or licensing exams for particular professions (e.g., nursing and teaching), as well as on admissions tests for graduate school (e.g., master's and doctoral degree programs) and professional school (e.g., law school and medical school). Since you're likely to take multiple-choice tests frequently in high school and beyond, this section of the text is devoted to a detailed discussion of strategies for taking such tests. These strategies are also applicable to *true–false* questions, which are really essentially multiple-choice questions with two choices: true or false.

1. **Read the question and think of the answer in your head before looking at the possible answers.** If the answer you thought of is in the list of possible answers, it is likely that is the correct answer. However, if you see an answer that is similar but you feel is more correct, select that answer. Thinking of the answer in your head allows you to recall what you studied before recognizing it.
2. **Read all choices listed and use a *process-of-elimination* approach.** Search for the correct answer by first eliminating choices that are clearly wrong; continue to do so until you're left

174 ■ **Chapter 7:** Test-Taking Skills and Strategies

A process-of-elimination approach is an effective test-taking strategy to use when answering difficult multiple-choice questions.

with one choice that represents the best option. Keep in mind that the correct answer is often the one that has the highest probability or likelihood of being true; it doesn't have to be absolutely true—just truer than all the other choices listed.

3. **For a choice to be correct, the *entire statement* must be true.** If any part of the statement is inaccurate or false, eliminate it because it's an incorrect answer.

4. **Use *test-wise* strategies when you cannot narrow down your choice to one answer.** Your first strategy on any multiple-choice question should be to choose an answer based on your knowledge of the material, not by guessing the correct answer based on how the question is worded. However, if you've relied on your knowledge, used the process-of-elimination strategy to eliminate clearly wrong choices, and you're still left with two or more answers that appear to be correct, then you should turn to being *test wise*—use the wording or placement of the test question itself to increase your chances of selecting the correct answer (Flippo & Caverly, 2009). Here are three test-wise strategies you can use for multiple-choice questions when more than one choice appears to be correct:

    • **Pick the answer that contains qualifying words.** Correct answers are more likely to contain modifying words such as "usually," "probably," "often," "likely," "sometimes," "perhaps," or "may." Knowledge often doesn't come neatly packaged as absolute or unqualified truths, so choices are more likely to be false if they make broad generalizations or contain words such as "always," "every," "never," "only," "must," and "completely."

    • **Pick the longest answer.** True statements often require more words to make them true.

    • **Pick a middle answer rather than the first or last answer.** If you've narrowed down the correct answer to either "a" or "c," go with "c." Similarly, if you've narrowed your choices to "b" or "d," your best bet may be to go with "b." Studies show that teachers have a tendency to place the correct answer in the middle, rather than as the first or last choice (Miller, Linn, & Gronlund, 2012)—perhaps because they think the correct answer will be too obvious or stand out if it's placed at the top or bottom of the list.

5. **Check to be sure that your answers are aligned with the right questions.** When looking over your test before turning it in, search carefully for questions you may have skipped and intended to go back to later. Sometimes you may skip a test question on a multiple-choice test and forget to skip the number of that question on the answer form. This will throw off all your other answers by one space or line and result in a disastrous "domino effect" of wrong answers that can do major damage to your total test score. To prevent this from happening, check the alignment of all your answers to be sure there are no blank spaces on your column of answers and that your order of answers line up with the order or test questions.

6. **Don't feel that you must remain locked into your first answer.** When reviewing your answers on multiple-choice and true–false tests, don't be afraid to change an answer after you've given it more thought. Don't buy into the common belief that your first answer is always your best answer. There have been numerous studies on the topic of changing answers on multiple-choice and true–false tests, dating all the way back to 1928 (Kuhn, 1988). These studies consistently show that most changed test answers go from being incorrect to correct, resulting in improved test scores (Bauer, Kopp, & Fischer, 2007; Prinsell, Ramsey, & Ramsey, 1994). In one study of more than 1,500 students' midterm exams in an introductory psychology course, it was discovered that when students changed answers, 75% of the time they changed from an incorrect to correct answer (Kruger, Wirtz, & Miller, 2005). These results probably reflect the fact that students often catch mistakes when reading the question again or when they find some information later in the test that causes them to reconsider (and correct) their first answer to an earlier test question.

If you have good reason to think an answer change should be made, don't be afraid to make it. The only exception to this general rule is when you find yourself changing many of your original answers; this may indicate that you were not well prepared for the exam and are just doing a lot of guessing and second-guessing.

However, be sure you don't overthink the question and talk yourself into changing a correct answer. Sometimes "go with your gut" is the best decision if you are not sure. Don't change an answer if you are not sure the new answer is correct.

Think About It—Journal Entry 7.4

On multiple-choice exams, do you ever change your original choice?
_____

If you do make changes, what's your usual reason for doing so?
_____
_____
_____
_____
_____

Strategies for Answering Essay Questions

Along with multiple-choice questions, essay questions are among the most common types of test questions on high school exams. The following strategies are recommended for strengthening your performance on essay questions.

1. **Look for "mental action" verbs in the question that point to the type of thinking your teacher expects you to demonstrate in your answer. Box 7.2** contains a list of thinking verbs you're likely to see in essay questions and the type of mental action typically called for by each of these verbs. As you read this list, place a check mark next to the verbs that represent a type of thinking you've rarely or never been asked to do in the past.

BOX 7.2

Mental Action Verbs Commonly Found in Essay-Test Questions

Analyze. Break the topic down into its key parts and evaluate the parts in terms of their accuracy, strengths and weaknesses.

Compare. Identify the similarities and differences between major concepts.

Contrast. Identify the differences between ideas, particularly sharp differences and clashing viewpoints.

Describe. Provide details (e.g., who, what, where, and when).

Discuss. Analyze (break apart) and evaluate the parts (e.g., strengths and weaknesses).

Document. Support your judgment and conclusions with scholarly references or research evidence.

Explain. Provide reasons that answer the questions "why?" and "how?"

> "I keep six honest serving men. They taught me all I knew. Their names are what and why and how and when and where and who."
> —Rudyard Kipling, "The Elephant's Child," The Just-So Stories

Illustrate. Supply concrete examples or specific instances.

Interpret. Draw your own conclusion and explain why you came to that conclusion.

Support. Back up your ideas with logical reasoning, persuasive arguments, or statistical evidence.

Think About It—Journal Entry 7.5

Which of the mental actions listed in **Box 7.2** was most often required on your high school writing assignments?

_____
_____
_____
_____

Which was least often (or never) required?

_____
_____
_____
_____

2. **Make an outline of your key ideas before you start writing sentences.** First, do a quick "information dump" by jotting down the main points you plan to make in your essay answer in outline form. Outlines are effective for several reasons:
   - **An outline ensures you don't forget to include your most powerful points.** The points listed in your outline serve as memory-retrieval cues that help you remember the "big picture" before getting lost in all the details.
   - **An outline earns you points by improving your answer's organizational quality.** In addition to reminding you of the points you need to make, an outline gives you a plan for ordering your ideas in a sequence that flows smoothly from beginning to middle to end. One factor teachers consider when awarding points for an essay answers is how well that answer is organized. An outline will make your answer's organization clearer and more coherent to the reader, which will increase the amount of points you're awarded.
   - **An outline helps reduce test anxiety.** By organizing your points ahead of time, you can focus on expressing (writing) those points without the added stress of figuring out *what* you're going to say at the same time you're trying to figure out *how* to say it.
   - **An outline can add points to answers you don't have time to complete.** If you run out of test time before writing out your full answer to an essay question, an outline shows your teacher what you planned to include in your written answer. The outline itself is likely to earn you some points because it demonstrates your knowledge of the major points called for by the question.

Exhibit 1

Margin notes:
- Identical twins
- Adoption
- Parents/family tree
- 6/6

1. There are several different studies that scientists conduct, but one study that they conduct is to find out how genetics can influence human behavior in <u>identical twins</u>. Since they are identical, they will most likely end up very similar in behavior because of their identical genetic makeup. Although environment has some impact, genetics are still a huge factor and they will, more likely than not, behave similarly. Another type of study is with <u>parents and their family trees</u>. Looking at a subject's family tree will explain why a certain person is bipolar or depressed. It is most likely caused by a gene in the family tree, even if it was last seen decades ago. Lastly, another study is with adopted children. If an <u>adopted child</u> acts a certain way that is unique to that child, and researchers find the parents' family tree, they will most likely see similar behavior in the parents and siblings as well.

Margin notes:
- No freewill
- No afterlife
- 6/6

2. The monistic view of the mind-brain relationship is so strongly opposed and criticized because there is a belief or assumption that <u>free will</u> is taken away from people. For example, if a person commits a horrendous crime, it can be argued "monistically" that the chemicals in the brain were the reason, and that a person cannot think for themselves to act otherwise. This view limits responsibility.

   Another reason that this view is opposed is because it has been said that <u>there is no afterlife</u>. If the mind and brain are one and the same, and there is <u>NO</u> difference, then once the brain is dead and is no longer functioning, so is the mind. Thus, it cannot continue to live beyond what we know today as life. <u>And</u> this goes against many religions, which is why this reason, in particular, is heavily opposed.

A student's answers to short essay questions that demonstrate effective use of bulleted lists or short outlines (in the side margin) to ensure recall of key points.

3. **Get directly to the point on each question.** Avoid elaborate introductions that take up your test time (and your teacher's grading time) but don't earn you any points. An answer that begins with the statement "This is an interesting question that we had a great discussion on in class . . ." is pointless because it doesn't add points to your test score. Timed essay tests often leave you pressed for time; don't waste that time on flowery introductions that contribute nothing to your test grade.

    One effective way to get directly to the point on essay questions is to include part of the question in the first sentence of your answer. For example, suppose the test question asks you to, "Argue for or against capital punishment by explaining how it will or will not reduce the nation's homicide rate." Your first sentence could be, "Capital punishment will not reduce the homicide rate for the following reasons . . ." Thus, your first sentence becomes your thesis statement—it points you directly to the major points you're going to make in your answer and earns immediate points for your answer.

4. **Answer essay questions with as much detail as possible.** Don't assume that your teacher already knows what you're talking about or will be bored by details. Instead, take the approach that you're

writing to someone who knows little or nothing about the subject—as if you're an expert teacher who is explaining it from scratch.

5. **Support your points with evidence—facts, statistics, quotes, or examples.** When you're answering essay questions, take on the mindset of a lawyer: make your case by presenting concrete evidence (exhibit A, exhibit B, etc.).
6. **Leave space between your answers to each essay question.** This strategy will enable you to easily add information to your original answer if you recall something later in the test that you would like to include.
7. **Proofread your answers for spelling and grammar.** Before turning in your test, proofread what you've written and correct any spelling or grammatical errors you find. Catching and correcting clerical errors will improve your test score. Even if your teacher doesn't explicitly state that grammar and spelling count toward your grade, these mechanical mistakes are still likely to influence your teacher's overall evaluation of your written work.
8. **Neatness counts.** Many years of research indicate that neatly written essays are scored higher than sloppy ones, even if the answers are essentially the same (Huck & Bounds, 1972; Hughes, Keeling, & Tuck, 1983; Pai et al., 2010). These findings aren't surprising when you consider that grading essay answers is a time-consuming, labor-intensive task that requires your teacher to plod through multiple answers written by students with multiple styles of handwriting—ranging from crystal clear to quasi-cryptic. If you make your teacher's job a little easier by writing as clearly as possible and cleaning up any sloppy markings before turning in your test, you're likely to earn more points for your answers.

> **NOTE**
>
> As a general rule, it's better to over-explain than under-explain your answers to essay questions.

Strategies for Online Tests

More teachers are using technology to enhance their courses. It is very possible that you could have to take an online test even when you are not taking an online course. When taking a test online, you should always read the instructions carefully. Below are some things you should consider when taking online tests.

1. **Online tests are often timed.** Because you are taking these tests outside of class, you are able to use your notes and books. For this reason, many teachers will place a time limit on the test. If you do not complete the test in time, it will shut off when your time is up and you won't be able to do the rest of the test. Be sure to study for online timed tests. You will not have enough time to look up all of the answers, and if you don't study, you won't do well.
2. **Backtracking might be prohibited.** Sometimes you have to answer a question before you can move on to the next question, and once you move on, you cannot go back and change an answer. If this is a timed test, be sure to use your time wisely and don't spend too much time on any one question.

If you have not taken an online test before, be sure to ask your teacher what to expect. Online tests can be created just like an in-class test. Don't assume that online tests will be made up of only multiple-choice and true–false questions.

Be sure you do not wait until the last minute to take your online test. Because you are dealing with technology something can (and often will) go wrong. Be prepared for something to go wrong (e.g., you lose your internet connection in the middle of the test) by giving yourself enough time to deal with any problems that might arise during the test.

When taking online tests, be sure you are using a reliable computer and you are free from anything that could take your focus away from the test (e.g., cell phone, children, etc.). If something does go wrong during the test, be sure to contact your teacher immediately.

Post-Test Strategies: What to Do *After* Receiving Your Test Results

Successful test performance involves both forethought (preparation before the test) and afterthought (reflection after the test). Often, when students get a test back, they check to see what grade they got, then stuff it in a binder or toss it into the nearest wastebasket. Don't fall prey to this unproductive habit; instead, use your test results as feedback to improve your future performance. Reflect on your results and ask yourself: How can I learn from this? How can I put it to use to correct my mistakes and repeat my successes? Remember: A test score isn't an end result; it may tell you where you are now, but it doesn't tell you where you'll end up. Use your results as a means to another end—a higher score on the next test.

> "When you make a mistake, there are only three things you should do about it: admit it; learn from it; and don't repeat it."
> —Paul "Bear" Bryant, legendary college football coach

Think About It—Journal Entry 7.6

What do you usually do with tests and assignments after they're returned to you? Why?

_____
_____
_____
_____
_____
_____

NOTE

If you do poorly on an exam, don't get bitter—get better. View your mistakes in terms of what they can do for you, not to you. A poor test performance can be turned into a productive learning experience, particularly if it occurs early in the course when you're still learning the rules of the game. You can use your test results as a valuable source of feedback for improving your future performance and final course grade.

In the movie and record industry, if the first cut isn't successful, additional "takes" ("take two," "take three," etc.) are made until it's done right. Successful students do the same thing: If they make a mistake on "take one," they stick with it and continue working to improve their performance on the next take.

©Lightspring/Shutterstock.com

In the movies, a clipboard is used to signal the next take (shooting) if the previous take was unsuccessful. Take the same approach to your test performances. If you make a mistake, consider it "take one," learn from it, and approach the next take with the mindset that you're going to improve your previous performance.

"A man who has committed a mistake and doesn't correct it is committing another mistake."
—Confucius, ancient Chinese philosopher and educator

Listed below are strategies you can use to transform your test results into performance-enhancing feedback.

1. **When you get a test back, determine where you gained points and lost points.** Pinpoint what went right so you do it again, and troubleshoot what went wrong so you don't make the same mistake again. On test questions where you lost points, use the strategies summarized in **Box 7.3** to pinpoint the source of the problem.

BOX 7.3

Strategies for Pinpointing the Source of Lost Points on Tests

On test questions where you lost points, identify the stage in the learning process where the breakdown occurred by asking yourself the following questions.

- **Did I have the information I needed to answer the question correctly?** If you didn't have the information needed to answer the question, where should you have acquired it in the first place? Was it information presented in class that didn't get into your notes? If yes, consider adopting strategies for improving your classroom listening and note-taking. If the missing information was contained in your assigned reading, check whether you're using effective reading strategies. (See Chapter 5.)

- **Did I have the information but didn't study it because I didn't think it was important?** If you didn't expect the information to appear on the test, review the strategies for detecting the most important information delivered during class classes and in reading assignments.

- **Did I study it, but didn't retain it?** Not remembering information you studied may mean one of three things:

  (a) You didn't learn it deeply and didn't lay down a strong enough memory trace in your brain for you to recall it at test time. This suggests you need to put in more study time or use a different study strategy to learn it more deeply. (See Chapter 5.)

BOX 7.3 (CONT)

(b) You may have tried to cram in too much study time just before the exam and may have not given your brain time enough to "digest" (consolidate) the information and store it in long-term memory. The solution may be to distribute your study time more evenly in advance of the next exam and take advantage of the "part-to-whole" study method. (See **p. 100.**)

(c) You studied hard and didn't cram, but you may need to study smarter or more strategically. (See strategies on **p. 119.**)

- Did I study the material but didn't really understand it or learn it deeply? This suggests you may need to self-monitor your comprehension more carefully while studying to track whether you're truly understanding the material and moving beyond "shallow" or "surface" learning. (See **pp. 125–126.**)

- Did I know the material but lost points due to careless test-taking mistakes? If this happened, the solution may simply be to take more time to review your test after completing it and check for absent-minded errors before turning it in. Or, your careless errors may have resulted from test anxiety that interfered with your concentration and memory. If you think this was the factor, consider using strategies for reducing test anxiety. (See **pp. 184–186.**)

2. **Get feedback from your teacher.** Start by noting any written comments your teacher made on your exam; keep these comments in mind when you prepare for the next exam. You can seek additional feedback by making an appointment to speak with your teacher during office hours. Come to the appointment with a positive mindset about improving your next test performance, not complaining about your last test grade.

3. **Seek feedback from professionals in your Learning Center or Academic Support Center.** Tutors and other learning support professionals can also be excellent sources of feedback about adjustments you can make in your test preparation and test-taking strategies. Ask these professionals to take a look at your tests and seek their advice about how to improve your test performance.

4. **Seek feedback from your classmates.** Your peers can also be a valuable source of information on how to improve your performance. You can review your test with other students in class, particularly with students who did well. Their test answers can provide you with models of what type of work your teacher expects on exams. You might also consider asking successful students what they did to be successful, such as how they prepared for the test and what they did during the test.

   Teaming up after tests and assignments *early in the term* is especially effective because it enables you to get a better idea of what the teacher will expect from students throughout the remainder of the course. You can use this information as early feedback to diagnose your initial mistakes, improve your next performance, and raise your overall course grade—while there's still plenty of time in the term to do so. (See **Box 7.4** for a summary of the type of feedback you should seek from others to best strengthen your academic performance.)

BOX 7.4

Key Features of Performance-Enhancing Feedback

When asking for feedback from others on your academic performance, seek feedback that has the following performance-improvement features:

- Effective feedback is *specific*. Seek feedback that identifies precisely what you should do to improve your performance and how you should go about doing it. After a test, seek feedback that provides you with more than information about what your grade is, or why you lost points. Seek specific information about what particular adjustments you can make to improve your next performance.

- Effective feedback is *prompt*. After receiving your grade on a test or assignment, *immediately* review your performance and seek feedback as soon as possible. This is the time when you're likely most motivated to find out what you got right and wrong, and it's also the time when you're most likely to retain the feedback you receive.

- Performance-enhancing feedback is *proactive*. Seek feedback *early* in the learning process. Be sure to ask for feedback at the start of the term. This will leave you with plenty of time and opportunity to use the feedback throughout the term to accumulate points and earn a higher final grade.

Think About It—Journal Entry 7.7

How would you rate your general level of test anxiety during tests? (Circle one.) Explain.

        high   moderate   low

What types of tests or subjects tend to produce the most test stress or anxiety for you?

_____

_____

_____

_____

Why?

_____

_____

_____

_____

_____

Strategies for Reducing Test Anxiety

High levels of anxiety can interfere with the ability to recall information that's been studied and increases the risk of making careless concentration-related errors on tests—such as, overlooking key words in test questions (Fernández-Castillo & Caurcel, 2014; Tobias, 1993). Studies also show that students who experience high levels of test anxiety are more likely to use ineffective "surface"-level study practices that rely on memorization, rather than more effective "deep-learning" strategies that involve seeking meaning and understanding (Biggs & Tang, 2007; Ramsden, 2003). The strategies listed below can help you recognize and minimize test anxiety.

1. **Understand what test anxiety is and what it's not.** Don't confuse anxiety with stress. Stress is a physical reaction that prepares your body for action by arousing and energizing it; this heightened level of arousal and energy can actually strengthen your performance. In fact, to be totally stress-free during an exam may mean that you're too laid back and could care less about how well you're doing. Peak levels of performance—whether academic or athletic—are not achieved by completely eliminating stress. Research shows that experiencing a *moderate* level of stress (neither too high nor too low) during exams and other performance-testing situations serves to maximize alertness, concentration, and memory (Sapolsky, 2004). The key is to keep stress at a manageable level so you can capitalize on its capacity to get you pumped up or psyched up, but prevent it from reaching a level where you become stressed out or psyched out.

    If you often experience the following physical and psychological symptoms during tests, it probably means your stress level is too high and may be accurately called *test anxiety*.

    - You feel bodily symptoms of tension during the test, such as pounding heartbeat, rapid pulse, muscle tension, sweating, or a queasy stomach.
    - You have difficulty concentrating or maintaining your focus of attention while answering test questions.
    - Negative thoughts and feelings rush through your head, such as fear of failure or self-putdowns (e.g., "I always mess up on exams.")
    - You rush through the test just to get it over with and get rid of the uncomfortable feeling you're experiencing.
    - Even though you studied and know the material, you go blank during the test and forget much of what you studied. However, after turning in the test and leaving the test situation, you're often able to remember the information you were unable to recall during the exam.

2. **Use effective test preparation strategies prior to the test.** Test-anxiety research indicates that high school students who prepare well for tests and use effective study strategies prior to tests—such as those discussed in this chapter—experience less test anxiety during

tests (Zeidner, 1995; Zohar, 1998). Studies also show that there is a strong relationship between test anxiety and procrastination—that is, students who put off studying to the very last minute are more likely to report higher levels of test anxiety (Carden, Bryant, & Moss, 2004). The high level of pretest tension caused by last minute rushing to prepare for an exam often carries over to the test itself, resulting in higher levels of tension during the exam. Furthermore, late night cramming deprives the brain of stress-relieving dream (REM) sleep (Voelker, 2004), causing the sleep-deprived student to experience higher levels of anxiety the following day—the day of the test.

3. **Stay focused on the test in front of you, not the students around you.** Don't spend valuable test time looking at what others are doing and wondering whether they're doing better than you are. If you came to the test well prepared and still find the test difficult, it's very likely that other students are finding it difficult too. If you happen to notice that other students are finishing before you do, don't assume they breezed through the test or that they're smarter than you. Their faster finish may simply reflect the fact that they didn't know many of the answers and decided to give up and get out, rather than prolong the agony.

4. **During the test, concentrate on the here and now.** Devote your attention fully to answering the test question that you're currently working on; don't spend time thinking (and worrying) about the test's outcome or what your grade will be.

5. **Focus on the answers you're getting right and the points you're earning, rather than worrying about what you're getting wrong and how many points you're losing.** Our thoughts can influence our emotions (Ellis, 2004), and positive emotions—such as those associated with optimism and a sense of accomplishment—can improve mental performance by enhancing the brain's ability to process, store, and retrieve information (Fredrickson & Branigan, 2005). One way to maintain a positive mindset is to keep in mind that high school tests are often designed to be more difficult than middle school tests, so it's less likely that students will get 90% to 100% of the total points. You can still achieve a good grade on a high school test without having to achieve a near-perfect test score.

6. **Don't forget that it's just a test, not a measure of your intelligence, academic ability, or self-worth.** No single test can measure your true intellectual capacity or academic talent. In fact, the test grade you earn may not be a true indicator of how much you've actually learned. A low test grade also doesn't mean you're not capable of doing better work or destined to end up with a poor grade in the course—particularly if you adopt a "growth mindset" that views mistakes as learning opportunities and uses test results as feedback for improving future performance.

7. **If you continue to experience test anxiety after trying to overcome it on your own, seek assistance from a professional in your Learning (Academic Support) Center or Counseling Office.** You can try to overcome test anxiety (or any other personal issue) through the use of self-help strategies. However, if the problem persists after you've done your best to overcome it,

there's no need to keep struggling on your own; instead, it's probably time to seek help from others. This doesn't mean you're weak or incompetent; it means you have the emotional intelligence and resourcefulness to realize your limitations and capitalize on the support networks available to you.

CHAPTER SUMMARY AND HIGHLIGHTS

Effective performance on high school tests involves strategies used in advance of the test, during the test, and after test results are returned. Good test performance starts with good test preparation and awareness of the type of test questions you will be expected to answer (e.g., multiple-choice or essay). Test questions can be classified into two major categories, depending on the type of memory required to answer them: (1) *recognition* questions and (2) *recall* questions. Each of these types of questions tests your knowledge and memory in a different way.

Recognition test questions ask you to select or choose the correct answer from choices provided for you. Falling into this category are multiple-choice, true–false, and matching questions. These test questions don't require you to supply or produce the correct answer on your own; instead, you recognize or pick out the correct answer. Since recognition test questions ask you to recognize or select the correct answer from among answers provided for you, reviewing your class notes and textbook highlights may be an effective study strategy for multiple-choice and true–false test questions because it matches the type of mental activity you'll be asked to perform on the exam—which is to read test questions and look for the correct answer.

Recall test questions, on the other hand, require you to retrieve information you've studied and reproduce it on your own. This means you have to recall (re-call or "call back") the information you studied and supply it yourself. Recall test questions include essay and short answer questions; these questions don't involve answer recognition, but answer *production*—you produce the answer in writing. Studying for these types of test questions require *retrieval*—such as reciting the information without looking at it.

Effective test performance not only involves effective test-preparation strategies, but also effective test-taking strategies. For multiple-choice tests, effective test-taking strategies include using a *process-of-elimination* approach to weed out incorrect answers before identifying the best option, and *test-wise* strategies that use the wording of test questions to increase the likelihood of choosing the correct answer (e.g., choosing the longest answer and eliminating answers that contain absolute truths or broad generalizations).

Lastly, effective test performance involves carefully reviewing test results and using them as feedback to improve your future performance and final course grade. When test results are returned, determine where you earned and lost points. Pinpoint what went right so you continue doing it, and troubleshoot what went wrong so you prevent it from happening again.

Learning More through the World Wide Web: Internet-Based Resources

For additional information on strategic test-taking and managing test anxiety, see the following websites:

Test-Taking Strategies:
https://miamioh.edu/student-life/rinella-learning-center/academic-counseling/self-help/test-taking/index.html
https://www.stmarys-ca.edu/academics/academic-resources-support/student-academic-support-services/tutorial-academic-skills-8

Overcoming Test Anxiety:
http://www.studygs.net/tstprp8.htm
http://www.sic.edu/files/uploads/group/34/PDF/TestAnxiety.pdf

References

Bauer, D., Kopp, V., & Fischer, M. R. (2007). Answer changing in multiple choice assessment: change that answer when in doubt—and spread the word! *BMC Medical Education*, 7, 28–32.

Biggs, J., & Tang, C. (2007) *Teaching for quality learning at university* (3rd ed.) Buckingham: SRHE and Open University Press.

Carden, R., Bryant, C., & Moss, R. (2004). Locus of control, test anxiety, academic procrastination, and achievement among college students. *Psychological Reports*, 95(2) 581–582.

Carey, B. (2014). *How we learn*. London: Random House.

Ellis, A. (2004) Rational emotive behavior Therapy: It works for me—It can work for you. Amherst, NY: Prometheus Books.

Fernández-Castillo, A., & Caurcel, M. J. (2014). State test-anxiety, selective attention and concentration in university students. *International Journal of Psychology*, 50(4), 265–271.

Flippo, R. F., & Caverly, D. C. (2009). *Handbook of college reading and study strategy research* (2nd ed.). New York: Lawrence Erlbaum Associates.

Fredrickson, B. L., & Branigan, C. (2005). Positive emotions broaden the scope of attention and thought-action repertoires. *Cognition & Emotion*, 19, 313–332.

Glenberg, A, M. (1997). What memory is for. *Behavioral and Brain Sciences*, 20, 1–55.

Glenberg, A. M., Schroeder, J. L., & Robertson, D. A. (1998). Averting the gaze disengages the environment and facilitates remembering. *Memory & Cognition*, 26(4), 651–658.

Godden, D., & Baddeley, A. (1975). Context dependent memory in two natural environments. *British Journal of Psychology*, 66(3), 325–331.

Haas, R. (1994). *Eat smart, think smart*. New York: HarperCollins.

Huck, S., & Bounds, W. (1972). Essay grades: An interaction between graders' handwriting clarity and the neatness of examination papers. *American Educational Research Journal*, 9(2), 279–283.

Hughes, D. C., Keeling, B., & Tuck, B. F. (1983). Effects of achievement expectations and handwriting quality on scoring essays. *Journal of Educational Measurement*, 20(1), 65–70.

Jensen, E. (2005). *Teaching with the brain in mind* (2nd ed.). Alexandria, VA: Association for Supervision and Curriculum Development.

Kruger, J., Wirtz, D., & Miller, D. (2005). Counterfactual thinking and the first instinct fallacy. *Journal of Personality and Social Psychology*, 88, 725–735.

Kuhn, L. (1988). What should we tell students about answer changing? *Research Serving Teaching*, 1(8).

Miller, M. D., Linn, R. L., & Gronlund, N. E. (2012). *Measurement and assessment in teaching* (7th ed.). Englewood Cliffs, NJ: Pearson.

National Resource Center for the First-Year Experience and Students in Transition (2004). *The 2003 Your First College Year (YFCY) Survey*. Columbia, SC: Author.

Pai, M. R., Sanji, N., Pai, P. G. & Kotian, S. (2010). Comparative assessment in pharmacology multiple choice questions versus essay with focus on gender differences. *Journal of Clinical and Diagnostic Research* [serial online], 4(3), 2515–2520.

Phillips, G. W. (2005). Does eating breakfast affect the performance of college students on biology exams? *Bioscene, 30*(4), 15–19.

Prinsell, C. P, Ramsey, P. H., & Ramsey, P. P. (1994). Score gains, attitudes, and behaviour changes due to answer-changing Instruction. *Journal of Educational Measurement, 31,* 327–337.

Ramsden, P. (2003). *Learning to teach in higher education* (2nd ed.). London: RoutledgeFalmer.

Rankin CH, Abrams T, Barry RJ, Bhatnagar S, Clayton DF, Colombo J, Coppola G, Geyer MA, Glanzman DL, Marsland S, McSweeney FK, Wilson DA, Wu CF, Thompson RF (2009) Habituation revisited: an updated and revised description of the behavioral characteristics of habituation. Neurobiol Learn Mem 92:135–138

Reed, S. K. (2013). *Cognition: Theory and applications* (3rd ed.). Belmont, CA: Wadsworth/Cengage.

Roediger, H., & Karpicke, J. (2006). The power of testing memory: Basic research and implications for educational practice. *Perspectives on Psychological Science, 1*(3), 181–210.

Sapolsky, R. (2004). *Why zebras don't get ulcers.* New York: W. H. Freeman.

Schab, F. R., & Crowder, R.G. (2014). *Memory for odors.* New York: Psychology Press.

Schroll, R. M. (2006). Effects of breakfast on memory retention of students at the college level. *Saint Martin's University Biology Journal, 1,* 35–50.

Smith, S., & Vela, E. (2001). Environmental context-dependent memory: A review and meta-analysis. *Psychonomic Bulletin & Review, 8*(2), 203–220.

Sprenger, M. (1999). *Learning and memory: The brain in action.* Alexandria, VA: Association for Supervision and Curriculum Development.

Thayer, R. E. (1997). *The origin of everyday moods: Managing energy, tension, and stress.* New York: Oxford University Press.

Tobias, S. (1993). *Overcoming math anxiety.* New York: W.W. Norton.

Tulving, E. (1983). *Elements of episodic memory.* Oxford: Clarendon Press/Oxford University Press.

Ueda, Y., Wang, M. F., Irei, A. V., Sarukura, N., Sakai, T., & Hsu, T. F. (2011). Effect of dietary lipids on longevity and memory in SAMP8 mice. *Journal of Nutritional Science Vitaminol, 57*(1), 36-41.

Ulus, I. H., Scally, M. C., & Wurtman, R. C. (1977). Choline potentiates the induction of adrenal tyrosine hydroxylase by reserpine, probably by enhancing the release of acetylcholine. Life Sci 21:145–148.

Voelker, R. (2004). Stress, sleep loss, and substance abuse create potent recipe for college depression. *Journal of the American Medical Association, 291,* 2177–2179.

Willingham, D. B. (2009). *Cognition: The thinking animal.* Upper Saddle River, NJ: Pearson.

Zeidner, M. (1995). Adaptive coping with test situations: A review of the literature. *Educational Psychologist, 30*(3), 123–133.

Zohar, D. (1998). An additive model of test anxiety: role of exam-specific expectations. *Journal of Educational Psychology, 90,* 330–340.

CHAPTER 7 EXERCISES

7.1 QUOTE REFLECTIONS

Review the sidebar quotes contained in this chapter and select two that were especially meaningful or inspirational to you.

For each quote, provide a three- to five-sentence explanation why you chose it.

7.2 SELF-ASSESSMENT OF TEST-TAKING HABITS AND STRATEGIES

Rate yourself in terms of how frequently you use these test-taking strategies according to the following scale:
4 = always, 3 = sometimes, 2 = rarely, 1 = never

1.	I take tests in the same seat I usually sit in to take class notes.	4 3 2 1
2.	I answer easier test questions first.	4 3 2 1
3.	I use a process-of-elimination approach on multiple-choice questions to eliminate choices until I find one that is correct or appears to be the most accurate option.	4 3 2 1
4.	Before answering essay questions, I look for key action words indicating what type of thinking I should display in my answer (e.g., "analyze," "compare").	4 3 2 1
5.	On essay questions, I outline or map out the major ideas I'll include in my answer before I start writing sentences.	4 3 2 1
6.	I look for information included on the test that may help me answer difficult questions or that may help me remember information I've forgotten.	4 3 2 1
7.	I leave extra space between my answers to essay questions in case I want to come back and add more information later.	4 3 2 1
8.	I carefully review my work, double-checking for errors and skipped questions before turning in my tests.	4 3 2 1

Self-Assessment Reflections

Which of the above strategies do you already use?

Of the ones you don't use, which one are you *most* likely to implement and *least* likely to implement? Why?

190 ■ Chapter 7: Test-Taking Skills and Strategies

7.3 MIDTERM SELF-EVALUATION

Using the form below, list the courses you're taking this term and the grades you are currently receiving in each of these courses. If you don't know what your grade is, take a few minutes to check your syllabus for your teacher's grading policy and add up your scores on completed tests and assignments; this should give you at least a rough idea of where you stand in your courses. If you're having difficulty determining your grade in a course, even after checking your course syllabus and returned tests or assignments, ask your teacher how you could estimate your current grade.

         Course Title   **Grade**

1. _____
2. _____
3. _____
4. _____
5. _____

Reflection Questions

1. Were these the grades you *expected*? If not, were they better or worse than you anticipated?
2. Were these the grades you were *hoping* for? Are you pleased or disappointed?
3. Do you see any patterns in your performance that suggest what you're doing well and what you need to improve?
4. If you had to pinpoint one action you could immediately take to improve your lowest course grades, what would it be?

7.4 CHAPTER 7 REFLECTION

What are some ways that you currently prepare for tests that do not seem to be working? Why do you think these methods of preparing for tests do not work?

List and explain three ways you can change your current methods of preparing for tests that you believe will help you perform better on tests.

1.

2.

3.

What are two things you can do during the test that will help you perform better?

1.

2.

What are two things you can do after you get your test back that can help you perform better on future tests?

1.

2.

FINANCIAL LITERACY

Managing Money and Minimizing Debt

CHAPTER PREVIEW

Effective money management strategies will help you minimize unnecessary spending, reduce accumulation of debt, and improve your overall quality of life. This chapter provides you with specific strategies for tracking cash flow, minimizing and avoiding debt, balancing time spent on schoolwork and employment, and making wise decisions about spending and saving. You can use many of these strategies in high school and others can be used if and when you decide to enroll in college.

LEARNING GOAL

Become more aware, knowledgeable, and strategic about managing money, financing your high school education and handling your future finances.

THOUGHT STARTER

 Think About It—Journal Entry 8.1

Complete the following sentence with the first thought that comes to mind:

To me, money is . . .

_____
_____
_____
_____

From *Thriving in the Community College & Beyond: Strategies for Academic Success and Personal Development*, Third Edition, by Joseph Cuseo, Aaron Thompson, and Julie McLaughlin. Copyright © 2016 by Kendall Hunt Publishing Company. Reprinted by permission.

One reason why money management is growing in importance for high school students is the availability and convenience of credit cards. It's never been easier for students to access, use, and abuse credit cards. Credit agencies and bureaus now closely monitor students' credit card payments and routinely report their "credit score" to credit card companies and banks. Since research shows that there is a statistical relationship between using credit cards responsibly and being a responsible employee (Ring, 1997; Susswein, 1995), employers check these credit scores and use them as indicators or predictors of how responsible a student will be as an employee. Thus, being irresponsible with credit while in school can affect a student's ability to land a job after (or during) high school. Students' credit scores also affect their likelihood of qualifying for car loans and home loans as well as their ability to rent an apartment (Pratt, 2011). High school graduates today can do everything right while they are in high school or in the workplace, such as get good grades, get involved on school, and working or getting work experience before graduating, but a poor credit history can do harm in the short and long term by reducing their chance of obtaining credit, their job prospects, and buy a home. (Nellie Mae, 2005; Sallie Mae, 2009).

Furthermore, accumulating high levels of debt while in school is associated with higher levels of student stress (Nelson et al., 2008), lower academic performance (Susswein, 1995), and greater risk of withdrawing (Ring, 1997). On the positive side of the ledger, studies show that when students learn to use effective money management strategies (such as those discussed below), they can reduce unnecessary spending, minimize accumulation of debt, and lower their overall level of stress (Health & Soll, 1996; Kidwell & Turrisi, 2004; Walker, 1996).

Even now is a good time for you to be thinking about your finances. Keep in mind that, depending on your situation, high school and any type of post-secondary training will have a cost. Be thinking about how you will manage that cost now. If you plan on working right out of high school, then you too must think about how you will support yourself.

Sources of Income for Financing a College Education

If you decide to go to college, your income will likely come from three sources.

- Loans that must be repaid,
- Scholarships or grants that are not repaid, and
- Salary earned from part-time or full-time work.

The *Free Application for Federal Student Aid (FAFSA)* is the application used by the U.S. Department of Education to determine financial aid eligibility for students. It asks for personal and family financial information to determine a student's eligibility for federal, state, and college-sponsored financial aid, including grants, loans, and work-study employment. A formula is used to determine the student's *estimated family contribution (EFC)*—the amount of money estimated by the government that a family can contribute to the educational costs incurred by a family member attending college.

No fee is charged to complete the application, so you should complete an application every year to determine your eligibility for financial aid. (See the Financial Aid Office on your campus for a copy of the FAFSA form and for help completing it.)

Student Loans

Loans need to be repaid after a student graduates from college. Listed below are some of the more well-known, federally funded student loan programs.

- *The Federal Perkins Loan*: a low-interest loan awarded to exceptionally needy students. Repayment of the loan begins nine months after a student is no longer enrolled at least half-time.
- *The Federal Subsidized Stafford Loan*: available to students enrolled at least half-time, has a fixed interest rate established each year on July 1. The federal government pays the interest on the loan while the student is enrolled. Repayment for this loan begins six months after a student is no longer enrolled at least half-time.
- *The Federal Unsubsidized Stafford Loan*: a loan not based on need that has the same interest rate as the Federal Subsidized Stafford Loan. Students are responsible for paying the interest on this loan while they're enrolled in high school. Repayment for this loan begins 6 months after a student is no longer enrolled at least half-time.

Keep in mind that federal loans and private loans differ in the following ways:

- *Federal* loans have fixed interest rates that are comparatively low (currently less than 7%) and cannot go higher.
- *Private* loans have variable interest rates that are very high (currently more than 15%) and can go higher at any time.

Despite the much higher interest rate of private loans, they're the fastest-growing type of loans taken out by college students—largely because of aggressive, and sometimes misleading, irresponsible, or unethical advertising on loan-shopping websites. Students sometimes think they're getting a federal loan only to find out later they've taken on a more expensive private loan (Hamilton, 2012; Kristof, 2008).

Keep in mind that not all loans are created equal. Compared to private loans, federally guaranteed student loans are relatively low-cost and may be paid off slowly after graduation. On the other hand, private lenders of student loans are like credit card companies; they charge extremely high interest rates (that can go even higher at any time) and the loans must be paid off quickly. Private loans should not be used as a primary loan to help pay for college and they should only be used as a last resort—when no other options are available for covering college expenses.

> "Apply for as much grant aid as possible before borrowing, and then seek lower-interest federal student loans before tapping private ones. There is a lot of student aid that can help make the expense [of college] more manageable."
> —*Sandy Baum, senior policy analyst, College Board (quoted in Gordon, 2009)*

In addition, keep in mind that federal and state regulations require that if you're receiving financial aid, you must maintain "satisfactory academic progress." In most cases, this means you must do the following:

1. Maintain a satisfactory GPA—such as, 2.0 or above. Your entire academic record will be reviewed, even if you have paid for some of the classes with your own resources.
2. Make satisfactory academic progress—such as, 12 to 15 units per semester for full-time students and 6 to 9 hours for part-time students. You must successfully complete approximately 70% of the classes you attempt. Your academic progress will be evaluated at least once per year, usually at the end of each spring semester.
3. Complete a degree or certificate program with a reasonable number of units. There is a maximum number of course hours you can attempt per degree. (Check with your institution's Financial Aid Office for details.)

Student Loans and Credit Scores

Be aware that students loans are a type of loan and can affect your credit score. For many college students, credit is now a reality and will be when they graduate from college. College loans can hurt or enhance your credit score depending on how you treat the loan.

Your credit score is a number that tells lenders and creditors how financially responsible you are. It assists them in judging the level of risk you present to them as a borrower.

This score will dictate how easily you can obtain credit cards, loans, houses, and renting an apartment. The score is based on the following percentages:

- 35% based on payment history: how consistently you pay bills on time
- 30% based on how much you currently owe
- 15% based on credit history: have you had credit before and handled it responsibly?
- 10% based on new credit: how many new applications and acceptances of other credit you've had
- 10% based on types of credit: credit card, student loan, and auto loan.

Thus, having loans (including student loans) can be good or bad and sometimes both, depending on how you use them and how you repay them. Making your student loan payments in full and on time each month will assist your credit score and help you to establish a good credit history. However, missing payments or not paying at all can be devastating to your credit and credit score.

Lastly, if you find yourself temporarily short of funds and need just a small loan to recover, many colleges have an *emergency student loan program*, whereby they provide students with an immediate, interest-free loan to help them cover short-term expenses (e.g., cost of textbooks) or deal with financial emergencies (e.g., accidents and illnesses). Emergency student loans are typically granted within 24 to 48 hours, sometimes even the same day, and usually need to be repaid within two months.

Scholarships

Scholarships are available from many sources, including the institution you choose to attend. They are awarded based on various criteria that may include a written essay, ACT or SAT scores, and high school grade point average (GPA). In addition to academic scholarships, scholarships are awarded based on organizations you may have been a part of, race or ethnicity, the region of the country you live in, athletics, artistic talents, and so on. It is important to remember that all scholarships are competitive and deadlines are observed by the awarding agencies or institutions. Be aware of the application material deadlines and submit your materials well in advance of these deadlines.

You should contact the Financial Aid Office of the institution you are attending to find available scholarships. You can also conduct an Internet search to find many sites that offer scholarship information (like www.fastweb.com), but it is important to remember that you should not enter credit card or bank account information on any site.

Grants

Grants are considered to be gift aid, which typically does not have to be repaid. About two-thirds of all high school students receive grant aid, which, on average, reduces their tuition bills by more than half. The Federal Pell Grant is the largest grant program; it provides need-based aid to low-income undergraduate students. The amount of the grant depends on criteria such as: (1) the anticipated contribution of the family to the student's education (EFC), (2) the cost of the post-secondary institution that the student is attending, and (3) the enrollment status of the student (part-time or full-time). Even though grants do not need to be paid back, students must maintain certain academic standards to remain eligible to receive their grant money.

Planning on joining the Armed Services?

The Montgomery GI Bill–Active Duty, called MGIB for short, provides up to 36 months of education benefits to eligible veterans. Benefits may include, but are not limited to, tuition and fees, a housing allowance, and a books and supplies stipend. Veterans must maintain certain academic standards to receive the benefits. Visit the Office of Veterans Affairs on your campus to get more information (see the following website for more detail: http://www.vba.va.gov/VBA/benefits/factsheets/index.asp#BM4).

Developing a Money Management Plan
Gain Financial Self-Awareness

Development of any good habit begins with the critical first step of self-awareness. Developing effective money-management habits begins with awareness of your *cash flow*—the amount of money you

Chapter 8: Financial Literacy

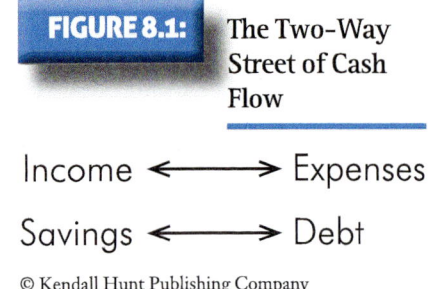

FIGURE 8.1: The Two-Way Street of Cash Flow

Income ⟷ Expenses
Savings ⟷ Debt

© Kendall Hunt Publishing Company

> "Never spend your money before you have it."
> —Thomas Jefferson, third president of the United States and founder of the University of Virginia

have coming in and going out. As illustrated in **Figure 8.1**, cash flow is tracked by monitoring:

- Income—the amount of money you have coming in versus the amount going out (expenses or expenditures), and
- Savings—the amount of money you've earned and not spent versus the amount you've borrowed and haven't paid back (debt).

Once you're aware of the amount of money you have coming in (and from what sources) plus the amount of money you're spending (and for what reasons), your next step is to develop a plan for managing your cash flow. The bottom line is to ensure that the sum of money you have coming in (income) is equal to or greater than the sum of money you have going out (expenses). If the amount of money going out exceeds the amount coming in, you're "in the red" or have "negative cash flow."

Track Your Cash Flow

You can track cash flow by using any of the following tools:

- Checking accounts
- Credit cards
- Charge cards
- Debit cards

Checking Accounts

Long before credit cards were created, a checking account was the method most people used to keep track of their money. Many people still use checking accounts in addition to (or instead of) credit cards. A checking account may be obtained from a bank or credit union; its typical costs include a deposit ($20–$25) to open the account, a monthly service fee (e.g., $10), and small fees for checks. Some banks charge customers a service fee based on the number of checks written; this is a good option if you don't plan to write many checks each month. Look for a checking account that doesn't charge you if your balance drops below a certain minimum figure. If you maintain a high enough *balance* (deposited money in your account) the bank may not charge any extra fees, and if you're able to maintain an even higher balance, some banks may also pay you interest—known as an interest-bearing checking account.

Along with your checking account, banks usually provide you with an automatic teller machine (ATM) card that you can use to get cash. Look for a checking account that offers a free service along with your checking account, rather than one that charges a separate fee for ATM transactions.

A checking account has several advantages:

- You can carry checks instead of cash.
- You have access to cash at almost any time through an ATM.
- You can keep a visible track record of your income and expenses in your checkbook.

- If you manage a checking account responsibly, it can serve as a good credit reference for future loans and purchases.

To make the best use of your checking account, apply the following strategies:

- Whenever you write a check or make an ATM withdrawal, immediately subtract its amount from your *balance* (the amount of money remaining in your account) and determine your new balance.
- Keep a running balance in your checkbook; this will ensure you know exactly how much money you have in your account at all times. It also reduces your risk of *bouncing* a check—writing a check for an amount that exceeds the total amount you have in your account. If you do bounce a check, you'll probably have to pay a charge to the bank and possibly to the business that attempted to cash your bounced check.
- Double-check your checkbook balance with each monthly statement you receive from the bank. Be sure to include the service charges your bank makes to your account; these charges will appear on your monthly statement. Checking your checkbook on a regular basis will enable you to catch errors that you've made or the bank has made. (Banks can and do occasionally make mistakes.)

Credit Cards

A credit card is basically money loaned to you by the credit card company issuing the card, which you pay back to the company on a monthly basis. You can pay the whole bill or a portion of the bill each month—as long as some minimum payment is made. However, for any remaining (unpaid) portion of your bill, you're charged a high interest rate—which can be as much as 30%. Consequently, if you decide to use a credit card, be sure you're able to pay off your whole bill (loan) each month.

If a credit card is used responsibly, it has some key advantages as a money management tool:

- It helps you track your spending habits because the credit card company sends you a monthly statement with an itemized list of all your card-related purchases. This list supplies you with a "paper trail" of what you purchase each month and when you purchased it.
- It provides a convenient way for you to purchase things you need online, which can save time and money that would otherwise be spent traveling to and from stores.
- It allows access to cash whenever and wherever you need it because any bank or ATM that displays your credit card's symbol will give you cash up to a certain limit (usually for a small transaction fee). Keep in mind that some credit card companies charge a higher interest rate for cash *advances* than credit card *purchases*.

- It enables you to establish a personal credit history. If you use a credit card responsibly, you can establish a good credit history that can be used later in life for big ticket purchases—such as a car or home. In effect, responsible use of a credit card shows others from whom you wish to seek credit (or borrow money) that you will pay it back. However, don't buy into the belief that the only way you can establish a good credit history is by using a credit card. It's not your only option; you can also establish a good credit history by responsible use of a checking account and by paying your bills on time.

If you decide to use a credit card, pay attention to its *annual percentage rate (APR)*—the interest rate you pay for previously unpaid monthly balances. This rate can vary from one credit card company to another. Credit card companies also vary in terms of their annual service fee. You'll find that companies charging higher interest rates also charge lower annual fees, and vice versa. As a general rule, if you expect to pay the full balance every month, you're probably better off choosing a credit card that doesn't charge you an annual service fee. On the other hand, if you think you'll need more time to make the full monthly payments, you're probably better off with a credit card company that offers a low interest rate.

Credit card companies also differ from one another in terms of whether they allow a *grace period*—the amount of time you have after receiving your monthly statement to pay back the company without paying additional interest fees. Some companies may allow you a grace period of a full month, while others may provide no forgiveness period and begin charging interest immediately after a payment isn't received by the bill's due date.

Credit cards also differ in terms of their *credit limit* (also known as a "credit line" or "line of credit"), which is the maximum amount of money the credit card company will make available to you. If you're a new customer, most companies will set a credit limit beyond which no additional credit will be granted.

There are advantages of using a credit card, but those advantages are only reaped by using credit cards strategically. If not, its advantages are quickly and greatly outweighed by its disadvantages. Listed here are some strategies for using a credit card in ways that maximize its advantages and minimize its disadvantages.

- **Use a credit card for making purchases conveniently and for tracking the purchases you make; don't use it as a tool for obtaining a long-term loan.** A credit card's main money-management advantage is that it enables you to make purchases with plastic instead of cash. It saves you the inconvenience of having to carry cash or checks and conveniently supplies you with a monthly statement of your purchases, making it easier for you to track and analyze your spending habits.

    The credit provided by a credit card should be seen simply as a short-term loan that must be paid back at the end of every month. Don't use credit cards for long-term credit or long-term loans because their interest rates are outrageously high. Paying such a high rate of interest for a loan is an ineffective (and irresponsible) money-management strategy.

- **Limit yourself to one credit card.** Having more than one credit card means having more accounts to keep track of and more opportunities to accumulate debt. You don't need additional credit cards from department stores, gas stations, or any other profit-making business because they duplicate what your personal credit card already does (plus they typically charge extremely high interest rates for late payments).
- **Make sure you know the specific terms of the agreement.** Credit card companies vary in terms of what they will charge you for not paying your full bill on time and what restrictions they will impose on further use of your card if you accumulate debt. Be sure to read the fine print on your contract; if you have any doubts or questions, contact a representative of the credit card company.
- **Pay off your balance each month** *in full* **and** *on time.* If you pay the full amount of your bill each month, this means you're using your credit card effectively to obtain an interest-free, short-term (1-month) loan. You're just paying *principal*—the total amount of money borrowed and nothing more. However, if your payment is late and you end up paying interest, you're paying more for the items you purchased than their actual ticket price. For instance, if you have an unpaid balance of $500 on your monthly credit bill for merchandise purchased the previous month and you're charged the typical 18% credit card interest rate for late payment, you end up paying $590: $500 (merchandise) + $90 (18% interest to the credit card company).

> "What I don't do that I know I should do is pay my bills on time, like my cell phone and credit cards."
> —First-year student

Credit card companies make their profit by the interest they collect from cardholders who don't pay back their credit on time. Just as procrastinating about completing schoolwork is a poor time-management habit that hurts your grades, procrastinating about paying your credit card bills is a poor money-management habit that hurts your pocketbook by forcing you to pay high interest rates.

> "I need to pay attention to my balance more closely and actually allot certain amounts for certain things."
> —First-year student

Don't allow credit card companies to make profit at your expense. Pay your total balance on time and avoid paying exorbitantly high interest rates. If you can't pay the total amount owed at the end of the month, instead of making the minimum monthly payment, pay as much as you possibly can. If you keep making only the minimum payment each month, you'll begin piling up huge amounts of debt.

> "You'll never get your credit card debt paid off if you keep charging on your card and make only the minimum monthly payment. Paying only the minimum is like using a Dixie cup to bail water from a sinking boat."
> —Eric Tyson, financial counselor and national best-selling author of Personal Finance for Dummies

NOTE

If you keep making charges on your credit card while you have an unpaid balance (debt), you no longer have a grace period to pay back your charges; instead, interest is charged immediately on all your purchases.

BOX 8.1

Credit Cardholders' Bill of Rights Act of 2009

Congress passed legislation in 2009 that enacted certain protections for consumers who use credit cards. Here are the specific reforms that affect college students:

- Creditors are forbidden from offering credit to consumers under the age of 18 (unless they are emancipated under state law, or the consumer's parent or legal guardian is the primary account holder).
- College students without a cosigner will have their credit line limited to the greater amount of 20 percent of their annual gross income or $500. The collective amount of credit available on all credit cards will be limited to 30 percent of the student's annual gross income.
- Creditors are not allowed to open a credit-card account for a college student who does not have a verifiable annual gross income or already has a credit-card account with that creditor or any of its affiliates (Chan, 2009).

Think About It—Journal Entry 8.2

Do you have a credit card? Do you have more than one?

_____

_____

If you have at least one credit card, do you pay off your entire balance each month?

_____

If you don't pay off your entire balance each month:

(a) What's your average unpaid balance per month?

_____

_____

_____

_____

(b) What changes would you have to make in your money-management habits to be able to pay off your entire balance each month?

_____

_____

_____

_____

Charge Cards (a.k.a Smart Cards)

A charge card works similar to a credit card in that you're given a short-term loan for one month; the only difference is that you must pay your bill in full at the end of each month and you cannot carry over any debt from one month to the next. Its major disadvantage relative to a credit card is that it has less flexibility—no matter what your expenses may be for a particular month, you must still pay up or lose your ability to obtain credit for the following month. However, if you're someone who consistently has trouble paying your monthly credit card bill on time, this is an advantage of a charge card because it will prevent you from accumulating debt.

Debit Cards

A debit card looks almost identical to a credit card (e.g., it has a *MasterCard* or *Visa* logo), but it works differently. When you use a debit card, money is immediately taken out or subtracted from your checking account. Like a check or ATM withdrawal, any purchase you make with a debit card is immediately subtracted from your balance. Thus, you can only use money that's already in your account (rather than borrowing money). At the end of the month, you don't receive a bill; instead, you get a statement with information about checks you deposited and cashed, as well as your debit card transactions. If you attempt to purchase something with a debit card that costs more than the amount of money you have in your account, your card will not allow you to do so. Similar to a bounced check, a debit card will not permit you to pay out any money that's not in your account.

Like a credit card, a major advantage of the debit card is that it provides you with the convenience of plastic; however, unlike a credit card, it prevents you from spending beyond your means and accumulating debt. For this reason, many financial advisors recommend using a debit card rather than a credit card (Knox, 2004; Tyson, 2012).

BOX 8.2

Minimize Your Risk of Identity Theft

Identity thieves steal your personal information to make transactions or purchases in your name. This can damage your credit status and cost you time and money to restore your financial credibility. Listed below are key strategies for reducing your risk of identity theft. Even as high school students this is something to be vigilant about. Check your credit report. You are allowed a free credit report every year. There are services that provide credit monitoring, your local bank most likely has this available for a fee.

- Don't share personal identity information over the phone with anyone you don't know and trust, especially your social security or credit card number.
- Don't share identity information over the phone with anyone who claims to be an Internal Revenue Service (IRS) agent and threatens you with arrest or deportation, or who requests personal

BOX 8.2 (CONT)

information the purpose of sending you a refund. The IRS will contact you in writing if it needs anything.
- Don't respond to e-mails from anyone claiming to be from the IRS. This is always a scam because the IRS doesn't initiate contact with taxpayers by e-mail or social media to request personal or financial information. (The only legitimate communication you will receive from the IRS is through postal mail.)
- Don't click on links or open e-mail attachments from anyone unfamiliar to you. Scam artists create fake websites and send "phishing" e-mails—which are attempts to acquire personal information such as usernames, passwords, and credit card details, often using the names of trustworthy electronic sources (e.g., an Internet service provider).
- Don't enter your credit card or bank account information on any websites.
- Install firewalls and virus detection software on your computer, to protect yourself against "cyber crime."
- When using your laptop in public, shield your screen from "shoulder surfers."
- Don't carry your Social Security (SSN) card in your wallet or write it on your checks. Only give out your SSN to people you know and trust.
- Conceal your personal identification number (PIN). Don't supply it to anyone and don't keep it in your wallet.
- Shred documents containing personal information you no longer need. (Some identity thieves are "dumpster divers" who go through the garbage to get your personal information.)
- Compare your receipts with your account statements and credit card statements to be sure there are no transactions you didn't authorize. If you have an online account, you can check your account at any time. It's a good idea to get in the habit of checking it at least once a week (e.g., every Sunday evening).
- If you believe you've been victimized by identity theft, contact your local police department and any of the following credit reporting companies to place a fraud alert:

Experian: https://www.experian.com/freeze/center.html

TransUnion: https://freeze.transunion.com/sf/securityFreeze/landingPage.jsp

Equifax: https://www.freeze.equifax.com/Freeze/jsp/SFF_PersonalIDInfo.jsp

Sources:
Prevent and Report Identity Theft: https://www.irs.gov/Individuals/Identity-Protection

Identity Protection Tips - Internal Revenue Service: www.irs.gov/Individuals/Identity-Protection-Tips

Tips to Avoid Identity Theft: http://www.bbb.org/sacramento/news-events/consumer-tips/2015/03/how-to-avoid-identity-theft/

Developing a Plan for Managing Money and Minimizing Debt

The ultimate goal of money management is to save money and dodge debt. Here are some strategies for accomplishing both of these goals.

Prepare a personal budget. A budget is simply a plan for coordinating income and expenses in a way that ensures you're left with sufficient money to cover your expenses. It enables you to be your own accountant who keeps an accurate account of your own income and expenses.

Sources of expense for high school students typically fall into three categories:

1. *Basic needs or essential necessities*—these are "fixed" expenses because you can't live without them—such as, expenses for food, housing, tuition, textbooks, phone, transportation to and from school, and health-related costs
2. *Incidentals or extras*—these are "flexible" expenses because they're optional or discretionary—you choose to spend at your own discretion or judgment. These expenses usually include:
    - money spent on entertainment, enjoyment, or pleasure (e.g., music, movies, and spring break vacations), and
    - money spent on promoting personal status or self-image (e.g., buying expensive brand name products, fashionable clothes, jewelry, and other personal accessories)
3. *Emergency expenses*—unpredicted, unforeseen, or unexpected expenditures (e.g., costs incurred by unanticipated car repairs or medical services)

Think About It—Journal Entry 8.3

What are your most expensive incidentals (optional purchases)?

What could you do to reduce or eliminate these expenses?

Similar to managing your time, the first step in planning and managing money is to prioritize. Identify your most important expenses—the indispensable necessities you can't live without—and separate them from incidentals—dispensable luxuries you can live without and can be reduced or eliminated if necessary. People easily confuse *essentials* (things they really *need*) with *desirables* (stuff they just

"I shouldn't buy random stuff (like hair dye) and other stuff when I don't need it."
—First-year student

want). For instance, if a piece of merchandise happens to be on sale, it may be a desirable purchase at that time because of its reduced price; however, it's not an essential purchase if you don't need that piece of merchandise at that particular time.

> **NOTE**
>
> Remaining aware of the distinction between essentials that must be purchased and incidentals that may or may not be purchased is an important first step toward budgeting effectively and minimizing debt.

> "I need to save money and not shop so much and impulse buy."
> —First-year student

Postponing short-term satisfaction of material desires is a key element of long-term financial success. Unfortunately, humans are often more motivated by short-range thinking because it produces quicker results and more immediate gratification (Goldstein & Hogarth, 1997; Lowenstein, Read, & Baumeister, 2003). This is why so many people pile up credit card debt; they choose to experience the short-term pleasure of the immediate purchase instead of postponing gratification to save money in the long run.

We need to remain mindful of whether we're spending money *impulsively* on what we want rather than *reflectively* on what we need. The truth is that humans spend money for a host of psychological reasons (conscious or subconscious), many of which are unrelated to actual need. Some people spend money to build their self-esteem or self-image, to combat personal boredom, or because of an emotional "high" they experience when they buy things for themselves (Dittmar, 2004; Furnham & Argyle, 1998). Other people can become obsessed with spending money, shop compulsively, and develop an addiction to purchasing products. Just as Alcoholics Anonymous (AA) functions as a support group for alcoholics, Debtors Anonymous serves as a support group for shopaholics and includes a similar 12-step recovery program.

> "My money management skills are poor. If I have money, I will spend it unless somebody takes it away from me. I am the kind of person who lives from paycheck to paycheck."
> —First-year student

> **NOTE**
>
> What you're willing to sacrifice and save for, and what you're willing to spend money on and go into debt for, says a lot about who you are and what you value.

Make all your bills visible and, if possible, pay them as soon as you see them. When bills are in your sight, they're on your mind and you're less likely to forget to pay them, or forget to pay them on time. Try to get in the habit of paying a bill as soon as you open it and have it in your hands, rather than setting it aside and running the risk of forgetting to pay it (or losing it altogether).

You can increase the visibility of your bill payments by creating and posting a financial calendar on which you record key fiscal deadlines for the academic year (e.g., due dates for tuition payments, residential bills, and financial aid applications). In addition, consider setting up an online banking program that will enable you to visually track your transactions and make credit card payments automatically. The advantage of an online account is that it's paperless and you don't have to deal with bills sent to you through postal mail. However, its disadvantage is that it doesn't appear in tangible form in your mailbox—which provides you with clear, visual reminder to pay it. Therefore, if you set up an online account, get into an ongoing habit of checking it. Otherwise, what's out of sight stays out of mind and your bills may not get paid on time.

Live within your means. Simply stated: Don't purchase what you can't afford. If you're spending more money than you're taking in, it means you're living *beyond* your means. To begin living *within* your means, you have two options:

1. Decrease your expenses (reduce your spending), or
2. Increase your income (earn more money).

AUTHOR'S EXPERIENCE

I remember my mom always telling me to make sure I turned the lights off when I left the room. At the time, I didn't understand nor did I care much about it. As I grew older, I understood why she was always looking for ways to save money. My mother raised two boys on her own and had to make ends meet with a tight budget. Every dollar saved put food on the table and clothes on my back. She always looked for ways to stretch a dollar. At times, school shopping was a yard sale or she would bring home discounted groceries from work. I soon learned to watch carefully how I spent my money... and, yes, I use discount coupons to this day. For most people, money is a finite resource. Thus, learning how to manage it is a valuable skill.

—*Shane Shope*

Most students work while attending school (Kingkade, 2014) and they work so many hours that it interferes with their academic performance and educational progress (King, 2005). Thus, for most students who find themselves in debt, their best option is not to work more hours for more money, but to reduce their spending on nonessentials and live within their means.

> "We choose to spend more money than we have today. Choose debt, or choose freedom, it's your choice."
> —Bill Pratt, *Extra Credit: The 7 Things Every College Student Needs to Know About Credit, Debt & Cash*

 Think About It—Journal Entry 8.4

Are you working while attending high school?

If you're working:
a) How many hours per week do you currently work?

b) Are you working for things you need or want?

_____

_____

c) Do you think that working is interfering with your academic performance or progress? Why or why not?

_____

_____

_____

_____

> **NOTE**
> Advertising creates product familiarity, not product quality. The more money manufacturers pay for advertising and creating well-known brands, the more money we pay for their product.

Economize. Intelligent consumers use critical thinking skills when purchasing products. We can be frugal or thrifty without compromising the quality of our purchases. We could pay less to see the same movie in the late afternoon than to see it at night. Why pay more for brand name products that are exactly the same as less expensive products? For instance, why pay 33% more for Advil or Tylenol when we can get the same pain-relieving ingredient (ibuprofen or acetaminophen) from a generic brand? When we buy brand name products, what we're often paying for is all the advertising these brand name companies pay the media and celebrities to promote their products.

Downsize. Cut down or cut out spending for products you don't need. Avoid conspicuous consumption or exhibitionistic (look-at-me) spending just to keep up with or show off to your friends. Don't allow peer pressure to determine your spending habits; your consumer decisions should reflect your ability to think critically, not your desire to conform socially.

> "It is preoccupation with possessions, more than anything else, that prevents us from living freely and nobly."
> —Bertrand Russell, British philosopher and mathematician

Save money by living with others rather than living alone. You lose some privacy when you share living quarters, but you save a substantial amount of money. Living with others may also bring with it the fringe social benefit of spending time with people (roommates or housemates) with whom you're compatible and whose company you enjoy.

> "If you would be wealthy, think of saving as well as getting."
> —Benjamin Franklin, 18th-century inventor, newspaper writer, and cosigner of the Declaration of Independence

Give gifts of time instead of money. Spending money on gifts for family, friends, and romantic partners isn't the only way to show you care. The point of gift giving isn't to show others you aren't cheap, it's to show you care. You can demonstrate caring by making something special or doing something meaningful for those you care about. Gifts of time and kindness are often more personal and special than store-bought gifts.

AUTHOR'S EXPERIENCE

When my wife (Mary) and I were first dating, I was trying to gain weight because I was on the thin side. One day when I came home from school, I found this hand-delivered package in front of my apartment door. I opened it up and there was a homemade loaf of whole wheat bread made from scratch by Mary. That gift didn't cost her much money, but she took the time to do it and she remembered to do something that was important to me (gaining weight). That gift really touched me; it's a gift I've never forgotten. Since I eventually married Mary and we're still happily married, I guess you could say that inexpensive loaf of bread was a "gift that kept on giving."

—*Joe Cuseo*

Develop your own money-saving strategies and habits. You can save money by doing little things that eventually add up to big savings over time. The following tips for saving money were suggested by students in a college-success course. Some of these strategies may work for you as well.

- Don't carry a lot of extra money in your wallet. (It's just like food; if it's easy to get to, you'll be more likely to eat it up.)
- Shop with a list—get in, get what you need, and get out.
- Put all your extra change in a jar.
- Put extra cash in a piggy bank that requires you to smash the piggy to get at it.
- Seal your savings in an envelope.
- When you get extra money get it immediately into the bank (and out of your hands).
- Bring (don't buy) your lunch.
- Hide your credit card or put it in the freezer so that you don't use it on impulse.
- Use cash (instead of credit cards) because you can set aside a certain amount of it for yourself and you can clearly see how much of it you have at the start of a week (as well as how much is left at any point during the week).

> "The safest way to double your money is to fold it over and put it in your pocket."
> —Kin Hubbard, American humorist, cartoonist, and journalist

Think About It—Journal Entry 8.5

Do you use any of the money-saving strategies on the above list? Which one(s)?

_____
_____
_____
_____
_____

Chapter 8: Financial Literacy

What money-saving strategies do you use that could be added to the above list?

_____

_____

_____

_____

_____

Do's

Pay yourself first and learn to save. Make it a habit. Plan ahead. Know what you're spending your money on before you receive it. Give yourself an allowance and stick to it.

Track your spending. Know what you spend on living expenses and fun activities.

Understand your benefits. Be aware of your insurance benefits and medical costs.

Establish credit but make sure you are paying the balance off within a few months. Start with a small credit card limit and manage it carefully.

Talk to a financial advisor. It's never too early to have a conversation about long-term financial goals.

When using financial aid for college or any other post-secondary training, apply for Federal Subsidized Loans that do not require you to pay the interest on the money borrowed.

Monitor your credit report and banking accounts for any activity that you did not initiate.

Review your expenses annually, to make sure you are receiving the best insurance rate for your car, renters or homeowner's insurance, cable, internet and phone.

Check your bank accounts daily or at a minimum weekly.

Consider using a credit-monitoring service to protect you from identity theft.

Don'ts

Apply for high- interest credit cards.

Apply for loans from predatory lenders (i.e. payday loans or car-title loans).

Spend recklessly by making impulsive purchases that can destroy your budget.

Make only a minimum payment on any credit account.

Purchase the latest gadget or fad just because everyone else has it.

Spend your savings on impulse purchases.

Co-sign any loans.

Apply for private loans to pay for educational expenses after high school.

Ignore your online accounts

AUTHOR'S EXPERIENCE

When I was a four-year-old boy living in the mountains of Kentucky, it was safe for a young lad to walk the roads and railroad tracks alone. Knowing this, my mother would send me to the general store to buy a variety of small items we needed for our household. Since we had very little money, she was very aware of the fact that we needed to be cautious and spend money only on the basic necessities for survival. I could only purchase items from the general store that my mother strictly ordered me to buy. In the early 1960s, most of these items cost less than a dollar and many times you could buy multiple items for a dollar. At the store's checkout counter there were jars with different kinds of candy or gum. You could buy two pieces for one cent. I didn't think there would be any harm in rewarding myself for completing my shopping errand with two pieces of candy. I could even devour the evidence of my disobedience during my slow walk home. When I returned home from the store, my mother—being the protector of the vault and the sergeant-of-arms in our household—would count each item I bought to make sure I had been charged correctly. My mother never failed to notice if I was even one cent short! She always found that I had either been overcharged by one cent or that I had spent one cent. After she gave me a scolding, she would say: "Boy, you better learn how to count your money if you're ever going to be successful in life." I learned the value of saving money and the danger of overspending at a very young age!

—*Aaron Thompson*

When making purchases, always factor in their total, long-term cost. Short-term thinking leads to poor long-term money management and financial planning. Those small (monthly) installment plans that businesses offer to entice you to buy expensive products may make the cost of those products appear attractive and affordable in the short run. However, when you factor in the interest rates you pay on monthly installment plans, plus the length of time (number of months) you're making installment payments, you get a more accurate picture of the product's total cost in the long run. Taking this long-range perspective can quickly alert you to the reality that a product's sticker price represents its partial and seemingly affordable short-term cost—not its total long-term cost—which is much less affordable and more likely to exceed your budget.

Furthermore, the total long-term cost for purchases sometimes involves additional "hidden costs" that don't relate directly to the product's initial price but must be paid to enable you to continue using the product. For example, the sticker price paid for clothes doesn't include the hidden, long-term costs of having those clothes dry-cleaned. By just taking a moment to check the inside label, you can save yourself this hidden, long-term cost by purchasing clothes that are machine washable. Similarly, deciding to buy a new car instead of a used car brings with it not only the cost of a higher sticker price, but also the higher hidden costs of licensing and insuring the new car (plus any interest fees that must be paid if the new car was purchased on an installment plan). When you add in these hidden, long-term payments to a new car's total cost, buying a good used car is clearly a much more effective money-management strategy.

Keep in mind that not all debt is bad. Debt can be good if it represents an investment in something that will appreciate with time—that is, something that will gain in value and eventually turn into profit for the investor. Investing in a college education on credit is a good

> "Ask yourself how much of your income is being eaten up by car payments. It may be time to admit you made a mistake . . . sell it [and] replace it with an older or less sporty model."
> —Bill Pratt, *Extra Credit: The 7 Things Every high school Student Needs to Know About Credit, Debt & Cash*

> "Unlike a car that depreciates in value each year that you drive it, an investment in education yields monetary, social, and intellectual profit. A car is more tangible in the short term, but an investment in education (even if it means borrowing money) gives you more bang for the buck in the long run."
> —Eric Tyson, financial counselor and national best-selling author of *Personal Finance for Dummies*

investment because you're investing in yourself and your future, which, over time, will *appreciate*—that is, increase its monetary return in the form of higher salaries and benefits accumulated over the remainder of your life. In contrast, purchasing a new car is a bad long-term investment because it begins to *depreciate* or lose monetary value immediately after it's purchased. The instant you drive that new car off the dealer's lot, you become the proud owner of a used car that's worth much less than what you just paid for it.

You may have heard the expression: "Time is money." One way to interpret this expression is that the more money you spend, the more time you must spend making money. Students who spend more time earning money to cover the costs of material things they want, but don't need, typically spend less time studying, complete fewer classes, and earn lower grades. You can avoid this negative cycle by viewing academic work as work that "pays" you back in terms of completed courses and higher grades. If you put in more academic time to earn more course credits in less time, you're paid back sooner by graduating sooner and beginning to earn the full-time salary of a graduate—which will pay you much more per hour than you'll earn doing part-time work without a diploma (plus additional "fringe benefits" like health insurance and paid vacation time). Furthermore, the time you put into earning higher grades in high school will earn you more pay in your first full-time position after high school because research shows that students graduating with higher grades earn higher starting salaries (Pascarella & Terenzini, 2005).

> "If a man empties his purse into his head, no one can take it away from him. An investment in knowledge always pays the best interest."
> —Benjamin Franklin, 18th-century scientist, inventor, and a founding father of the United States

Think About It—Journal Entry 8.6

In addition to a college education, what might be other good, long-term investments you could make now or in the near future?

___

BOX 8.3

Financial Literacy: Understanding the Language of Money Management

As you can tell from the number of financial terms used in this chapter, there's an entire language we must master to be *financially literate*. As you read the financial terms listed below, place a checkmark next to any term you didn't know.

Account. A formal business arrangement in which a bank provides financial services to a customer (e.g., checking account or savings account).

Annual Fee. Yearly fee paid to a credit card company to cover the cost of maintaining the cardholder's account.

BOX 8.3 (CONT)

Annual Percentage Rate (APR). Interest rate that must be paid when monthly credit card balances aren't paid in full.

Balance. Amount of money in a person's account or amount of unpaid debt.

Bounced Check. A check written for a greater amount of money than the amount contained in a personal checking account; it typically requires the person paying a charge to the bank and possibly to the business that attempted to cash the bounced check.

Budget. A plan for balancing income and expenses to ensure that sufficient money is available to cover personal expenses.

Cash Flow. Amount of money flowing in (income) and flowing out (expenses); "negative cash flow" occurs when the amount of money going out exceeds the amount coming in.

Credit. Money obtained with the understanding that it will be paid back.

Credit History. Past record of how timely and completely a credit card holder has paid off credit.

Credit Line (a.k.a. Credit Limit). The maximum amount of money (credit) made available to a borrower.

Credit Score. Measure used by credit card companies to determine if someone applying for a credit card is "credit worthy," that is, likely to repay. (An applicant with a low credit score may be denied credit.)

Debt. Amount of money owed.

Default. Failure to meet a financial obligation (e.g., a student who fails to repay a high school loan "defaults" on that loan).

Emergency Student Loan. Immediate, interest-free loan provided by a institutions of learning to help financially strapped students cover short-term expenses (e.g., cost of textbooks) or deal with financial emergencies (e.g., accidents and illnesses). Emergency student loans are typically granted within 24 to 48 hours, sometimes even the same day, and usually need to be repaid within two months.

Deferred Student Payment Plan. A plan allowing student borrowers to temporarily defer or postpone loan payments for some acceptable reason (e.g., to pursue an internship or do volunteer work after high school).

Estimated Family Contribution (EFC). Amount of money the government has determined a family can contribute to the educational costs of a family member attending high school.

Fixed Interest Rate. A loan with an interest rate that stays the same for the entire term of the loan.

Free Application for Federal Student Aid (FAFSA). Free application that asks for personal and family financial information to determine a student's eligibility for federal, state, and high school-sponsored financial aid, including grants, loans, and work-study employment.

Grace Period. Amount of time a credit card holder has—after a monthly credit card statement has been issued—to pay back the company without paying added interest fees.

Grant. Money received that doesn't have to be repaid.

Gross Income. Income generated before taxes and other expenses are deducted.

Identity Theft. A crime committed by obtaining someone's personal identity information and assumes that person's identity to make financial transactions or purchases.

Insurance Premium. Amount of money paid in regular installments to an insurance company to remain insured.

Interest. Amount of money paid to a customer for deposited money (as in a bank account) or paid by a customer for borrowed money (e.g., interest on a loan). Interest is usually calculated as a percentage of the total amount of money deposited or borrowed.

Interest-Bearing Account. A bank account that earns interest if the customer keeps a minimum amount of money in the bank.

Loan Consolidation. Consolidating (combining) separate student loans into one larger loan to make the process of tracking, budgeting, and repayment easier. Loan consolidation typically requires the borrower to pay slightly more interest.

BOX 8.3 (CONT)

Loan Premium. The amount of money loaned without interest.

Merit-Based Scholarship. Money awarded to a student on the basis of performance or achievement that doesn't have to be repaid.

Need-Based Scholarship. Money awarded to a student on the basis of financial need that doesn't have to be repaid.

Net Income. Money earned after all expenses and taxes have been paid.

Principal. Total amount of money borrowed or deposited, not counting interest.

Variable Interest Rate. An interest rate on a loan that can vary (up or down) over the term of the loan.

Work Study. Financial assistance that high school students earned by working on campus (funded by the federal government).

Yield. Revenue gained beyond amount invested or paid. (For example, revenue gained by high school graduates through higher lifetime salaries beyond the amount they paid for a high school education.)

Think About It—Journal Entry 8.7

Which of the terms in Box 8.3 were unfamiliar to you?

_____
_____
_____
_____
_____

Which of these unfamiliar terms apply to your current financial decisions or money management plans?

_____
_____
_____
_____
_____
_____
_____

CHAPTER SUMMARY AND HIGHLIGHTS

Similar to time management, if you manage your money effectively and gain control of how you spend it, you gain greater control over the quality of your life.

In this chapter, effective strategies for money management were identified and discussed, such as the following:

- **Financing your college education wisely.** Explore all sources of income for financing your high school education, including FAFSA, scholarships, grants, loans, salary earnings, and personal savings.
- **Utilizing Financial Aid Counseling.** Check periodically to see if you qualify for additional sources of income, such as part-time employment on campus, low-interest loans, grants, or scholarships.
- **Gaining financial self-awareness.** Become aware of your cash flow—amount of money coming in versus going out.
- **Managing money effectively.** Use available financial tools and instruments to track and maximize cash flow, such as checking accounts, credit cards, or debit cards.
- **Preparing a personal budget.** Keep an accurate account of your money to ensure you have sufficient amount to cover your expenses.
- **Paying your bills when they arrive.** Take care of bills when you first get them to reduce the risk of forgetting to pay them or paying them late.
- **Living within your means.** Don't purchase what you can't afford.
- **Economizing.** Be an intelligent consumer who uses critical thinking skills to evaluate and prioritize purchases.
- **Downsizing.** Don't buy products you don't need and don't allow peer pressure to dictate your spending habits.

Learning More through the World Wide Web: Internet-Based Resources

For additional information on fiscal literacy, money management, and financial planning, see the following websites.

Fiscal Literacy & Money Management:
www.360financialliteracy.org
www.cashcourse.org

Financial Aid & Federal Funding Sources for a College Education:
www.students.gov
https://studentloans.gov/myDirectLoan/index.action

Student Loan Management Strategies:
https://firsttechfed.studentchoice.org/.../managing.../student-loan-repayment strategies

Spending Habits & Consumer Self-Awareness:
beyondthepurchase.org

References

Astin, A. W. (1993). *What matters in college?* San Francisco: Jossey-Bass.

Cermak, K., & Filkins, J. (2004). *On-campus employment as a factor of student retention and graduation.* DePaul University. Retrieved from http://oipr.depaul.edu/open/gradereten/oce.asp

Cude, B. J., Lawrence, F.C., Lyons, A.C., Metzger, K., LeJeune, E., Marks, L., & Machtmes, K. 2006. College students and financial literacy: What they know and what we need to learn. *Proceedings of the Eastern Family Economics and Resource Management Association Conference* (pp. 102–109).

Dittmar, H. 2004. Understanding and diagnosing compulsive buying. In R. Coombs (Ed.), *Handbook of addictive disorders: A practical guide to diagnosis and treatment* (pp. 411–450). New York, NY: Wiley.

Engle, J. Bermeo, A., & O'Brien, C. (2006). *Straight from the source: What works for first-generation college students.* Washington, DC: The Pell Institute for the Study of Opportunity in Higher Education.

Furnham, A., & Argyle, M. (1998). *The psychology of money.* New York: Routledge.

Goldstein, W. M., & Hogarth, R. M. (Eds.) 1997. *Research on judgment and decision making,* Cambridge, UK: Cambridge University Press.

Gordon, L. (2009, Oct. 21). College costs up in hard times. *Los Angeles Times,* p. A13.

Hamilton, H. 2012. Student loan blues. *Los Angeles Times,* pp. B1, B8.

Health, C., & Soll, J. (1996). Mental budgeting and consumer decisions. *Journal of Consumer Research, 23,* 40–52.

Kidwell, B., & Turrisi, R. (2004). An examination of college student money management tendencies. *Journal of Economic Psychology, 25*(5), 601–616.

King, J. E. (2002). *Crucial choices: How students' financial decisions affect their academic success.* Washington, DC: American Council on Education.

King, J. E. (2005). Academic success and financial decisions: Helping students make crucial choices. In R. S. Feldman (Ed.), *Improving the first year of college: Research and practice* (pp. 3–26). Mahwah, NJ: Lawrence Erlbaum.

Kingkade, T. (2014, August 27). "Sleepy college students are worried about their stress levels." *The Huffington Post.* Retrieved from http://www.huffingtonpost.com/2014/08/27/college-students-sleep-stress_n_5723438.html.

Knox, S. (2004). *Financial basics: A money management guide for students.* Columbus: Ohio State University Press.

Kristof, K. M., 2008. Hooked on debt: Students learn too late the costs of private loans. *Los Angeles Times,* pp. A1, A18-19.

Leonard, G. (2008). *A study on the effects of student employment on retention.* Retrieved from uc.iupui.edu/Portals/155/uploadedFiles/.../StudEmpRetentionRprt.pdf

Levine, A., & Cureton, J. S. (1998). *When hopes and fears collide.* San Francisco: Jossey-Bass.

Lowenstein, G., Read, D., & Baumeister, R. G. (Eds.) (2003). *Time and decision: Economic and psychological perspectives on intertemporal choice.* New York: Russell Sage Foundation.

Nellie Mae (2005). *Undergraduate students and credit cards in 2004: An analysis of usage rates and trend.* Wilkes-Barre, PA: Nellie Mae.

Nelson, M. C., Lust, K., Story, M., & Ehlinger, E. (2008). Credit card debt, stress and key health risk behaviors among college students. *American Journal of Health Promotion, 22*(6), 400–407.

Niederjohn, M.S. 2008. First-year experience course improves students' financial literacy. *ESource for College Transitions* [Electronic newsletter published by the National Resource Center for the First-Year Experiencee and Students in Transition], 6(1), 9–11.

Orszag, J. M., Orszag, P. R., & Whitmore, D. M. (2001). *Learning and earning: Working in college.* Retrieved from http://www.brockport.edu/career01/upromise.htm.

Pascarella, E., & Terenzini, P. (1991). *How college affects students: Findings and insights from twenty years of research.* San Francisco: Jossey-Bass.

Pascarella, E., & Terenzini, P. (2005). *How college affects students: A third decade of research* (Vol. 2). San Francisco: Jossey-Bass.

Perna, L. W., & DuBois, G. (Eds.). (2010). *Understanding the working college student: New research and its implications for policy and practice.* Sterling, VA: Stylus.

Pratt, B. 2008. *Extra credit: The 7 things every college student needs to know about credit, debt, & cash.* Keedysville, MD: ExtraCreditBook.com.

Pratt, B. (2011). *Extra credit: The 7 things every college student needs to know about credit, debt & cash* (2nd ed.). Winterville, NC: Financial Relevancy.

Ring, T. (1997, October). Issuers face a visit to the dean's office. *Credit Card Management, 10,* 34–39.

Sallie Mae (2009, April). *How undergraduate students use credit cards: Sallie Mae's national study of usage rates and trends 2009.* Retrieved from http://static.mgnetwork.com/rtd/pdfs/20090830_iris.pdf.

Susswein, R. (1995). College students and credit cards: A privilege earned? *Credit World, 83,* 21–23.
Tinto, V. (1993). *Leaving college: Rethinking the causes and cures of student attrition* (2nd ed.). Chicago: University of Chicago Press.
Tinto, V. 2012. *Completing College: Rethinking Institutional Action.* University of Chicago Press, Chicago, IL.
Tyson, E. (2012). *Personal finance for dummies* (7th ed.). Hoboken, NJ: John Wiley & Sons. Walker, C. M. (1996). Financial management, coping, and debt in households under financial strain. *Journal of Economic Psychology, 17,* 789–807.

CHAPTER 8 EXERCISES

8.1 QUOTE REFLECTIONS

Review the sidebar quotes contained in this chapter and select two that were especially meaningful or inspirational to you.

For each quote, provide a three- to five-sentence explanation why you chose it.

8.2 WHO'S AT FAULT?

Next week all of your friends are going to a concert to see a group you have always wanted to see perform. You are conflicted because you just bought a car and the payment is due next week and you only have enough to cover the cost of payment. Your parents told you that you are responsible for the payment. You decide to go to the concert and forgo the car payment this month. Over the next several months you continue to miss payments and finally one day the car is gone—repossessed. You can't believe you are that far behind. You ask mom and dad to help and they tell you, again, this is your responsibility.

What could have you done differently in this situation?

8.3 SELF-ASSESSMENT OF FINANCIAL ATTITUDES AND HABITS

Answer the following questions about yourself as accurately and honestly as possible.

		Agree	Disagree
1.	I pay for some of my expenses.	_____	_____
2.	I have a job after school and during the summer.	_____	_____
3.	I monitor my bank accounts to keep current with my balances.	_____	_____
4.	I set aside money each month for savings.	_____	_____
5.	I have a credit card and keep current on my payments.	_____	_____
6.	I pay my cell phone bill in full each month.	_____	_____
7.	I believe it's important to buy the things I want when I want them.	_____	_____
8.	Borrowing money to pay for school is a smart thing to do.	_____	_____
9.	I have a monthly or weekly budget that I follow faithfully.	_____	_____
10.	The thing I enjoy most about making money is spending money.	_____	_____
11.	I have one credit card.	_____	_____
12.	Getting a degree will get me a good job and a good income.	_____	_____

Sources: Cude, et al. (2006), Niederjohn (2008).

Give yourself one point for each item that you marked "agree"—except for items 7, 9, and 10. For these items, give yourself a point if you marked "disagree."

A perfect score on this short survey would be 12.

Reflection Questions:

1. What was your total score?

2. Which items lowered your score?

3. Do you detect any pattern across the items that lowered your score?

4. Do you see any realistic way(s) for improving your score on this test?

8.4 FINANCIAL SELF-AWARENESS: MONITORING MONEY & TRACKING CASH FLOW

Step 1. Use the "Financial Self-Awareness" worksheet that follows Step 3. to *estimate* your income and expenses per month, and enter them in column 2.

Step 2. Check with your parents/guardians regarding the expenses for the household. Based on the number of people living in your home, identify your portion of the monthly expenses for each month.

Step 3. After one month of tracking your cash flow, answer the following questions.

   a. How much money will you need to earn monthly to live as you currently live? In other words, how much will you need to live a lifestyle that's comfortable for you?

   b. Do you see areas that you could save money?

   c. How much money do you think you will need once you pay your expenses?

   d. Based on this exercise, do you see a need to regularly review your expenses and develop a personal budget plan?

Financial Self-Awareness Worksheet

	Estimate	Actual
Income Sources		
Parents/Family		
Work/Job		
Grants/Scholarships		
Loans		
Savings		
Other:		
TOTAL INCOME		
Essentials (Fixed Expenses)		
Living Expenses:		
Food/Groceries		
Rent/Room & Board		
Utilities (gas/electric)		
Clothing		
Laundry/Dry Cleaning		
Cell Phone		
Computer		
Household Items (dishes, etc.)		
Medical Insurance Expenses		
Debt Payments (loans/credit cards)		
Other:		
School Expenses:		
Tuition		
Books		
Supplies (print cartridges, etc.)		
Special Fees (lab fees, etc.)		
Other:		
Transportation:		
Public Transportation (bus fees, etc.)		
Car Insurance		
Car Maintenance		
Fuel (gas)		
Car Payments		
Other:		
Incidentals (Variable Expenses)		
Entertainment:		
Movies/Concerts		
Digital Downloads		
Restaurants (eating out)		
Other:		

Financial Self-Awareness Worksheet *(cont)*

	Estimate	Actual
Personal Appearance/Accessories:		
Hairstyling/Coloring		
Cosmetics/Manicures		
Fashionable Clothes		
Jewelry		
Other:		
Hobbies		
Travel (trips home, vacations)		
Gifts		
Other:		
TOTAL EXPENSES		

8.5 CHAPTER 8 REFLECTION

Do you feel you have good or poor money management skills? Explain.

List and describe at leave five principles discussed in this chapter that you can use to better manage your money.

1.

2.

3.

4.

5.

Now explain HOW you can put these principles into practice.

CHAPTER 9

DIVERSITY AND THE HIGH SCHOOL EXPERIENCE

Learning about and from Human Differences

CHAPTER PREVIEW

This chapter clarifies what "diversity" truly means and demonstrates how experiencing diversity can deepen:

- Learning,
- Promote critical and creative thinking, and
- Contribute to your personal and professional development.

Simply stated, we learn more from people who differ from us than we do from people similar to us. There is more diversity among high school students today than at any other time in history. This chapter will help you capitalize on this learning opportunity.

LEARNING GOAL

Gain greater appreciation of human differences and develop skills for making the most of diversity in high school and beyond.

THOUGHT STARTER

 Think About It—Journal Entry 9.1

Complete the following sentence:

When I hear the word *diversity*, the first thing that comes to my mind is . . .

_____

_____

From *Thriving in the Community College & Beyond: Strategies for Academic Success and Personal Development*, Third Edition, by Joseph Cuseo, Aaron Thompson, and Julie McLaughlin. Copyright © 2016 by Kendall Hunt Publishing Company. Reprinted by permission.

What Is Diversity?

Literally translated, the word *diversity* derives from the Latin root *diversus*, meaning "various" or "variety." Thus, human diversity refers to the variety that exists in humanity (the human species). The relationship between humanity and diversity may be compared to the relationship between sunlight and the variety of colors that make up the visual spectrum. Similar to how sunlight passing through a prism disperses into the variety of colors that comprise the visual spectrum, the human species on planet earth is dispersed into a variety of different groups that comprise the human spectrum (humanity). **Figure 9.1** illustrates this metaphorical relationship between diversity and humanity.

As depicted in the above figure, human diversity is manifested in a multiplicity of ways, including differences in physical features, national origins, cultural backgrounds, and sexual orientations. Some dimensions of diversity are easily detectable, others are very subtle, and some are invisible.

FIGURE 9.1: Humanity and Diversity

"We are all brothers and sisters. Each face in the rainbow of color that populates our world is precious and special. Each adds to the rich treasure of humanity."
—Morris Dees, civil rights leader and cofounder of the Southern Poverty Law Center

SPECTRUM of DIVERSITY

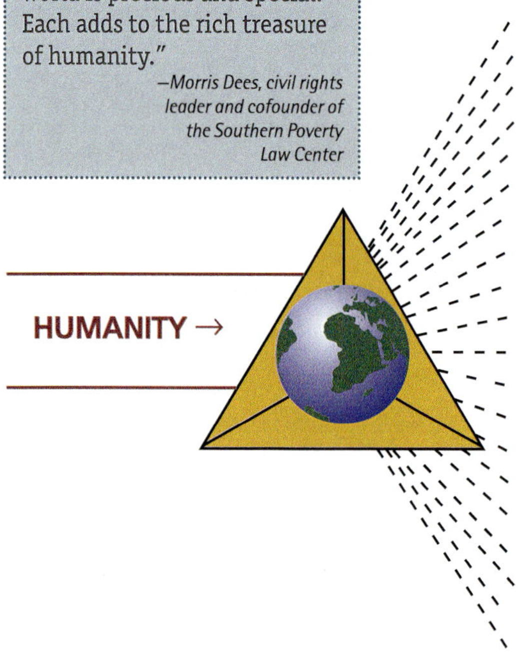

HUMANITY →

- *Gender* (male-female)
- *Age* (stage of life)
- *Race* (e.g., White, Black, Asian)
- *Ethnicity* (e.g., Native American, Hispanic, Irish, German)
- *Socioeconomic* status (job status/income)
- National *citizenship* (citizen of U.S. or another country)
- *Native* (first-learned) *language*
- National *origin* (nation of birth)
- National *region* (e.g., raised in north/south)
- *Generation* (historical period when people are born and live)
- *Political* ideology (e.g., liberal/conservative)
- *Religious/spiritual* beliefs (e.g., Christian/Buddhist/Muslim)
- *Family* status (e.g., single-parent/two-parent family)
- *Marital* status (single/married)
- *Parental* status (with/without children)
- *Sexual* orientation (heterosexual/homosexual/bisexual)
- *Physical* ability/disability (e.g., able to hear/deaf)
- *Mental* ability/disability (e.g., mentally able/challenged)
- *Learning* ability/disability (e.g., absence/presence of dyslexia)
- *Mental* health/illness (e.g., absence/presence of depression)

_ _ _ _ _ _ = dimension of diversity

*This list represents some of the major dimensions of human diversity; it does not constitute a complete list of all possible forms of human diversity. Also, disagreement exists about certain dimensions of diversity (e.g., whether certain groups should be considered races or ethnic groups).

© Kendall Hunt Publishing Company

Think About It—Journal Entry 9.2

Look at the diversity spectrum in Figure 9.1 and look over the list of groups that make up the spectrum. Do you notice any groups missing from the list that should be added, either because they have distinctive backgrounds or because they've been targets of prejudice and discrimination?

_____

_____

_____

_____

_____

Diversity includes discussion of equal rights and social justice for minority groups, but it's a broader concept that involves much more than political issues. In a national survey of American voters, the vast majority of respondents agreed that diversity is more than just "political correctness" (National Survey of Women Voters, 1998). Diversity is also an *educational* issue—an integral element of education that contributes to the learning, personal development, and career preparation of *all* students. It enhances the quality of the high school experience by bringing multiple perspectives and alternative approaches to *what* is being learned (the content) and *how* it's being learned (the process).

> "Ethnic and cultural diversity is an integral, natural, and normal component of educational experiences for all students."
> —National Council for Social Studies

What Is Racial Diversity?

A *racial group (race)* is a group of people who share distinctive physical traits, such as skin color or facial characteristics. The variation in skin color we now see among humans is largely due to biological adaptations that have evolved over thousands of years among groups of humans who migrated to different climatic regions of the world. Currently, the most widely accepted explanation of the geographic origin of modern humans is the "Out of Africa" theory. Genetic studies and fossil evidence indicate that all Homo sapiens inhabited Africa 150,000–250,000 years ago; over time, some migrated from Africa to other parts of the world (Mendez et al., 2013; Meredith, 2011; Reid & Hetherington, 2010). Darker skin tones developed among humans who inhabited and reproduced in hotter geographical regions nearer the equator (e.g., Africans). Their darker skin color helped them adapt and survive by providing them with better protection from the potentially damaging effects of intense sunlight (Bridgeman, 2003). In contrast, lighter skin tones developed over time among humans inhabiting colder climates that were farther from the equator (e.g., Scandinavia). Their lighter skin color enabled them to absorb greater

NOTE

Diversity is a *human* issue that embraces and benefits *all* people; it's not a code word for "some" people. Although one major goal of diversity is to promote appreciation and equitable treatment of particular groups of people who've experienced discrimination, it's also a *learning* experience that strengthens the quality of a high school education, career preparation, and leadership potential.

amounts of vitamin D supplied by sunlight, which was in shorter supply in those regions of the world (Jablonksi & Chaplin, 2002).

Currently, the U.S. Census Bureau has identified five races (U.S. Census Bureau, 2012):

White: a person whose lineage may be traced to the original people inhabiting Europe, the Middle East, or North Africa.

Black or African American: a person whose lineage may be traced to the original people inhabiting Africa.

American Indian or Alaska Native: a person whose lineage may be traced to the original people inhabiting North and South America (including Central America), and who continue to maintain their tribal affiliation or attachment.

Asian: a person whose lineage may be traced to the original people inhabiting the Far East, Southeast Asia, or the Indian subcontinent, including: Cambodia, China, India, Japan, Korea, Malaysia, Pakistan, the Philippine Islands, Thailand, and Vietnam.

Native Hawaiian or Other Pacific Islander: a person whose lineage may be traced to the original people inhabiting Hawaii, Guam, Samoa, or other Pacific islands.

It's important to keep in mind that racial categories are not based on scientific evidence; they merely represent group classifications constructed by society (Anderson & Fienberg, 2000). No identifiable set of genes distinguishes one race from another; in fact, there continues to be disagreement among scholars about what groups of people constitute a human race or whether distinctive races actually exist (Wheelright, 2005). In other words, you can't do a blood test or some type of internal genetic test to determine a person's race. Humans have simply decided to categorize themselves into races on the basis of certain external differences in their physical appearance, particularly the color of their outer layer of skin. The U.S. Census Bureau could have decided to divide people into "racial" categories based on other physical characteristics, such as eye color (blue, brown, and green), hair color (brown, black, blonde, or red), or body length (tall, short, or mid-sized).

AUTHOR'S EXPERIENCE

My father stood approximately six feet tall and had straight, light brown hair. His skin color was that of a Western European with a very slight suntan. My mother was from Alabama; she was dark in skin color with high cheekbones and had long curly black hair. In fact, if you didn't know that my father was of African American descent, you would not have thought he was black.

All of my life I've thought of myself as African American and all people who know me have thought of me as African American. I've lived half of a century with that as my racial identity. Several years ago, I carefully reviewed records of births and deaths in my family history and discovered that I had less than 50% African lineage. Biologically, I am no longer black; socially and emotionally, I still am. Clearly, my "race" has been socially constructed, not biologically determined.

—*Aaron Thompson*

While humans may display diversity in the color or tone of their external layer of skin, the reality is that all members of the human species are remarkably similar at an internal biological level. More than 98% of the genes of all humans are exactly the same, regardless of what their particular race may be (Bronfenbrenner, 2005). This large amount of genetic overlap accounts for our distinctively "human" appearance, which clearly distinguishes us from all other living species. All humans have internal organs that are similar in structure and function, and despite variations in the color of our outer layer of skin, when it's cut, all humans bleed in the same color.

AUTHOR'S EXPERIENCE

I was sitting in a coffee shop in the Chicago O'Hare airport while proofreading my first draft of this chapter. I looked up from my work for a second and saw what appeared to be a white girl about 18 years of age. As I lowered my head to return to work, I did a double-take and looked at her again because something about her seemed different or unusual. When I looked more closely at her the second time, I noticed that although she had white skin, the features of her face and hair appeared to be those of an African American. After a couple of seconds of puzzlement, I figured it out: she was an *albino* African American. That satisfied my curiosity for the moment, but then I began to wonder: Would it still be accurate to say she was "black" even though her skin was not black? Would her hair and facial features be sufficient for her to be considered or classified as black? If yes, then what would be the "race" of someone who had black skin tone, but did not have the typical hair and facial features characteristic of black people? Is skin color the defining feature of being African American or are other features equally important?

I was unable to answer these questions, but found it amusing that all of these thoughts were crossing my mind while I was working on a chapter dealing with diversity. On the plane ride home, I thought again about that albino African American girl and realized that she was a perfect example of how classifying people into "races" isn't based on objective, scientific evidence, but on subjective, socially constructed categories.

—*Joe Cuseo*

Categorizing people into distinct racial or ethnic groups is becoming even more difficult because members of different ethnic and racial groups are increasingly forming cross-ethnic and interracial families. By 2050, the number of Americans who identify themselves as being of two or more races is projected to more than triple, growing from 5.2 million to 16.2 million (U.S. Census Bureau, 2008).

Think About It—Journal Entry 9.3

What race(s) do you consider yourself to be?

_____

Would you say you identify strongly with your racial identity, or are you rarely conscious of it?

_____

_____

_____

Why?

_____
_____
_____
_____
_____

AUTHOR'S EXPERIENCE

I attended a high school that had very little racial diversity. During my first year of college, I met an African-American student (Paul) who was a resident assistant in my dorm. Paul was from Toledo and I was from southern Ohio. He grew up in an urban setting and I grew up in a rural area. Paul was a junior and was well acclimated to college life, whereas I had much to learn about living in an environment along with others from diverse backgrounds. Paul and I became good friends and I often visited his room to watch television and talk. On one occasion, I remember sitting in his room and several other African-American friends of his stopped in to pay a visit. As I sat there, I felt very uncomfortable until one of his friends (who I knew well) said: "Shope, what's wrong with you? Why are you so quiet?" Before I could answer, one of the other guys said: "Man, leave him alone; this is the first time in his life where he's the minority in the group." Everyone laughed, but it was true.

I never forgot the lesson I learned that day. I felt out of place and alone. I was lucky because Paul and the other guys never let me feel like I didn't belong. The conversation broke the ice and made me feel accepted. That experience always reminds me how it feels to be different than others; it was my first real lesson in empathy. I don't want anyone ever to feel a lack of belongingness caused by some superficial physical difference that doesn't really matter. I've learned to value people for their inner qualities rather than focusing on their outer features.

—*Shane Shope*

What Is an Ethnic Group?

A group of people who share the same culture is referred to as an *ethnic group*. Thus, "culture" refers to *what* an ethnic group shares in common (e.g., language and traditions) and "ethnic group" refers to the *people* who share the same culture that's been *learned* through common social experiences. Members of the same racial group—whose shared physical characteristics have been *inherited*—may be members of different ethnic groups. For instance, white Americans belong to the same racial group, but differ in terms of their ethnic group (e.g., French, German, Irish) and Asian Americans belong to the same racial group, but are members of different ethnic groups (e.g., Japanese, Chinese, Korean).

Currently, the major cultural (ethnic) groups in the United States include:

- Native Americans (American Indians)
  - Cherokee, Navaho, Hopi, Alaskan natives, Blackfoot, etc.

- European Americans (Whites)
  - Descendents from Western Europe (e.g., United Kingdom, Ireland, Netherlands), Eastern Europe (e.g., Hungary, Romania, Bulgaria), Southern Europe (e.g., Italy, Greece, Portugal), and Northern Europe or Scandinavia (e.g., Denmark, Sweden, Norway)
- African Americans (Blacks)
  - Americans whose cultural roots lie in the continent of Africa (e.g., Ethiopia, Kenya, Nigeria) and the Caribbean Islands (e.g., Bahamas, Cuba, Jamaica)
- Hispanic Americans (Latinos)
  - Americans with cultural roots in Mexico, Puerto Rico, Central America (e.g., El Salvador, Guatemala, Nicaragua), and South America (e.g., Brazil, Columbia, Venezuela)
- Asian Americans
  - Americans whose cultural roots lie in East Asia (e.g., Japan, China, Korea), Southeast Asia (e.g., Vietnam, Thailand, Cambodia), and South Asia (e.g., India, Pakistan, Bangladesh)
- Middle Eastern Americans
  - Americans with cultural roots in Iraq, Iran, Israel, etc.

Think About It—Journal Entry 9.4

What ethnic group(s) are you a member of, or do you identify with? What would you say are the key cultural values shared by your ethnic group(s)?

_____
_____
_____
_____

European Americans are still the majority ethnic group in the United States; they account for more than 50% of the American population. Native Americans, African Americans, Hispanic Americans, and Asian Americans are considered to be *minority* ethnic groups because each of these groups represents less than 50% of the American population.

> "I'm the only person from my race in class."
> —Hispanic student commenting on why he felt uncomfortable in his class on race, ethnicity, and gender

The Relationship between Diversity and Humanity

As previously noted, diversity represents variations on the same theme: being human. Thus, humanity and diversity are interdependent, complementary concepts. To understand human diversity is to understand both our differences and *similarities* (Public Service Enterprise Group, 2009). Diversity appreciation includes appreciating both the unique perspectives of different cultural groups as well as universal aspects of the human experience that are common to all groups—whatever their particular cultural background happens to be. Members of all racial and ethnic groups live in communities, develop personal relationships, have emotional needs, and undergo life experiences that affect their self-esteem and personal identity. Humans of all races and ethnicities experience similar emotions and reveal those emotions with similar facial expressions (see **Figure 9.2**).

Other characteristics that anthropologists have found to be shared by all humans in every corner of the world include: storytelling, poetry, adornment of the body, dance, music, decoration with artifacts, families, socialization of children by elders, a sense of right and wrong, supernatural beliefs, and mourning of the dead (Pinker, 2000).

FIGURE 9.2:

Humans all over the world display the same facial expressions when experiencing and expressing different emotions. See if you can detect the emotions being expressed in the following faces.
(To find the answers, turn your book upside down.)

Answers: The emotions shown. Top, left to right: anger, fear, and sadness. Bottom, left to right: disgust, happiness, and surprise.

All images ©JupiterImages Corporation.

Although different cultural groups may express these shared experiences in different ways, they are universal experiences common to all human cultures.

 Think About It—Journal Entry 9.5

In addition to those already mentioned, can you think of another important human experience that is universal—that is experienced by all humans?

_____

_____

_____

_____

You may have heard the question: "We're all human, aren't we?" The answer to this important question is "yes and no." Yes, we are all the same, but not in the same way. A good metaphor for understanding this apparent contradiction is to visualize humanity as a quilt in which we're all united by the common thread of humanity—the universal bond of being human. (Much like the quilt below.) The different patches comprising the quilt represent diversity—the distinctive or unique cultures that comprise our shared humanity. The quilt metaphor acknowledges the identity and beauty of all cultures. It differs from the old American "melting pot" metaphor, which viewed cultural differences as something to be melted down and eliminated. It also differs from the old "salad bowl" metaphor that depicted America as a hodgepodge or mishmash of cultures thrown together without any common connection. In contrast, the quilt metaphor suggests that the unique cultures of different human groups should be preserved, recognized, and valued; at the same time, these cultural differences join together to form a seamless, unified whole. This blending of diversity and unity is captured in the Latin expression *E pluribus unum* ("Out of many, one")—the motto of the United States—which you'll find printed on all its currency.

> "We are all the same, and we are all unique."
> —Georgia Dunston, African American biologist and research specialist in human genetics

> "We have become not a melting pot but a beautiful mosaic."
> —Jimmy Carter, 39th president of the United States and winner of the Nobel Peace Prize

©steven r. hendricks/Shutterstock.com

NOTE

When we appreciate diversity in the context of humanity, we capitalize on the variety and versatility of human differences while preserving the collective strength and synergy of human unity.

AUTHOR'S EXPERIENCE

When I was 12 years old and living in New York City, I returned from school one Friday and my mother asked me if anything interesting happened at school that day. I told her that the teacher went around the room asking students what they had for dinner the night before. At that moment, my mother became a bit concerned and nervously asked me: "What did you tell the teacher?" I said: "I told her and the rest of the class that I had pasta last night because my family always eats pasta on Thursdays and Sundays." My mother exploded and fired back the following question at me in a very agitated tone, "Why didn't you tell her we had steak or roast beef?" For a moment, I was stunned and couldn't figure out what I'd done wrong or why I should have lied about eating pasta. Then it dawned on me: My mom was embarrassed about being Italian American. She wanted me to hide our family's ethnic background and make it sound like we were very "American."

As I grew older, I understood why my mother felt the way she did. She grew up in America's "melting pot" generation—a time when different American ethnic groups were expected to melt down and melt away their ethnicity. They were not to celebrate their diversity; they were to eliminate it.

—*Joe Cuseo*

NOTE

While it's valuable to learn about differences between different human groups, there are substantial individual differences among people within the same racial or ethnic group that should neither be ignored nor overlooked. Don't assume that individuals with the same racial or ethnic characteristics share the same personal characteristics.

> "I realize that I'm black, but I like to be viewed as a person, and this is everybody's wish."
> —*Michael Jordan, Hall of Fame basketball player*

> "Every human is, at the same time, like all other humans, like some humans, and like no other human."
> —*Clyde Kluckhohn, American anthropologist*

What Is Individuality?

It's important to keep in mind that there are individual differences among members of any racial or ethnic group that are greater than the average difference between groups. Said in another way, there's more variability (individuality) within groups than between groups. For example, among members of the same racial group, individual differences in their physical attributes (e.g., height and weight) and psychological characteristics (e.g., temperament and personality) are greater than any average difference that may exist between their racial group and other racial groups (Caplan & Caplan, 2008).

As you proceed through your high school experience, keep the following key distinctions in mind:

- **Humanity.** All humans are members of the *same group*—the human species.
- **Diversity.** All humans are members of *different groups*—such as, different racial and ethnic groups.
- **Individuality.** Each human is a *unique individual* who differs from all other members of any group to which he or she may belong.

Major Forms or Types of Diversity in Today's World

Ethnic and Racial Diversity

America is rapidly becoming a more racially and ethnically diverse nation. Minorities now account for 36.6% of the total population—an all-time high; in 2011, for the first time in U.S. history, racial and ethnic minorities made up more than half (50.4%) of all children born in America (Nhan, 2012). By the middle of the 21st century, minority groups are expected to comprise 54% of the American population and more than 60% of the nation's children will be members of minority groups (U.S. Census Bureau, 2008).

More specifically, by 2050 the American population is projected to be more than 30% Hispanic (up from 15% in 2008), 15% Black (up from 13% in 2008), 9.6% Asian (up from 5.3% in 2008), and 2% Native Americans (up from 1.6% in 2008). The Native Hawaiian and Pacific Islander population is expected to more than double between 2008 and 2050. During this same timeframe, the percentage of white Americans will decline from 66% (2008) to 46% (2050). As a result of these demographic trends, today's ethnic and racial minorities will become the "new majority" of Americans by the middle of the 21st century (see **Figure 9.3**).

The growing racial and ethnic diversity of America's population is reflected in the growing diversity of students enrolled in its institutions of learning. In 1960, whites made up almost 95% of the total college population; in 2010, that percentage had decreased to 61.5%. Between 1976 and 2010, the percentage of ethnic minority students in higher education increased from 17% to 40% (National Center for Education Statistics, 2011). This rise in ethnic and racial diversity on American schools is particularly noteworthy when viewed in light of the historical treatment of minority groups in the United States. In the early 19th century, education was not a right, but a privilege available only to those who could afford to attend private schools. It was experienced largely by Protestants of European descent (Luhman, 2007).

FIGURE 9.3: The "New Majority"

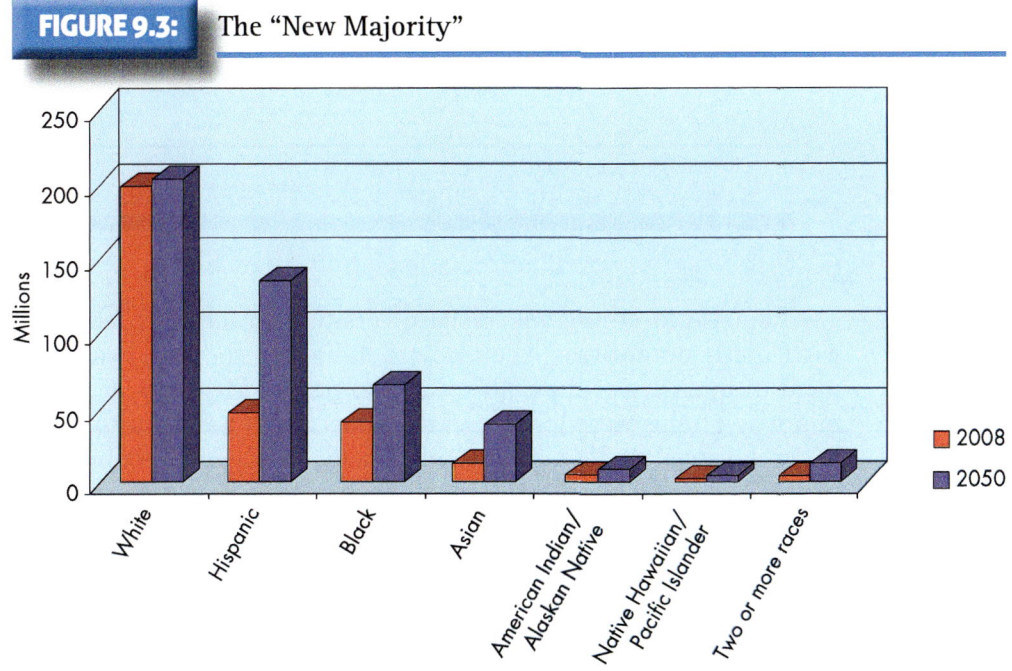

©Kendall Hunt Publishing Company

Think About It—Journal Entry 9.6

1. What diverse groups do you see represented on your school?

   _____
   _____
   _____
   _____
   _____

2. Are there groups on school you didn't expect to see or to see in such large numbers?

   _____
   _____
   _____
   _____
   _____

3. Are there groups on school you expected to see but don't see or, see in smaller numbers than you expected?

   _____
   _____
   _____
   _____
   _____

> "Of all the civil rights for which the world has struggled and fought for 5,000 years, the right to learn is undoubtedly the most fundamental."
> —W. E. B. Du Bois, African American sociologist, historian, and civil rights activist

The rise in ethnic and racial diversity on American schools is particularly noteworthy when viewed in light of the historical treatment of minority groups in the United States. Members of certain minority groups were left out of the educational process altogether, or were forced to be educated in racially segregated settings. For example, Americans of color were once taught in separate, segregated schools that were typically inferior in terms of educational facilities. It was not until the groundbreaking Supreme Court ruling in *Brown v. Board of Education* (1954) that the face of education for people of color changed with the ruling that "separate educational facilities are inherently unequal." The decision made it illegal for Kansas and 20 other states to deliver education in segregated classrooms.

AUTHOR'S EXPERIENCE

My mother was a direct descendent of slaves and moved with her parents from the Deep South at the age of 17. My father lived in an all-Black coal mining camp, into which my mother and her family moved in 1938. My father remained illiterate because he was not allowed to attend public schools in eastern Kentucky. In the early 1960s my brother, my sister, and I were integrated into the White public schools. Physical violence and constant verbal harassment caused many other Blacks to forgo their education and opt for jobs in the coal mines at an early age. But my father remained constant in his advice to me: "It doesn't matter if they call you n_____; but don't you ever let them beat you by walking out on your education." He would say to me, "Son, you will have opportunities that I never had. Just remember, when you do get that education, you'll never have to go in those coal mines and have them break your back. You can choose what you want to do, and then you can be free man."

My parents, who could never provide me with monetary wealth, truly made me proud of them by giving me the gift of insight and an aspiration for achievement.

—*Aaron Thompson*

Socioeconomic Diversity

Human diversity also exists among groups of people in terms of their socioeconomic status (SES), which is determined by their level of education, level of income, and the occupational prestige of the jobs they hold. Groups are stratified (divided) into lower, middle, or upper classes, and groups occupying lower social strata have less economic resources and social privileges (Feagin & Feagin, 2007).

Young adults from high-income families are more than seven times likely to have earned a college degree and hold a prestigious job than those from low-income families (Olson, 2007). Sharp discrepancies also exist in income level among different racial, ethnic, and gender groups. In 2012, the median income for non-Hispanic white households was $57,009, compared to $39,005 for Hispanics and $33,321 for African Americans (DeNavas-Walt, Proctor, & Smith, 2013). From 2005 to 2009, household wealth fell by 66% for Hispanics, 53% for Blacks, and 16% for Whites, largely due to the housing and mortgage collapse—which had a more damaging effect on lower-income families (Kochlar, Fry, & Taylor, 2011).

Despite its overall wealth, the United States is one of the most impoverished of all developed countries in the world (Shah, 2008). The poverty rate in the United States is almost twice the rate of other economically developed countries around the world (Gould & Wething, 2013). In 2012, more than 16% of the American population, and almost 20% of American children, lived below the poverty line ($23,050 yearly income for a family of four) (U.S. Census Bureau, 2013).

> "Being born in the elite in the U.S. gives you a constellation of privileges that very few people in the world have ever experienced. Being born poor in the U.S. gives you disadvantages unlike anything in Western Europe, Japan and Canada."
>
> —David I. Levine, economist and social mobility researcher

 Think About It—Journal Entry 9.7

Are you the first in your family to attend high school?

Whether yes or no, how does that make you feel?

_____

_____

_____

Generational Diversity

Humans are also diverse with respect to the historical time period in which they grew up. The term "generation" refers to a cohort (group) of individuals born during the same period in history whose attitudes, values, and habits have been shaped by events that took place in the world during their formative years of development. People growing up in different generations are likely to develop different attitudes and beliefs because of the different historical events they experienced during their upbringing.

Box 9.1 contains a brief summary of different generations, the key historical events they experienced, and the personal characteristics commonly associated with each generational group (Lancaster & Stillman, 2002).

BOX 9.1

Generational Diversity: A Snapshot Summary

- **The Traditional Generation (a.k.a. "Silent Generation")** (born 1922–1945). This generation was influenced by events such as the Great Depression and World Wars I and II. Characteristics associated with people growing up at this time include loyalty, patriotism, respect for authority, and conservatism.
- **The Baby Boomer Generation** (born 1946–1964). This generation was influenced by events such as the Vietnam War, Watergate, and the civil rights movement. Characteristics associated with people growing up at this time include idealism, emphasis on self-fulfillment, and concern for social justice and equal rights.
- **Generation X** (born 1965–1980). This generation was influenced by Sesame Street, the creation of MTV, AIDS, and soaring divorce rates. They were the first "latchkey children"—youngsters who used their own key to let themselves into their home after school—because their mother (or single mother) was working outside the home. Characteristics associated with people growing up at this time include self-reliance, resourcefulness, and ability to adapt to change.
- **Generation Y (a.k.a. "Millennials")** (born 1981–2002). This generation was influenced by the September 11, 2001, terrorist attack on the United States, the shooting of students at Columbine High School, and the collapse of the Enron Corporation. Characteristics associated with people growing up at this time include a preference for working and playing in groups, familiarity with technology, and willingness to engage in volunteer service in their community (the "civic generation"). This is also the most ethnically diverse generation, which may explain why they're more open to diversity than previous generations and are more likely to view diversity positively.

BOX 9.1 (CONT)

> "You guys [in the media] have to get used to it. This is a new day and age, and for my generation that's a very common word. It's like saying 'bro.' That's how we address our friends. That's how we talk."
>
> —Matt Barnes, 33-year-old, biracial professional basketball player, explaining to reporters after being fined for using the word "niggas" in a tweet to some of his African American teammates

- Generation Z (a.k.a. "The iGeneration") (born 1994–present). This generation includes the latter half of Generation Y. They grew up during the wars in Afghanistan and Iraq, terrorism, the global recession, and climate change. Consequently, they have less trust in political systems and industrial corporations than previous generations. During their formative years, the world wide web was in place, so they're quite comfortable with technology and rely heavily on the Internet, Wikipedia, Google, Twitter, MySpace, Facebook, Instant Messaging, image boards, and YouTube. They expect immediate gratification through technology and accept the lack of privacy associated with social networking. For these reasons, they're also referred to as the "digital generation."

Think About It—Journal Entry 9.8

Look back at the characteristics associated with your generation. Which of these characteristics accurately reflect your personal characteristics and those of your closest friends? Which do not?

_____
_____
_____
_____
_____
_____

Sexual Diversity

These acronyms refer to lesbian, gay, bisexual, transgender, queer or questioning, and asexual or ally but all of the different identities within "LGBT" are often grouped together. These groups are very present on college campuses and there are specific needs and concerns related to each individual identity.

Humans experience and express sexuality in diverse ways. "Sexual diversity" refers to differences in human *sexual orientation*—the gender (male or female) an individual is physically attracted to, and *sexual identity*—the gender an individual identifies with or considers himself or herself or to be. The spectrum of sexual diversity includes:

Heterosexuals—males who are sexually attracted to females, and females who are sexually attracted to males.

Gays—males who are sexually attracted to males.

Lesbians—females who are sexually attracted to females.

Bisexuals—individuals who are sexually attracted to males and females.

Transgender—individuals who do not identify with the gender they were assigned at birth, or don't feel they belong to a single gender (e.g., transsexuals, transvestites, and bigender).

High schools across the country are increasing their support for GLBT (gay, lesbian, bisexual, transgendered) students, creating centers and services to facilitate their acceptance and adjustment. These centers and services play an important role in combating homophobia and related forms of sexual prejudice on campus, while promoting awareness and tolerance of all forms of sexual diversity. By accepting individuals who span the spectrum of sexual diversity, we acknowledge and appreciate the reality that heterosexuality isn't the one-and-only form of human sexual expression (Dessel, 2012). This growing acknowledgment is reflected in the Supreme Court's historic decision to legalize same-sex marriage nationwide (Dolan & Romney, 2015).

The Benefits of Experiencing Diversity

Thus far, this chapter has focused on *what* diversity is; we now turn to *why* diversity is worth experiencing.

Diversity Increases Self-Awareness and Self-Knowledge

Interacting with people from diverse backgrounds increases self-knowledge and self-awareness by enabling you to compare your life experiences with others whose experiences may differ sharply from your own. When you step outside yourself to contrast your experiences with others from different backgrounds, you move beyond ethnocentrism and gain a *comparative perspective*—a reference point that positions you to see how your particular cultural background has shaped the person you are today.

A comparative perspective also enables us to learn how our cultural background has advantaged or disadvantaged us. For instance, learning about cross-cultural differences in education makes us aware of the limited educational opportunities people have in other countries have to attend high school and how advantaged we are in America—where a high school education is available to everyone, regardless of their race, gender, age, or prior academic history.

Diversity Deepens Learning

Research consistently shows that we learn more from people who differ from us than we do from people similar to us (Pascarella, 2001; Pascarella & Terenzini, 2005). Learning about different cultures and interacting with people from diverse cultural groups provides our brain with more varied routes or pathways through which to connect (learn) new ideas. Experiencing diversity "stretches" the brain beyond its normal "comfort zone," requiring it to work harder to assimilate something unfamiliar. When we encounter the unfamiliar, the brain has to

> "It is difficult to see the picture when you are inside the frame."
> —An old saying (author unknown)

NOTE

The more you learn from people who are different than yourself, the more you learn about yourself.

engage in extra effort to understand it by comparing and contrasting it to something we already know (Acredolo & O'Connor, 1991; Nagda, Gurin, & Johnson, 2005). This added expenditure of mental energy results in the brain forming neurological connections that are deeper and more durable (Willis, 2006). Simply stated, humans learn more from diversity than they do from similarity or familiarity. In contrast, when we restrict the diversity of people with whom we interact (out of habit or prejudice), we limit the breadth and depth of our learning.

Diversity Promotes Critical Thinking

Studies show that students who experience high levels of exposure to various forms of diversity while in high school—such as participating in multicultural courses and school events and interacting with peers of different ethnic backgrounds—report the greatest gains in:

- thinking *complexity*—ability to think about all parts and sides of an issue (Association of American Colleges & Universities, 2004; Gurin, 1999),
- *reflective* thinking—ability to think deeply about personal and global issues (Kitchener, Wood, & Jensen, 2000), and
- *critical* thinking—ability to evaluate the validity of their own reasoning and the reasoning of others (Gorski, 2009; Pascarella et al., 2001).

These findings are likely explained by the fact that when we're exposed to perspectives that differ from our own, we experience "cognitive dissonance"—a state of cognitive (mental) disequilibrium or imbalance that "forces" our mind to consider multiple perspectives simultaneously; this makes our thinking less simplistic, more complex, and more comprehensive (Brookfield, 1987; Gorski, 2009).

Diversity Stimulates Creative Thinking

Cross-cultural knowledge and experiences enhance personal creativity (Leung et al., 2008; Maddux & Galinsky, 2009). When we have diverse perspectives at our disposal, we have more opportunities to shift perspectives and discover "multiple partial solutions" to problems (Kelly, 1994). Furthermore, ideas acquired from diverse people and cultures can "cross-fertilize," giving birth to new ideas for tackling old problems (Harris, 2010). Research shows that when ideas are generated freely and exchanged openly in groups comprised of people from diverse backgrounds, powerful "cross-stimulation" effects can occur, whereby ideas from one group member trigger new ideas among other group members (Brown, Dane, & Durham, 1998). Research also indicates that seeking out diverse alternatives, perspectives, and viewpoints enhances our ability to reach personal goals (Stoltz, 2014).

Diversity Enhances Career Preparation and Career Success

Whatever line of work you decide to pursue, you're likely to find yourself working with employers, coworkers, customers, and clients from diverse cultural backgrounds. America's workforce is now more diverse than at any other time in history and will grow ever more

> "When the only tool you have is a hammer, you tend to see every problem as a nail."
> —Abraham Maslow, humanistic psychologist, best known for his self-actualization theory of human motivation

> "What I look for in musicians is generosity. There is so much to learn from each other and about each other's culture. Great creativity begins with tolerance."
> —Yo-Yo Ma, French-born, Chinese-American virtuoso cellist, composer, and winner of multiple Grammy Awards

NOTE

By drawing on ideas generated by people from diverse backgrounds and bouncing your ideas off them, divergent or expansive thinking is stimulated; this leads to *synergy* (multiplication of ideas) and *serendipity* (unexpected discoveries).

> "When all men think alike, no one thinks very much."
> —Walter Lippmann, distinguished journalist and originator of the term "stereotype"

diverse throughout the 21st century; by 2050, the proportion of American workers from minority ethnic and racial groups will jump to 55% (U.S. Census Bureau, 2008).

National surveys reveal that policymakers, business leaders, and employers seek graduates who are more than just "aware" of or "tolerant" of diversity. They want graduates who have actual *experience* with diversity (Education Commission of the States, 1995) and are able to collaborate with diverse coworkers, clients, and customers (Association of American Colleges & Universities, 2002; Hart Research Associates, 2013). Over 90% of employers agree that all students should have experiences in high school that teach them how to solve problems with people whose views differ from their own (Hart Research Associates, 2013).

The current "global economy" also requires skills relating to international diversity. Today's work world is characterized by economic interdependence among nations, international trading (imports/exports), multinational corporations, international travel, and almost instantaneous worldwide communication—due to rapid advances in the world wide web (Dryden & Vos, 1999; Friedman, 2005). Even smaller companies and corporations have become increasingly international in nature (Brooks, 2009). As a result, employers in all sectors of the economy now seek job candidates who possess the following skills and attributes: sensitivity to human differences, ability to understand and relate to people from different cultural backgrounds, international knowledge, and ability to communicate in a second language (Fixman, 1990; Hart Research Associates, 2013; National Association of Colleges & Employers, 2007; Office of Research, 1994).

> "Technology and advanced communications have transformed the world into a global community, with business colleagues and competitors as likely to live in India as in Indianapolis. In this environment, people need a deeper understanding of the thinking, motivations, and actions of different cultures, countries and regions."
> —The Partnership for 21st Century Skills

As a result of these domestic and international trends, *intercultural competence* has become an essential skill for success in the 21st century (Thompson & Cuseo, 2014). Intercultural competence may be defined as the ability to appreciate and learn from human differences and to interact effectively with people from diverse cultural backgrounds. It includes "knowledge of cultures and cultural practices (one's own and others), complex cognitive skills for decision making in intercultural contexts, social skills to function effectively in diverse groups, and personal attributes that include flexibility and openness to new ideas" (Wabash National Study of Liberal Arts Education, 2007).

Think About It—Journal Entry 9.9

What intercultural skills do you think you already possess?

_____
_____
_____
_____
_____

What intercultural skills do you think you need to develop?

_____

_____

_____

_____

_____

_____

> **NOTE**
>
> The wealth of diversity in schools today represents an unprecedented educational opportunity. You may never again be a member of a community with so many people from such a wide variety of backgrounds. Seize this opportunity to strengthen your education and career preparation.

Overcoming Barriers to Diversity

Before we can capitalize on the benefits of diversity, we need to overcome obstacles that have long impeded our ability to appreciate and seek out diversity. These major impediments are discussed below.

Stereotyping

"Stereotype" derives from two different roots: *stereo*—to look at in a fixed way—and *type*—to categorize or group together, as in the word "typical." Thus, to stereotype is to view individuals of the same type (group) in the same (fixed) way.

Stereotyping overlooks or disregards individuality; all people sharing the same group characteristic (e.g., race or gender) are viewed as having the same personal characteristics—as in the expression: "You know how they are; they're all alike." Stereotypes can also involve *bias*—literally meaning "slant"—a slant that can tilt toward the positive or the negative. Positive bias results in favorable stereotypes (e.g., "Asians are great in science and math"); negative bias leads to unfavorable stereotypes (e.g., "Asians are nerds who do nothing but study"). Here are some other examples of negative stereotypes:

- Muslims are religious terrorists.
- Whites can't jump (or dance).
- Blacks are lazy.
- Irish are alcoholics.
- Gay men are feminine; lesbian women are masculine.
- Jews are cheap.
- Women are weak.

While few people would agree with these crass stereotypes, overgeneralizations are often made about members of certain groups. Such negative overgeneralizations malign the group's reputation, rob group members of their individuality, and can weaken their self-esteem and self-confidence (as illustrated by the following experience).

AUTHOR'S EXPERIENCE

When I was six years old, I was told by a six-year-old girl from a different racial group that all people of my race could not swim. Since I couldn't swim at that time and she could, I assumed she was correct. I asked a boy, who was a member of the same racial group as the girl, whether her statement was true. He responded emphatically: "Yes, it's true!" Since I was from an area where few other African Americans were around to counteract this belief about my racial group, I continued to buy into this stereotype until I finally took swimming lessons as an adult. After many lessons, I am now a lousy swimmer because I didn't even attempt to swim until I was an adult. Moral of this story: Group stereotypes can limit the confidence and potential of individual members of the stereotyped group.

—*Aaron Thompson*

Think About It—Journal Entry 9.10

1. Have you ever been stereotyped based on your appearance or group membership? If so, what was the stereotype and how did it make you feel?

   _____
   _____
   _____
   _____
   _____
   _____

2. Have you ever unintentionally perceived or treated a person in terms of a group stereotype rather than as an individual? What assumptions did you make about that person? Was that person aware of, or affected by, your stereotyping?

   _____
   _____
   _____
   _____
   _____
   _____
   _____

Prejudice

If all members of a stereotyped group are judged and evaluated in a negative way, the result is *prejudice*. The word "prejudice" literally means to "pre-judge." Typically, the prejudgment is negative and involves *stigmatizing*—ascribing inferior or unfavorable traits to people who belong to the same group. Thus, prejudice may be defined as a negative stereotype held about a group of people that's formed before the facts are known.

People who hold a group prejudice typically avoid contact with members of that group. This enables the prejudice to continue unchallenged because there's little opportunity for the prejudiced person to have a positive experience with members of the stigmatized group that could contradict or disprove the prejudice. Thus, a vicious cycle is established in which the prejudiced person continues to avoid contact with individuals from the stigmatized group; this, in turn, continues to maintain and reinforce the prejudice

> When you see me, do not
>   look at me with disgrace.
> Know that I am an
>   African-American
> Birthed by a woman of style
>   and grace.
> Be proud
> To stand by my side.
> Hold your head high
> Like me.
> Be proud. To say you know me.
> Just as I stand by you, proud
>   to be me.
> —Poem by Brittany Beard,
> first-year student

 Think About It—Journal Entry 9.11

Prejudice and discrimination can be subtle and only begin to surface when the social or emotional distance among members of different groups grows closer. Rate your level of comfort (high, moderate, or low) with the following situations.

Someone from another racial group:

1. Going to your school   high   moderate   low
2. Working in your place of employment   high   moderate   low
3. Living on your street as a neighbor   high   moderate   low
4. Living with you as a roommate   high   moderate   low
5. Socializing with you as a personal friend   high   moderate   low
6. Being your most intimate friend or romantic partner   high   moderate   low
7. Being your partner in marriage   high   moderate   low

For any item you rated "low," what do you think was responsible for the low rating?

_____

_____

_____

_____

_____

> See that man over there? Yes.
>
> "Well, I hate him.
> But you don't know him.
> That's why I hate him."
> —Gordon Allport,
> influential social
> psychologist and author
> of The Nature of Prejudice

Once prejudice has been formed, it often remains intact and resistant to change through the psychological process of *selective perception*—the

> "We see what is behind our eyes."
> —Chinese proverb

tendency for biased (prejudiced) people to see what they *expect* to see and fail to see what contradicts their bias (Hugenberg & Bodenhausen, 2003). Have you ever noticed how fans rooting for their favorite sports team tend to focus on and "see" the calls of referees that go against their own team, but don't seem to react (or even notice) the calls that go against the opposing team? This is a classic example of selective perception. In effect, selective perception transforms the old adage, "seeing is believing," into "believing is seeing." This can lead prejudiced people to focus their attention on information that's consistent with their prejudgment, causing them to "see" what supports or reinforces it and fail to see information that contradicts it.

Making matters worse, selective perception is often accompanied by *selective memory*—the tendency to remember information that's consistent with one's prejudicial belief and to forget information that's inconsistent with it or contradicts it (Judd, Ryan, & Parke, 1991). The mental processes of selective perception and selective memory often work together and often work *unconsciously*. As a result, prejudiced people may not even be aware they're using these biased mental processes or realize how these processes are keeping their prejudice permanently intact (Baron, Byrne, & Brauscombe, 2008).

Think About It—Journal Entry 9.12

Have you witnessed selective perception or selective memory—people seeing or recalling what they believe is true (due to bias), rather than what's actually true? What happened and why do you think it happened?

_____
_____
_____
_____
_____

Discrimination

Literally translated, the term *discrimination* means "division" or "separation." Whereas prejudice involves a belief, attitude or opinion, discrimination involves an *act* or *behavior*. Technically, discrimination can be either positive or negative. A discriminating eater may only eat healthy foods, which is a positive quality. However, discrimination is most often associated with a harmful act that results in a prejudiced person treating another individual, or group of individuals, in an unfair manner. Thus, it could be said that discrimination is prejudice put into action. For instance, to fire or not hire people on the basis of their race, gender, or sexual orientation is an act of discrimination.

Box 9.2 contains a summary of the major forms of discrimination, prejudice, and stereotypes that have plagued humanity. As you read through the following list, place a check mark next to any item that you, a friend, or family member has experienced.

BOX 9.2

Stereotypes, Prejudices, and Forms of Discrimination: A Snapshot Summary

- **Ethnocentrism**: viewing one's own culture or ethnic group as "central" or "normal," while viewing different cultures as "deficient" or "inferior."
  Example: Viewing another culture as "abnormal" or "uncivilized" because its members eat animals our culture views as unacceptable to eat, although we eat animals their culture views as unacceptable to eat.
- **Stereotyping**: viewing all (or virtually all) members of the same group in the same way—as having the same personal qualities or characteristics.
  Example: "If you're Italian, you must be in the Mafia, or have a family member who is."
- **Prejudice**: negative prejudgment about another group of people.
  Example: Women can't be effective leaders because they're too emotional.
- **Discrimination**: unequal and unfair treatment of a person or group of people—prejudice put into action.
  Example: Paying women less than men for performing the same job, even though they have the same level of education and job qualifications.
- **Segregation**: intentional decision made by a group to separate itself (socially or physically) from another group.
  Example: "White flight"—white people moving out of neighborhoods when people of color move in.
- **Racism**: belief that one's racial group is superior to another group and expressing that belief in attitude (prejudice) or action (discrimination).
  Example: Confiscating land from American Indians based on the unfounded belief that they are "uncivilized" or "savages."
- **Institutional Racism**: racial discrimination rooted in organizational policies and practices that disadvantage certain racial groups.

> "Let us all hope that the dark clouds of racial prejudice will soon pass away and . . . in some not too distant tomorrow the radiant stars of love and brotherhood will shine over our great nation."
> —Martin Luther King, Jr., Civil rights leader, humanitarian, and youngest recipient of the Nobel Peace Prize

  Example: Race-based discrimination in mortgage lending, housing, and bank loans.
- **Racial Profiling**: investigating or arresting someone solely on the basis of the person's race, ethnicity, or national origin—without witnessing actual criminal behavior or possessing incriminating evidence.
  Example: Police making a traffic stop or conducting a personal search based solely on an individual's racial features.
- **Slavery**: forced labor in which people are considered to be property, held against their will, and deprived of the right to receive wages.
  Example: Enslavement of Blacks, which was legal in the United States until 1865.
- **"Jim Crow" Laws**: formal and informal laws created by Whites to segregate Blacks after the abolition of slavery.
  Example: laws in certain parts of the United States that once required Blacks to use separate bathrooms and be educated in separate schools.
- **Apartheid**: an institutionalized system of "legal racism" supported by a nation's government. (Apartheid derives from a word in the Afrikaan language, meaning "apartness.")
  Example: South Africa's national system of racial segregation and discrimination that was in place from 1948 to 1994.

BOX 9.2 (CONT)

> "Never, never, and never again shall it be that this beautiful land will again experience the oppression of one by another."
> —Nelson Mandela, anti-apartheid revolutionary, first Black president of South Africa after apartheid, and winner of the Nobel Peace Prize

> "Rivers, ponds, lakes and streams— they all have different names, but they all contain water. Just as religions do— they all contain truths."
> —Muhammad Ali, three-time world heavyweight boxing champion, member of the International Boxing Hall of Fame, and recipient of the Spirit of America Award as the most recognized American in the world

- **Hate Crimes:** criminal action motivated solely by prejudice toward the crime victim.
  Example: Acts of vandalism or assault aimed at members of a particular ethnic group or persons of a particular sexual orientation.
- **Hate Groups:** organizations whose primary purpose is to stimulate prejudice, discrimination, or aggression toward certain groups of people based on their ethnicity, race, religion, etc.
  Example: The Ku Klux Klan—an American terrorist group that perpetrates hatred toward all non-white races.
- **Genocide:** mass murdering of a particular ethnic or racial group.
  Example: The Holocaust, in which millions of Jews were systematically murdered during World War II. Other examples include the murdering of Cambodians under the Khmer Rouge regime, the murdering of Bosnian Muslims in the former country of Yugoslavia, and the slaughter of the Tutsi minority by the Hutu majority in Rwanda.
- **Classism:** prejudice or discrimination based on social class, particularly toward people of lower socioeconomic status.
  Example: Acknowledging the contributions made by politicians and wealthy industrialists to America, while ignoring the contributions of poor immigrants, farmers, slaves, and pioneer women.
- **Religious Intolerance:** denying the fundamental human right of people to hold religious beliefs, or to hold religious beliefs that differ from one's own.
  Example: An atheist who forces nonreligious (secular) beliefs on others, or a member of a religious group who believes that people who hold different religious beliefs are infidels or "sinners" whose souls will not be saved.
- **Anti-Semitism:** prejudice or discrimination toward Jews or people who practice the religion of Judaism.
  Example: Disliking Jews because they're the ones who "killed Christ."
- **Xenophobia:** fear or hatred of foreigners, outsiders, or strangers.
  Example: Believing that immigrants should be banned from entering the country because they'll undermine our economy and increase our crime rate.
- **Regional Bias:** prejudice or discrimination based on the geographical region in which an individual is born and raised.
  Example: A northerner thinking that all southerners are racists.
- **Jingoism:** excessive interest and belief in the superiority of one's own nation—without acknowledging its mistakes or weaknesses—often accompanied by an aggressive foreign policy that neglects the needs of other nations or the common needs of all nations.
  Example: "Blind patriotism"—failure to see the shortcomings of one's own nation and viewing any questioning or criticism of one's own nation as being disloyal or "unpatriotic." (As in the slogan, "America: right or wrong" or "America: love it or leave it!")

> "Above all nations is humanity."
> —Motto of the University of Hawaii

- **Terrorism:** intentional acts of violence committed against civilians that are motivated by political or religious prejudice.
  Example: The September 11, 2001, attacks on the United States.

Chapter 9: Diversity and the High School Experience 247

BOX 9.2 (CONT)

- **Sexism:** prejudice or discrimination based on sex or gender.
    Example: Believing that women should not pursue careers in fields traditionally filled only by men (e.g., engineering or politics) because they lack the innate qualities or natural skills to do so.
- **Heterosexism:** belief that heterosexuality is the only acceptable sexual orientation.
    Example: Believing that gays should not have the same legal rights and opportunities as heterosexuals.
- **Homophobia:** extreme fear or hatred of homosexuals.

  Example: Creating or contributing to anti-gay websites, or "gay bashing" (acts of violence toward gays).
- **Ageism:** prejudice or discrimination toward certain age groups, particularly toward the elderly.
    Example: Believing that all "old" people have dementia and shouldn't be allowed to drive or make important decisions.
- **Ableism:** prejudice or discrimination toward people who are disabled or handicapped (physically, mentally, or emotionally).
    Example: Intentionally avoiding social contact with people in wheelchairs.

Think About It—Journal Entry 9.13

As you read through the above list, did you, a friend, or family member experience any of the form(s) of prejudice listed? If yes, what happened and why do you think it happened?

_____
_____
_____
_____
_____

> "I grew up in a very racist family. Even just a year ago, I could honestly say 'I hate Asians' with a straight face and mean it. My senior AP language teacher tried hard to teach me not to be judgmental. He got me to be open to others, so much so that my current boyfriend is half Chinese."
>
> —First-year college student

Strategies for Overcoming Stereotypes and Prejudices

We may hold prejudices, stereotypes, or subtle biases that bubble beneath the surface of our conscious awareness. The following practices and strategies can help us become more aware of our unconscious biases and relate more effectively to individuals from diverse groups.

Consciously avoid preoccupation with physical appearances. Remember the old proverb: "It's what inside that counts." Judge others by the quality of their inner qualities, not by the familiarity of their outer features. Get beneath the superficial surface of appearances and relate to people not in terms of how they look but who they are and how they act.

> "Stop judging by mere appearances, and make a right judgment."
>
> —Bible, John 7:24

> "You can't judge a book by the cover."
> —1962 hit song by Elias Bates, a.k.a. Bo Diddley
> (Note: a "bo diddley" is a one-stringed African guitar)

Form impressions of others on a person-to-person basis, not at the basis of their group membership. This may seem like an obvious and easy thing to do, but research shows that humans have a natural tendency to perceive individuals from unfamiliar groups as being more alike (or all alike) than members of their own group (Taylor, Peplau, & Sears, 2006). Thus, we need to remain mindful of this tendency and make a conscious effort to perceive and treat individuals of diverse groups as unique human beings, not according to some general (stereotypical) rule of thumb.

NOTE

It's valuable to learn about different cultures and the common characteristics shared by members of the same culture; however, this shouldn't be done while ignoring individual differences. Don't assume that all individuals who share the same cultural background share the same personal characteristics.

Think About It—Journal Entry 9.14

Your comfort level while interacting with people from diverse groups is likely to depend on how much prior experience you've had with members of those groups. Rate the amount or variety of diversity you have experienced in the following settings:

1. The high school you attended   high   moderate   low

2. The neighborhood in which you
   grew up   high   moderate   low

3. Places where you have been
   employed   high   moderate   low

Which setting had the *most* and the *least* diversity?

_____
_____
_____
_____

What do you think accounted for this difference?

_____
_____
_____
_____

> "I am very happy with the diversity here, but it also frightens me. I have never been in a situation where I have met people who are Jewish, Muslim, atheist, born-again, and many more."
> —First-year student (quoted in Erickson, Peters, & Strommer, 2006)

Place yourself in situations and locations on school where you will come in regular contact with individuals from diverse groups. Distancing ourselves from diversity ensures we'll never experience diversity and benefit from it. Research in social psychology shows that relationships are more likely to form among people who come in regular contact with one another (Latané et al., 1995), and research on diversity reveals that when there's regular contact between members of different racial or ethnic groups, stereotyping is sharply reduced and intercultural friendships are more likely to develop (Pettigrew, 1997, 1998). You can create these conditions by making an intentional attempt to sit near diverse students in the classroom, library, or student café, and by joining them for class discussion groups or group projects.

Take advantage of social media to "chat" virtually with students from diverse groups on your own school, or students on other schools. Electronic communication can be a convenient and comfortable way to initially interact with members of diverse groups with whom you have had little prior experience. After interacting *online*, you're more likely to feel more comfortable about interacting *in person*.

Be on the lookout for diversity implications associated with topics you're reading about or discussing in class. Consider the multicultural and cross-cultural ramifications of material you're studying and use examples of diversity to support or illustrate your points. If you're allowed to choose a topic for a research project, select one that relates to diversity or has implications for diversity.

> "Empirical evidence shows that the actual effects on student development of emphasizing diversity and of student participation in diversity activities are overwhelmingly positive."
> —Alexander Astin, *What Matters in College*

Seek out the views and opinions of classmates from diverse backgrounds. Discussions among students of different races and cultures can reduce prejudice and promote intercultural appreciation, but only if each member's cultural identity and perspective is sought out and valued by members of the discussion group (Baron, Byrne, & Brauscombe, 2008). During class discussions, you can demonstrate leadership by seeking out views and opinions of classmates from diverse backgrounds and ensuring that the ideas of people from minority groups are included and respected. Also, after class discussions, you can ask students from different backgrounds if there was any point made or position taken in class that they would have strongly questioned or challenged.

> "The classroom can provide a 'public place' where community can be practiced."
> —Susanne Morse, *Renewing Civic Capacity: Preparing College Students for Service and Citizenship.*

If there is little or no diversity among students in class, encourage your classmates to look at the topic from diverse perspectives. For instance, you might ask: "If there were international students here, what might they be adding to our discussion?" or, "If members of certain minority groups were here, would they be offering a different viewpoint?"

If you are given the opportunity to form your own discussion groups and group project teams, join or create groups composed of students from diverse backgrounds. You can gain greater exposure to diverse perspectives by intentionally joining or forming learning groups with students who differ in terms of gender, age, race, or ethnicity. Including diversity in your discussion groups not only creates social variety, it also enhances the quality of your group's work by allowing members to gain access to and learn from multiple perspectives.

Form collaborative learning teams with students from diverse backgrounds. A learning *team* is more than a discussion group that tosses around ideas; it moves beyond discussion to *collaboration*—its members "co-labor" (work together) to reach the same goal. Research from kindergarten through high school indicates that when students collaborate in teams, their academic performance and interpersonal skills are strengthened (Cuseo, 1996). Also, when individuals from different racial groups work collaboratively toward the same goal, racial prejudice is reduced and interracial friendships are more likely to be formed (Allport, 1954; Amir, 1976; Brown et al., 2003; Dovidio, Eller, & Hewstone, 2011). These positive developments may be explained, in part, by the fact that when members of diverse groups come together on the same team, nobody is a member of an "out" group ("them"); instead, everybody belongs to the same "in" group ("us") (Pratto et al., 2000; Sidanius et al., 2000).

In an analysis of multiple studies involving more than 90,000 people from 25 different countries, it was found that when interaction between members of diverse groups took place under the conditions described in **Box 9.3**, prejudice was significantly reduced (Pettigrew & Tropp, 2000) and the greatest gains in learning took place (Johnson, Johnson, & Smith, 1998; Slavin, 1995).

BOX 9.3

Tips for Teamwork: Creating Diverse and Effective Learning Teams

1. **Intentionally form learning teams with students who have different cultural backgrounds and life experiences.** Teaming up only with friends or classmates whose backgrounds and experiences are similar to yours can actually impair your team's performance because teammates can get off track and onto topics that have nothing to do with the learning task (e.g., what they did last weekend or what they're planning to do next weekend).

2. **Before jumping into group work, take some time to interact informally with your teammates.** When team members have some social "warm up" time (e.g., time to learn each other's names and learn something about each other), they feel more comfortable expressing their ideas and are more likely to develop a stronger sense of team identity. This feeling of group solidarity can create a foundation of trust among group members, enabling them to work together as a team, particularly if they come from diverse (and unfamiliar) cultural backgrounds.

   The context in which a group interacts can influence the openness and harmony of their interaction. Group members are more likely to interact openly and collaboratively when they work in a friendly, informal environment that's conducive to relationship building. A living room or a lounge area provides a warmer and friendlier team-learning atmosphere than a sterile classroom.

3. **Have teammates work together to complete a single work product.** One jointly created product serves to highlight the team's collaborative effort and collective achievement (e.g., a completed sheet of answers to questions, or a comprehensive list of ideas). Creating a common final product helps keep individuals thinking in terms of "we" (not "me") and keeps the team moving in the same direction toward the same goal.

4. **Group members should work interdependently**—they should depend on each other to reach their common goal and each member should have equal opportunity to contribute to the team's final product. Each teammate should take responsibility for making an indispensable contribution to the team's end product, such as contributing: (a) a different piece of *information* (e.g., a specific chapter from the textbook or a particular section of class notes), (b) a particular

BOX 9.3 (CONT)

form of *thinking* to the learning task (e.g., analysis, synthesis, or application), or (c) a different *perspective* (e.g., national, international, or global). Said in another way, each group member should assume personal responsibility for a piece that's needed to complete the whole puzzle.

Similar to a sports team, each member of a learning team should have a specific role to play. For instance, each teammate could perform one of the following roles:
- manager—whose role is to assure that the team stays on track and keeps moving toward its goal;
- moderator—whose role is to ensure that all teammates have equal opportunity to contribute;
- summarizer—whose role is to monitor the team's progress, identifying what has been accomplished and what still needs to be done;
- recorder—whose role is to keep a written record of the team's ideas.

5. After concluding work in diverse learning teams, take time to reflect on the experience. The final step in any learning process, whether it be learning from a class or learning from a group discussion, is to step back from the process and thoughtfully review it. Deep learning requires not only effortful action but also thoughtful reflection (Bligh, 2000; Roediger, Dudai, & Fitzpatrick, 2007). You can reflect on your experiences with diverse learning groups by asking yourself questions that prompt you to process the ideas shared by members of your group and the impact those ideas had on you. For instance, ask yourself (and your teammates) the following questions:

What major similarities in viewpoints did all group members share? (What were the common themes?)
- What major differences of opinion were expressed by diverse members of our group? (What were the variations on the themes?)
- Were there particular topics or issues raised during the discussion that provoked intense reactions or emotional responses from certain members of our group?
- Did the group discussion lead any individuals to change their mind about an idea or position they originally held?

When contact among people from diverse groups takes place under the five conditions described in this box, group work is transformed into *teamwork* and promotes higher levels of thinking and deeper appreciation of diversity. A win-win scenario is created: Learning and thinking are strengthened while bias and prejudice are weakened (Allport, 1979; Amir, 1969; Aronson, Wilson, & Akert, 2013; Cook, 1984; Sherif et al., 1961).

Think About It—Journal Entry 9.15

Have you had an experience with a member of an unfamiliar racial or cultural group that caused you to change your attitude or viewpoint toward that group? Explain.

_____
_____
_____
_____

Take a stand against prejudice or discrimination by constructively disagreeing with students who make stereotypical statements and prejudicial remarks. By saying nothing, you may avoid conflict, but your silence may be perceived by others to mean that you agree with the person who made the prejudicial remark. Studies show that when members of the same group observe another member of their own group making prejudicial comments, prejudice tends to increase among all group members—probably due to peer pressure of group conformity (Stangor, Sechrist, & Jost, 2001). In contrast, if a person's prejudicial remark is challenged by a member of one's own group, particularly a fellow member who is liked and respected, that person's prejudice decreases along with similar prejudices held by other members of the group (Baron, Byrne, & Brauscombe, 2008). Thus, by taking a leadership role and challenging peers who make prejudicial remarks, you're likely to reduce that person's prejudice as well as the prejudice of others who hear the remark. In addition, you help create a school climate in which students experience greater satisfaction with with their high school experience and are more likely to complete their degree. Studies show that a school climate which is hostile toward students from minority groups lowers students' level of high school satisfaction and high school completion rates of both minority and majority students (Cabrera et al., 1999; Eimers & Pike, 1997; Nora & Cabrera, 1996).

> **NOTE**
>
> By actively opposing prejudice on school, you demonstrate diversity leadership and moral character. You become a role model whose actions send a clear message that valuing diversity is not only the smart thing to do, it's the *right* thing to do.

Think About It—Journal Entry 9.16

If you heard another student telling an insulting racial or gender joke, do you think you would do anything about it? Why?

_____

_____

_____

_____

CHAPTER SUMMARY AND HIGHLIGHTS

Diversity refers to the variety of groups that comprise humanity (the human species). Humans differ from one another in multiple ways, including physical features, religious beliefs, mental and physical abilities, national origins, social backgrounds, gender, and sexual orientation. Diversity involves the important political issue of securing equal rights and social justice for all people; however, it's also an important *educational* issue—an integral element of the high school experience that enriches learning, personal development, and career preparation.

When a group of people share the same traditions and customs, it creates a culture that serves to bind people into a supportive, tight-knit community. However, culture can also lead its members to view the world solely through their own cultural lens (known as ethnocentrism), which can blind them to other cultural perspectives. Ethnocentrism can contribute to stereotyping—viewing individual members of another cultural group in the same (fixed) way, in which they're seen as having similar personal characteristics.

Stereotyping can result in prejudice—a biased prejudgment about another person or group of people that's formed before the facts are known. Stereotyping and prejudice often go hand in hand because if the stereotype is negative, members of the stereotyped group are then judged negatively. Discrimination takes prejudice one step further by converting the negative prejudgment into behavior that results in unfair treatment of others. Thus, discrimination is prejudice put into action.

Once stereotyping and prejudice are overcome, we are positioned to experience diversity and reap its multiple benefits—which include sharper self-awareness, deeper learning, higher-level thinking, and better career preparation.

Learning More through the World Wide Web: Internet-Based Resources

For additional information on diversity, see the following websites:

Stereotyping:
ReducingStereotypeThreat.org at www.reducingstereotypethreat.org

Prejudice & Discrimination:
Southern Poverty Law Center at www.splcenter.org/

Human Rights:
Amnesty International at www.amnesty.org/en/discrimination
Center for Economic & Social Justice at www.cesj.org

Sexism in the Media:
"Killing Us Softly" at www.youtube.com/watch?v=PTlmho_RovY

LGBT Acceptance & Support:
"It Gets Better Project," at www.itgetsbetter.org

References

Acredolo, C., & O'Connor, J. (1991). On the difficulty of detecting cognitive uncertainty. *Human Development, 34*, 204–223.

Allport, G. W. (1954). *The nature of prejudice*. Cambridge, MA: Addison-Wesley.

Allport, G. W. (1979). *The Nature of prejudice* (3rd ed.). Reading, MA: Addison-Wesley.

American Association of Community Colleges (2009). 2009 Fact Sheet. Retrieved from http://www.aacc.nche.edu/About/Documents/factsheet2009.pdf.

Amir, Y. (1969). Contact hypothesis in ethnic relations. *Psychological Bulletin, 71*, 319–342.

Amir, Y. (1976). The role of intergroup contact in change of prejudice and ethnic relations. In P. A. Katz (Ed.), *Towards the elimination of racism* (pp. 245–308). New York: Pergamon Press.

Anderson, M. & Fienberg, S. 2000. *Race and ethnicity and the controversy over the US Census. Current Sociology*, 48(3): 87–110.

Aronson, E., Wilson, T. D., & Akert, R. M. (2013). *Social psychology* (8th ed.). Upper Saddle River, NJ: Pearson/Prentice Hall.

Association of American Colleges & Universities (AAC&U) (2002). *Greater expectations: A new vision for learning as a nation goes to college*. Washington, DC: Author.

Association of American Colleges & Universities (AAC&U) (2004). *Our students' best work*. Washington, DC: Author.

Baron, et al., 2008. *Social psychology*, (12th ed.) Boston, MA: Allyn & Bacon.

Bligh, D.A. (2000). *What's the use of lectures?* San Francisco: Jossey Bass.

Bridgeman, B. 2003. *Psychology and evolution: The origins of mind*. Thousand Oaks, CA: Sage Publications.

Bronfenbrenner, U. (Ed.) (2005). *Making human beings human: Bioecological perspectives on human development*. Thousand Oaks, CA: Sage.

Brookfield, S. D. (1987). *Developing critical thinkers*. San Francisco: Jossey-Bass.

Brooks, I. 2009. Organisational Behaviour, 4th Edition. Englewood Cliffs, NJ: Prentice Hall.

Brown, T. D., Dane, F. C., & Durham, M. D. (1998). Perception of race and ethnicity. *Journal of Social Behavior and Personality*, 13(2), 295–306.

Brown, K. T, Brown, T. N., Jackson, J. S., Sellers, R. M., & Manuel, W. J. (2003). Teammates on and off the field? Contact with Black teammates and the racial attitudes of White student athletes. *Journal of Applied Social Psychology*, 33, 1379–1403.

Cabrera, A., Nora, A., Terenzini, P., Pascarella, E., & Hagedorn, L. S. (1999). Campus racial climate and the adjustment of students to college: A comparison between White students and African American students. *The Journal of Higher Education*, 70(2), 134–160.

Caplan, P. J., & Caplan, J. B. (2008). *Thinking critically about research on sex and gender* (3rd ed.). New York: HarperCollins College Publishers.

Cook, S. W. (1984). Cooperative interaction in multiethnic contexts. In N. Miller & M. B. Brewer (Eds.), *Groups in contact: The psychology of desegregation (pp. 291–302)*. New York: Academic Press.

Cuseo, J. B. (1996). *Cooperative learning: A pedagogy for addressing contemporary challenges and critical issues in higher education*. Stillwater, OK: New Forums Press.

DeNavas-Walt, C., Proctor, B. D., & Smith, J. C. (2013). *Income, poverty, and health insurance coverage in the United States, 2012*. U.S. Census Bureau, Current Population Reports, P60–245, Washington, DC: U.S. Government Printing Office.

Dessel, A. (2012). Effects of intergroup dialogue: Public school teachers and sexual orientation prejudice. *Small Group Research*, 41(5), 556–592.

Dolan, M., & Romney, L. (2015). "Law in California is now a right for all." *Los Angeles Times*. June 27, pp. A1 & A8.

Dovidio, J. F., Eller, A., & Hewstone, M. (2011). Improving intergroup relations through direct, extended and other forms of indirect contact. *Group Processes & Intergroup Relations*, 14, 147–160.

Dryden, G., & Vos, J. (1999). *The learning revolution: To change the way the world learns*. Torrance, CA and Auckland, New Zealand: The Learning Web.

Education Commission of the States (1995). *Making quality count in undergraduate education*. Denver, CO: ECS Distribution Center.

Eimers, M. T., & Pike, G. R. (1997). Minority and nonminority adjustment to college: Differences or similarities. *Research in Higher Education*, 38 (1), 77–97.

Erickson, B. L., Peters, C. B., & Strommer, D. W. (2006). *Teaching first-year college students*. San Francisco: Jossey-Bass.

Feagin, J. R., & Feagin, C. B. (2007). *Racial and ethnic relations*, (8th ed.) Englewood Cliffs, NJ: Prentice Hall.

Fixman, C. S. (1990). The foreign language needs of U.S. based corporations. *Annals of the American Academy of Political and Social Science*, 511, 25–46.

Friedman, T. L. 2005. *The world is flat: A brief history of the twenty-first century: Revitalizing the civic mission of schools*. Alexandria, VA.

Gorski, P. C. (2009). *Key characteristics of a multicultural curriculum*. Critical Multicultural Pavilion: Multicultural Curriculum Reform (An EdChange Project). Retrieved from www.edchange.org/multicultural/curriculum/characteristics.html.

Gould, E. & Wething, H. (2013). *Health Care, the Market and Consumer Choice. Inquiry* 50 (1):85–86.

Gurin, P. (1999). New research on the benefits of diversity in college and beyond: An empirical analysis. *Diversity Digest* (spring). Retrieved from http://www.diversityweb.org/Digest/Sp99/benefits.html.

Harris, (2010). Leading system transformation. *School Leadership and Management* 30 (Jul).

Hart Research Associates (2013). *It takes more than a major: Employer priorities for college learning and student success.* Washington, DC: Author.

Hugenberg, K., & Bodenhausen, G. V. (2003). Facing prejudice: Implicit prejudice and the perception of facial threat. *Psychological Science, 14*, 640–643.

Jablonski, N. G., & Chaplin, G. (2002). Skin deep. *Scientific American* (October), 75–81.

Johnson, D., Johnson, R., & Smith, K. (1998). Cooperative learning returns to college: What evidence is there that it works? *Change, 30*, 26–35.

Judd, C. M., Ryan, C. S., & Parke, B. (1991). Accuracy in the judgment of in-group and out-group variability. *Journal of Personality and Social Psychology, 61*, 366–379.

Kelly, K. (1994). *Out of control: The new biology of machines, social systems, and the economic world.* Reading, MA: Addison-Wesley.

Kitchener, K., Wood, P., & Jensen, L. (2000, August). *Curricular, co-curricular, and institutional influence on real-world problem-solving.* Paper presented at the annual meeting of the American Psychological Association, Boston.

Kochlar, R., Fry, R., & Taylor, P. (2011). "Wealth gaps rise to record highs between Whites, Blacks, Hispanics, twenty-to-one." *Pew Research Social and Demographics Trends* (July). Retrieved from http://www.pewsocialtrends.org/2011/07/26/wealth-gaps-rise-to-record-highs-between-whites-blacks-hispanics/.

Lancaster, L., & Stilman, D. (2002). *When generations collide: Who they are. Why they clash.* New York: HarperCollins.

Latané, B., Liu, J. H., Nowak, A., Bonevento, N., & Zheng, L. (1995). Distance matters: Physical space and social impact. *Personality and Social Psychology Bulletin, 21*, 795–805.

Leung, A. K., Maddux, W. W., Galinsky, A. D., & Chie-yue, C. (2008). Multicultural experience enhances creativity: The when and how. *American Psychologist, 63*(3), 169–181.

Luhman, R. (2007). *The sociological outlook.* Lanham, MD: Rowman & Littlefield.

Maddux, W.W. & Galinsky, A.D. 2009. *Cultural borders and mental barriers: the relationship between living abroad and creativity.* Journal of Personality and Social Psychology, 96(5):1047-61.

Mendez, F., Krahn, T., Schrack, B., Krahn, A. M., Veeramah, K., Woerner, A., Fomine, F. L. M., Bradman, N., Thomas, M., Karafet, T., & Hammer, M. (2013). An African American paternal lineage adds an extremely ancient root to the human Y chromosome phylogenetic tree. *The American Journal of Human Genetics, 92*, 454–459.

Meredith, M. (2011). *Born in Africa: The quest for the origins of human Life.* New York: Public Affairs.

Nagda, B. R., Gurin, P., & Johnson, S. M. (2005). Living, doing and thinking diversity: How does pre-college diversity experience affect first-year students' engagement with college diversity? In R. S. Feldman (Ed.), *Improving the first year of college: Research and practice* (pp. 73–110). Mahwah, NJ: Lawrence Erlbaum.

National Association of Colleges & Employers, 2003, 2007

National Association of Colleges and Employers (NACE). (2003). Job outlook 2003 survey. Bethlehem, PA: Author.

National Center for Education Statistics. (2011). *Digest of education statistics, table 237. Total fall enrollment in degree-granting institutions, by level of student, sex, attendance status, and race/ ethnicity: Selected years, 1976 through 2010.* Alexandria, VA: U.S. Department of Education. Retrieved from http://neces. ed/gov/programs/digest/d11/tables/dt11_237.asp

National Association of Colleges and Employers (NACE). (2007). Job outlook 2007 survey. Bethlehem, PA: Author

National Survey of Women Voters (1998). *Autumn overview report conducted by DYG Inc.* Retrieved from http://www.diversityweb.org/research_and_trends/research_evaluation_impact_/campus_community_connections/ national_poll.cfm

Nhan, D. (2012). "Census: Minorities constitute 37 percent of U.S. population." *National Journal: The Next America-Demographics 2012.* Retrieved from http://www.nationaljournal.com/thenextamerica/demographics/census-minorities- constitute-37-percent-of-u-s-population-20120517

Nora, A., & Cabrera, A. (1996). The role of perceptions of prejudice and discrimination on the adjustment of minority college students. *The Journal of Higher Education, 67* (2), 119–148.

Office of Research (1994). *What employers expect of college graduates: International knowledge and second language skills.* Washington, DC: Office of Educational Research and Improvement, U.S. Department of Education.

Olson, L. (2007). What does "ready" mean? *Education Week, 40*, 7–12.

Pascarella, E. T. (2001, November/December). Cognitive growth in college: Surprising and reassuring findings from the National Study of Student Learning. *Change*, pp. 21–27.

Pascarella, E., Palmer, B., Moye, M., & Pierson, C. (2001). Do diversity experiences influence the development of critical thinking? *Journal of College Student Development, 42*(3), 257–291.

Pettigrew, T. F. (1997). Generalized intergroup contact effects on prejudice. *Personality and Social Psychology Bulletin, 23,* 173–185.

Pettigrew, T. F. (1998). Intergroup contact theory. *Annual Review of Psychology, 49,* 65–85.

Pettigrew, T. F. & Tropp, L. R. (2000). Does intergroup contact reduce prejudice? Recent meta-analytic findings. S. Oskamp (Ed.), *Reducing prejudice and discrimination* (pp. 93–114). Mahwah, NJ: Lawrence Erlbaum Associates.

Pinker, S. (2000). *The language instinct: The new science of language and mind.* New York: Perennial.

Pratto, F., Liu, J. H., Levin, S., Sidanius, J., Shih, M., Bachrach, H., & Hegarty, P. (2000). Social dominance orientation and the legitimization of inequality across cultures. *Journal of Cross-Cultural Psychology, 31,* 369–409.

Public Service Enterprise Group (PSEG) (2009). *Diversity.* Retrieved from www.pseg.com/info/environment/sustainability/2009/.../diversity.jsp

Reid, G. B. R., & Hetherington, R. (2010). *The climate connection: Climate change and modern evolution.* Cambridge, UK: Cambridge University Press.

Roediger, H. L., Dudai, Y., & Fitzpatrick, S. M. (2007). *Science of memory: concepts.* New York, NY: Oxford University Press.

Shah, A. (2009). *Global issues: Poverty facts and stats.* Retrieved from http://www.globalissues.org/artoc;e/26/poverty-facts-and-stats.

Sherif, M., Harvey, D. J., White, B. J., Hood, W. R., & Sherif, C. W. (1961). *The Robbers' cave experiment.* Norman, OK: Institute of Group Relations.

Sidanius, J., Levin, S., Liu, H., & Pratto, F. (2000). Social dominance orientation, anti-egalitarianism, and the political psychology of gender: An extension and cross-cultural replication. *European Journal of Social Psychology, 30,* 41–67.

Slavin, R. E. (1995). *Cooperative learning* (2nd ed.). Boston: Allyn & Bacon.

Stangor, C., Sechrist, G. B., & Jost, J. T. (2001). Changing racial beliefs by providing consensus information. *Personality and Social Psychology Bulletin, 27,* 484–494.

Stoltz, P. G. (2014). *Grit: The new science of what it takes to persevere, flourish, succeed.* San Luis Obispo: Climb Strong Press.

Taylor, S. E., Peplau, L. A., & Sears, D. O. (2006). *Social psychology* (12th ed.). Upper Saddle River, NJ: Pearson/Prentice-Hall.

Thompson, A., & Cuseo, J. (2014). *Diversity and the college experience.* Dubuque, IA: Kendall Hunt.

U.S. Census Bureau (2008). *Bureau of Labor Statistics.* Washington, DC: Author.

U.S Census Bureau (2013). *Poverty.* Retrieved from https://www.census.gov/hhes/www/poverty/data/threshld/.

Wabash National Study of Liberal Arts Education (2007). *Liberal Arts outcomes.* Retrieved from http:www.liberalarts.wabash.edu/ study-overview/.

Wheelright, J. (2005, March). Human, study thyself. *Discover,* pp. 39–45.

Willis, J. (2006). *Research-based strategies to ignite student learning: Insights from a neurologist and classroom teacher.* Alexandria, VA: ASCD.

CHAPTER 9 EXERCISES

9.1 QUOTE REFLECTIONS

Review the sidebar quotes contained in this chapter and select two that were especially meaningful or inspirational to you.

For each quote, provide a three- to five-sentence explanation why you chose it.

9.2 REALITY BITE

Hate Crime: A Racially Motivated Murder

Jasper County, Texas, has a population of approximately 31,000 people. In this county, 80% of the people are White, 18% are Black, and 2% are of other races. The county's poverty rate is considerably higher than the national average, and its average household income is significantly lower. In 1998, the mayor, the president of the Chamber of Commerce, and two councilmen were Black. From the outside, Jasper appeared to be a town with racial harmony, and its Black and White leaders were quick to state that there was no racial tension in Jasper.

However, one day, James Byrd Jr.—a 49-year-old African American man—was walking home along a road one evening and was offered a ride by three White males. Rather than taking Byrd home, Lawrence Brewer (age 31), John King (age 23), and Shawn Berry (age 23), three men linked to White-supremacist groups, took Byrd to an isolated area and began beating him. They then dropped his pants to his ankles, painted his face black, chained Byrd to their truck, and dragged him for approximately three miles. The truck was driven in a zigzag fashion to inflict maximum pain on the victim. Byrd was decapitated after his body collided with a culvert in a ditch alongside the road. His skin, arms, genitalia, and other body parts were strewn along the road, while his torso was found dumped in front of a Black cemetery. Medical examiners testified that Byrd was alive for much of the dragging incident.

When they were brought to trial, the bodies of Brewer and King were covered with racist tattoos; they were eventually sentenced to death. As a result of the murder, Byrd's family created the James Byrd Foundation for Racial Healing. A wrought iron fence that separated Black and White graves for more than 150 years in Jasper Cemetery was removed in a special unity service. Members of the racist Ku Klux Klan have since visited the gravesite of Byrd several times, leaving racist stickers and other marks that angered the Jasper community and Byrd's family.

Source: Louisiana Weekly (February 3, 2003).

Reflection Questions

1. What factors do you think were responsible for this incident?
2. Could this incident have been prevented? If yes, how? If no, why not?
3. How likely do you think an incident like this could take place in your hometown or near your school?
4. If this event happened to take place place in your hometown, how do you think members of your community would react?

258 ◆ Chapter 9: Diversity and the High School Experience

9.3 GAINING AWARENESS OF YOUR GROUP IDENTITIES

We are members of multiple groups at the same time and our membership in these overlapping groups can influence our personal development and identity. In the following figure, consider the shaded center circle to be yourself and the six unshaded circles to be six different groups you belong to and that you think have influenced your development.

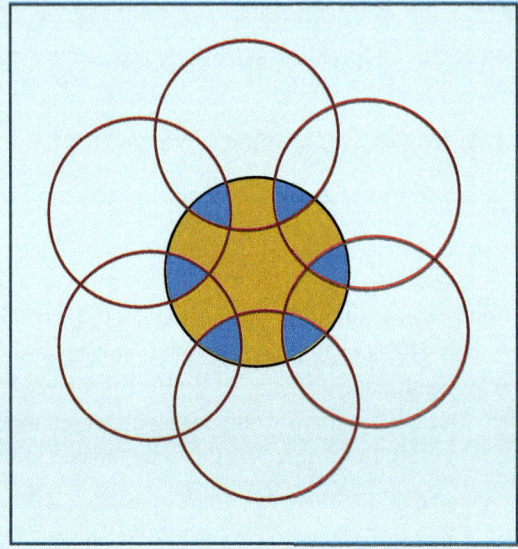

©Kendall Hunt Publishing Company

Fill in the unshaded circles with the names of groups to which you think you belong that have had the most influence on your personal development and identity. You can use the diversity spectrum (**p. 224**) to help you identify different groups to which you may be a member. Don't feel you have to fill in all six circles. What's more important is to identify those groups that you think have had a significant influence on your personal development or identity.

Reflection Questions:

1. Which one of your groups has had the greatest influence on your personal development or identity? Why?
2. Have you ever felt limited or disadvantaged by being a member of any your group(s) to which you belonged? Why?
3. Have you ever felt advantaged or privileged by your membership in any group(s)? Why?

9.4 INTERCULTURAL INTERVIEW

1. Identify a person on your school who is a member of an ethnic or racial group that you've had little previous contact. Ask that person for an interview, and during the interview, include the following questions:
   - What does "diversity" mean to you?
   - What prior experiences have affected your current viewpoints or attitudes about diversity?
   - What would you say have been the major influences and turning points in your life?
   - Who would you cite as your positive role models, heroes, or sources of inspiration?
   - What societal contributions made by your ethnic or racial group would you like others to be aware of and acknowledge?
   - What do you hope will never again be said about your ethnic or racial group?

2. If you were the interviewee instead of the interviewer, how would you have answered the above questions?
3. What do you think accounts for the differences (and similarities) between your answers to the above questions and those provided by the person you interviewed?

9.5 HIDDEN BIAS TEST

Go to www.tolerance.org/activity/test-yourself-hidden-bias and take one or more of the hidden bias tests on this website. These tests assess subtle bias with respect to gender, age, ethnic minority groups, religious denominations, sexual orientations, disabilities, and body weight.

1. After completing the test, answer the following questions:
2. Did the results reveal any biases you weren't unaware of?
3. Did you think the assessment results were accurate or valid?
4. What do you think best accounts for or explains your results?

If your closest family member and best friend took the test, how do you think their results would compare with yours?

CHAPTER 9 REFLECTION

After reading this chapter, has your definition of diversity changed? Explain.

List and describe five ways appreciating diversity will assist you in being successful in high school and/or life.

1.

2.

3.

4.

5.

Are there any areas of diversity you feel you need to be more comfortable with? What are the areas and HOW will you become more comfortable with them?

CHAPTER 10

CAREER EXPLORATION, PREPARATION, AND READINESS

Making Wise Choices about Your Future Life Path

CHAPTER PREVIEW

Even though career entry may be years away, career exploration and preparation should begin in the first term of college. Career planning gives you a practical, long-range goal to strive for and gets you thinking about how the skills you're using and developing in high school align with the skills that promote your professional success beyond high school. This chapter will help you develop a plan for making educational and career decisions that will best enable you to reach your long-term goals.

LEARNING GOAL

Equip you with effective strategies for pursuing a career path that's compatible with your personal interests, talents, and goals.

THOUGHT STARTER

 Think About It—Journal Entry 10.1

At this point in your high school experience, are you decided or undecided about a career?
_____

If you're undecided, what fields are you considering as possible careers?
_____
_____

From *Thriving in the Community College & Beyond: Strategies for Academic Success and Personal Development*, Third Edition, by Joseph Cuseo, Aaron Thompson, and Julie McLaughlin. Copyright © 2016 by Kendall Hunt Publishing Company. Reprinted by permission.

2. If you're decided:

   a) What's your choice?

   _____

   b) What led you to this choice?

   _____
   _____
   _____
   _____

   c) How sure are you about this choice? (Circle one.)

   absolutely sure   fairly sure   not too sure   likely to change

The Importance of Career Planning

After finishing your education, most of the remaining hours of your life will be spent working; the only other single activity you'll spend more time doing is sleeping. Since such a sizable portion of your life is spent on your vocation, it's easy to see why your career can have such a strong influence on your identity and personal happiness. Choosing a career path is one of the most important decisions you'll make in your life, so the process of career exploration and choice should begin right now.

Even if you have decided on a career that you've been dreaming about since you were a preschooler, you still need to confirm this choice and will likely need to decide on a specialization within your chosen field. For instance, if you're interested in pursuing a career in law, you'll need to decide what branch of law you will practice (criminal law, corporate law, family law, etc.). You will also need to decide what employment sector or type of industry you'd like to work in (e.g., nonprofit, for-profit, education, or government). Thus, no matter how certain or uncertain you are about your career path, you still need to explore specific career options and begin to devise a career development plan.

> "Love and work . . . work and love . . . what else is there really? Love and work are the cornerstones to our humanness."
> —Sigmund Freud, famous psychologist, responding to the question: What do you humans need to be happy?

Strategies for Career Exploration and Preparation

Reaching an effective decision about a career path involves four key steps:

1.
| Awareness of *yourself*—insight into your personal, interests, talents, needs, and values |

↓

2.
| Awareness of your *career options*—knowing the different career choices available to you |

↓

3.
| Awareness of what career options provide the *best "fit"* for you—knowing what career(s) best match your personal interests, talents, needs, and values |

↓

4.
| Awareness of the key *steps and strategies* needed to reach your career goal—knowing how to prepare for and gain entry to the career of your choice |

In short, effective career decision-making begins with a clear understanding of who you are, where you can go, where you will go, and how you will get there.

Step 1. Awareness of Self

The career you decide to pursue says a lot about who you are, what you want from life, and how you want to impact the lives of others. Thus, self-awareness is the critical first step in the process of career planning. A wise career choice begins with a clear understanding of who you are; from there you can determine where you want to go and how to get there. You must know yourself before you know what career is best for you. While this may seem obvious, self-awareness and self-discovery are often overlooked aspects of the career decision-making process. By deepening your self-awareness, you put yourself in a better position to choose a career path that's true to the person you are and the person you want to be.

Self-awareness is the first and most important step in the career planning process. Meaningful career goals and effective career choices are built on a deep understanding of self.

> "The unexamined life is not worth living."
> —Socrates, ancient Greek philosopher and a founding father of Western philosophy

You can increase your self-awareness by asking yourself questions that stimulate introspection—reflection on your inner qualities and personal priorities. Introspective questions launch you on an inner quest for self-insight and self-discovery which leads you to a career that's consistent with who you are and who you want to be. You can begin this introspective process by asking yourself questions relating to your personal:

- **Interests:** what you *like* doing;
- **Talents:** what you're *good* at doing;
- **Needs:** what you find personally *satisfying* or *fulfilling*; and
- **Values:** what you believe is *important* to do or is *worth* doing.

> "In order to succeed, you must know what you are doing, like what you are doing, and believe in what you are doing."
> —Will Rogers, Native American humorist and actor

AUTHOR'S EXPERIENCE

I often get asked about by students about what they should do after high school and what should they do to move forward in their careers. I typically start by asking about their interests and passions, which usually leads us to some ideas about a future career path. In almost every case, I always encourage them to pick a path that provides them future choices. When you reach the proverbial fork in the road, having a choice.

—*Shane Shope*

Think About It—Journal Entry 10.2

Complete the following sentences:

- My primary interests are . . .

_____
_____
_____
_____
_____

- My strongest abilities or talents are . . .

_____
_____
_____
_____
_____

- What brings me the greatest sense of personal satisfaction and fulfillment is ...

_____

_____

_____

_____

_____

- What I value the most is ...

_____

_____

_____

_____

_____

One way to gain greater self-awareness is by taking psychological tests or assessments. These assessments allow you to see how your interests and values compare with other students and with working professionals who are satisfied and successful with their careers. This comparative perspective provides you with an important reference point for assessing whether your level of interest in a career is high, average, or low relative to other students and to professionals working in that field. To take a career interest test, as well as other career exploration assessments, consult the Counseling Office on your campus.

Multiple Intelligences

One personal characteristic you should be aware of when choosing a career is your mental strengths, abilities, and talents. Intelligence was once considered to be a single, general trait that could be identified by one intelligence test score. Scholars have since discovered that intelligence doesn't come conveniently wrapped in a one-size-fits-all package. The singular word "intelligence" has been replaced by the plural word "intelligences" to reflect the fact that humans display intelligence (mental ability) in a variety of forms other than that measured by their score on an IQ or SAT test.

Based on studies of gifted and talented individuals, experts in different lines of work, and research on the human brain, psychologist Howard Gardner (1993, 1999, 2006) has identified the multiple

> "Exceptional individuals have a special talent for identifying their own strengths and weaknesses."
> –*Howard Gardner,* Extraordinary Minds

forms of intelligence listed in **Box 10.1.** Keep these forms of intelligence in mind when you're choosing a career because different careers emphasize different mental skills (Brooks, 2009). Ideally, you want to pursue an academic field that allows you to utilize your strongest mental attributes and talents. If you do, you're likely to master the concepts and skills required by your career more efficiently and more deeply.

BOX 10.1

Multiple Forms of Intelligence

As you read through the following forms of intelligence, place a checkmark next to the type that you think represents your strongest ability or talent. (You can possess more than one type.)

1. *Linguistic* Intelligence: ability to comprehend the meaning of words and communicate through language (e.g., verbal skills relating to speaking, writing, listening, and learning foreign languages).
2. *Logical–Mathematical* Intelligence: aptitude for understanding logical patterns (e.g., making and following logical arguments) and solving mathematical problems (e.g., working well with numbers and quantitative calculations).
3. *Spatial* Intelligence: aptitude for visualizing relationships among objects arranged in different spatial positions and ability to perceive or create visual images (e.g., forming mental images of three-dimensional objects; detecting detail in objects or drawings; drawing, painting, sculpting, and graphic design; strong sense of direction and capacity to navigate unfamiliar places).
4. *Musical* Intelligence: ability to appreciate or create rhythmical and melodic sounds (e.g., playing, writing, or arranging music).
5. *Interpersonal (Social)* Intelligence: ability to relate to others and accurately identify their needs, motivations, or emotional states; effective at expressing emotions and feelings to others (e.g., interpersonal communication skills, ability to accurately "read" the feelings of others and meet their emotional needs).
6. *Intrapersonal (Self)* Intelligence: ability to introspect and understand your own thoughts, feelings, and behaviors (e.g., capacity for personal reflection; emotional self-awareness; self-insight into personal strengths and weaknesses).
7. *Bodily–Kinesthetic (Psychomotor)* Intelligence: ability to control one's own body skillfully and learn through bodily sensations or movements; skilled at tasks involving physical coordination, working well with hands, operating machinery, building models, assembling things, and using technology.

> "I used to operate a printing press. In about two weeks I knew how to run it and soon after I could take the machine apart in my head and analyze what each part does, how it functioned, and why it was shaped that way."
> —Response of college sophomore to the questions: "What are you really good at? What comes easily or naturally to you?"

8. *Naturalist* Intelligence: ability to carefully observe and appreciate features of the natural environment; keen awareness of nature or natural surroundings; ability to understand causes and consequences of events occurring in the natural world.
9. *Existential* Intelligence: ability to conceptualize phenomena and ponder experiences that go beyond sensory or physical evidence, such as questions involving the origin of human life and the meaning of human existence.

Sources: Gardner (1993, 1999, 2006).

Think About It—Journal Entry 10.3

Look back at the nine forms of intelligence listed in **Box 10.1**.

Which of these types of intelligence do you think represents your strongest talent(s)?

_____

_____

_____

_____

Which career(s) do you think may best match your natural talents?

_____

_____

_____

_____

_____

In addition to your personal interests and talents, another factor you should consider when choosing a career is your personal needs. A *need* may be described as something stronger than an interest. When you do something that satisfies a personal need, you're doing something that you find highly motivating and personally fulfilling (Melton, 1995). Psychologists have identified several important human needs that vary in strength or intensity from person to person (Ryan, 1995; Ryan & Deci, 2000). Listed in **Box 10.2** are personal needs that are especially important to consider when making a career choice.

> "I believe following my passion is more crucial than earning money. I think that would come itself eventually."
> —College sophomore responding to the question, "What are you looking for in a career?"

BOX 10.2

Personal Needs to Consider When Making Career Choices

After reading about each need in this box, make a note indicating how strong that need is for you (high, moderate, or low).

1. **Autonomy.** Need for working independently without close supervision or control. Individuals with a high need for autonomy experience greater fulfillment working in careers that allow them to be their own boss, make their own choices or decisions, and control their own work schedule. Individuals low in this need may experience greater satisfaction working in careers that are more structured and allow them to work with a supervisor who provides direction, assistance, and frequent feedback.

BOX 10.2 (CONT)

> "Our research [on happiness] indicates prosperity is not the most important factor. Personal freedom is more important, and it's freedom in all kinds of ways... political freedom and freedom of choice."
> —Ronald Inglehart, happiness researcher, University of Michigan

2. **Affiliation (Belongingness).** Need for social interaction, a sense of belonging, and the opportunity to collaborate with others. Individuals with a high need for affiliation experience greater fulfillment working in careers that involve teamwork and frequent interpersonal interaction with coworkers. Individuals low in this need are more likely to be satisfied working alone or in competition with others.

> "To me, an important characteristic of a career is being able to meet new, smart, interesting people."
> —First-year student

3. **Achievement (Competence).** Need to experience challenge and a sense of personal accomplishment. Individuals with high achievement needs to feel a more fulfilled working in careers that push them to solve problems, generate creative ideas, and continually learn new information or master new skills. Individuals with a low need for achievement are likely to be more satisfied with careers that don't continually test their abilities and don't repeatedly challenge them to stretch their skills with new tasks and different responsibilities.

> "I want to be able to enjoy my job and be challenged by it at the same time. I hope that my job will not be monotonous and that I will have the opportunity to learn new things often."
> —First-year student

4. **Recognition.** Need for prestige, status, and respect from others. Individuals with high recognition needs are likely to feel satisfied working in high-status careers that society perceives as prestigious. Individuals with a low need for recognition would feel comfortable working in a career that they find self-satisfying, regardless of how impressive or enviable their career appears to others.

5. **Sensory Stimulation.** Need for experiencing variety, change, and risk. Individuals with high sensory stimulation needs are more likely to be satisfied working in careers that involve frequent changes of pace and place (e.g., travel), unpredictable events (e.g., work tasks that require them to think on their feet), and some stress (e.g., working under pressure of competition or deadlines). Individuals with a low need for sensory stimulation may feel more comfortable working in careers that involve regular routines, predictable situations, and minimal risk or stress.

> "For me, a good career is very unpredictable and interest-fulfilling. I would love to do something that allows me to be spontaneous."
> —First-year student

Sources: Baumeister & Leary (1995); Chua & Koestner (2008); Deci & Ryan (2002); Ryan (1995)

AUTHOR'S EXPERIENCE

As a college junior with half of my degree completed, I had an eye-opening experience. I wish this experience had happened in my first year, but better late than never. When I chose a career during my first year of college, my decision-making process was not systematic and didn't involve critical thinking. I chose a major based on what sounded prestigious and would pay me the most money. Although these are not necessarily bad factors, my failure to use a systematic and reflective process to evaluate my career choice. In my junior year I asked one of my professors why he decided to get his Ph.D. and become a professor. He simply answered, "I wanted autonomy." This was an epiphany for me. He explained that when he reflected on what mattered most to him, he realized that he needed a career that offered independence. So, he began looking at career options that would allow him to work independently. After hearing his explanation, "autonomy" became my favorite word, and this story became a guiding force in my life. After going through a critical introspective process, I determined that autonomy was exactly what I desired and a professor is what I became.

—*Aaron Thompson*

Think About It—Journal Entry 10.4

Looking back at the five needs listed in **Box 10.2**, which one(s) did you identify as being strong needs for you?

What career or careers do you think would best match your strongest needs?

_____
_____
_____
_____
_____
_____
_____

> "Don't expect a recluse to be motivated to sell, a creative thinker to be motivated to be a good proofreader day in and day out, or a sow's ear to be happy in the role of a silk purse."
>
> —Pierce Howard, author of The Owner's Manual for the Brain

In sum, four key personal characteristics should be considered when exploring and choosing a career: abilities, interests, values, and needs. As illustrated in **Figure 10.1**, these core characteristics are the pillars that provide the foundational support for making effective career choices and decisions. Ideally, you want to be in a career that you're good at, interested in, passionate about, and brings you a sense of personal satisfaction and fulfillment.

FIGURE 10.1: Personal Characteristics Providing the Foundation for Effective Career Choice

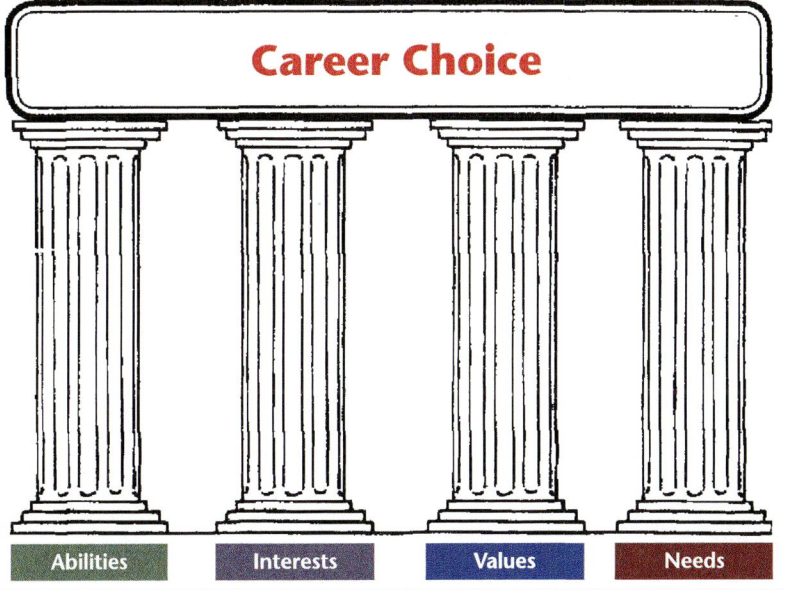

©Kendall Hunt

> "Know thyself and to thine own self be true."
> —Polonius in Hamlet, a play by William Shakespeare

The opportunity to make a reasonable amount of money is certainly one factor to consider when choosing a career, but a good career choice involves more factors than just starting salary. It's a decision that should also involve deep awareness and strong consideration of your special abilities, what you're passionate about, and what is meaningful to you. It's noteworthy that the word *vocation* derives from the Latin "vocatio" meaning "a calling." This suggests that a career is more than a money-making venture; it should call out to you and call forth your true talents and interests.

Step 2. Awareness of Career Options

In addition to self-awareness and knowledge about yourself, effective career decision-making requires knowledge about your range of career options and the realities of the work world. If you were to ask people to name as many careers as they could, they would not come close to naming the 900 career titles listed by the federal government in its Occupational Information Network. There are many more career choices in today's work world than there were for our early ancestors. When you look at the list of occupations in **Box 10.3**—none of which existed 10 years ago—you can see how the nature of today's work world is changing more rapidly than at any other time in history.

BOX 10.3

Occupations that Didn't Exist 10 Years Ago

1. **App developer:** When you hear "there's an app for that" it's because a career track emerged for program developers who have professional knowledge and skills into the world of mobile devices.
2. **Market research data miner:** Ever wonder how retailers know how to create customized advertisements especially for you? Market researcher data miners collect data on consumer behaviors and predict trends for advertisers to use to develop marketing strategies.
3. **Educational or admissions consultant:** Some parents take extra steps to ensure their children are accepted at the "right" school (from preschool to college). Educational or admissions consultants are hired to guide families through the application and interview process.
4. **Millennial generation expert:** It's now very common to find people from different generations working together in the same organization. Millennial generation experts help employers maximize the potential of their staff by providing advice on working with their youngest employees and mentoring them for future success.
5. **Social media manager:** The business world now makes greater use of social media to market and advertise their products and services. Social media managers target their marketing to users of different social media sites.
6. **Chief listening officer:** Similar to a social media manager, a chief listening officer uses social media to monitor consumer discussions and shares this information with marketing agents so they can design strategies that appeal to various segments of the population.
7. **Cloud computing services:** Most websites used every day by consumers store incredibly large amounts of data. Computer engineers with expertise in data management, store, and index tremendous volumes of bytes for companies—about a quadrillion!

> **BOX 10.3 (CONT)**
>
> 8. **Elder care:** Life expectancy is increasing and along with it the need for individuals who possess the knowledge, skills, and compassion to serve the elderly, their families, and the agencies and companies that assist them.
> 9. **Sustainability expert:** For environmental and economic reasons, companies are now seeking ways to minimize their carbon emissions. This has created a demand for professionals with expertise in the science of sustainability and the ability to develop "green" business practices that are also cost-effective.
> 10. **User experience design:** User experience designers do exactly what their titles suggest: they create experiences for consumers through technology. These designers use current technology to create color, sound and images by using tools like HTML, Photoshop, and CSS.
>
> Source: Casserly (2012)

Career Information Resources

Listed below are some of the best sources of information about careers. The primary place on campus for locating these sources is likely to be your Counseling Office. In addition to helping you assess your career interests and abilities, this is also the place where you can learn about the nature of different careers and locate career-related work experiences. The Library is another campus resource where you can find a wealth of reading material on careers, either in print or online.

Dictionary of Occupational Titles **(DOT) (www.occupationalinfo.org).** This is the largest printed resource on careers; it contains concise definitions of more than 17,000 jobs. It also includes information on:

- Work tasks typically performed in different careers.
- Background experiences of people working in different careers that qualified them for their positions.
- Types of knowledge, skills, and abilities required for different careers.
- Personal interests, values, and needs of individuals in different occupations who are satisfied and successful in their line of work.

Occupational Outlook Handbook **(OOH) (www.bls.gov/oco).** This is one of the most widely available and used resource on careers. It contains descriptions of approximately 250 positions, including information on: the nature of the work; work conditions; places of employment; training or education required for career entry and advancement; salaries and benefits; and additional sources of information about particular careers (e.g., professional organizations and governmental agencies associated with a career). A distinctive feature of this resource is that it also contains information about the *future employment outlook* for different careers.

Encyclopedia of Careers and Vocational Guidance **(Chicago: Ferguson Press).** As the name suggests, this is an encyclopedia of information on entry qualifications, salaries, and advancement opportunities for a wide variety of careers.

***Occupational Information Network (O*NET) Online* (www.online.onetcenter.org).** This is America's most comprehensive online source of online information about careers. It contains up-to-date descriptions of almost 1,000 careers, plus lots of other career-related information similar to what you would find in the *Dictionary of Occupational Titles*.

In addition to these general sources of information, your Counseling Office and College Library should have resources relating to specific careers or occupations. You can also learn a great deal about specific careers by simply reading advertisements for position openings in your local newspaper or online (e.g., www.careerbuilder.com and college.monster.com). When reading position descriptions, make special note of the tasks, duties, or responsibilities they involve and ask yourself whether these positions are compatible with your personal talents, interests, needs, and values.

Career Fairs

Periodically during the academic year, your campus is likely to offer programs devoted to career exploration and career preparation. For example, the Counseling Office may sponsor career exploration or career planning workshops that you can attend for free. Research indicates that career development workshops are effective in helping students plan for and choose careers (Brown & Krane, 2000; Hildenbrand & Gore, 2005). Your Counseling Office may also organize career fairs, at which professionals working in different career fields have booths where you can visit with them and ask questions about their careers. (See **p. 296** for interview questions you can ask working professions about their career.)

Information Interviews

One of the best and most overlooked ways to get accurate information about a career is to interview professionals working in that career. Career development specialists refer to this strategy as information interviewing. Don't assume that working professionals aren't interested in taking time to speak with a student; most are open to being interviewed and many report they like doing it (Crosby, 2002).

Information interviews provide you with "inside information" about what the career is really like because you're getting it directly from the horse's mouth—the person actually working in the career on a day-to-day basis. Information interviewing also helps you gain experience and confidence in interview situations, which may help you prepare for future job interviews. Furthermore, if you make a good impression during information interviews, the people you interview may suggest that you contact them again after graduation to see if there's a position opening. If there is an opening, you might find yourself being the interviewee instead of the interviewer, and find yourself being hired.

Because interviews can supply you with valuable information about careers and provide possible contacts for future employment, we strongly encourage you to complete the information interview assignment at the end of this chapter.

Career Observation (Shadowing)

In addition to reading about careers and interviewing professionals, you can also learn about careers by observing professionals performing their daily duties in their place of work. Two college-sponsored programs may be available on your campus that will allow you to observe working professionals:

Job Shadowing Program. Following (shadowing) and observing a professional during a typical workday.

Visit your Counseling Office to learn about what job shadowing or externship programs may be available on your campus. If you're unable to find a campus program for the career field you're exploring, consider finding one on your own by using strategies similar to the recommendations for information interviews at the end of this chapter. It's basically the same process; the only difference is that instead of asking the person for an interview, you're asking if you could observe that person at work. In fact, you could ask the person who granted you an information interview if you could observe (shadow) that person at work. Just a day or two of job shadowing can give you valuable information about a career.

AUTHOR'S EXPERIENCE

My father was a high school teacher. Ever since I was old enough to stand at a counter, I accompanied him to extracurricular activities and sporting events. He was a teacher first and foremost; for him, every experience was a teachable moment—whether it was on vacation, building a fence, cleaning out pig pens, or attending church. He also coached volleyball and softball, sponsored a National Honor Society, the Student Council, and served in a variety of other leadership roles. One of those roles was serving as the concession stand supervisor (which is where my early experience at a counter took place). I worked with hundreds of teenagers over the years making change, cooking and serving food, interacting with customers, conversing with adults, and solving problems. All my friends wore jeans and a t-shirt, but I was expected to dress my best, interact with people, and speak clearly. I didn't realize it at the time, but what I was doing was job shadowing at an early age. I was learning early on how to commit to a job, work hard and responsibly, communicate effectively, and think on my feet.

Fast forward . . . When I became a principal, my students soon became tired of hearing me say things like: "No matter what you do, do it well," "Whatever you do, do it better than anyone else," "Everything you do is man interview for the next thing you do." I probably said the following a thousand times, "I don't care if you flip burgers; flip them like nobody has ever done it before." Find something that you love to do and make it a career, not work.

At my high school, we allowed seniors to job shadow at businesses in our community. One senior (Brittany) forgot to sign up on time for her shadowing opportunity, so the only place left on the list was the local funeral home. She was not happy. She agreed to at least go and meet with the owner. Two weeks later, she worked as a receptionist, greeter at funerals, and was given many other roles because of her positive attitude and people skills. She eventually applied to and was accepted at mortuary school. She now works full-time at a funeral home in a job that enables her to support her family.

My father passed away last year. When I went to his visitation, the first person at the door to greet and comfort me was Brittany.

—*J.R. Roush*

Think About It—Journal Entry 10.5

If you were to interview or observe a working professional in a career that interests you, what type of work would that person be doing?

Information interviewing, job shadowing, and externships supply you with great information about a career. However, information is not experience. To get career-related work *experience*, you've got four major options:

- Internships
- Cooperative education programs
- Volunteer work or service learning
- Part-time work

Internships

In contrast to job shadowing and externships—which involve observing someone at work—an internship actively involves you in the work itself and gives you an opportunity to perform career-related work duties. A distinguishing feature of internships is that you can receive academic credit and sometimes financial compensation for the work you do. Usually, an internship involves a total of 120 to 150 work hours, which may be completed at the same time you're enrolled in classes, or at a time when you're not taking classes (e.g., summer internship).

A key advantage of internships is that they enable you to escape the classic catch-22 situation that graduates often run into when interviewing for their first career position. The interview scenario usually goes something like this: The potential employer asks the graduate, "What work experience have you had in this field?" The recent graduate replies, "I haven't had any work experience because I've been a full-time student." You can avoid this scenario by completing an internship. Participating in at least one internship while you're enrolled in school will enable you to beat the "no experience" rap after graduation and distinguish yourself from other graduates. Surveys show that more than 75% of employers prefer candidates with internships (National Association of Colleges & Employers, 2010); students with internships are more likely to acquire career-relevant work skills while in school and find immediate employment after college (Hart Research Associates, 2006, 2014; Pascarella & Terenzini, 2005).

You can pursue internships on your own by consulting published guides that list various career-related internships and provide information on how to apply for them (e.g., Peterson's Internships and the Vault Guide to Top Internships). You can also find internships on websites such as www.internships.com or www.vaultreports.com. Lastly, information on internships may be available from the local chamber of commerce in your hometown, or in the city where your school is located.

When employers are asked to rank various factors they consider important when hiring new employees, internships receive the highest ranking (National Association of Colleges & Employers, 2012, 2014). Employers also report that when full-time positions open up in their organization or company, they usually turn first to their own interns and co-op students (National Association of Colleges & Employers, 2013).

Volunteer Work or Service Learning

Volunteer service not only gives you the opportunity to serve your community, it also gives you the opportunity to explore different work environments and gain work experience in career fields relating to your area of service. For example, volunteer work performed for different age groups (children, adolescents, or the elderly) and in different work environments (hospital, school, or laboratory) provides you with firsthand, resume-building experience and the opportunity to test your interest in careers related to these age groups and work environments. Volunteer experience also enables you to network with professionals who can serve as personal references for you and provide you with letters of recommendation. Furthermore, if these professionals are impressed with your service they may hire you on a part-time basis while you're still in college, or full-time after you graduate.

To get an idea of the wide range of career-related service opportunities that may be available to you, go to: www.usa.service.org. You may also get volunteer experience through *service learning* courses at your college that integrate these experiences into coursework. Volunteer service may be incorporated into the course as a required or optional assignment whereby you participate in the volunteer experience and then reflect on your experience in a paper or class presentation.

Another course-integrated option for gaining work experience is by enrolling in courses that include a *practicum* or *field work*. For instance, if you're interested in working with children, courses in child psychology or early childhood education may offer experiential learning opportunities in a preschool or daycare center on campus.

Lastly, it may be possible to do volunteer work on campus in different college offices, or by assisting a faculty member. Volunteering as a research or teaching assistant can be a very valuable experience if you intend to go to graduate school. If you have a good relationship with faculty members in an academic field that interests you, consider asking them whether they would like some assistance with their teaching or research responsibilities.

AUTHOR'S EXPERIENCE

I was once advising two first-year students, Kim and Christopher. Kim was thinking about becoming a physical therapist and Chris was thinking about becoming an elementary school teacher. To help Kim get a better idea if physical therapy was the career for her, I suggested that she visit a hospital near our college to inquire about whether she could do volunteer work in the physical therapy unit. As it turned out, the hospital did need volunteers, so she volunteered in the physical therapy unit and loved it. That volunteer experience confirmed for Kim that a physical therapist is what she wanted to be. She completed a degree in physical therapy and is now a professional physical therapist.

Similarly, I suggested to Chris that he test his interest in possibly becoming an elementary school teacher by visiting some local schools to ask about whether they could use a volunteer teacher's aide. One of the schools did need his services, so Chris volunteered as a teacher's aide for about 10 weeks. About two weeks into his volunteer experience, he came into my office to tell me that the kids were just about driving him crazy and he no longer had any interest in becoming a teacher! He ended up majoring in communications.

Kim and Chris were the first two students I advised to get involved in volunteer work to test their career interests. Their volunteer experiences proved to be so useful in helping them identify their career path that I continued to encourage all students I advised to get volunteer experience in the career field they were considering.

—Joe Cuseo

Think About It—Journal Entry 10.6

If you have participated in volunteer experiences, what did you learn about yourself from these experiences that might influence your career plans, or acquire skills that could be applied to a future career?

_____
_____
_____
_____
_____

Part-Time Work

Jobs you hold during the academic year or summer break shouldn't be overlooked as career development experiences. Part-time work can supply you with opportunities to develop skills and personal qualities that may be relevant to any future career you decide to pursue, such as organizational skills, communication skills, and ability to work effectively with coworkers from diverse backgrounds and cultures. It's also possible that work in a part-time position may eventually turn into a full-time career—as illustrated in the following story.

> **AUTHOR'S EXPERIENCE**
>
> While he was enrolled in college, a former student of mine (Matt), an English major, worked part time for an organization that provides special assistance to mentally handicapped children. After he completed his English degree, the organization offered him a full-time position that he accepted. While working full-time at this position with handicapped children, Matt decided to go to graduate school part-time and eventually completed a master's degree in special education. This degree qualified him for a promotion to a more advanced position in the organization, which he also accepted. Moral of the story: Part-time work in college can play an important role in opening up a future career path.
>
> —*Joe Cuseo*

There's simply no substitute for gaining knowledge about careers than direct, hands-on learning experience in actual work settings—such as shadowing, internships, volunteer services, and part-time work. These firsthand experiences represent the ultimate career "reality test." They allow you direct access to what careers are really like—as opposed to the glamorized and unrealistic picture of them portrayed in the media.

> "As entertainment, TV shows are great. As reality, they fall a little short. So enjoy your TV and movies, but don't make career decisions based on them."
> —*Katharine Brooks, author,* You Majored in What? Mapping Your Path from Chaos to Career

> **NOTE**
>
> A key characteristic of effective goal setting is to set goals that are realistic. In the case of career goals, getting firsthand experience in actual work settings allows you to get a much more realistic view of what work in a field is really like—before committing to that field as your career goal.

Tying it altogether, experiencing work in real-life work settings has five powerful career advantages:

- You get a realistic picture of what work is like in a particular field.
- You get to test your interests and skills for certain types of work.
- You strengthen your resume by adding experiential learning to academic (classroom) learning.
- You acquire contacts who can serve as personal references and sources for letters of recommendation.
- You network with employers who may hire you or refer you for a position after graduation.

To locate and participate in work experiences that relate to your career interests, use all resources available to you, including campus resources (e.g., the Counseling Office and Financial Aid Office), local resources (e.g., Chamber of Commerce), and personal contacts (e.g., family and friends). Take these experiences seriously, learn as much as you can from them, and build relationships with the people you work with—these are the people who can provide you with future contacts, references, and referrals. Don't forget that almost three of every four jobs are obtained through personal relationships, aka "networking" (Brooks, 2009).

Think About It—Journal Entry 10.7

1. Have you had work experiences that may influence your future career plans, or provided you with skills you can include on your resume? What are they?

   _____
   _____
   _____
   _____
   _____
   _____

2. If you could get work experience in any career field right now, what would it be? Why?

   _____
   _____
   _____
   _____
   _____
   _____

Step 3. Awareness of Career Options that Provide the Best "Fit" for You

As we've emphasized throughout this chapter, the factor that should carry the greatest weight in career decision-making is the match between your career choice and your personal talents, interests, needs, and values. Since a career choice is a long-range decision that affects your life well beyond college, the process of self-awareness should not only involve reflection on who you are now, but also on how your career choice relates to where you see yourself in the future.

> "More people today have the means to live, but no meaning to live for."
> —Viktor Frankl, Austrian neurologist, psychiatrist, and Holocaust survivor

Think About It—Journal Entry 10.8

Answer the following questions about a career you're considering or have chosen:

1. Why are you attracted to this career? (What led or caused you to become interested in it?)

> "I think that a good career has to be meaningful for a person. It should give a person a sense of fulfillment."
> —First-year student

2. Would you say that your interest in this career is characterized primarily by *intrinsic* motivation—something "inside" of you, such as your personal abilities, interests, needs, and values? Or, would you say that your interest in the career is driven by *extrinsic* motivation—something "outside" of you, such as starting salary, pleasing your family, or meeting expectations of your gender (i.e., an expected career role for a male or female)? Explain.

3. If money weren't an issue and you could earn a comfortable living working in another career, would you still continue to pursue the same career you're currently considering? Why or why not?

> "It's easy to make a buck. It's a lot tougher to make a difference."
> —Tom Brokaw, award-winning television journalist and author

Step 4. Awareness of the Major Steps Needed to Reach Your Career Goal

Whether you're keeping your career options open or think you have a particular career in mind, there are three paths to career readiness: (1) develop career-readiness skills in high school (such as those recommended in this chapter) and seek a job immediately after graduation,

(2) continue your education after high school by enrolling in a two-year community, technical junior college, or (3) continue your education after high school by enrolling in a four-year college or university. These three paths are illustrated in **Figure 10.2**.

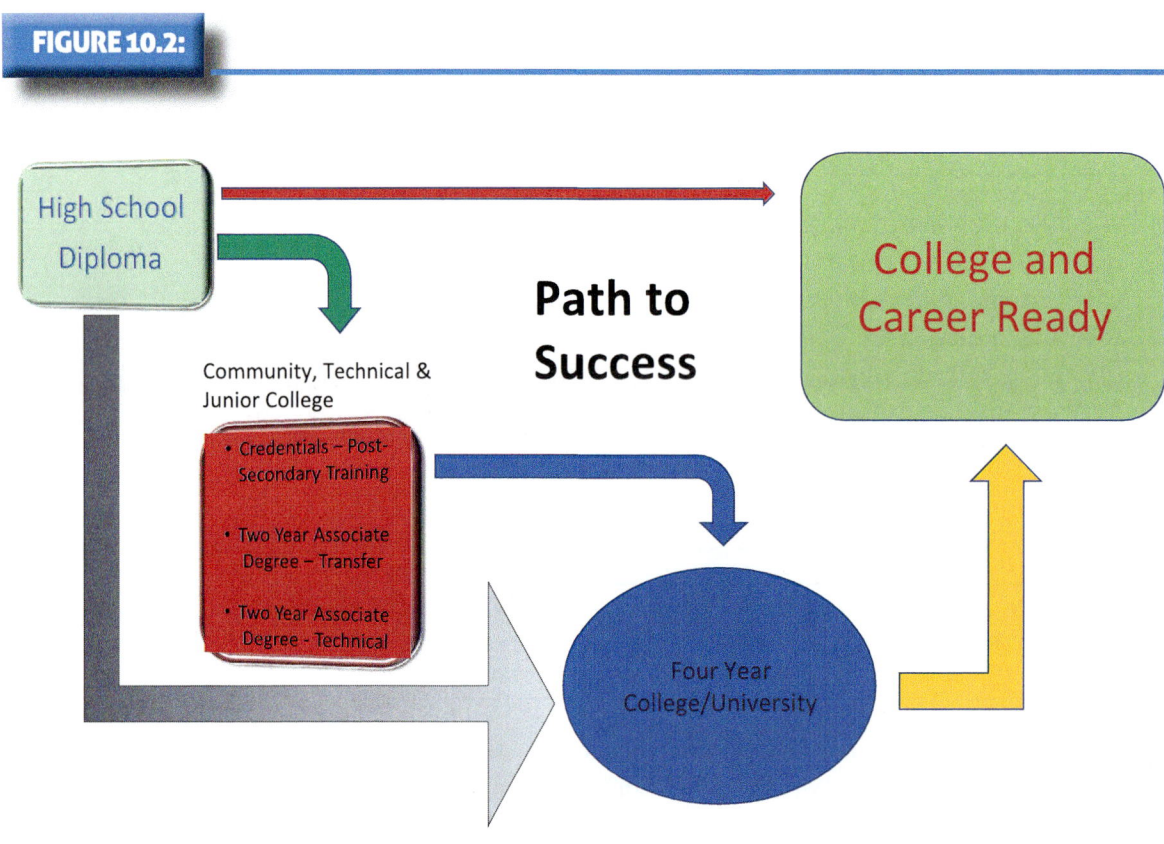

FIGURE 10.2:

You should be aware that American employers have been dissatisfied with the career-readiness skills of high school graduates (Gewertz, 2016). Our country has shifted from being a manufacturing-based economy to a more service-oriented, knowledge-based economy, creating a demand for workers with more advanced skills that require some education beyond high school. By 2020, almost two-thirds of jobs in the United States will require some form of education beyond high school (Carnevale, Smith, & Strohl, 2013). Simply stated, there are now substantially more job opportunities for students with a college degree or credential than there are for students with a high school diploma. In addition to more opportunities for employment, pursuing a college credential puts you in a better position to choose a career path that matches your interests and talents.

Self-Monitoring: Watching and Tracking Your Skills and Attributes

Keep in mind that the *academic* skills you're developing in school are also *professional* skills you'll use in your career. Said in another way, learning skills become earning skills. When you're engaged in the process of completing academic tasks—such as note-taking, reading, writing papers, and taking tests—you're also developing career-relevant skills—such as listening, interpreting, analyzing, and problem solving.

What matters more to employers of graduates than their degree credentials or the courses on their transcript are the skills and personal qualities they've developed and can bring to the position (Education Commission of the States, 1995; Figler & Boles, 2007) You can start building these skills and qualities through effective *self-monitoring*—that is, monitoring (watching) yourself and tracking the skills you're using and developing during in school. Skills are habits, and like other habits which are repeatedly practiced, their development can be so gradual and subtle that you may not even notice how much growth has taken place (like watching grass grow). Thus, career development specialists recommend that you consciously and carefully reflect on the skills you're using so you remain aware of their development and are able to articulate them to potential employers (Lock, 2004).

One way to track your developing skills is by keeping a *learning journal* in which you reflect on the academic tasks and assignments you've completed, along with the skills you developed while completing them. Your journal should also include skills developed outside the classroom—such as those acquired through co-curricular experiences, leadership development programs, volunteer experiences, and part-time jobs.

Since skills are actions, it's best to track and record them in your journal as *verbs*. You're likely to find that many of these action verbs reflect the type of work-related skills that employers seek in today's job candidates. **Box 10.4** contains a sample of action-oriented career skills you're likely to develop in college that are relevant to successful performance in a variety of careers.

BOX 10.4

Transferable Skills Relevant to Successful Career Performance

The following behaviors represent a sample of flexible skills that are relevant to success in virtually all careers (Bolles, 1998; Figler & Bolles, 2007). As you track your learning experiences in high school, remain mindful of whether you're developing these (and other) skills, both inside and outside the classroom.

advise	delegate	motivate	resolve
assemble calculate	design evaluate	negotiate	sequence
coach	explain	present	summarize
coordinate	initiate	produce	supervise
create	measure	research	synthesize

In addition to tracking your skills, also keep track of the positive traits and attributes you're developing. While skills are best recorded as *verbs* because they represent actions you can perform for anyone who hires you, personal attributes are best recorded as *adjectives* because they describe who you are and what positive qualities you can bring to any position. **Box 10.5** identifies examples of personal traits and attributes that are relevant to successful performance in any career.

BOX 10.5

Personal Traits and Attributes Relevant to Successful Career Performance

As you proceed through high school, keep track of these and other personal attributes or character traits you are developing.

collaborative	energetic	loyal	positive	reflective
conscientious	enthusiastic	observant	precise	sincere
considerate	ethical	open-minded	prepared	tactful
curious	flexible	outgoing	productive	team player
dependable	imaginative	patient	prudent	thorough
determined	industrious	persuasive	punctual	thoughtful

Think About It—Journal Entry 10.9

Look back at the personal skills and traits listed in **Boxes 10.5** and **10.6**. Underline or highlight those that you think are relevant to the career(s) you're considering.

_____
_____
_____
_____
_____

AUTHOR'S EXPERIENCE

After class one day, I had a conversation with a student of mine (Max) about his personal interests. He said he was considering a career in the music industry and was working part-time as a disc jockey at a night club. I asked him what it took to be a good disc jockey, and in less than five minutes of talking about his part-time work, we discovered that there were many transferable career skills embedded in his job than he realized. Each night he worked he was responsible for organizing three to four hours of music; he had to read the reactions of his audience (customers) and adapt or adjust his selections to their musical tastes; he had to arrange his selections in a sequence that varied the tempo of music he played throughout the night; and he had to continually research and update his music collection to track the latest trends in hits and popular artists. His job also required him to deliver public announcements, which enabled him to overcome his fear of public speaking.

Although we were just having a short, friendly conversation after class about his part-time work, Max ended up reflecting on and identifying multiple skills he was developing on the job. We both agreed that it would be a good idea for him to get these skills down in writing so that he could use them as selling points for future jobs in the music field, or any other line of work he might eventually pursue.

—*Joe Cuseo*

NOTE

Embedded in your work and class experiences are transferable skills and personal qualities that are applicable to a variety of careers. Tracking these skills and qualities and articulating them to potential employers is as important to successful entry into a future career as the courses listed on your transcript and the major listed on your resume.

Self-Marketing: Packaging and Presenting Your Personal Strengths and Achievements

Studies show that students who convert their degree into a successful career have two common characteristics: personal initiative and a positive attitude (Pope, 1990). They don't take a passive approach and assume a good position will just fall into their lap; nor do they believe they are owed a position simply because they have a degree or credential. Instead, they take an active role involved in defining their strengths and showcasing them in the job-search process (Brown & Krane, 2000).

One way you can convert your degree into gainful employment is to view yourself (a graduate) as a product and view employers as customers who may be interested in purchasing your product (your skills and attributes). As a high school student, it could be said that you're in the early stages in the process of developing your product. Begin the process now by identifying and packaging your skills and attributes so by the time you graduate you'll have a well-developed product that potential employers will be interested in purchasing.

By developing an effective self-marketing plan, you give employers a clear idea of what you can bring to the table and do *for them*. You can market your personal skills, qualities, and achievements to future employers through the following formats.

"Man who stand on hill with mouth open will wait long time for roast duck to drop in."
—*Confucius, Chinese philosopher who emphasized sincerity and social justice*

"The bottom line for most employers is 'Will this person fit in our environment?' One of the keys to marketing yourself is to make a connection, to get out of your mindset and into your audience's."
—*Katharine Brooks, author,* You Majored in What? Mapping Your Path from Chaos to Career

Extracurricular Experiences

Participation in student clubs, campus organizations, and other types of extracurricular activities represent a valuable source of experiential learning that complements classroom-based learning and contributes to career preparation and development. A sizable body of research supports the power of these experiences for career success (Astin, 1993; Hart Research Associates, 2006, 2014; Kuh, 1993;

Pascarella & Terenzini, 1991, 2005). Extracurricular experiences that are especially relevant to career development and career success are those that:

- Allow you to develop leadership and mentoring skills—such as, participating in leadership retreats, student government, college committees, peer counseling, or peer tutoring.
- Enable you to interact with others from diverse ethnic and racial groups—such as, multicultural or international clubs and organizations.
- Relate to your career interests—such as, involvement in student clubs in your intended college major or career field.

Don't forget that extracurricular experiences are also resume-building experiences; they serve as evidence of social responsibility to your communities on and off campus. Be sure to showcase these experiences to prospective employers. Also, don't forget that campus professionals with whom you may interact while participating in extracurricular activities (e.g., the director of student activities or dean of students) can serve as valuable references and provide you with letters of recommendation to future employers, graduate schools, or professional schools.

Personal Resume

A resume may be described as a listed or bulleted summary of your most important accomplishments, skills, and credentials. If you haven't yet accumulated enough experiences to construct a fully developed resume, you can start building a "skeletal resume" that contains major categories or headings (the skeleton) which you'll eventually flesh out with your specific experiences and accomplishments. (See **Box 10.6** for a sample skeleton resume.)

Portfolio

Unlike a resume, which simply lists your experiences, a portfolio contains actual products or samples of your work. You may have heard the word "portfolio" referred to as a collection of artwork that professional artists put together to showcase or advertise their artistic ability. However, the term *portfolio* has a broader meaning; it can be a collection of any material that depicts a person's skills and talents, or demonstrates educational and personal development. For example, a portfolio could include items such as:

- Outstanding papers, exam performances, research projects, and lab reports
- Work samples and photos from service learning experiences and internships
- Video footage of oral presentations and public performances
- Performance evaluations received from teachers and employers
- Letters of recognition from teachers and employers

BOX 10.6

Constructing a Skeletal Resume

Use this skeletal resume as an outline or template or blueprint to begin constructing your personal resume and setting future goals. (If you have already created a resume, use this template to identify and add categories that may be missing from your current one.)

NAME
(First, Middle, Last)

Current Addresses:
Postal address
E-mail address
Phone no.

Permanent Addresses:
Postal address
E-mail address
Phone no.

EDUCATION: Name of School, City, State
Degree Name (e.g., Bachelor of Science)
College Major (e.g., Accounting)
Graduation Date
GPA (if 3.0 or higher)

RELATED WORK EXPERIENCES: Position Title, City, State   Start and stop dates
(Begin the list with your most recent experiences.)
(List skills you used or developed.)

VOLUNTEER (COMMUNITY SERVICE) EXPERIENCES
(List skills you used or developed.)

NOTABLE COURSEWORK
(e.g., leadership, interdisciplinary, or intercultural courses)

EXTRACURRICULAR EXPERIENCES
(e.g., student government or peer leadership)
(List skills used or developed.)

PERSONAL SKILLS AND POSITIVE QUALITIES
(List as bullets; be sure to include those that are especially relevant to the position for which you're applying.)

HONORS AND AWARDS
(Include those received prior to school and outside of school)

REFERENCES
(Names and contact information for those who can speak to your work experience)

As a high school student, you can begin the process of portfolio development right now by saving your best work and performances, including those done in classes, co-curricular experiences on campus, or service and work experiences off campus. Store them in a traditional portfolio folder, or save them on a flash drive to create an electronic portfolio. You could also create a website and upload your materials there. Eventually, you should be able to build a well-stocked portfolio that showcases your skills and demonstrates your achievements to future employers or future schools.

Think About It—Journal Entry 10.10

What do you predict will be your best work products in high school—those that you would most likely showcase in a portfolio?

_____
_____
_____

Why?

_____
_____
_____

Letters of Recommendation (Letters of Reference)

The quality of your letters of recommendation will be strengthened if you give careful thought to (a) who will serve as your references, (b) how to approach them, and (c) what to provide them. Specific strategies for doing so are summarized in **Box 10.7**.

BOX 10.7

The Art and Science of Requesting Letters of Recommendation: Effective Strategies and Common Courtesies

1. **Select recommendations from people who know you well.** Think about individuals with whom you've had an ongoing relationship, who know you by name, and who have observed your strongest performances and skills. Good candidates are teachers who you've had for more than one course, an academic advisor whom you see often, or an employer who has witnessed your work habits for an extended period of time.

2. **Seek a balanced blend of letters from people who have observed your performance in different settings or situations.** The following are performance-based settings where people may have observed how well you performed:
   - The classroom—a teacher who can speak on your academic performance
   - On campus—someone who can comment on your contributions to a club or organization
   - Off campus—a professional for whom you've performed volunteer service, part-time work, or an internship

3. **Pick the right time and place to make your request.** Be sure to request letters of recommendation well in advance of the letter's deadline date (at least two weeks). First, ask the person if he or she is willing to write you a letter of recommendation. Don't approach the person with the form in your hand because it may send the message that you have assumed the person will say yes or are pressuring the person to say yes. This isn't the most socially sensitive message to send someone whom you're about to ask a favor.

   Also, pick a place and time where the person can give full attention to your request. Make a personal visit to the person's office,

BOX 10.7 (CONT)

rather than making the request in a busy hallway or in front of a classroom full of students.

4. **Provide your references with a fact sheet about yourself.** Include your experiences and achievements—both inside and outside the classroom. This will help make your references' job a little easier by providing points for them to focus on. It's also likely to make your letter stronger because it will contain specific examples that draw directly from your personal experiences and accomplishments. On your fact sheet, be sure to include high grades you may have earned in certain courses, as well as volunteer services, leadership experiences, awards or forms of recognition, and special interests or talents relevant to your career choice. Your fact sheet is the place to "toot your own horn," so don't fear coming across as a braggart. You're not being boastful or showboating; you're just highlighting your strengths.

5. **If the letter is to be mailed, provide your references with a stamped, addressed envelope.** This is a simple courtesy that makes their job easier and demonstrates your social sensitivity.

6. **Waive your right to see the letter.** If you have the option to waive (give up) your right to see the letter of recommendation, waive your right—as long as you feel reasonably certain that you will receive a good letter of recommendation. By waiving your right to see the letter, you show confidence that the letter will be positive and assures the person reading the letter that you didn't inspect or screen it to ensure it was good before sending it.

7. **Follow up with a thank you note.** Send this note at about the time your letter of recommendation should be sent. This is the right thing to do because it shows your appreciation; it's also the smart thing to do because if the letter hasn't been sent, the thank you note serves as a gentle reminder to your reference that the letter should be sent soon.

8. **Let your references know the outcome of your application.** If you've been offered the position or been admitted to the school to which you applied, let your references know. This is the socially sensitive thing to do, and your references are likely to notice and remember your social sensitivity—which should strengthen the quality of any future letters of recommendation you may request from them.

Think About It—Journal Entry 10.11

Have you met anyone at school who you could be in a position to write a letter of recommendation for you?

_____

_____

If you have, who is this person, and what position does he or she hold at school?

_____

_____

_____

_____

If you haven't, who might be a good future candidate?

_____
_____
_____
_____

Networking

Would it surprise you to learn that 80% of jobs are never advertised? This means that jobs you see listed in a classified section of the newspaper and posted an employment center represent only 20% of available openings at any given time. Almost one-half of all job hunters find employment through people they know or have met, such as friends, family members, and casual acquaintances. When it comes to locating positions, *who* you know can be as important as *what* you know or how good your resume looks. Consequently, it's important to continually expand the circle of people who are aware of your career interests and abilities, because they can be a valuable source of information about employment opportunities.

Also, be sure to share copies of your resume with friends and family members, just in case they come in contact with employers who are looking for somebody with your career interests and qualifications.

Personal Interview

A personal interview is your opportunity to make a positive in-person impression. You can make a strong first impression during any interview by showing that you've done your homework and have come prepared. In particular, you should come to the interview with knowledge about yourself and your audience.

You can demonstrate knowledge about yourself by bringing a mental list of your strongest selling points to the interview and being ready to speak about them when the opportunity arises. You can demonstrate knowledge of your audience by doing some homework on the organization you are applying to, the people who are likely to be interviewing you, and the questions they are likely to ask you. Try to acquire as much information about the organization and its key employees as is available to you online and in print. When you know your audience (who your interviewers are likely to be and what they're likely to ask), and when you know yourself well (what about yourself you're going to say), you should then be ready to answer what probably is the most important interview question of all: "What can *you* do for *us*?"

Once you begin to participate in actual interviews, make note of the questions you are asked. Although you may be able to anticipate some of the more general questions that are asked in almost any interview, there likely will be unique questions asked of you that relate specifically to your personal qualifications and experiences. If these questions are asked in one of your interviews, there's a good chance they'll be asked in a future interview. As soon as you complete an interview, mentally review it and attempt to recall the major questions you were asked before they slip your mind. Consider developing an index card catalog of questions that you've been asked during interviews, with the question on one side and your prepared response on the reverse side. By being better prepared for personal interviews, you'll increase the quality of your answers and decrease your level of anxiety. You should also have a list of questions to ask at the interview. This shows that you are interested and did your homework. Finally, remember to dress appropriately for an interview. If you are unsure how to dress, consult a professional you trust on campus.

Lastly, remember to send a thank you note to the person who interviewed you. This is not only the courteous thing to do, but also the smart thing to do because it demonstrates your interpersonal sensitivity and reinforces the person's memory of you.

Technology and Career Placement

Once you start looking for a job, internship, or co-op, it is very important to consider how you use technology:

1. **Your e-mail address.** Make sure it is professional and would not offend anyone.
2. **Your cell phone.** Consider your "ring-back tone." If it is music that has offensive language, remove it. Also, make sure your voicemail message is short and professional. Time is precious and people don't want to listen to a two-minute voicemail message, no matter what it is about.
3. **Facebook, Twitter, etc.** Make sure anything you post would not turn off any potential employers. Even if your page is marked "private," employers are hiring people to get all the dirt on you!

It is important when you are looking for a job to put your best self out there—this includes your digital self.

CHAPTER SUMMARY AND HIGHLIGHTS

Reaching an effective decision about a career path involves four forms of awareness (involved in setting):

1. Awareness of *self*—insight into your personal interests, talents, needs, and values
2. Awareness of your *career options*—knowledge of different career fields available to you
3. Awareness of what options provide the *best "fit" for you*—knowing what careers most closely match your personal interests, talents, needs, and values

4. Awareness of the major *steps needed to reach your career goal*—knowing how to prepare for and gain entry into the career of your choice

You can gain valuable information about careers by:

- Accessing printed and online career resources (e.g., *Dictionary of Occupational Titles; Occupational Outlook Handbook*)
- Attending career fairs on campus
- Conducting information interviews with professionals in careers that interest you
- Shadowing (observing) professionals at work
- Engaging in service learning or internships

After graduating from high school, you have three primary career pathways available to you. These three pathways, along with strategies for taking them, are summarized in **Figure 10.3**.

FIGURE 10.3: Career Pathways Planning Matrix

JOB-RELATED CAREER TRAINING AFTER HIGH SCHOOL
- Career Interest Inventories
- Occupational search for in-demand jobs
- Experiential opportunities: Co-ops/Internships/Job shadowing
- Vocational programs
- Trade schools

COLLEGE PATH AFTER HIGH SCHOOL
- Career Interest Inventories
- Select college-prep coursework
- Investigate Career Pathway
- Match your desired career pathway with a college major
- Experiential opportunities: Co-ops/Internships/Job shadowing

IMMEDIATE EMPLOYMENT AFTER HIGH SCHOOL
- Career Interest Inventories
- Military: ASVAB/Talk to local recruiters/Join ROTC
- Find employment in your area of interest
- Participate in apprenticeships
- Utilize local and state agencies that provide employment lists.

Learning More through the World Wide Web: Internet-Based Resources

For additional information related to career exploration, preparation, and readiness, see the following websites.

Developing a Personalized Career Plan:
www.mapping-your-future.org

Navigating the Job Market:
www.mymajors.com

Career Descriptions and Future Employment Outlook:
www.bls.gov/

Position Openings & Opportunities:
www.rileyguide.com
www.monster.com

Resume Writing & Job Interviewing:
www.quintcareers.com

References

Astin, A. W. (1993). *What matters in college?* San Francisco: Jossey-Bass.

Baumeister, R., & Leary, M. R. (1995). The need to belong: Desire for interpersonal attachments as a fundamental human motivation. *Psychological Bulletin, 117,* 497–529.

Bolles, R.N., 1998. *The new quick job-hunting map.* Toronto, Ontario, Canada: Ten Speed Press.

Brooks, K. (2009). *You majored in what? Mapping your path from chaos to career.* New York: Penguin.

Brown, S. D., & Krane, N. E. R. (2000). Four (or five) sessions and a cloud of dust: Old assumptions and new observations about career counseling. In S. D. Brown & R. W. Lent (Eds.), *Handbook of counseling psychology* (3rd ed., pp. 740–766). New York: Wiley.

Carnevale, A. P., Smith, N., & Strohl, (2013). *Recovery: Projection of jobs and education requirements through 2020.* Washington DC: Georgetown University, Center on Education and the Workforce.

Casserly, M. (2012). "10 jobs that didn't exist 10 years ago." *Forbes.* Retrieved from http://www.forbes.com/sites/meghancasserly/2012/05/11/10-jobs-that-didnt-exist-10-years-ago/.

Chua, S. N., & Koestner, R. (2008). A Self-Determination Theory perspective on the role of autonomy in solitary behavior. *The Journal of Social Psychology, 148*(5), 645–647.

Crosby, O. (2002). Informational interviewing: Get the scoop on careers. *Occupational Outlook Quarterly* (Summer), 32–37.

Deci, E., & Ryan, R. (Eds.). (2002). *Handbook of self-determination research.* Rochester, NY: University of Rochester Press.

Education Commission of the States. (1995). *Making quality count in undergraduate education.* Denver, CO: ECS Distribution Center.

Figler, H., & Bolles, R. N. (2007). *The career counselor's handbook.* Berkeley, CA: Ten Speed Press.

Gardner, H. (1993). *Frames of mind: The theory of multiple intelligences* (2nd ed.). New York: Basic Books.

Gardner, H. (1999). *Intelligence reframed: Multiple intelligences for the 21st century.* New York: Basic Books.

Gardner, H. (2006) *Changing Minds. The art and science of changing our own and other people's minds.* Boston MA: Harvard Business School Press.

Gewertz, C. (2016, April 5). "Only 8 percent of students complete college- and career-ready curriculum." Retrieved August 15, 2017, from *Education Week,* at http://blogs.edweek.org/edweek/high_school_and_beyond/2016/04/only_8_percent_of_students_complete_college_or_career_ready_curriculum.html

Hart Research Associates. (2006). *How should colleges prepare students to succeed in today's global economy?* Based on surveys among employers and recent college graduates. Conducted on behalf of the Association of American Colleges and Universities. Washington, DC: Author.

Hart Research Associates. (2014. July). *How should colleges prepare students to succeed in today's global economy?* Retrieved from http://dpdproject.info/details/how-should-colleges-prepare-students-to-succeed-in-todays-global-economy-peter-d-hart-research-associates/.

Hildenbrand, M., & Gore, P. A., Jr. (2005). Career development in the first-year seminar: Best practice versus actual practice. In P. A. Gore (Ed.), *Facilitating the career development of students in transition* (Monograph No. 43, pp. 45–60). Columbia: National Resource Center for the First-Year Experience and Students in Transition, University of South Carolina.

Kuh, G. D. (1993). In their own words: What students learn outside the classroom. *American Educational Research Journal, 30*, 277–304.

Lock, R. D. (2004). *Taking charge of your career direction* (5th ed.). Belmont, CA: Brooks Cole. Melton, 1995

National Association of Colleges & Employers (2012). *Internship and co-op survey*. Bethlehem, PA: Author.

National Association of Colleges & Employers (2013). *Job outlook: The candidate skills/qualities employers want*. Retrieved from http://www.naceweb.org/s10022013/job-outlook-skills-quality.aspx.

National Association of Colleges & Employers (2014). *2014 Internship and co-op survey*, **executive summary**. Retrieved from https://www.naceweb.org/uploadedFiles/Content/static-assets/downloads/executive-summary/2014-internship-co-op-survey-executive-summary.pdf.

National Center for Education Statistics (2014). *Fast facts: Most popular majors*. Washington, DC: U.S. Department of Education. Retrieved from http://nces.ed.gov/fastfacts/display.asp?id=37.

Pascarella, E., & Terenzini, P. (1991). *How college affects students: Findings and insights from twenty years of research*. San Francisco: Jossey-Bass.

Pascarella, E., & Terenzini, P. (2005). *How college affects students: A third decade of research* (Vol. 2). San Francisco: Jossey-Bass.

Pope, L. (1990). *Looking beyond the Ivy League*. New York: Penguin Press.

Ryan, R. (1995). Psychological needs and the facilitation of integrative processes. *Journal of Personality, 63*, 397–427.

Ryan, R. M., & Deci, E. L. (2000). Self-determination theory and the facilitation of intrinsic motivation, social development, and well-being. *American Psychologist, 55*, 68–78.

CHAPTER 10 EXERCISES

10.1 QUOTE REFLECTIONS

Review the sidebar quotes contained in this chapter and select two that were especially meaningful or inspirational to you.

For each quote, provide a three- to five-sentence explanation why you chose it.

10.2 REALITY BITE

Career Choice: Conflict and Confusion

Josh is a high school student whose family has made a great financial sacrifice to support his education. He deeply appreciates the sacrifice his family members has made and wants to pay them back as soon as possible. Consequently, he's been looking into careers that offer the highest starting salaries immediately after graduation. Unfortunately, none of these careers seem to match Josh's natural abilities and personal interests. He's now conflicted, confused, and worried.

Reflection and Discussion Questions

1. If you were Josh, what would you do?
2. Do you see any way that Josh might balance his desire to pay back his family as soon as possible with his desire to pursue a career that's compatible with his interests and talents?
3. What questions or factors do you think Josh should consider before making his decision about a career?
4. Can you relate to Josh's story, or do you know of students in a similar predicament?

10.3 GAINING SELF-AWARENESS OF PERSONAL INTERESTS, TALENTS, AND VALUES

No one is in a better position to discover who you are, and who you want to be, than *you*. One effective way to gain deeper self-insight is through self-questioning. You can become more self-aware by asking yourself questions that cause you to think carefully about your inner qualities and characteristics. Responding honestly to the following questions can sharpen awareness of your true interests, abilities and values, and help you determine what career is a good "fit" for you. As you read each question, briefly note what thought(s) come to mind about yourself.

Personal Interests

1. What tends to grab your attention and hold it for long periods of time?
2. What sorts of things are you naturally curious about or frequently intrigue you?
3. What do you really enjoy doing and do as often as you possibly can?
4. What do you look forward to, or get excited about?
5. What are your favorite hobbies or pastimes?
6. When you're with your friends, what do you like to talk about or spend time doing?

Chapter 10: Career Exploration, Preparation, and Readiness

7. What has been your most stimulating or enjoyable learning experience?
8. If you've had previous work or volunteer experience, what jobs or tasks did you find most interesting or stimulating?
9. When time seems to "fly by" for you, what are you usually doing?
10. What do you like to read about?
11. When you open a newspaper or log onto the Internet, where do you tend to go first?
12. When you find yourself daydreaming or fantasizing about your future, what is it usually about?

From your responses to the above questions, identify a career that appears to be most compatible with your personal *interests*? In the space below, note the career and your interests that are compatible with it.

Personal Talents and Abilities

1. What seems to come naturally to you?
2. What would you say is your greatest talent or personal gift?
3. What are your most advanced or well-developed skills?
4. What seems to come easily to you that others have to work harder to do?
5. What would you say has been your greatest personal accomplishment or achievement in life thus far?
6. What about yourself are you most proud of, or that you take most pride in doing?
7. When others come to you for advice or assistance, what is it usually for?
8. What would your best friend(s) say is your best quality, trait, or characteristic?
9. When you've done something that left you feeling like you really were successful, what was it that you did?

> "Never desert your line of talent. Be what nature intended you for and you will succeed."
> —Sydney Smith, 18th-century English writer and defender of the oppressed

10. If you have received awards or other forms of recognition, what have they been for?
11. On what types of learning tasks or activities have you experienced the most success?
12. In what types of courses do you tend to earn the highest grades?

From your responses to the above questions, identify a career that appears to be most compatible with your personal *talents and abilities*? In the space below, note the career and your talents and abilities that are compatible with it.

Personal Values

1. What matters most to you?
2. If you were to single out one thing you really stand for or believe in, what would it be?
3. What would you say are your highest priorities in life?
4. Whenever you get the feeling you've done what was good or right, what was it that you did?

> "To love what you do and feel that it matters—how could anything be more fun?"
> —Katharine Graham, former CEO of the Washington Post and Pulitzer Prize–winning author

5. If there were one thing in the world you could change, improve, or make a difference in, what would it be?
6. When you have extra spending money, what do you usually spend it on?

7. When you have free time, what do you usually find yourself doing?

8. What does living a "good life" mean to you?

9. How would you define success? (What would it take for you to feel that you achieved success?)

10. How do you define happiness? (What would it take for you to be happy?)

11. Do you have a hero or anyone you admire, look up to, or feel has set an example worth following? (If yes, who and why?)

12. Would you rather be thought of as:

    (a) smart,

    (b) wealthy,

    (c) creative, or

    (d) caring?

(Rank from 1 to 4, with 1 being the highest)

> "Success is getting what you want. Happiness is wanting what you get."
> —Dale Carnegie, author of the best-selling book, How to Win Friends and Influence People and founder of The Dale Carnegie Course—a worldwide program for business based on his teachings

> "Do what you value; value what you do."
> —Sidney Simon, author of Values Clarification and In Search of Values

From your responses to the above questions, identify a career that appears to be most compatible with your personal *values*? In the space below, note the career and your values that are compatible with it.

10.4 CONDUCTING AN INFORMATION INTERVIEW

One of the best ways to acquire accurate information about a career is to interview a working professional in that career. This career exploration strategy is known as an *information interview*. An information interview enables you to (a) get an insider's view of what the career is really like, (b) network with a professional in the field, and (c) gain confidence in interview situations that prepares you for future job interviews.

Steps in the Information Interview Process

1. Select a career you may be interested in pursuing. Even if you're currently keeping your career options open, pick a career that might be a possibility. You can use the resources cited on **pp. 272–273** in this chapter to help you identify a career that may be most appealing to you.

2. Find someone in the career you've selected and set up an information interview with that person. To locate possible interview candidates, consider members of your family, friends of family members, and family members of your friends. Any of these people may be working in the career you are considering and may be good interview candidates, or they may know others who could be good candidates. The Internet may be another source for locating interview candidates.

3. Once you've identified someone you would like to interview, send that person a short letter or e-mail, or give them a call, asking about the possibility of scheduling a short interview and mention that you would be willing to conduct the interview in person or by phone—whichever would be more convenient. If you don't hear back within a reasonable period (7–10 days), send a follow-up message. If you don't receive a response to the follow-up message, try contacting someone else.

4. After you have found someone to interview, here are some strategies for conducting the interview:
   - Thank the person for taking the time to speak with you. This should be the first thing you do after meeting the person—before you officially begin the interview.
   - Prepare your interview questions in advance. Here are some questions that you might consider asking:
     1) During a typical day's work, what tasks occupy most of your time?
     2) What do you like most about your career?
     3) What are the most difficult or frustrating aspects of your career?
     4) What personal skills or qualities do you see as being critical for success in your career?
     5) How did you decide on your career?
     6) What personal qualifications or prior experiences enabled you to enter your career?
     7) How does someone find out about openings in your field?
     8) What steps did you take to locate your current position?
     9) What advice would you give high school students about what they might do at this stage of their life to begin preparing for a career in your field?
     10) How does someone advance in your career?
     11) Are there any moral issues or ethical challenges that tend to arise in your career?
     12) Are members of diverse groups likely to be found in your career? (This is an especially important question to ask if you're a member of an ethnic, racial, or gender group that is underrepresented in the career field.)
     13) What impact does your career have on your home life or personal life outside of work?
     14) If you had to do it all over again, would you choose the same career?
     15) Would you recommend that I speak with anyone else to obtain additional information or a different perspective on your career field? (If the answer is "yes," you may follow up by asking: "May I mention that you referred me?") It's always a good idea to obtain more than one person's perspective before making any important choice, such as your career choice.

Chapter 10: Career Exploration, Preparation, and Readiness 297

- **Take notes during the interview.** This not only helps you remember what was said, it also sends a positive message to the persons you interview because it shows them that their ideas are important and noteworthy (worth taking notes on).
- **If the interview goes well, consider asking if it might be possible to observe or shadow that person at work.**

Self-Assessment Questions

After completing your interview, take a moment to reflect on it and answer the following questions:

1. What information did you receive that impressed you about the career?

2. What information did you receive that distressed (or depressed) you about the career?

3. What was the most useful piece of information you took away from the interview?

4. Based on the information you acquired during the interview, would you still be interested in pursuing a career in this field? Why?

CHAPTER 10 REFLECTION

What would your ideal career be?

What would your work day be like?

What are some things you can utilize from this chapter to make it happen?

INDEX

A

ableism, 247
academic self-efficacy, 58
academic skills, 122, 281
academic success
   active involvement (engagement), 24–29
   capitalizing on school resources (resourcefulness), 30–31
   fear of, 88
   vs. goal setting, 49–50
   interpersonal interaction and collaboration (social integration), 31–38
   reflection and self-awareness (mindfulness), 38–40
   tips for, 6–9
account, 212
achievement (competence), 268
active class participation, 27
active involvement (engagement)
   active class participation, 27
   active reading, 27
   in learning process, 25
   and note taking, 25, 26
active listening, 25, 26
active reading, 27
adduction, 140
affiliation (belongingness), 268
ageism, 247
analytical thinking, 137
annual fee, 212
annual percentage rate (APR), 200, 213
anti-semitism, 246
apartheid, 245
app developer, 270
applied thinking, 137–139
aptitudes, 39
attendance, 10
auditory-sequential learning, 123

B

Baby Boomer Generation, 236
backtracking, 179–180
balance, 199, 213
balanced thinking, 137, 140–142
bisexuals, 238
bodily–kinesthetic (psychomotor) intelligence, 266
bounced check, 199, 203, 213
brainstorming, 149
budget, 213

C

capitalizing on school resources (resourcefulness)
   disability services, 29
   guidance counseling, 30
   media center library, 29–30
   seek advice, 31
   student development opportunities, 30–31
capital punishment, 178
career choice, 267–268
   personal characteristics, 269
career exploration
   career options, awareness of, 270–279
   major steps needed to reach your career goal, 279–280
   self awareness, 263–270
career fairs, 272
career information resources
   Dictionary of Occupational Titles (DOT), 271
   Encyclopedia of Careers and Vocational Guidance, 271
   Occupational Information Network (O*NET), 272
   Occupational Outlook Handbook (OOH), 271
career observation (shadowing), 273–274
career paths, 16
career placement, 289
career planning
   abilities and talents, 265–270
   advantages, 277
   career fairs, 272
   career transition, 48
   exploration and preparation, 263–270
   extracurricular experiences, 283–284
   importance of, 262
   information interviews, 272
   information resources, 271–272
   internships, 274–275
   letters of recommendation, 286–287
   networking, 288
   observation (shadowing), 273–274
   part-time work, 276–280
   personal interview, 288–289
   personal strengths and achievements, 283
   portfolio, 284–285
   skills and attributes, 281–282
   strategies for, 263–270
   successful performance, 281, 282
   technology and career placement, 289
   volunteer work/service learning, 275
career preparation, strategies for, 263–270
career-readiness skills, 280
career success, 239–240
cash flow
   defined, 197, 213
   negative, 198
   track your, 198–214
   two-way street, 198
charge cards, 203
chief listening officer, 270
classism, 246

classroom behavior
  avoid inappropriate and uncivil, 11–14
  avoid plagiarism, 14–15
Cloud computing services, 270
co-curricular experiences, 30
collaborative learning
  library research teams, 37
  note-taking teams, 37
  reading teams, 37
  study teams, 37–38
  test review teams, 38
  writing teams, 37
convergent thinking, 149
Cornell Note-Taking System, 105
counselor
  interacting with your guidance, 33
  seek advice, 31
creative thinking, 137, 148–149
  diversity stimulates, 239
creativity strategies, 154–155
Credit Cardholders' Bill of Rights Act of 2009, 202
credit cards
  annual percentage rate (APR), 200, 213
  credit limit, 200
  in full and on time, 201
  grace period, 200
  limit yourself to, 201
  money management tool, 199–200
credit history, 196, 197, 213
credit line, 200, 213
credit scores, 194, 196–197, 213
critical thinking, 137, 142–143
  diversity promotes, 239
cyberbullying, 12

D

debit cards, 203
debt, 213
  credit card, 201
  minimizing, 204–212
decontextualization, 126
deep learning
  defined, 100–101
  effective class-listening and note-taking strategies, 101–102
  listening and note-taking strategies, 103–105
  make meaningful associations, 116–125
  post-class strategies, 105–107
  pre-class strategies, 102–103
  reading process, 109–111
  strategic reading, 107–108
  strategic studying, 114–115
default, 213
deferred student payment plan, 213

dialectic/dialogic thinking, 141
disability services, 29
discrimination, 244–245
divergent thinking, 149
diversity
  benefits of, 238–240
  deepens learning, 238–239
  defined, 224–225, 232
  enhances career preparation and career success, 239–240
  ethnic and racial diversity, 232–234
  generational diversity, 236–237
  vs. humanity, 229–231
  increases self-awareness and self-knowledge, 238
  overcoming barriers to, 241–245
  for overcoming stereotypes and prejudices, 247–252
  promotes critical thinking, 239
  sexual diversity, 237–238
  socioeconomic diversity, 235
  stimulates creative thinking, 239
  types of, 232–238
downsize, 208
dual coding, 120
dualistic thinking, 141

E

economize, 208
educational/admissions consultant, 270
elder care, 271
e-mail
  connect with your teachers through, 33
  how to e-mail (or not) your teacher, 14–15
emergency student loan program, 196, 213
emotion
  inferential reasoning, 147
  learn with, 125–127
essay test questions, 176–179
estimated family contribution (EFC), 195, 213
ethnic diversity, 232–234
ethnic group, 228–229
ethnocentrism, 245
existential intelligence, 266
extracurricular activities, 30

F

face-to-face interaction, 33
fear of failure, 88
fear of success, 88
Federal loans, 195
Federal Pell Grant, 197
Federal Perkins Loan, 195
Federal Subsidized Stafford Loan, 195

Federal Unsubsidized Stafford Loan, 195
feedback
  defined, 183
  proactive, 183
  prompt, 183
  specific, 183
  from your classmates, 182
  from your teacher, 182
field work, 275
Financial Aid Office, 195–197
financial literacy
  cash flow, 198–214
  charge cards, 203
  checking accounts, 198–199
  college education, income sources for, 194–197
  credit cards, 199–201
  credit score, 194, 196–197
  debit cards, 203
  developing money management plan, 197–198, 204–212
  grants, 197, 213
  minimizing debt, 204–212
  planning on joining the armed services, 197
  scholarships, 197
  student loans, 195–197
fixed interest rate, 195, 213
fixed mindset (FM), 63
Free Application for Federal Student Aid (FAFSA), 194, 213

G

gays, 238
generational diversity, 236–237
Generation X, 236
Generation Y, 236
Generation Z, 237
genocide, 246
goal setting
  important of, 52–53
  internal locus of control, 57–58
  maintaining motivation and progress, strategies for, 53–57
  self-efficacy, 58
  SMART method of, 51
  vs. success, 49–50
  successful people, characteristics of, 57–58
  well-designed, 50–53
grace period, credit cards, 200, 213
grade point average (GPA), 4, 9, 102, 196, 197
grants, 197, 213
grit
  persistence, 59
  resilience, 59–61
  self-control, 61

self-discipline, 61–62
tenacity, 59
gross income, 213
growth mindset (GM), 63–65
guidance counseling, 30

H

habituation, 122
hate crimes, 246
hate groups, 246
heterosexism, 247
heterosexuals, 237
higher-level thinking
    analytical thinking, 137
    applied thinking, 137–139
    balanced thinking, 137, 140–142
    creative thinking, 137, 148–149
    critical thinking, 137, 142–143
    defined, 136
    increasing creativity, strategies for, 154–155
    inferential reasoning, 143–144
    multidimensional thinking, 137, 139
    self-questioning strategies, 152–153
    seven major forms of, 137
    skills to improve academic performance, 150–151
    synthesis (integrative thinking), 137, 138
high school
    attendance, 10
    career paths, 16
    effective classroom behavior, 11–13
    first year in, 9–10
    four steps to success, 24–40
    how to e-mail (or not) your teacher, 14–15
    middle school *vs.* college, 2–4
    transitioning from middle school to, 9
    use of personal technology, 11–12
homophobia, 247
humanity, 232
    vs. diversity, 229–231

I

identity theft, 203–204, 213
indecisiveness, 88
individuality, 232
inferential reasoning
    ad hominem argument, 146
    authority/prestige, 146–147
    circular reasoning, 146
    dogmatism, 145
    double standard, 145
    emotion, 147
    empirical (observable) evidence, 143–144
    errors, 144–147
    false analogy, 145
    false cause and effect, 145
    glittering generality, 146
    hasty generalization, 145
    logical reasoning, 143
    non sequitur, 144–145
    popularity/majority, 147
    red herring, 146
    rhetorical deception, 146
    selective perception, 145
    slippery slope, 146
    smoke screen, 146
    straw man argument, 146
    tradition/familiarity, 147
    wishful thinking, 145
information interviews, 272
institutional racism, 245
insurance premium, 213
intercultural competence, 240
interest-bearing account, 198, 213
interests, 195, 198, 213, 264
internal locus of control, 57–58
international diversity, 240
internships, 274–275
intrapersonal intelligence, 266
interpersonal interaction and collaboration (social integration)
    collaborative learning, 35–38
    with high school teachers, 32–33
    with guidance counselor, 33
    making connections with members, school community, 32
    with peers (student–student interaction), 34–35
introspection, 38

J

Jim Crow laws, 245
jingoism, 246
job shadowing program, 273–274

K

kinesthetic learning, 123

L

learner, self-aware, 8
learning habits, 39
learning journal, 281
learning styles, 39, 122–124
lesbians, 238
letters of recommendation, 286
    effective strategies and common courtesies, 286–287
line of credit *see* credit limit
linguistic intelligence, 266
loan consolidation, 213
loan premium, 214
logical-mathematical intelligence, 266
long-term loan, 200–201
long-term memory, 111

M

market research data miner, 270
Maslow's theory of self-actualization, 35
massed practice, 119
meaningful associations
    build variety into study process, 122
    distribute study time across separate study sessions, 118–119
    integrate information from classes and readings, 118
    learning styles, 122–124
    learn with emotion, 125–127
    part-to-whole study method, 119–120
    visual learning, power of, 120–121
means-end analysis, 50
media center library, 29–30
memory
    improves your, 118–119
    long-term, 111
    selective, 244
    short-term, 105
memory block, 172
mental abilities, 265–270
merit-based scholarship, 214
metacognition, 151
middle school
    high school *vs.* college, 2–4
    transitioning from, 5
millennial generation expert, 270
mindset, 63
money management plan
    charge cards, 203
    checking accounts, 198–199
    credit cards, 199–201
    debit cards, 203
    do's and don'ts, 210
    downsize, 208
    economize, 208
    gain financial self-awareness, 197–198
    minimizing debt, 204–212
    money-saving strategies and habits, 209
    personal budget, 204–207
    track your cash flow, 198–214
Montgomery GI Bill–Active Duty (MGIB), 197
motivation, 54
multidimensional thinking, 137, 139
multiple-choice test questions, 173–175
multiple intelligences, 265–270
musical intelligence, 266

N

naturalist intelligence, 266
need-based scholarship, 214
needs, 264
    personal, 267–268
negative cash flow, 198
net income, 214
netiquette, 13
nonverbal cues, 104
note-taking
    in classroom, 25, 26
    strategies, 101–105

O

online tests, 179–180

P

part-time work, 276–280
passive learning, 25
perfectionism, 88
persistence, 59
personal abilities, 39
personal budget, 204–207
personal interests, 39
personal interview, 288–289
personality traits, 39
personal needs, 267–268
personal resume, 284
personal technology
    cyberbullying, 12
    text messaging, 12
    using cell phones, 11–12
    web surfing, 12
personal values, 39
plagiarism, 14–15
portfolio, 284–285
post-class strategies, 105–107
post-reading strategies, 111–112
post-test strategies, 180–183
practicum, 275
pre-class strategies, 102–103
prejudices
    defined, 242, 245
    strategies for, 247–252
preparing, for high school
    career planning transition, 48
    goal setting *vs.* success, 49–50
    grit, 59–62
    growth mindset (GM), 63–65
    motivation and progress, goals, 53–57
    successful people, characteristics of, 57–58
    well-designed goal, characteristics of, 50–53
    work and experience, 48–49
pre-reading strategies, 108–109
pre-test strategies
    creating retrieval cues, 167–169
    recall test questions, 166
    recitation, 167
    recognition test questions, 166
principal, 201, 214
private loans, 195
process-of-elimination approach, 173–174
procrastination
    divide and conquer strategy, 91
    location matters, 90
    myths that promote, 86
    organization matters, 89
    psychological causes of, 87–88
    strategies for preventing and overcoming, 88–91
    test anxiety, 185
professional skills, 281

R

racial diversity, 225–227, 232–234
racial profiling, 245
racism, 245
recall test questions, 166
recognition, 268
    test questions, 166
red herring, 146
reflection and self-awareness (mindfulness)
    self-assessment, 39
    self-awareness, 38
    self-monitoring, 39
reflective learners, 125
reflective thinking, 239
refutation, 140
regional bias, 246
religious intolerance, 246
resilience, 59–61
retrieval cues, 167–169

S

SCOT (Symptoms, Causes, Outcomes, and Therapies), 169
segregation, 245
self-assessment, 39
self-awareness
    career exploration and preparation, 263–265
    diversity increases, 238
    gain financial, 197–198
    mindfulness, 38
self-control, 61, 107
self-discipline, 61–62
self-efficacy, 58
self-knowledge, 238
self-marketing, 283
self-monitoring, 39, 281
self-satisfaction, 91
sensory stimulation, 268
service learning, 275
sexism, 247
sexual diversity, 237–238
sexual identity, 237
sexual orientation, 237
short-term memory, 105
slavery, 245
SMART (Specific, Meaningful, Actionable, Realistic, Time) method, 50–51
social media manager, 270
socioeconomic diversity, 235
socioeconomic status (SES), 235
spatial intelligence, 266
start-up stress, 89
stereotypes
    defined, 241, 245
    strategies for, 247–252
stigmatizing, 243
stroke of genius, 149
student development opportunities, 30–31
student loans, 195–197
student–student interaction, 34–35
student–teacher interaction, 33
studying strategic, 114–115
sustainability expert, 271
syllabus, 5–6
synthesis (integrative thinking), 137, 138

T

talents
    defined, 264
    multiple intelligences, 265–270
task management
    advantage of, 77
    analysis, 75
    gravity, 79
    itemizing, 75
    prioritize, 78
    prioritizing, 76
    urgency, 78–79
teachers
    connect with your, 32–33
    how to e-mail (or not) your, 14–15
tenacity, 59
terrorism, 246
test anxiety, 184–186
test-taking skills and strategies
    academic performance, nutritional strategies for, 170–171
    essay questions, 176–179
    multiple-choice test questions, 173–175

Index 303

online tests, 179–180
pinpointing source of lost points on tests, 181–182
post-test, 180–183
pre-test, 166–169
before test, 169–170
test anxiety, 184–186
during tests, 171–172
true–false questions, 173
test-wise strategies, 174
textbook reading comprehension and retention, 28
thinking complexity, 239
thrill seeking, 88
time management
advantage of, 77
analysis, 75
creating, 80–85
dealing with procrastination, 85
free time, productive use of, 81–82
importance of, 74–75
itemizing, 75
myths that promote procrastination, 86
plan transforms intention into action, 83
preparing, for high school, 48–49
prioritizing, 76
strategies for, 75–79
Traditional Generation, 236
transgender, 238
transition to high school
outside of school choices, 48
time management, 48–49
tips on, 49–50
work management, 49
true–false questions, 173

U

user experience design, 271

V

values, 264
variable interest rate, 195, 214
verbal cues, 104
visual learning, power of, 120–121
visual-spatial learning, 120, 123
volunteer work, 275

W

wishful thinking, 145
work experience, career-related, 274
work management, 49

X

xenophobia, 246

Y

yield, 214